# ARMY MODERNIZATION STRATEGY

# Attention Authors

Manas Publications is fighting a war to tell the world that India can win the battle not only by the bullet but also by pen. We are converting fighters into writers. There is no dearth of intellectuals in our country, however, their knowledge is confined to them only. No sincere effort has been made by any other publisher to channelise their knowledge, which is why the talent of every intellectual remains latent. An author always presents the raw material in the shape of a manuscript and it is the job of the publisher to convert it to a finished product. Manas has been continually motivating intellectuals and publishing their manuscripts for more than two decades and would like to publish your manuscript too. If you or your colleagues have a manuscript ready for publication or are working on it, contact us with a detailed synopsis and list of contents. Manas will also suggest you a suitable title for writing related to your area of expertise. Manas is known for its publishing quality. We take utmost care in publishing and also give wide publicity to the book and its author through our national and international distribution network.

# ARMY MODERNIZATION STRATEGY

Department of Defence, USA

Manas Publications
New Delhi-110002 (INDIA)

**MANAS PUBLICATIONS**
(Publishers, Distributors, Importers & Exporters)
4402/5-A, Ansari Road
(Opp. HDFC Bank)
Darya Ganj, New Delhi-110 002 (INDIA)
**Off. © 23260783, 23265523, Res. © 23842660**
**Fax: 011-23272766**
**E-mail: manaspublications@vsnl.com**
**www.manaspublications.in**



**ISBN** 978-81-7049-365-5
Rs. 995/-



*Typeset at*
**Manas Publications**

*Printed in India at*
R.K. Offset Works, Delhi
and published by Mrs Suman Lata for
**Manas Publications,** 4402/5-A, Ansari Road
(Opp. HDFC Bank),
Darya Ganj, New Delhi-110 002 (INDIA)

# Contents

# Preface

The Army's enduring mission is to protect and defend American Nation's vital security interests and to provide support to civil authorities in response to domestic emergencies. This requires an expeditionary, campaign-quality Army capable of dominating across the full spectrum of conflict, at any time, in any environment and against any adversary for extended periods of time. To do this the Army must continually review its structure and capabilities to ensure it remains adaptive and responsive to the evolving world security environment. While maintaining our mission focus on preparing forces and building readiness for counterinsurgency operations in Iraq and Afghanistan, the Army must remain ready to provide the Combatant Commanders with the forces and capabilities they need for full spectrum operations anywhere in the world both now and in the future. The Army Modernization Strategy provides a summary of the ends, ways and means through which the Army will equip itself and continue to modernize in support of this end. It describes the operational environment an era of persistent conflict and the Army's newest doctrine for dominating in that environment. It describes the challenges the Army is facing as it executes the current fight while preparing for the future, and the imperatives established by our senior leaders for restoring balance to the force. Finally, it details the four Elements of Modernization the specific ways in which the Army's equipping and modernization efforts support rebalancing the force and integrating capabilities necessary to ensure our success across the range of operations, from peacetime engagement to major combat operations

# Chapter 1

# The Army Modernization Strategy

## Introduction

The Army's enduring mission is to protect and defend our Nation's vital security interests and to provide support to civil authorities in response to domestic emergencies. This requires an expeditionary, campaign-quality Army capable of dominating across the full spectrum of conflict, at any time, in any environment and against any adversary—for extended periods of time. To do this the Army must continually review its structure and capabilities to ensure it remains adaptive and responsive to the evolving world security environment. While maintaining our mission focus on preparing forces and building readiness for counterinsurgency operations in Iraq and Afghanistan, the Army must remain ready to provide the Combatant Commanders with the forces and capabilities they need for full spectrum operations anywhere in the world—both now and in the future.

The Army Modernization Strategy provides a summary of the ends, ways and means through which the Army will equip itself and continue to modernize in support of

this end. It describes the operational environment—an "era of persistent conflict"—and the Army's newest doctrine for dominating in that environment. It describes the challenges the Army is facing as it executes the current fight while preparing for the future, and the imperatives established by our senior leaders for restoring balance to the force. Finally, it details the four Elements of Modernization—the specific "ways" in which the Army's equipping and modernization efforts support rebalancing the force and integrating capabilities necessary to ensure our success across the range of operations, from peacetime engagement to major combat operations.

## Strategic Environment – Era of Persistent Conflict

We have entered an era of persistent conflict, which for the foreseeable future will place us in a security environment much more ambiguous and unpredictable than that faced during the Cold War. A key current threat is a radical, ideology-based, long-term terrorist threat bent on using any means available – to include weapons of mass destruction – to achieve its political and ideological ends. And, unlike previous threats manifested in rationally-acting nation states, this one is not easily deterred nor defeated by the traditional elements of national power. We also face new security challenges influenced by the effects of globalization, especially in failing states and in ungoverned areas. Finally, we face a potential return to traditional security threats posed by emerging nearpeers as we compete globally for depleting natural resources and overseas markets. Specific trends of this evolving security environment include:

- An expanding, interconnected global economy supported by advancements in technology will continue to drive prosperity. However, this will also underscore wealth and power disparities between populations while providing the means to export terror and extremism around the world – to include the proliferation of weapons of mass destruction
- Radicalism influenced by extremist ideologies and separatist movements will remain attractive to those who feel threatened and victimized by the cultural and economic impacts of globalization
- Population growth – especially in less-developed countries – will expose a resulting "youth bulge" to

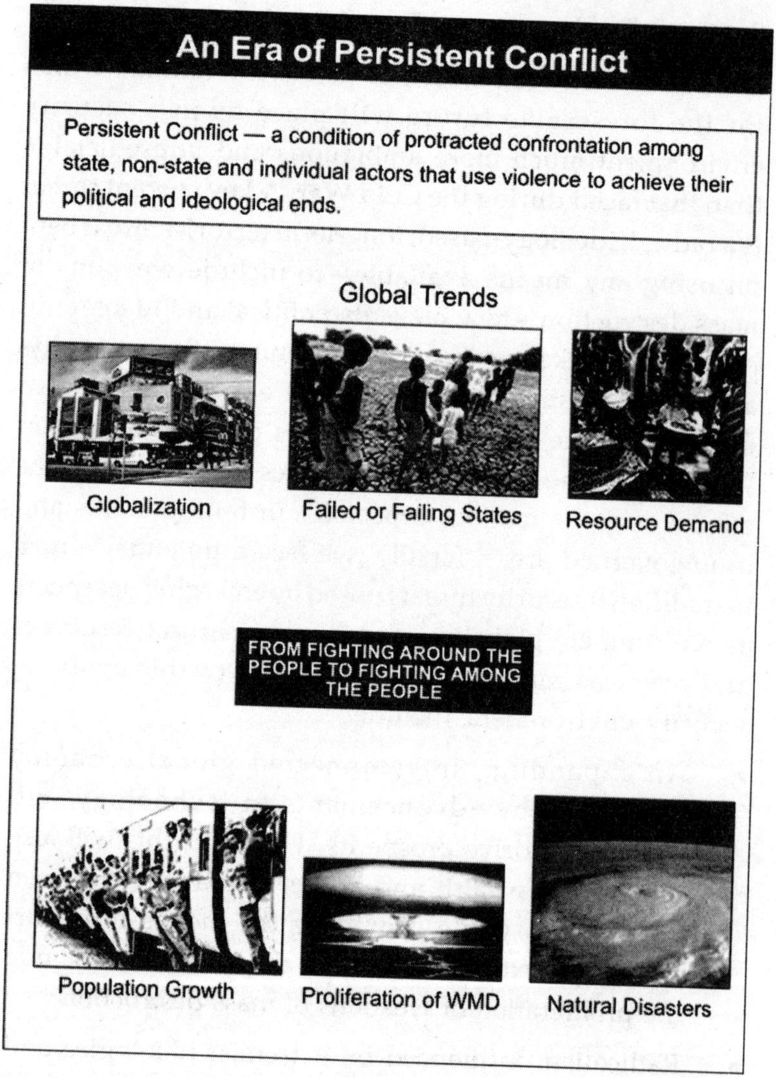


Figure 1– 1, "An era of persistent conflict" – Key trends driving the shape of the strategic environment are globalization, population growth, increasing resource demands, natural disasters, weapons of mass destruction proliferation, failed and failing states.

anti-government and radical ideologies that potentially threaten government stability

- Resource competition induced by growing populations and expanding economies will consume ever increasing amounts of food, water and energy. States or entities controlling these resources will leverage them as part of their security calculus
- Climate change and natural disasters will compound already difficult positions in many developing countries, thereby increasing the potential for humanitarian crises, epidemic disease and regionally destabilizing population migrations
- Proliferation of weapons of mass destruction and effects will create the potential for catastrophic attacks. Attacks of this nature will be destabilizing globally, and will undercut the confidence that spurs economic development
- Safe havens that create opportunities for global and regional groups to organize and export terror will be created by states unable or unwilling to exercise control within their borders. This will also enable these organizations to challenge central government authority and launch broader security threats.

Clearly, our most immediate concern is ensuring readiness to succeed in current operations. However, the evolving strategic environment will continue to place steady demands on the Army long after we conclude operations in Afghanistan and Iraq. We can expect future foes to be innovative and adaptive, and fully adept at exploiting a globalized world to their advantage. The implication for the Army is that we must continuously and aggressively modernize our capabilities to ensure we remain a dominant force, capable of operating in complex environments across the full spectrum of conflict.

## Army Out of Balance

The Army is engaged in the third longest war in our Nation's history and the longest ever with an All-Volunteer Force. Continual deployments in support of the Global War on Terrorism (GWOT) have caused the Army to become out of balance with the demand for forces exceeding the sustainable supply. The pace of operations coupled with insufficient time between deployments is forcing the Army to focus on counter-insurgency training and equipping to the detriment of preparing for full spectrum operations. In addition, equipment that is being used repeatedly in harsh environments is wearing out more rapidly than programmed and overall readiness is being consumed as fast as it is built. Most importantly, the lack of balance is reducing the Army's strategic depth and degrading our ability to readily respond to other contingencies.

Despite these challenges, the Army is committed to restoring balance in order to preserve the All-Volunteer Force, develop the necessary depth and breadth in Army capabilities and build essential capacity for the future by addressing these imperatives: **Sustain, Prepare, RESET** and **Transform**. The Army's modernization strategy specifically relates to imperatives Prepare, RESET and Transform.

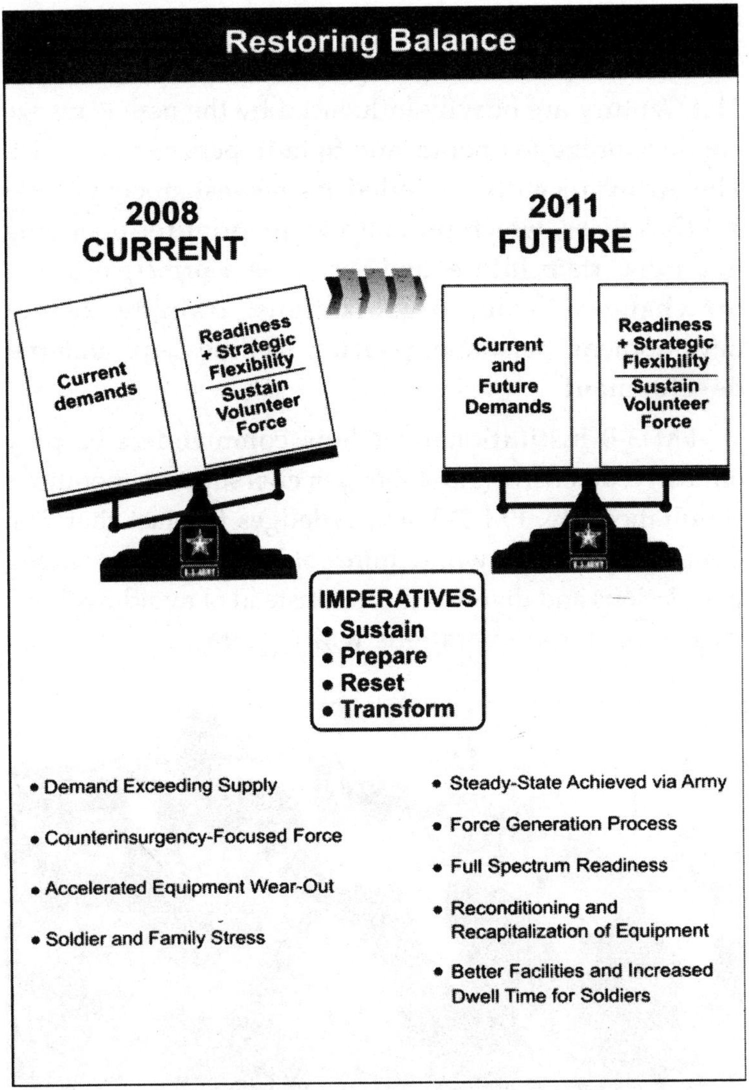


Figure 1–2, "Out of Balance" assessment = stretched and stressed All-Volunteer Force–Demand –exceeds supply –COIN-focused force – Accelerated equipment wear out – Soldier and Family stress

## Evolving Doctrine – Operations in an Uncertain Future

The full-spectrum capabilities necessary to fight in the 21st Century are heavily influenced by the new ways we are developing to operate and fight in persistent conflict. The Army recently unveiled its newest doctrine, *FM 3-0 Operations*, which provides a blueprint for operating in an uncertain future, and serves as a principal driver for changes in our organizations, training, leader development, personnel policies, facilities and **material development**.

FM 3-0 institutionalizes how commanders employ offensive, defensive and stability or civil support operations simultaneously. FM 3-0 acknowledges the fact that 21st Century operations will require soldiers to engage among populations and diverse cultures instead of avoiding them. Success in these operations will require the protracted

application of all aspects of national power and cause us to place equal emphasis on tactical tasks dealing with the people as with those related to the execution of combat operations. A primary purpose of the modernization strategy is ensuring the Army has a comprehensive balance of integrated capabilities for accomplishing its wide array of missions.

Conflict remains a fundamentally human endeavour. Although the operating concept defined within FM 3-0 provides a major impetus to the development of the strategy, Soldiers as the foundation and centerpiece of the Army remain its focus. Soldiers are the ultimate sensors, analysts, decision makers and shooters and they remain our most important advantage in an era of persistent conflict. It is imperative that we ensure our material solutions to provide the capabilities our Soldiers need to guarantee success.

## The Army Modernization Strategy–Ends, Ways and Means

### *Ends*

The Army is committed to never putting a Soldier in a "fair fight." Therefore, the Army Modernization Strategy strives to ensure that the Army continues to be equipped with capabilities that guarantee its stature as the pre-eminent land combat force in the world. To do this the Army must concentrate its equipping and modernization efforts on two mutually supporting ends—**restoring balance** and achieving **full-spectrum dominance**.

The Army Modernization Strategy directly supports restoring balance through the Army Imperatives:

Prepare, RESET and Transform. Specifically, to **Prepare** our Soldiers, units and equipment we must maintain a high level of equipment readiness for the current operational environments, especially in Iraq and Afghanistan. To **RESET** our force we must properly posture Soldiers, units and equipment for future deployments and other contingencies. Finally, to **Transform** our force, we must continuously improve our capabilities to meet the needs of the Combatant Commanders in a changing security environment.

Central to the efforts is the need to upgrade and mobilize equipment for our Soldiers in the current fight. This ensures readiness with units equipped to succeed in a variety of contingency scenarios and transformed as a part of joint, multinational or interagency efforts with modernized equipment.

The Army Imperatives recognize that restoring balance is about more than just addressing capacity shortfalls tied to the current fight. It is also about continuously improving our capabilities to ensure Soldiers and units remain equally adept at executing all types of operations—often times concurrently—from peace time engagement to major combat operations. This is full-spectrum dominance as executed by an expeditionary, campaign quality Army. Expeditionary capability ensures the Army is ready to deploy promptly, at any time, in any environment and against any adversary. Campaign quality means that once the Army is deployed it can operate for extended periods of time across the entire spectrum of conflict.

### *Ways–The Four Elements of Continuous Modernization*

An era of persistent conflict demands continuous modernization. In the past the Nation could anticipate a strategic pause at the end of a conflict that afforded an opportunity to rebuild military strength in advance of future conflict. Today's environment of persistent conflict offers no such luxury. Therefore, today's Army must build the capabilities it needs in the 21st century. This must be done while restoring the capacity to sustain operations over an extended period.

The figure below depicts the trends fuelling persistent conflict and the capabilities the Army requires in the 21st century.

The Army's Modernization Strategy methodically delivers needed capabilities through the following ways:

1. **Rapidly field the best new equipment** to the Current Force

## The Four Elements of Army Modernization

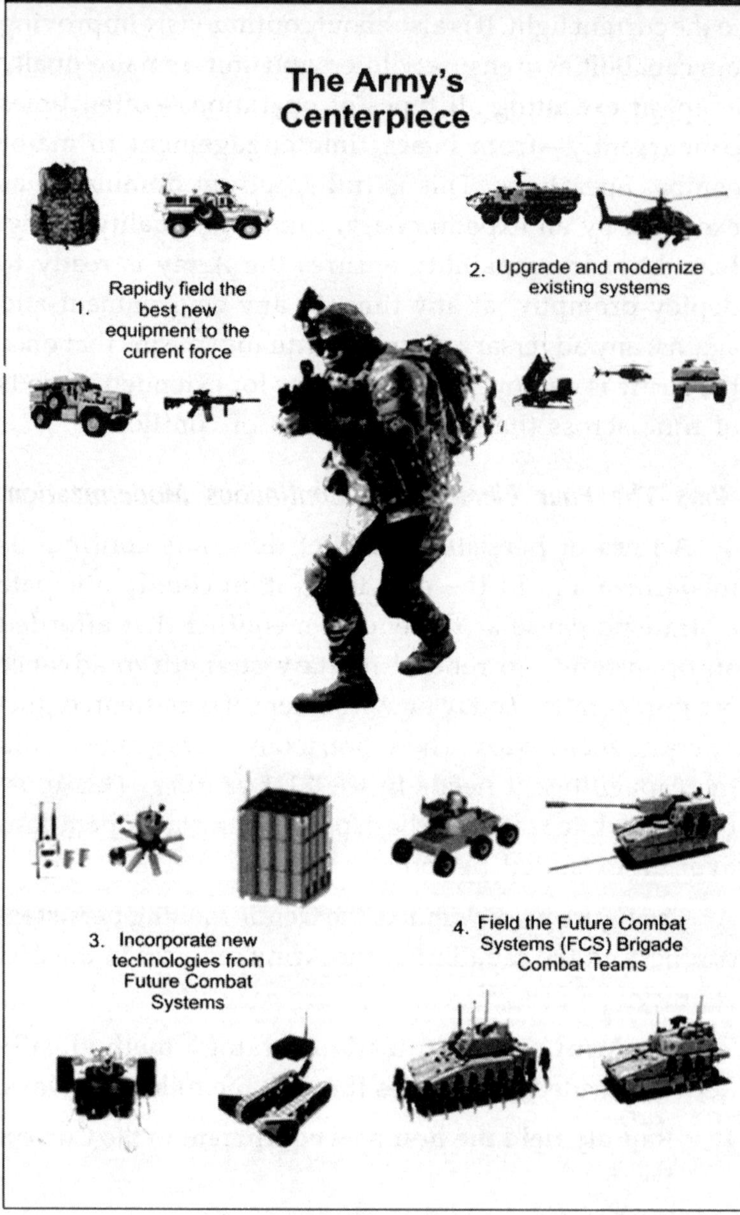

2. **Upgrade and modernize existing systems** within modular formations to ensure all Soldiers have the equipment they need

3. **Incorporate new technologies derived from Future Combat Systems (FCS)** research and development **(R&D)** as they become available

4. **Field Future Combat Systems** Brigade Combat Teams.

**Rapidly fielding new and better equipment** to the Current Force ensures the Army remains adaptive and responsive to evolving situations by providing the means to provide Soldiers with greater **protection**, and enhanced capabilities. Rapid fielding provides Soldiers and units the equipment they need now. Many of these initiatives mature into formal acquisition programmes. Virtually all these initiatives provide the Army with expeditious and informative means that facilitate Future Force development. Details of the Army's rapid equipping efforts are presented in Chapter 2.

**Upgrading and modernizing existing systems** allows us to better leverage the Army's considerable investments in its existing capabilities when it makes sense to do so. More specifically, it allows the Army to extend equipment utility while we work to bridge capacity in new technologies and formations. Modernizing existing capabilities through technology insertions also facilitates Future Force development while we maintain comparative operational capabilities within the Total Force mix.

The Army's primary modernization efforts are described in Chapter 3. Additional details on core modernization programmes, by functional area, are provided in Annexure A.

**Incorporating FCS-based technologies** into all Army Combat Brigades allows the Army to exploit and leverage FCS capabilities efforts sooner with mutually supporting technology enhancements across the force. This facilitates adding new capabilities quickly by leveraging current platforms that can accept technology insertions, and also serves to facilitate earlier integration across other Doctrine, Organizations, Training, Material, Leadership and Education, Personnel and Facilities (DOTMLPF) dimensions. Details of how the Army is facilitating development of the Future Force through the incorporation of FCS Spin-out technologies into the Current Force are provided in Chapter 4.

**Fielding FCS Brigade Combat Teams** fulfills the Army's vision for the future by integrating full spectrum capabilities in an integrated unit design. FCS is more than just a new type of Brigade Combat Team. FCS is the Army's modernization programme consisting of a family of manned and unmanned systems, connected by a common network that enables the Modular Force, providing our Soldiers and leaders with leading edge technologies and capabilities allowing them to dominate in complex environments. FCS is the core of the Army's modernization effort and serves as a principal driver behind many of our rapid fielding initiatives, R&D, and modernization programes. FCS is underpinned by a common platform that streamlines logistics and extends an advanced network to the tactical units that engage the enemy. FCS will provide our Soldiers with unparalleled understanding of their operational environment while also dramatically improving their lethality and survivability. The Family of Manned Ground Vehicles (MGV) is uniquely relevant for today's contemporary operating environment (COE) as well as any future battlefield. The enhanced protection, situational awareness, and networked capabilities will ensure our continued dominance. FCS is focused on delivering the capabilities the Army needs: enhanced **Soldier protection**, modular, scalable, and tailorable, **network** at the lowest level, strategic **force projection**– intra-theater operational manoeuvre and **sustainment**, **modular**, tailorable forces –**adaptable** to present and future threats, and lethal and non-lethal **overmatch**. Details of how the Army will field its FCS Brigade Combat Teams are provided in Chapter 5.

### *Means*

Implementing this strategy requires continuing support from Congress. The Army began the GWOT with a $56 billion shortfall in its equipment and modernization programmes. Although we have received significant funding support through wartime supplementals, most of it has served to sustain the Nation's war effort and has not been used to correct pre-existing deficiencies or support modernization. Full Congressional funding support to the Army's current and future needs is integral to maintaining readiness and modernizing for success in the 21st Century security environment.

The fiscal year 2008 Army equipping base budget provided $15.5 billion for rapid fielding of new equipment, $3.9 billion for upgrading and modernizing existing systems and over $3.4 billion for FCS research and procurement, including Spin-outs. Of note, FCS represents 28 percent of the Army's fiscal year 2008 overall budget for Research, Development, Test & Evaluation and four percent of the procurement budget. The Army will seek to increase modernization funding in its base budget in POM 10-15 to correct previous funding shortfalls and provide adequate funding support to critical programmes.

## A Comprehensive Approach

Sufficient investment in modernization provides an Army that is integral to Joint, interagency and multinational success, across the full-spectrum of conflict. Today's Army is moving rapidly in that direction. The Army Modernization Strategy features the Army's efforts to develop and field improved operational capabilities in order to restore balance and ensure full-spectrum dominance. Accompanying advancements in **DOTMLPF** supporting this strategy and providing integrated solutions which improve how the Army is organized, trained, and equipped are fully examined in Annexure B.

Given the challenges we face today, and are likely to face tomorrow, the Army cannot risk delaying execution of our modernization strategy over multiple decades, stretching out significant increments of modernization such that they may be obsolete as we field them. We must aggressively pursue efforts now to restore balance and achieve full spectrum dominance, in order to guarantee our success in an era of persistent conflict.

# Chapter 2

# Rapidly Field the Best Available Equipment to the Current Force

## Introduction

Significant equipping challenges remain for the Army for the foreseeable future as it simultaneously supports current operations, consistently improves the readiness of non-deployed units and transforms to the Future Force. In an era of persistent conflict the Army must be a relentlessly adaptive force. Our Soldiers and leaders have excelled in adapting to the enemy from the early days of operations in Afghanistan to the combat of today. The Army must ensure that the system that equips these brave Americans is equally agile and just as relentless in providing the best available equipment to ensure readiness. Rapidly fielding new and better equipment to the Current Force ensures the Army remains adaptive and responsive to evolving situations by providing the means which allow us to consider what may have not been previously considered or anticipated, thus providing Soldiers and units the equipment they need now.

## Drivers

The Army's equipping demands are influenced by a variety of factors. For more than three decades prior to the GWOT, the Nation and our Army accepted operational risk with a tiered readiness system that allowed certain follow-on, or late deploying units to be equipped to a lesser level, believing there would be sufficient time and resources to get them up to speed before they are deployed. Personnel and equipment demands of GWOT have made this way of doing business obsolete. Today's combined equipment demands of converting to a Modular Force, resourcing Military Transition Teams, supporting pre- and post- deployment training, increasing operational requirements, replacing Army Pre-Positioned Stocks and generating Theater Provided Equipment are all magnified by existing unit equipment shortages.

Operations in Iraq and Afghanistan also exposed Army capability gaps that resulted from years of constrained resources. The Army has not yet recovered from equipment shortfalls that existed at the start of the war, and in 2013 faces residual unfunded equipment requirements of $17.4 billion.

Wear and tear on equipment has also been accelerated due to increased OPTEMPO. In the current theater, increased usage and added weight from extra armour are wearing out equipment at up to six times the established peacetime usage rates.

In addition, the non-deployed force lacks the necessary equipment to meet unexpected National requirements. Army National Guard on hand equipment, identified as critical dual-use equipment, necessary for both deployments and emergency/disaster response, is critically short in some states. These critical shortages limit training, especially pre/post mobilization training and unit abilities to support their respective governors and provide support to other states and Federal agencies. Finally, the need to modernize will never end. While the current operations in Iraq and Afghanistan have forced the Army to address challenges with its operational capacities and sufficiencies, we have also had to reflect deeper on what the Army will require in the future to remain a pre-eminent force in this era of persistent conflict.

Collectively, these challenges limit our current ability to fully equip the Army and increase the Nation's strategic flexibility. A modernized Army will require a significant investment in resources over time in support of both current and future modernization to provide a more agile responsive force.

The Army remains committed to aggressively maintaining the best trained, best equipped, most fully manned and best led ground force in the world. To do this though, the Army needs predictable, sufficient and stable funding.

The Army's Modernization Strategy, supported by significant investment, will provide the Nation with a balanced, modernized Army, engaged in persistent conflict that meets all of today's operational needs while building the Army needed in the 21st Century.

## Expediting Capabilities to the Warfighter

The Army, as we entered this war, recognized that our processes were too slow, requiring as much as 18 to 24 months to get some of our major systems into the hands of Soldiers. We had to respond and adapt to changing situations, consider what had not been previously considered, and above all, ensure that the Current Force had useable equipment in all new operational environments. We have undertaken numerous initiatives to accelerate acquisition and equipment fielding—expediting capabilities to the warfighter.

## Army Force Generation (ARFORGEN)

ARFORGEN manages the Army's limited resources more effectively and rids the Army of have and have-not units. Under ARFORGEN, units progressively increase in readiness as they progress through three readiness pools:

- An initial RESET/Train pool for units either redeploying from long operations or who spent their available time in the Available Pool and did not deploy but were prepared to do so, if directed
- A ready pool that includes modular units assessed as "ready" to conduct mission preparation and training
- An available pool that includes modular units assessed as "available" to conduct missions in support of any Regional Combat Commander or serve as rapidly deployable contingency forces.

When a unit deploys, it is the best trained, and equipped unit capable of meeting the regional Combatant Commander mission requirements. However, the Army must also continue to invest in capability by supporting upgrades to current modular formations and by introducing emerging technologies to the force.

## Capabilities Development for Rapid Transition

Capabilities Development for Rapid Transition is a process that identifies non-programme of record, non-standard systems or pieces of equipment to be rapidly transitioned into an acquisition programme. It also identifies other non-equipment capabilities that merit consideration as potential enduring Army capabilities. In partnership with the Army Deputy Chief of Staff for Operations, TRADOC manages this process to assess systems in operational settings to determine whether or not they should become systems of record and be fielded to the entire Army.

The intent of the process is to enter the formal developments process at a later stage reducing time from the development cycle. An iteration of CDRT lasts six months. It primarily considers material capabilities and these issues are worked in close coordination with a variety of Army agencies, to include:

- TRADOC
- Army Deputy Chiefs of Staff for Intelligence, Operations, Logistics, Communications and Programmes
- Office of the Surgeon General
- Army Test and Evaluation Command
- Army Material Command
- Assistant Secretary of the Army for Acquisitions, Logistics, and Technology.

Lists of equipment candidate systems are streamlined for warfighter assessments. CDRT primarily considers material capabilities and is worked in close collaboration with HQ TRADOC, ARCIC FWD, HQDA G2, G3/5/7, G4, G6, G8, OTSG, ATEC, ASA (ALT), ATEC, AMC, all COIs and the Operating Force. Iterative lists of equipment candidate systems are streamlined for reasonable warfighter assessments. Its recommendations are ultimately briefed to the Army Vice Chief of Staff.

CDRT's force protection candidates that have become proven winners for our Soldiers are Interceptor Body Armour, IED Route Clearance Package, Armoured Security Vehicle and the Common Remote Operated Weapons System. CDRT's most recent candidates include, One System Remote Video Terminal, Green Laser—Z-Bolt, Specialized Search Dogs, Line of Communication Bridging and the Joint Automated Deep Operations Coordination System. CDRT is a relatively new and evolving

process that will continue to mature as its utility to the Army grows.

## Rapid Equipping Force

The Rapid Equipping Force mission is to quickly assess what the Army needs and fill those needs by providing commanders with off-the-shelf items, both government and commercial, that reduce risks to Soldiers and help increase their effectiveness. The REF works one-on-one with units, either in combat or preparing for it, to find innovative solutions for their immediate equipping needs. They accomplish this by partnering with industry and academia, and with senior leaders and Army organizations such as Army Material Command, TRADOC, the acquisition community and the Army Test and Evaluation Command. One main focus is on defeating Improvised Explosive Devices and providing direct support to the Joint IED Defeat

Organization and the Asymmetric Warfare Group. The Rapid Equipping Force also deploys teams forward to evaluate deployed force needs and capabilities. To date they have introduced more than 200 different types of equipment and have provided more than 47,000 items to units in Iraq and Afghanistan as well as other parts of the world.

## Rapid Fielding Initiative

In keeping with the "Soldier as a System" philosophy, the Rapid Fielding Initiative provides off-the-shelf technology and items of equipment to Soldiers to enhance their survivability, lethality and mobility. The Rapid Fielding Initiative list is composed of individual equipment that every Soldier receives and additional unit equipment that we field to Brigade Combat Teams. TRADOC updates the RFI list to keep it relevant to lessons learned from the war. The Rapid Fielding Initiative helps save Soldiers' lives by fielding items such as the Improved First Aid Kit, fielded to every Soldier in theater. We have issued more than a million sets of equipment to Soldiers.

## Reset

The requirement to reset equipment and return all Army units to full readiness when they return from deployment ensures Army ability to execute follow-on operations. Reset restores equipment and personnel to a desired level of combat capability commensurate with a unit's future mission. It restores readiness of equipment that has been damaged, or worn out and replaces equipment that was destroyed. Reset does not fix Army equipment shortfalls, but restores serviceability and

capability of equipment on hand, and replaces battle losses with new equipment. Reset planning is synchronized with unit training and deployment schedules.

A fully funded Army Reset programme ensures equipment is operationally ready for use by combat forces in Iraq and Afghanistan as well as other missions the Army is asked to perform for the Nation, and by forces that are training prior to deployment. Reset funding should match requirements and be provided in a timely manner to promote cost efficiencies while ensuring Soldiers have the proper equipment first in training, then while deployed conducting operations.

## How the Army is Managing Immediate Equipping Needs Life Cycle Management Commands

Established in 2004 by an agreement between ASA (ALT) and the Army Material Command, Life Cycle

Management Commands have enhanced support of Army equipment through improved collaboration between the acquisition, logistics and technology communities. They bring together acquisition, logistics and technology under integrated leadership to focus all efforts toward supporting the Soldier through the Army Sustainment Command as the single interface point. This construct not only assists the warfighter through improved responsiveness, but also ensures that solutions provided by the Material community provide the best balance between enhanced capability, speed of acquisition and long-term sustainment costs.

## Army Sustainment Command

The Army Sustainment Command provides field units a direct link for integrating logistics with Joint and strategic partners in the National sustainment base. In conjunction with the Army's Life Cycle Management Commands, the ASC coordinates and establishes an end-to-end distribution pipeline to the deployed warfighter and assists the U.S. Forces Command and Joint Forces Command in the rapid projection of forces to the Regional Commander and return. Through the global presence of AMC's Army Field Support Brigades, the ASC provides a single command structure that coordinates acquisition, logistics readiness and technology integration efforts in the field.

## Theater Provided Equipment

At the end of the Cold War, the "Peace Dividend" resulted in investment accounts being under-funded by \$100 billion resulting in a \$56 billion shortfall for all Army equipment shortages, modernization and operational needs at the start of GWOT. To help overcome these equipment

shortfalls a strategy was developed to maintain select equipment in theater for use by rotational forces. This strategy saves time and money by not shipping similar equipment to and from theater. This is the Army's Theater Provided Equipment pool, providing theater commanders with flexible response options and additional on-hand resources in theater. TPE also decreases direct and indirect costs for repeat transportation of rotational force equipment, reduces convoy exposure time to move equipment into and out of areas of operations, and increases equipment longevity at home by decreasing downtime associated with transporting and resetting equipment.

Theater Provided Equipment consists of items that have been deployed to and left behind in theater to support ongoing operations. As units finish their deployment, TPE is placed in a Soldier. Equipment left in theater is planned for Reset and for continued use.

## Left Behind Equipment

Left Behind Equipment processes ensure that equipment is maintained and accounted for to support ARFORGEN. When units redeploy from theater, a large amount of their equipment needs to be repaired and Reset, and their inventory is temporarily depleted. LBE is also equipment that is left at home station after a unit deploys. Other units deploying to theater leave some equipment at home, such as un-armoured trucks. The intent of this programme is to release AC units from responsibility for equipment they will not use in the conduct of their wartime mission. LBE is often used to help equip other units that are training and preparing to re-deploy. HQDA G-8 manages the re-equipping of units and management of G-8 items in accordance with HQDA G-3 priorities. This ensures redeploying units are fully equipped.

## Army Pre-positioned Stocks

Army Pre-positioned Stocks have provided Combatant Commanders with a modern fleet of equipment to directly support contingency operations throughout the world. APS consists of pre-positioned unit sets, operational stocks, sustainment stocks and War Reserve Stocks. These are critical warfighting stocks, located in strategic land and ship-based locations, thus reducing deployment response times for Army forces during contingencies. Pre-positioned stocks are important in reducing strategic lift requirements and improving force closure times.

Whether on specially-designed ships, or stored in various strategic locations, APS provides a flexible, sustainable and strategically responsive force that can rapidly engage in Army and Joint operations.

The Army has used equipment from all five of our pre-positioned sets to support OIF/OEF. Since 2003, the Army has been resetting and reconfiguring prepositioned stocks to match Army Modular Force designs. This includes heavy equipment such as Abrams tanks, as well as repair parts and other assets assigned to APS.

As a part of Reset, items drawn from APS stocks will not only be replenished to pre-war levels, but also modernized to a more current configuration that allows Soldiers to quickly operate this equipment in support of short notice, full spectrum military operations.

## ReUse

ReUse is the process the Army uses to ensure all available equipment, whether new or used, is redistributed to fill requirements for the Total Force. Driven by operational requirements, Army equippers use ARFORGEN, TPE and LBE programmes to ensure allocation of the right mix of equipment to provide to operationally ready units. This includes equipment needed by National Guard units to perform Homeland Security and Homeland Defence missions, and equipment required for the Army's training base. Currently the Army is managing more than 96,000 pieces of equipment through ReUse.

## Army Enterprise Equipping and ReUse Conference

The Army uses twice-yearly Army Enterprise Equipping and ReUse Conferences to synchronize Army Equipping Enterprise Architectures with equipment requirements, modernization plans and delivery of equipment. Army equippers, planners and force developers from all Army Commands, Army Service Component Commands and Direct Reporting Units use AEERCs to schedule deliveries of equipment from production, RESET, TPE and ReUse.

As a result of the latest AEERC conducted in January 2008, the Army was able to schedule over $56 billion of equipment distributions to Active and Reserve formations from January 2008 to 31 December 2009. This includes $34.6 billion to the Active Component, about $17.5 billion of equipment for the ARNG and over $4 billion of equipment for the USAR.

## Army Equipping Enterprise System (AE2S)

The Army Equipping Enterprise System (AE2S) provides Force Development, Army G-8 and HQDA Staff with an authoritative, analytical and collaborative set of tools. AE2S will seamlessly support the Equipping Process from requirements determination, resourcing and programming to delivery of capabilities to the Army. This initiative began in 2007 and in March 2008 the AE2S support contract was awarded that began the first phase of a multi-year effort to integrate the Army G-8 equipping systems into one collaborative equipping process application. The three major applications within AE2S are the Army Flow Model, Force Development Investment Information System and EQUIPFOR. One of the new tools to provide our staff and leaders with a comprehensive view of our equipping efforts resides in AE2S. The Strategic Common Operation Picture (shown in the chart on the following page) combines authoritative information concerning requirements, inventory, distribution and Future Years Defence Planning equipment procurements to project equipping postures for individual items and groups of items making up major capabilities. This tool is expected to serve as one of the major projection tools for the Army G-8's AEERC.

The AE2S also contains EQUIPFOR which is the Army G-8 distribution system that serves as the primary planning tool for the staff to distribute newly produced equipment or equipment modified and ready for distribution. Current initiatives to update and expand the use of EQUIPFOR include extending its use to the Army Material Command for critical AMC managed procurements.

## Reserve Component Equipping

Reserve Components are also part of the Army Equipping Enterprise. These units provide essential combat and support capabilities and comprise 55 percent of the Army's structure. Pre-war ARNG equipment levels were at 70 percent of "Army of Excellence" unit designs, most

## ARMY Equipping Enterprise

**EXAMPLE: Army Strategic Equipping Common Operational Picture**

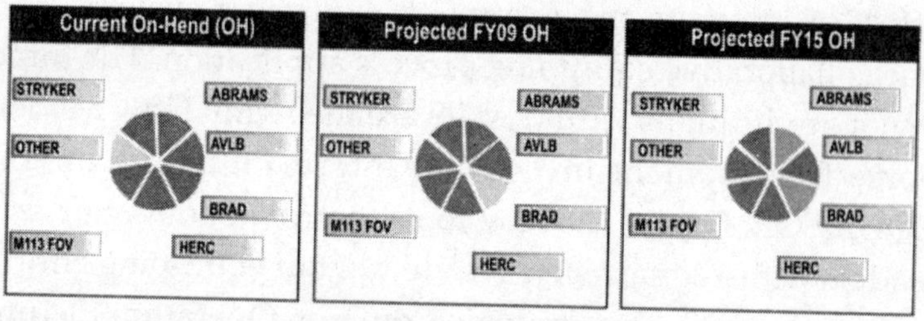


| LIN Family | Current % OH | FY09 % OH | FY15 % OH |
|---|---|---|---|
| ABRAMS | | | |
| ARMORED VEHICULAR LAUNCHED BRIDGE (AVLB) | | | |
| BRADLEY (BRAD) | | | |
| HERCULES (HERC) | | | |
| M113 FOV | | | |
| OTHER | | | |
| STRYKER | | | |

**MANOEUVRE CBT VEH**

**Legend**

is > = 90%

is < 90% > = 80%

is < 80% > = 65%

* Critical LIN

**As of Dates**

On-Hand: 23-Mar-2008

Required: 06-Dec-2007

Equip For: 26-Mar-2008

LQA: 26-Mar-2008

**Comments:**

**Acronyms:**

**TOTAL ARMY [MTOE & TDA - Without Subs)**

*LIN Family = Specific groups of LINs

*Current On - Hand = LIW on-hand with substitutions

*Projected on-Hand based on EQUIP FOR distribution

*Color codes based on SACS File requirements vs on-hand inventory

*On-hand inventory above requirements are not counted

**FOR OFFICAL USE ONLY**

The linkage between the Army G-3 Force Management Structure and Composition System for requirements, the Army G-4 Property Book Unit Supply -Enhanced (PBUSE) for inventory, EQUIPFOR for distributions and Force Development's Force Development Investment Information System (FDIIS) for procurement quantities allows the Army G-8 to synchronize information to support the equipping process.

of which was old, obsolete and worn equipment. The current shift from strategic reserve to an operational reserve force requires the assurance that RC units are equipped, trained, manned and structured like the AC to provide the required land forces to support the Nation's defence strategy and provide support to Civil Authorities. To accomplish this, the Army National Guard is being resourced $49.1 billion from 2001 through 2013, while the Reserve is being resourced $15.7 billion for the same time period. From January 2008 to December 2009, the Army delivered over 400,000 pieces of equipment worth about $17.5 billion to the ARNG and over 118,000 pieces of equipment worth $5 billion to USAR. The ARNG reached 77% equipment on hand (EOH) by the end of fiscal year 2008; and 74% EOH by the end of fiscal year 2009 based on fiscal year 2013 MTOEs.

## DoDD 1225.6 Paybacks

The Secretary of Defence provided specific guidance in DoD Directive that requires the Army to replace equipment transferred from one component to another on a one-for-one basis. The National Defence Authorization Act of 2007 reinforced this directive, making it a law. As per this guidance, the Army documents equipment transfers and develops payback plans coordinated between Department of the Army, the Army National Guard and Reserves and approved at Defence Department level. The Army is validating payback actions for equipment that was transferred out of RC to other units. To date, the Army has validated the transfer of more than 54,000 items of equipment from the ARNG and USAR to the AC to support deployed forces and

Soldiers in training. Currently, $2.5 billion worth of equipment has been validated for repayment. The Army is also reducing the amount of RC equipment being transferred, and is continuing to monitor and improve the process.

## Homeland Defence

The Army has a long tradition of support to Civil Authorities, while maintaining its primary mission of fighting and winning the Nation's wars. While the Army does not typically resource equipment specifically for Homeland Defence and support to Civil Authorities missions, it does recognize priority Army National Guard equipment as critical dual-use equipment which is used to support both combat and Civil Authorities support missions. We make an effort to field this equipment first.

The Army Staff, ARNG and the Army Reserve worked collaboratively to identify and prioritize the Baseline Equipment Set for Homeland Defence and Support to Civil Authorities. This Baseline Equipment Set currently consists of approximately 342 equipment types identified as dual-use items that are managed in 10 essential capabilities: Aviation, Engineering, Civil Support Teams, Security, Medical, Transportation, Maintenance, Logistics, Joint Force Headquarters and Communications.

## Response to Natural Disaster

The equipping levels for dual use equipment in the non-deployed ARNG units in some states could impact on the state's ability to respond to state emergencies. In those cases, neighbouring states provide equipment and unit support through the Emergency Management

## Sustaining the Army's Equipping Needs

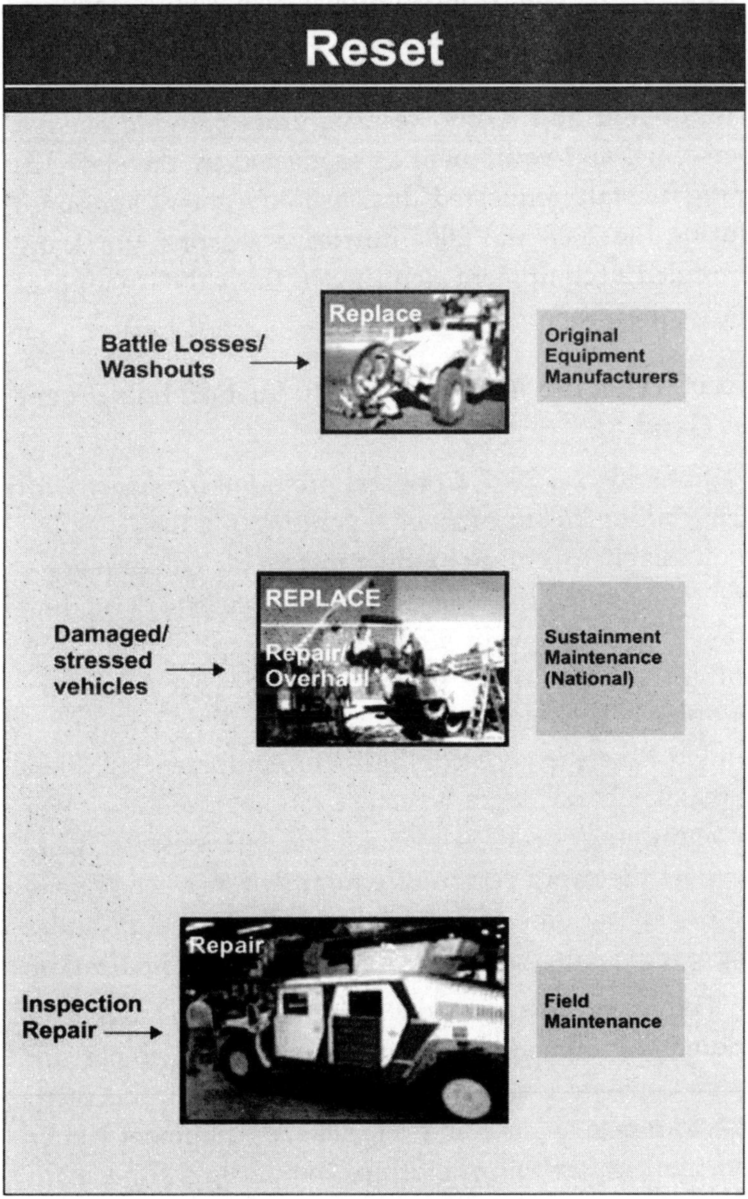

Assistance Compact. Response to natural disasters is not just an Army Guard mission but a Total Force mission. When a natural disaster hits a state where the ARNG does not have all of its required resources, Active Component and Army Reserve units provide needed personnel and equipment as requested by the state. To mitigate state requested dual use equipment shortages during the 2006 and 2007 hurricane seasons, the Army provided all equipment identified by the ARNG to support hurricane preparedness.

## Reset: What the Army is doing to Sustain Equipment on Hand

In fiscal year 2007, Congress provided the Army with $17.1 billion in supplemental funding for Reset, and is aggressively executing funding to provide equipment for deploying units. The majority of the procurement funding was obligated within 90 days of receipt, while OMA obligations occurred throughout the fiscal year as equipment was returned and repaired. Even when fully funded, Reset merely holds the line on equipment readiness so that it does not degrade further. It is not the final answer for improving overall Army readiness, but does effectively support the rapid return of equipment to a ready state for deploying units. In certain instances, Reset provides improved capabilities through equipment recapitalization.

The Army must continue to Reset equipment to rebuild readiness consumed in current operations, and prepare for future deployments. We must partner with our industrial base to repair, replace and recapitalize equipment lost or damaged in current operations, while upgrading both capacity and capabilities through our modernization efforts.

The Army will have to repair, replace and recapitalize equipment for a minimum of at least three years after the end of the current conflict. OIF/ OEF has forced the Army to adapt to a more formal integration of Reset processes, namely: Repair, Replace and Recapitalize.

## Replacement

Replacement is the procurement of new equipment to replace battle losses or equipment deemed too expensive to repair. Equipment lost due to combat action or that is not economically repairable is replaced from the industrial base. The Army procures the newest versions of equipment it can to replace battle losses, ensuring the longest possible shelf life within the Army Modular Force.

In addition to the replacement of end items, replacement also includes the purchase and installation of supply parts and assemblies installed into pre-existing Army equipment. Done primarily when a system

undergoes maintenance and repair, the incremental installation of improved parts provides significant improvements to Army equipment without having to remove the item from the unit's inventory.

### Recapitalization

Recapitalization is depot-level maintenance activity that extends the useful life of systems by completely rebuilding and introducing selected upgrades to the fleet. It is the Army's long-term investment strategy to sustain equipment readiness. RECAP is accomplished by rebuilding old, worn-out, or combat-damaged equipment to a "zero mile/zero hour" level with original performance specifications. This is done by using Research, Development, Test and Evaluation, procurement, or operation and maintenance funds. RECAP objectives include: (1) extend service life; (2) reduce operating and support costs; (3) improve reliability, maintainability, safety and efficiency and (4) enhance capability.

RECAP is an effort usually conducted at either a depot, contractor facility or a combination of the two. Items placed in RECAP are completely disassembled, have all outdated and worn parts stripped and are rebuilt from the frame up, using the latest parts and manufacturing processes. The end state of RECAP is a fully refurbished and modernized piece of equipment that has been restored to its original condition and has new capabilities. On an average, items placed through RECAP not only represent the most modern configuration, but are far more reliable and have their useful service life dramatically extended, reducing the burden on the acquisition community.

The Army's plan to recapitalize major combat systems ensures required capabilities are available for the next fight. Major systems being recapitalized include the Abrams Tank, Bradley Fighting Vehicle, 105-millimeter Light Howitzer, HMMWV and Apache Attack Helicopter. Recapitalization may include pre-planned product improvements, extended service programmes and major modifications, but these programmes alone are not recapitalization unless the system is restored to zero time/ zero mile condition.

## Repair

Repair of Army equipment involves inspection followed by repair and rebuild of equipment to meet Army maintenance standards. Repair is essential to maintaining not only readiness, but is also a primary means of providing incremental modernization. This occurs by installing better parts and using more efficient maintenance procedures.

Repair restores equipment to meet the Army operator's fully operational maintenance standards, and other unique requirements. As equipment is broken, worn-out or damaged, the Army repairs it to prescribed standards to provide fully mission capable equipment. In fiscal year 2007, the Army repaired 57 crash-damaged helicopters, 190 Abrams, 364 Bradleys, 1,600 wheeled vehicles and more than 35,000 small arms in depots. At field level, the Army repaired 563 aircraft and Reset 27 Brigades: 20 brigade combat teams, four aviation brigades, two support brigades and one fires brigade. When possible, repairs are performed directly on each system. For Reserve Component units, the Army has further streamlined this process by performing repairs at National Guard facilities. This allows the ARNG to prioritize requirements and return equipment to units under the control of state authorities sooner, increasing their capability to respond to domestic missions.

## Sustainment

For all Army Components, repairs that exceed field level capability are performed at depots by organic depot and material maintenance contractors. These depots ensure broken or damaged equipment is repaired to fully operational standard as a part of equipment Reset. The majority of these repairs are executed at Anniston, Corpus Christi, Letterkenny, Red River and Tobyhanna Army Depots.

A key part of Reset at the Sustainment level is the Automatic Reset Induction (ARI) programme. ARI is based on lessons learned from Army Material Command that identified a list of equipment that after use in combat is automatically returned for sustainment level Reset maintenance. This programme speeds the planning and programming of depot level equipment Reset operations and helps speed the equipment flow through the depot system.

## Depot Production & Capacity

Depots are resetting equipment and recapitalizing battle-damaged vehicles and equipment at historically high levels. From the beginning of combat operations through fiscal year 2006, more than 200,000 pieces of equipment have been Reset, including 1,798 aircraft, 2,263 tracked vehicles, 11,312 HMMWVs, 3,899 trucks, 2,193 trailers, 128,531 small arms and 8,284 generators. These figures are only a snapshot of this enormous effort. In fiscal year 2007, the Army Reset approximately 133,000 major items of equipment and hundreds of thousands more pieces of equipment. Currently, the capacities and capabilities of the Army's Industrial Base provides the Army not only with significant Reset and RECAP services, but also Battle Damage and Repair facilities that exceed both field and garrison-level operations.

The overall capacity of our depots has increased to its highest levels since the Vietnam War. Direct labour hours at the depots have increased as well, from 16.3 million in fiscal year 2004, to 24.2 million hours in fiscal year 2007. The Army's organic depots have steadily increased their capability while simultaneously increasing efficiencies. Examples include:

- The work at Red River Army Depot increased from 400 items per month in October 2006 to 700 per month in September 2007

- Anniston Army Depot increased its effort from 1,500 to 7,000 items per month by the end of fiscal year 2007

Timely receipt of the fiscal year 2007 $17.1 billion Reset Supplemental enabled the Army to manage Reset more efficiently and effectively, allowing depot growth to help eliminate carryover depot backlog requirements. This allowed for the Reset of 27 BCTs within fiscal year 2007 and projecting an elimination of the current HMMWV backlog in future.

## Reset Pilot

The purpose of the Reset Pilot test programme is to establish a balanced process following an extended deployment that systematically restores deployed units to a level of personnel and equipment readiness that permits the resumption of training for future missions. The Reset Pilot will act as a forcing function to force institutional change required to implement Reset. The focus of the Reset Pilot is unit, not individual, reconstitution. The Reset model, when fully implemented, will accelerate reconstitution of the force, increase unit readiness, and improve preparation for deployment for next to- deploy units. The Army is conducting a Reset Pilot test of eight AC and five RC redeploying units in order to determine institutional adjustments required to support implementation of ARFORGEN. The 4/25 Airborne Infantry BCT was the first unit to enter the pilot test on 12 December 2007 is proceeding on schedule. Reset Pilot will test the following units:

- 864 EN HVY BN
- 116 IBCT (ARNG)

- 3 ASG
- 111 EN BDE (ARNG)
- 478 EN BN (USAR)
- 325 MD (CSH) (USAR)
- 396 EN CO (USAR)
- 82 DIV HQ
- 1/3 ID
- 4/25IBCT (Abn)
- 2/82 IBCT (Abn)
- 173 IBCT (Abn)
- 82 CAB

This will be a three phase operation:

**Phase 1:** Return minus 180 days (AC/RC)

**Phase 2:** Return to Return plus 180 days (AC)/ Return to Return plus 12 months (RC)

**Phase 3:** Return plus 180 days to LAD (AC)/ Return plus 12 months to Return plus 24 months (RC) where "Return" is defined as 51% of personnel returned to home station.

Chief of Staff of the Army (CSA) has directed that we re-equip 8 A/C and 5 R/C units to S-2 in 180 days after return for Active and 360 days up on returning for Reserve. This is part of the CSA goal to rebalance the Army with a focus on readiness across the force and build combat power regardless of LAD. In real terms we assess the ability to execute Reset pilot equipping requirements in fiscal year 2008 and to implement this in broader terms in fiscal year 2009. Our old equipping strategy focused on equipping deliveries driven by LAD and MRE training, our Pilot strategy stresses equipping units upon return, not LADs.

## Reset Accountability

Reset is a strategic pillar of our modernization strategy—it restores readiness, rebuilds unit readiness and cohesion and builds on the experience of combat operations to build strategic depth for future challenges. Resetting our forces rebuilds and restores strategic depth consumed in six years of combat operations. The Army will fix, replace and upgrade our equipment and prepare all for future deployments and future contingencies. We must Reset to reverse the cumulative effects of sustained high operational tempo.

## Reset Task Force

To manage Reset the Army has established a Reset Task Force composed of elements throughout the Army Staff, Army Material Command, Forces Command, U.S. Army Europe, U.S. Army Pacific, U.S. Army Special Operations Command, the Army Reserve, the Army National Guard and other Army elements as required. The RTF tracks and coordinates Reset at Department of the Army level. For the past several years the Army has estimated Reset requirements to be around $13 billion annually. Because of the increase in forces and the extension of tours of duty needed to meet operational requirements, the Army expects this to potentially increase by $2.5-3.5 billion. Also, the Army recently downloaded two pre-positioned stocks sets of $2.2 billion worth of equipment to fill force requirements that have now been requested for replacement equipment. This level of Reset funding is a spike that reflected the surge of forces in theater. Reset funding is closely related to the size and intensity of operations that is expected to continue until at least two to three years after the conclusion of combat operations. The Army must continue to be resourced at these levels to maintain our equipment readiness.

The receipt of Reset funding early in the fiscal year is essential to keeping the programme on track and preparing next deploying units for their missions.

A majority of Reset are equipment costs resulting from wartime operations. Those costs are reflected in requests for supplemental appropriations, not in the President's Annual Budget Request. A small portion of Reset costs are unrelated to wartime operations and funded through the base budget. Section 1008 of the fiscal year 2007 NDAA requires the President to submit as part of his annual request for funds, for each fiscal year after 2007, a request for funds for ongoing military operations. That section requires Reset be part of base budget requests. Any initiative to move Reset funding into the base budget versus supplemental funding, as long as the Army's top line is appropriately adjusted upward, would ensure long-term success for many Army programmes.

Chapter **3**

# Upgrade and Modernize Existing Modular Formations

## Introduction

Army modernization employs the material solutions necessary to develop a networked, Modular Force that is agile, dominating, globally responsive and sustainable. FCS is the core of this effort. However, Current Force upgrades are also essential for increasing the capabilities of all Brigade Combat Teams in an FCS enabled force. In the coming years, the Nation will invest considerable resources to upgrade the Active and Reserve Components to include the Abrams and Bradley fleets as well as the tactical wheeled vehicles fleet. Aging ambulances, M113 command vehicles, and Nuclear, Biological and Chemical vehicles will be displaced throughout the force by Stryker variants. The plan accelerates aviation modernization efforts, as it restructures and standardizes attack and lift formations across the force, and upgrades an additional 96 Apache Attack helicopters in the Reserve and National Guard. Lastly, the Army will pure fleet the Patriot missile force transforming 1980s technology to more lethal missile defense systems. All of these efforts contribute to ensuring that our Army is relevant in the 21st century.

Upgrading and modernizing existing systems allows us to better leverage the Army's considerable investments in its existing capabilities when it makes sense to do so. More specifically, it allows the Army to extend equipment utility while we work to bridge capacity in new technologies and formations. Modernizing existing capabilities through technology insertions also facilitates Future Force development while we maintain comparative operational capabilities within the Total Force mix.

Modernization is also essential for closing both current and future capability gaps. Without adequately resourced modernization, the Army will not provide significantly improved capabilities, greatly increasing risks to Soldiers now and in the future. To ensure that upgrades align with the prioritization of capability gaps the Army is formally developing an Army Capability Gap list. The ARCIC provides the management structure for identifying capability gaps and describing the operational attributes of proposed solutions. TRADOC's force modernization proposals are reviewed by the Army Staff to ensure integration with Department-wide force management processes and priorities. The Army Requirements Oversight

Council (AROC), chaired by the Vice Chief of Staff, exercises the Chief of Staff's approval authority for force modernization initiatives.

## Core Material Modernization Programmes

Core materiel programme modernization upgrades to existing platforms are essential for increasing the capabilities of the Current Force. The Army has a comprehensive plan to upgrade ground combat vehicles to the most modern variants while displacing the oldest and least modernized variants with FCS Manned Ground Vehicles beginning in 2015. Leveraging investments in tracked vehicle modernization today is essential for ensuring that the Army increases the capabilities of the Heavy Brigade Combat Teams that will be in service beyond 2030 when the 15th FCS BCT is fielded. By supporting the Abrams and Bradley programme upgrades, the Army will maximize the advantages of these current platforms, while augmenting them with advanced digital capabilities found in the most modern variants. These capabilities are essential for maintaining relevance and connectivity in an FCS enabled force.

In the last six years the Army introduced 94 programmes at a cost of $100 billion that greatly enhanced our Soldiers' capabilities on the frontlines of freedom. Maintaining this momentum, the Army will introduce over 64 new programmes over the next 10 years to maintain a current qualitative advantage. All of these efforts contribute to ensuring that our Army is relevant in the 21st Century. A modernization overview of the Army's Core Material Programmes is organized in the following sections:

Section 1: Combat Platforms - Manoeuvre
Section 2: Soldier as a System
Section 3: Aviation Systems
Section 4: Air and Missile Defense
Section 5: Fire Support
Section 6: Chemical, Biological, Radiological and Nuclear Defense
Section 7: Battle Command
Section 8: Battlespace Awareness
Section 9: Engineer Equipment
Section 10: Tactical Wheeled Vehicles
Section 11: Combat Service Support
Section 12: Army Watercraft

## Combat Platforms – Manoeuvre Modernization Overview

The Army's Combat Platform modernization is focused on standardizing the Heavy Brigade Combat Teams (HBCTs) with two variants of the Abrams tank and the Bradley Infantry Fighting Vehicle. The Army has almost completed the modularity of the HBCTs which gives every brigade a common structure. The short term modernization goal is to populate these brigades with only two variants of the Abrams and the Bradley. The Abrams M1A2 Sep is being paired with its partner the Bradley M2A3, and the Abrams M1A1 AIM SA is being teamed with the Bradley M2A2 ODS. This modernization aligns compatible Combat Platforms in common modular formations. The long term goal for the Combat Platforms of the HBCTs

## Section 1: Combat Platform—Manoeuvre

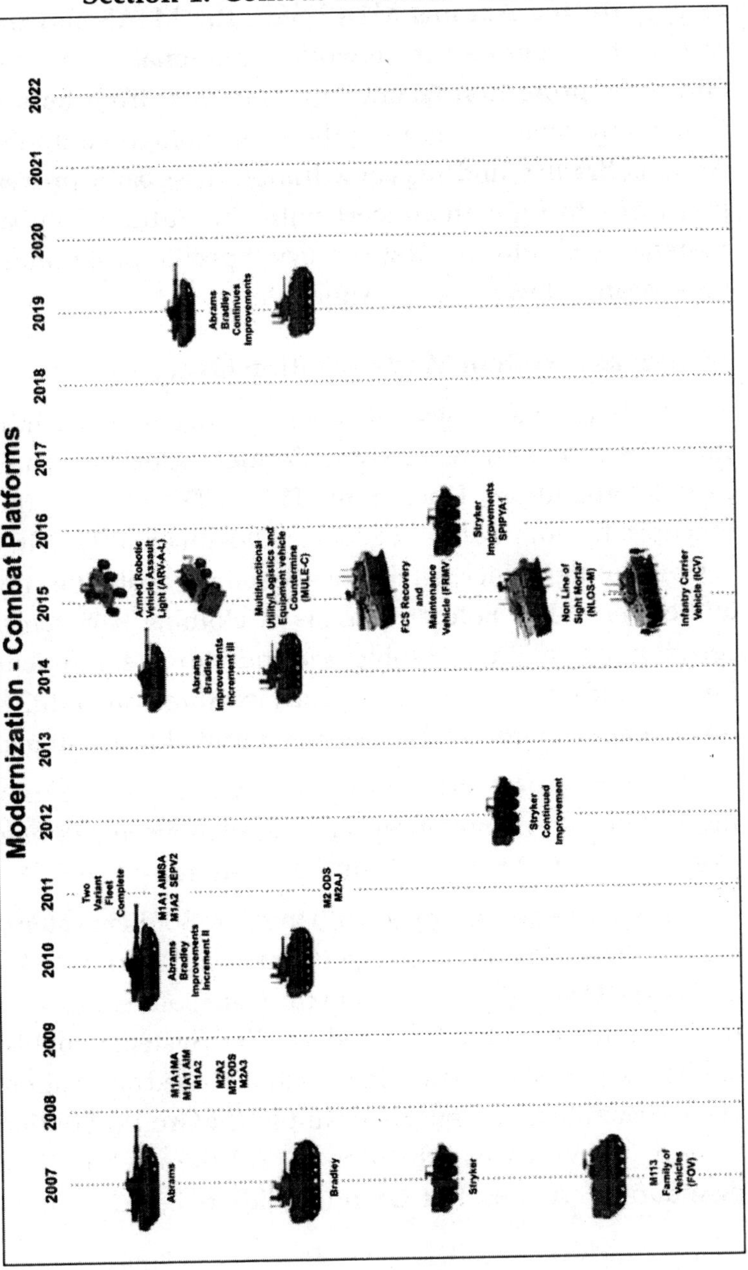

and the Stryker Brigade Combat Teams (SBCTs) will be to prepare the Abrams M1A2 SEP, the M2A3 and the Stryker to integrate the network, situational awareness and force protection technology Spin-outs from Future Combat Systems. Integrating these technologies onto the Abrams, Bradley, and Stryker will allow these battle proven platforms to fight in concert with the Future Combat Systems well into the 21st century. Specific programme details and status are in Annex A.

## Soldier as a System Modernization Overview

The Soldier as a System concept is documented in a Joint Requirements Oversight Council approved SaaS Initial Capabilities Document. This ICD serves as the lynchpin for four Soldier capability documents. The first is Core Soldier which establishes baseline capabilities for all Soldiers. Core Soldier consists of clothing bag items, select organizational clothing and individual equipment items required by all Soldiers. The next three capabilities documents are Ground, Mounted and Air Soldier Systems.

The embedded chart on the following page depicts the Soldier as a System concept and the relationships among Core, Ground, Air and Mounted Soldiers.

All Soldiers are equipped with the Core Soldier System, enabling them to train on and perform Basic Warrior Tasks and Battle Drills. When added to the Core Soldier System, the Ground, Air and Mounted Soldier Systems enable Soldiers to perform warfighting functions based on position and role within their unit. For example, the Ground Soldier System provides capabilities to Soldiers who fight dismounted. A subset of Ground Soldiers based on unit

## Section 2: The Soldier as a System

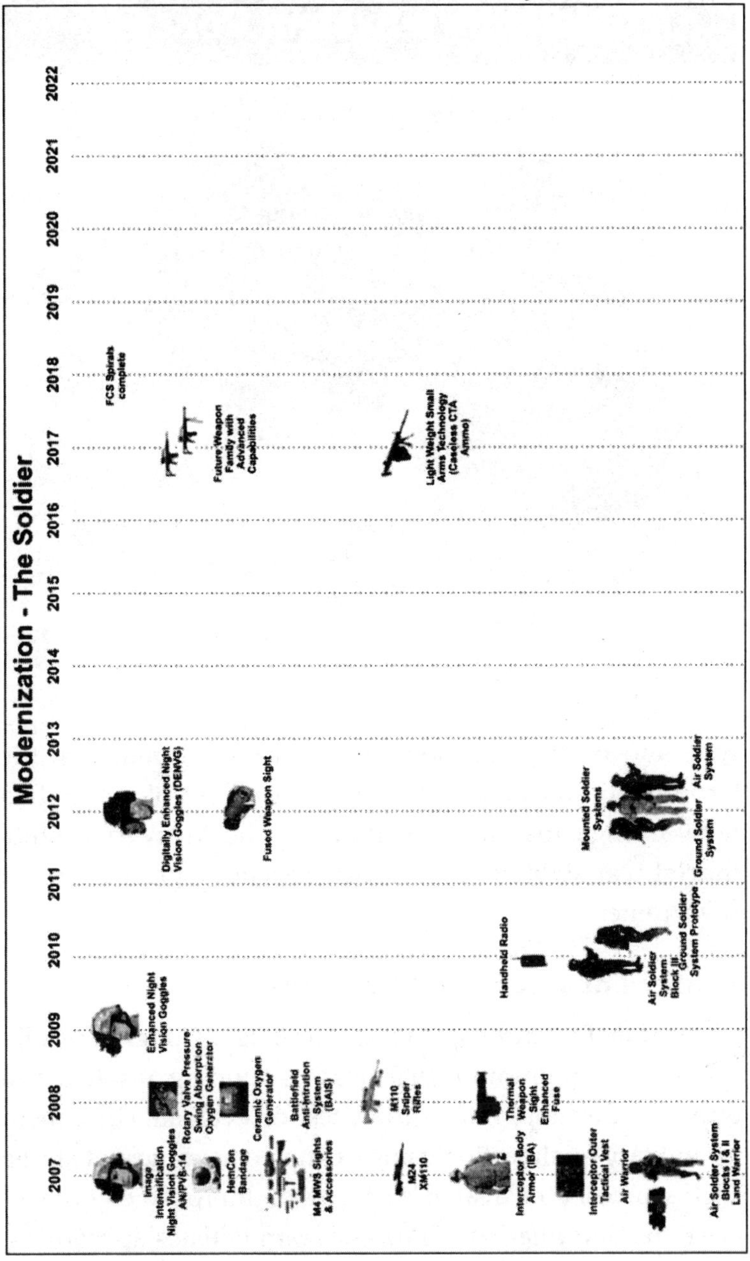

## Soldier as a System Concept

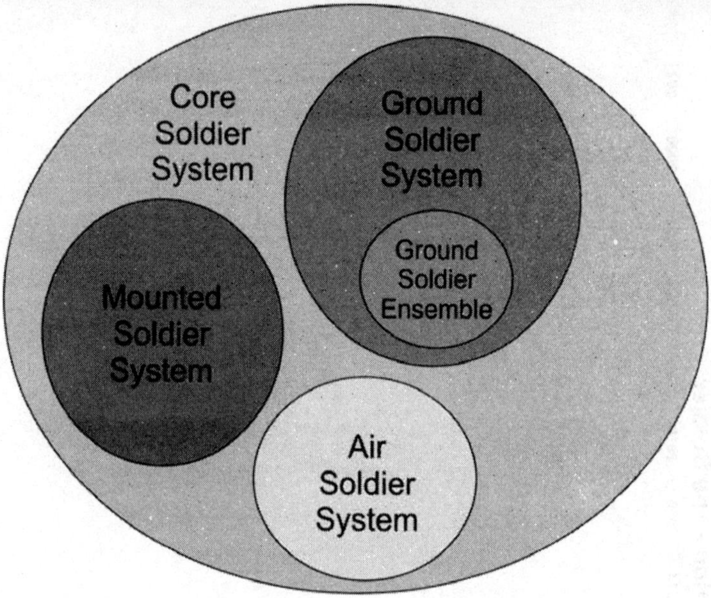


type and normal mission profile are equipped with the Ground Soldier Ensemble which provides voice and data networking capabilities. This allows the Army to provide the right capabilities to Soldiers to meet their specific mission requirements.

### Soldier Enhancement Programme

Soldier Enhancement Programme is a Congressionally sponsored programme that uses its funding resources to improve, develop, miniaturize, test or evaluate equipment for military qualification using existing or commercial off the shelf sources. If no available sources of improved equipment exist, the SEP Integrated Process Team initiates appropriate

## Section 3: Aviation Systems

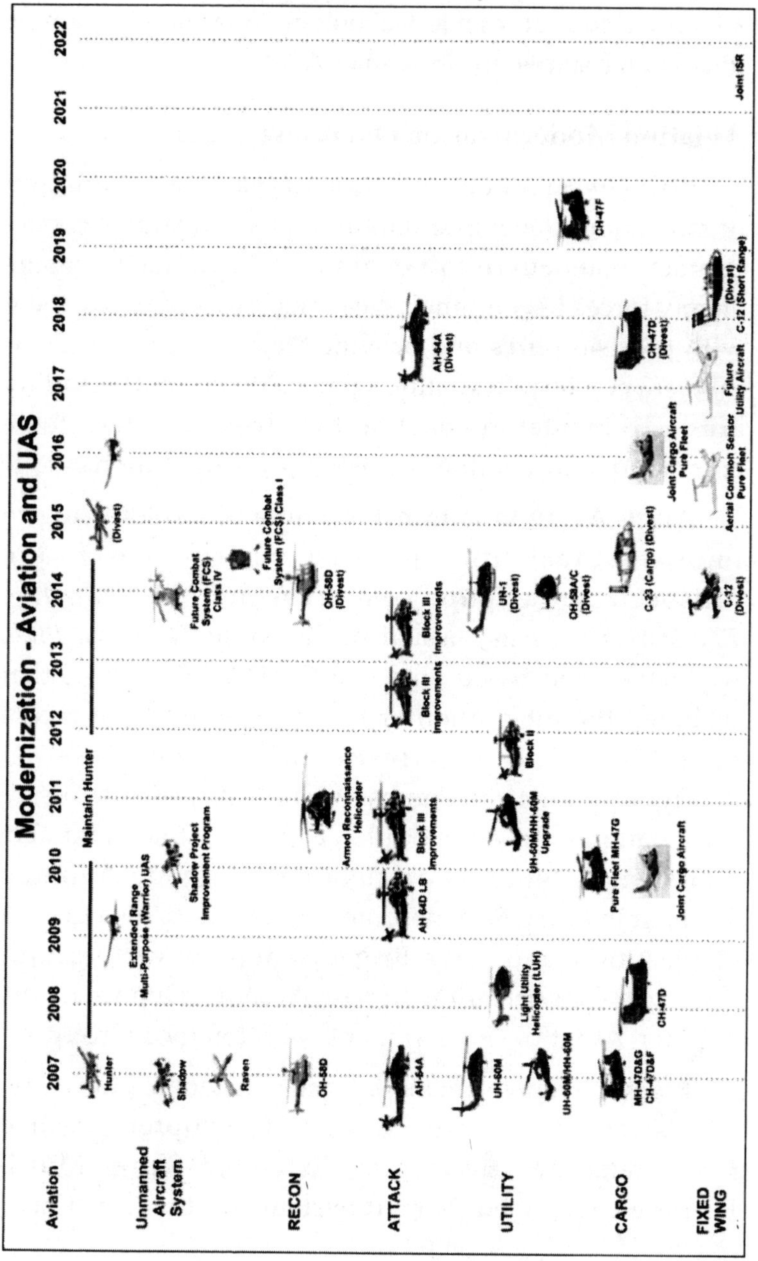

development efforts, three years or less, using the most advanced and affordable technology. Specific programme details and status are in Annex A.

## Aviation Modernization Overview

With its manned and unmanned assets, aviation organizations develop situations both in and out of enemy contact, manoeuvre to positions of advantage, engage enemy forces beyond their weapons' range, destroy them with precision fires and provide close air support. Their inherent mobility, flexibility, agility, lethality and versatility are instrumental in enabling the air-ground task force commander to conduct decisive Joint operations.

Army Aviation is transforming and modernizing to improve capabilities to meet current and future fullspectrum aviation requirements. *The Aviation Transformation Plan,* nested in the *Army Campaign Plan,* was developed based on a full DOTMLPF analysis that included the integration of lessons learned from recent operations. The Plan restructures Army Aviation warfighting units into Combat Aviation Brigades, ensuring the aviation units are modular, capable, lethal, tailorable and sustainable. We are fielding a Brigade Aviation Element in every Brigade Combat Team, a BAE(-) in each Stryker BCT and Fires Brigades and converting four Aviation Classification Repair Activity Depots to the Theater Aviation Sustainment Maintenance Group.

From the reinvestment of Comanche dollars the Army has selected a Light Utility Helicopter, Armed Reconnaissance Helicopter, Extended Range Multi-Purpose Unmanned Aircraft System and the Joint Cargo

## Section 3: Aviation Systems (Continued)

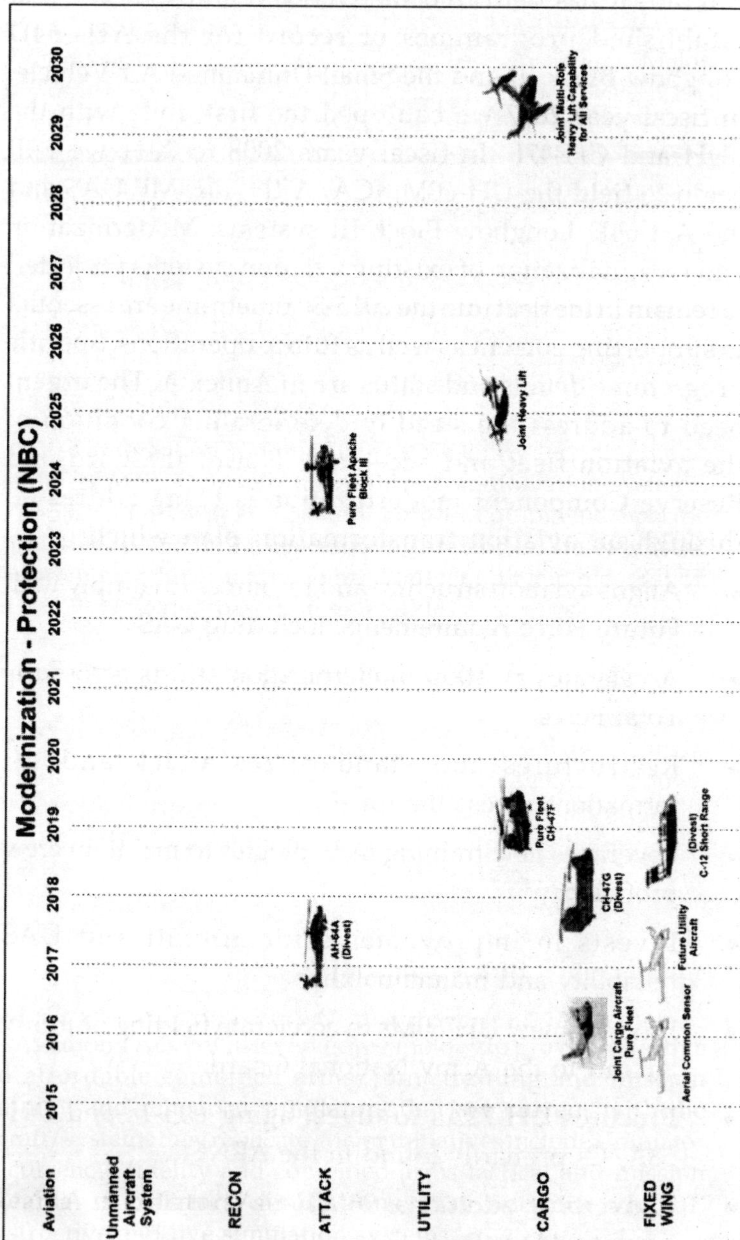

Aircraft. It has delivered the UH-60M and CH- 47F and established programmes of record for the AH- 64D Longbow Block III and the Small Unmanned Air Vehicle. In fiscal year 2007 we equipped the first units with the LUH and CH-47F. In fiscal years 2008 to 2011 we will begin to field the UH-60M, JCA, ARH, ER/MP UAS and the AH-64D Longbow Block III systems. Modernization and recapitalization of existing aviation systems projected to remain in the fleet into the 2015-30 timeframe are essential to supporting current as well as future operations. Specific programme details and status are in Annex A. The urgent need to address the steadily deteriorating condition of the aviation fleet and accelerate National Guard and Reserve Component modernization is being addressed through an aviation transformation plan which:

- Aligns aviation structure and resources to comply with Future Force requirements, including UAS
- Accelerates aviation modernization efforts across the Total Force
- Restructures and standardizes attack and lift formations across the force
- Leverages new training technologies to maintain crew proficiency
- Invests in improvements for aircraft and UAS reliability and maintainability
- Procures new UH-60Ms to accelerate fielding of utility aircraft to the Army National Guard
- Procures UH-72As to divest aging UH-1s and OH-58A/Cs primarily found in the ARNG
- Converts an additional 96 AH-64As located in ARNG units to AH-64Ds

- Procures ARHs to divest the OH-58D Kiowa
- Warriors and converts four ARNG AH-64A battalions to ARH
- Procures the Joint Cargo Aircraft to replace an aging fixed-wing fleet
- Procures ER/MP UAS and SUAS
- Invests in future Joint solutions such as Joint Multi-Role, and potentially a future Joint Medium Lift aircraft
- Continues to upgrade the aviation force with an improved infrared countermeasure suite capable of defeating the most advanced threat manportable air defence systems
- Converts CH-47D heavy-lift helicopter fleet to the CH-47F model with improved avionics, engines and airframe components.

## Future Combat Force Aviation

The Army plans to organize aviation assets into brigade formations at division and corps levels. Teaming UAS with manned systems will enhance operational fires, manoeuvre and intelligence collection capabilities for the commander. Future Force aviation modernization efforts incorporate lessons learned, the changing operational environment and emerging Joint force requirements. They leverage key technologies in areas such as electronics, communications, automation open systems architectures, UAS interoperability, propulsion systems and weaponization. These efforts include:

- Fielding SUAS, TUAV Shadow, Extended Range Multipurpose Warrior and FCS Class I and IV UAS

- Ensuring digital interoperability for effective Joint/combined force operations
- Fielding effective, affordable systems that enhance aviation survivability and improve Soldier stamina
- Improving aircraft operational readiness by leveraging technology to reduce costs and extend aircraft service life; strategy includes pursuit condition-based maintenance plus initiatives such as the aircraft component improvement programme, digital source collection and health usage monitoring
- Replacing obsolete air-traffic services equipment and maintaining compliance with future airspace usage requirements
- Digitizing aviation logistics and modernizing aviation ground support equipment and improving training
- Developing the technologies to ensure fielding of unmanned systems, interoperability of manned/unmanned aircraft and next generation and future system development

- Leveraging technology to reduce costs, extend aircraft service life and improve training
- Replacing OH-58D aircraft with the ARH to correct numerous capability gaps (interoperability, survivability, agility, versatility, lethality and sustainability)
- Procuring new UH-60M/HH-60M aircraft to grow fleet size to meet Modular Force requirements; recap the Black Hawk fleet by reducing the average age of the fleet while providing improved technology that increases reliability, maintainability and sustainability
- Replacing three aging fixed-wing aircraft (C-12, C-23 and C-26) with the JCA
- Continual modernization of the AH-64D to a Block III configuration with greater capabilities and increased reliability
- Remanufacturing 120 A Model Apaches to Apache D Model Block II Longbow configuration
- Replacing aging UH-1 and OH-58 aircraft with a COTS UH-72A
- Modernizing the CH-47D heavy-lift helicopter fleet with new-build and remanufactured CH-47F aircraft that incorporate updated avionics and major airframe improvements
- Procuring the Joint Air-to-Ground Missile as the replacement for the HELLFIRE, TOW and Maverick family of missiles for use by Army Aviation, USMC and USN.

## Section 4: Air and Missile Defence

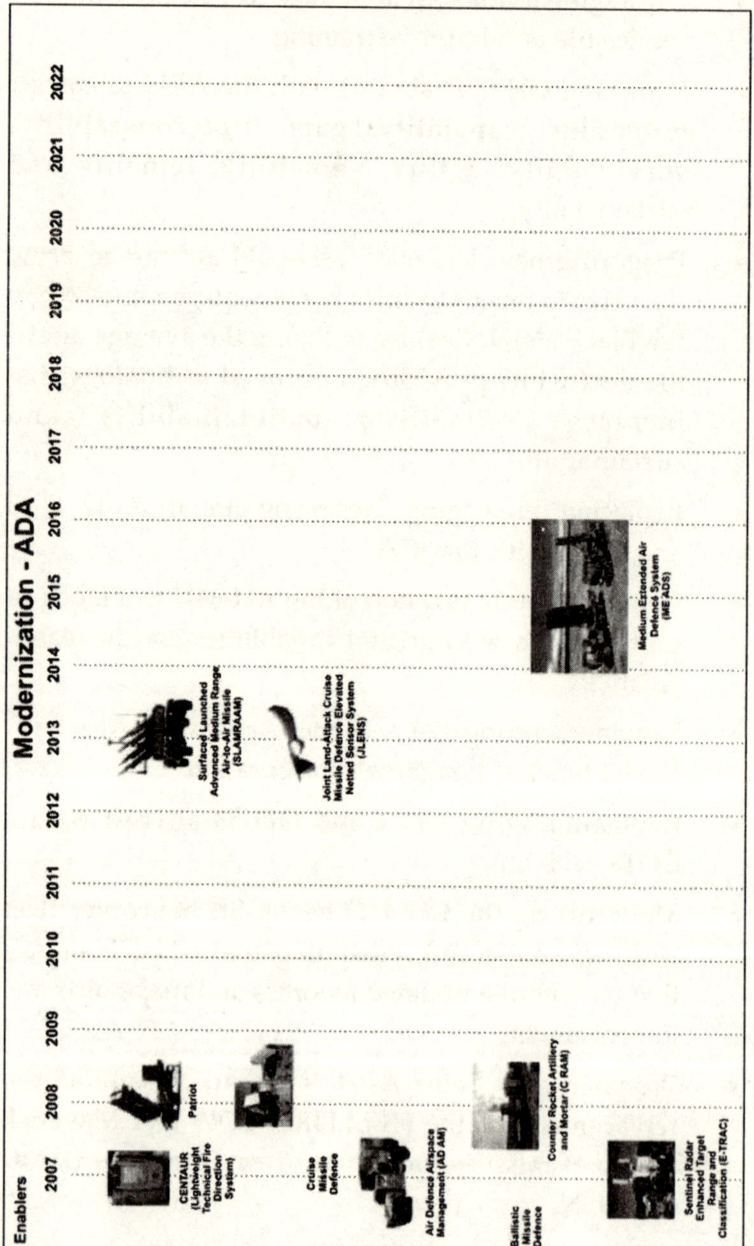

## Army Integrated Air and Missile Defence (AIAMD) System of Systems Modernization Overview

A relevant and ready AIAMD System of Systems (SoS) capability is crucial to supporting our National Security Strategy. Army Air and Missile Defence (AMD) units use specific systems with unique capabilities to dominate, enable, control or exploit the three dimensional battle space. Transforming Army AMD capabilities so they operate as integrated SoS facilitates the Joint force commander's ability to fully leverage the family of sensors and shooters at his disposal, optimizing their capabilities while mitigating their inherent limitations as they support the force. This transformation strategy is necessitated by the complex and changing operational environment where increased ballistic and cruise missiles, manned and unmanned aerial vehicles, rockets, artillery and mortars, coupled with WMD payloads are plausible for use against the homeland and from inside and outside a Joint force commander's AOR. AIAMD SoS will require an unprecedented degree of offensive/ defensive operations and capability integration within and among Joint force commands. This integration will enable Active AMD to provide a layered defense with multiple engagement opportunities against threats.

The regional fight may be constrained by limited assets due to strategic imperatives, short warning times for deployment, limited lift and immature AORs. The Joint force must mitigate these challenges through offensive/ defensive JIIM integration with AMD integrated platforms. AIAMD SoS will contribute to this mitigation by transforming current Army stovepiped, system-centric

AMD systems into integrated net-centric AMD system of systems via a command Army AMD Battle Command.

Joint, integrated AMD is a critical warfighting requirement that protects our homeland, deployed forces, friends and allies. This capability is achieved through an effective SoS application and synergy consisting of sensors, shooters and battle managers. Integrated Battle Command provides the IAMD SoS backbone. With the ability to provide fused, near real-time information with integrated fire control quality data, AIAMD SoS will be able to support key AMD capabilities such as Beyond Line of Sight and wide-area engagements. Currently, there is no Battle Command System that can provide fire control quality data throughout the Joint IAMD SoS network. As Joint net-centric enablers such as Joint SIAP or Joint IFC capability are developed, they may eventually provide a single AMD Battle Command solution among the Services and the Joint force. These Joint enablers will be integrated into the Army's IAMD SoS architecture as they become available and eventually integrated into Joint AMD programmes of record. The AIAMD SoS is designed to offset Army and Joint Service-specific systems limitations by enabling engagements to kinematics ranges, support the creation of a common operational air picture, contribute to persistent wide-area surveillance and detection and expand the protected battle space.

The AIAMD SoS programme is synchronized with other Services and in many aspects is leading the way to develop a Joint force AMD SoS to counter-ballistic missiles, cruise missiles, manned and unmanned aircraft, tactical air-to-surface missiles, rockets, artillery and mortars.

As the AIAMD SoS matures, the traditional system-centric paradigm that has driven AMD DOTMLPF will experience a corresponding evolution. The AMD force will continue to possess specific systems (Patriot and MEADS), which comprise shooters, sensors and battle managers. However, the pursuit of SoS has given rise to a conceptual construct of shooters, sensors and battle managers that will profoundly affect how Army DOTMLPF supports AMD. A mature AIAMD SoS will ultimately possess a common battle manager that will be supported by plug-and-fight shooters and sensors integrated into a network-centric Fire Control Quality Engagement Net. Our AMD units will be supported by Soldiers proficient in operating and maintaining Integrated Battle Command System, and a suite of shooters and sensors.

To prepare for these challenges, Army Air Defence is changing the way it organizes and fights with the development of composite ADA units that are modular, multifunctional and more readily provide the spectrum of AMD combat potential. These units offset the limitations of a single system, significantly increase the effectiveness of the area air defense commander's defense design, enhance modular or task force operations, reduce the limitations created by autonomous operations and conditions that have led to past fratricide, and increase the engagement battle space against AMD threats.

The ADA organizational vision is fully embedded with the Modular Army Future Force vision. All forces are considered pooled and available to support any future JIIM headquarters with mission-tailored packages. Army ADA transformation will optimize the synergy between

AC and RC forces to meet the requirements inherent in the Joint Operating Concepts.

Unit transformation began with battalions but stretches across all Army ADA echelons. Today, the Active Army ADA forces consist of nine Patriot Pure Battalions, and six composite battalions. The six composite battalions include a Headquarters and Headquarters Battery with a C2 system to integrate command and control of Patriot and Avenger capabilities, four Patriot batteries with six launchers per battery and one avenger battery with 24 avengers. Also included in the Active Force is one Manoeuvre AMD Avenger Battalion with 36 Avengers. The National Guard has six MAMD Battalions with 36 Avengers each. Beginning fiscal year 2009 all active Avenger weapon systems will convert to SLAMRAAM, fielding one composite battalion at a time, with the pure MAMD battalion scheduled last for conversion, planned for fiscal year 2017.

When fielded, THAAD will reside at the AMD BDE level and may be task organized to AMD Composite or Patriot Pure Battalions. ADA batteries or battery teams will be the primary battle elements to achieve effects on the battlefield from tactical to strategic levels. They can rapidly deploy, achieve one or more required lethal effects without augmentation and sustain unit operations. They can fight independently but generally will serve as subordinate, multifunctional AIAMD task force elements. All AIAMD combat units will be pooled at the theater-level under AIAMD brigades available for rapid integration into corps or division formations, in support of BCTs as the operational/ threat environment requires. Specific programme details and status are in Annex A.

## Army Air and Missile Defence Command

Senior Army ADA Battle Command headquarters at the theater level, and commands ADA brigades assigned to operate at that level. As a new structural approach, AAMDC has, in concert with the Joint force's area air defence commander, overall mission responsibility for the planning, integration and execution of Army AMD operations. AAMDCs are theater focused headquarters. The two Active Component AAMDCs conduct frequent, short notice deployments in support of USPACOM and USCENTCOM. The Reserve Component AAMDC is focused on defense of CONUS in support of USNORTHCOM and complements Theater headquarters in the other geographic Combatant Commanders' AORs. THAAD and JLENS batteries, along with their supporting command and maintenance units, will be assigned to regionally focused ADA brigades.

In summary, by using a plug and fight architecture that is enabled by an integrated Battle Command system, the AIAMD SoS optimizes the employment of current and future AMD systems in a given theater of operations. The modular, component based nature of this capability allows for a flexible, tailorable AMD force that can be tasked organized across multiple echelons to address the full spectrum of 3rd dimensional threats employed against JIIM forces.

## Fires Support Modernization Overview

Precision Strike is moving rapidly to achieve 21st Century Fires Support modernization, while simultaneously fighting the Global War on Terror. The

## Section 5: Fires Support Modernization

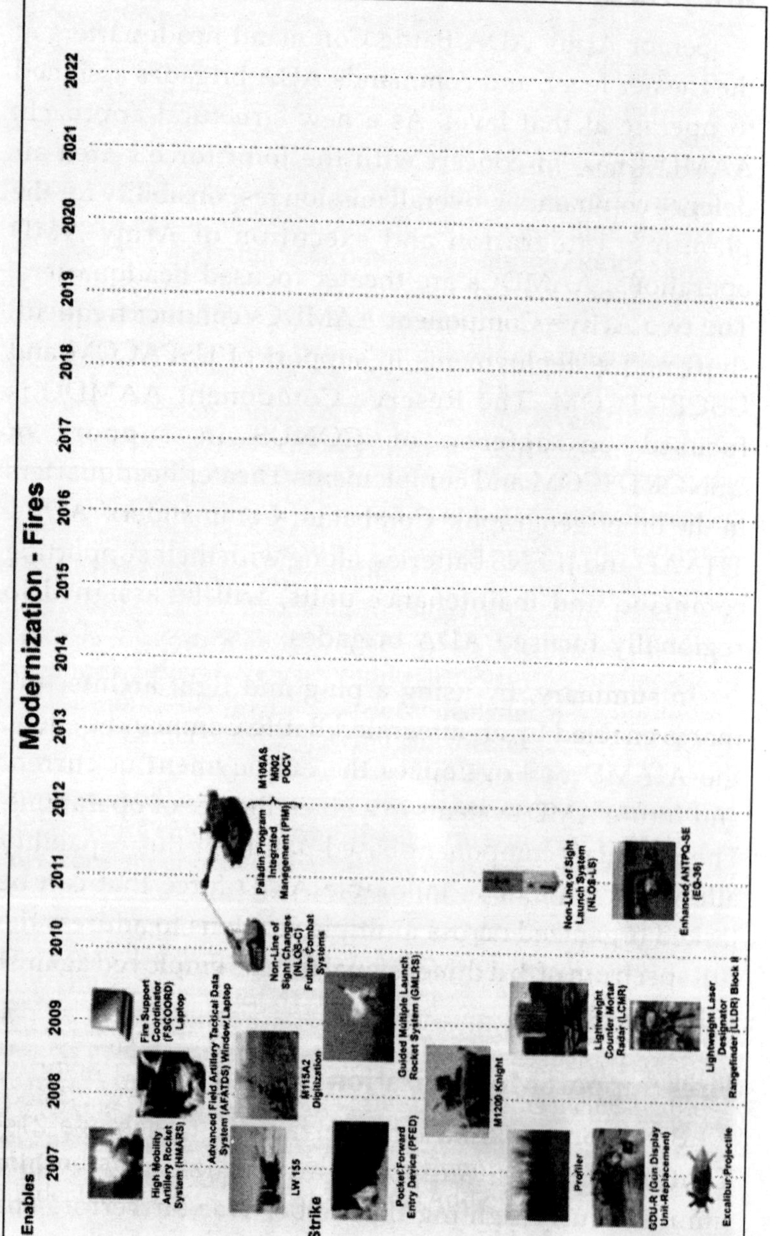

High Mobility Artillery Rocket System began fielding in 2005, and will complete Army wide fielding in 2013. The HIMARS provides Joint early entry forces, SOF, and BCTs with an indirect fire launch platform that provides extremely lethal, responsive, continuous, and all-weather, precision medium to long-range rocket and missile to a depth of 300 kilometers.

The Meteorological Measuring Set- Profiler AN/TMQ-52, began fielding in 2004, and will complete Army wide fielding's in 2012. Profiler provides a modernized, near real time meteorological capability for a wide range of indirect fire weapons and munitions over a 60 kilometer battle space with potential to extend coverage to 500 kilometers of battle space.

The Improved Position Azimuth Determining began fielding in 2004, and will complete Army wide fielding's in 2010. IPADS supports modernization of the Army's Field Artillery survey capabilities and provides exact position and directional data that is more accurate than that which is available from GPS.

Fire Support Command and Control is AFATDS, plus the four associated hand-held Computers that support AFATDS. FSC2 automates the process of Fire Support Coordination. Fire Support Coordination is the planning and execution of fires so that a weapon or group of weapons adequately covers targets. FSC2 functions at firing platoon through Echelons Above Corps.

The M777A2 Lightweight 155-millimeter HOWITZER began fielding in 2006, and will complete Army wide fielding in 2013. The M777A2 provides the Army with an advanced, towed, lightweight 155-millimeter howitzer, with self-locating and aiming capability that meets increased operational thresholds for mobility, survivability, deployability and sustainability. The Lightweight Counter Mortar Radar AN/TPQ- 48 was originally developed for the U.S. Special Operations Command in response to a 1999 MNS described by the 75th Ranger Regiment for automatic location of indirect fire weapons, with emphasis on mortars.

The M1200 KNIGHT began fielding in 2006, and will complete Army wide fielding in 2013. It is the natural progressive improvement to its predecessor the HMMWV based M707 KNIGHT. The M1200 KNIGHT is built upon an Armored Security Vehicle chassis which retains the essential mobility required for our Combat Observation Lasing Team operations while providing the increased force protection needed in theater today and for projected future operations.

The Guided Multiple Launch Rocket System began fielding in 2003, and will complete Army wide fielding in 2019. The GMLRS munitions are the Army's primary organic Joint Expeditionary, all-weather, all-terrain, 24/7, tactical range precision guided rockets employed by modular Fires Brigades supporting Brigade Combat Teams, Joint Expeditionary Force and Joint Special Operations Force Combatant Commands.

The Lightweight Laser Designator Rangefinder began fielding in 2005, and will complete Army wide fielding in 2014. LLDR provides Infantry, Stryker and Heavy BCTs with ability to locate, identify and designate during day and night to provide combat overmatch in symmetrical and asymmetrical environments.

## Section 6: Chemical, Biological, Radiological, Nuclear (CBRN) Defence

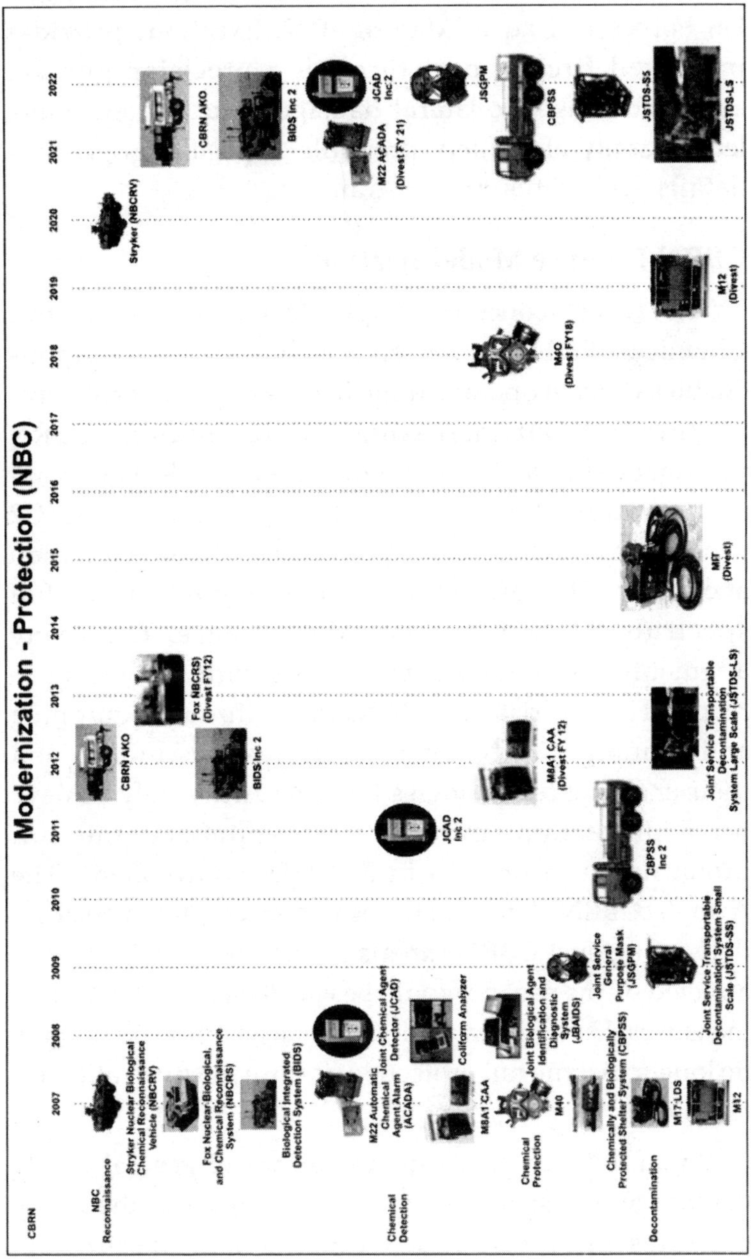

The EXCALIBUR cannon munition began fielding to US Forces in Iraq in May of 2007. Excalibur provides improved fire support through a precision-guided, extended range, collateral damage-reducing and more lethal family of artillery projectiles. Specific programme details and status are in Annex A.

## CBRN Defence Modernization

The Army's concept to employ focused defense against Chemical, Biological, Radiological, Nuclear weapons enables units to operate at the lowest required protective posture without increasing risk to Soldiers. CBRN reconnaissance and surveillance units, with their point and standoff detectors and battle management/C2 procedures, are the principal means of contamination avoidance. This protection extends throughout the full spectrum to include homeland defense. The Army augments installation commanders with the ability to respond to terrorist and CBRN attacks through equipping and training. CBRN defense systems, obscurants, and their enabling technologies help the Army fully achieve force protection, information dominance and full dimensional protection in a WMD environment. The Army's CBRN defence strategy is to employ a focused defence against CBRN threats so that only units directly affected by the hazard would be warned to take protective measures. Using focused defence, large numbers of units no longer assume full protective posture as a precautionary measure.

In addition to providing the means of general CBRN defence and obscuration common to all units, the Army provides increased CBRN defence and obscuration

**Section 6: Chemical, Biological, Radiological, Nuclear (CBRN) Defence (Continued)**

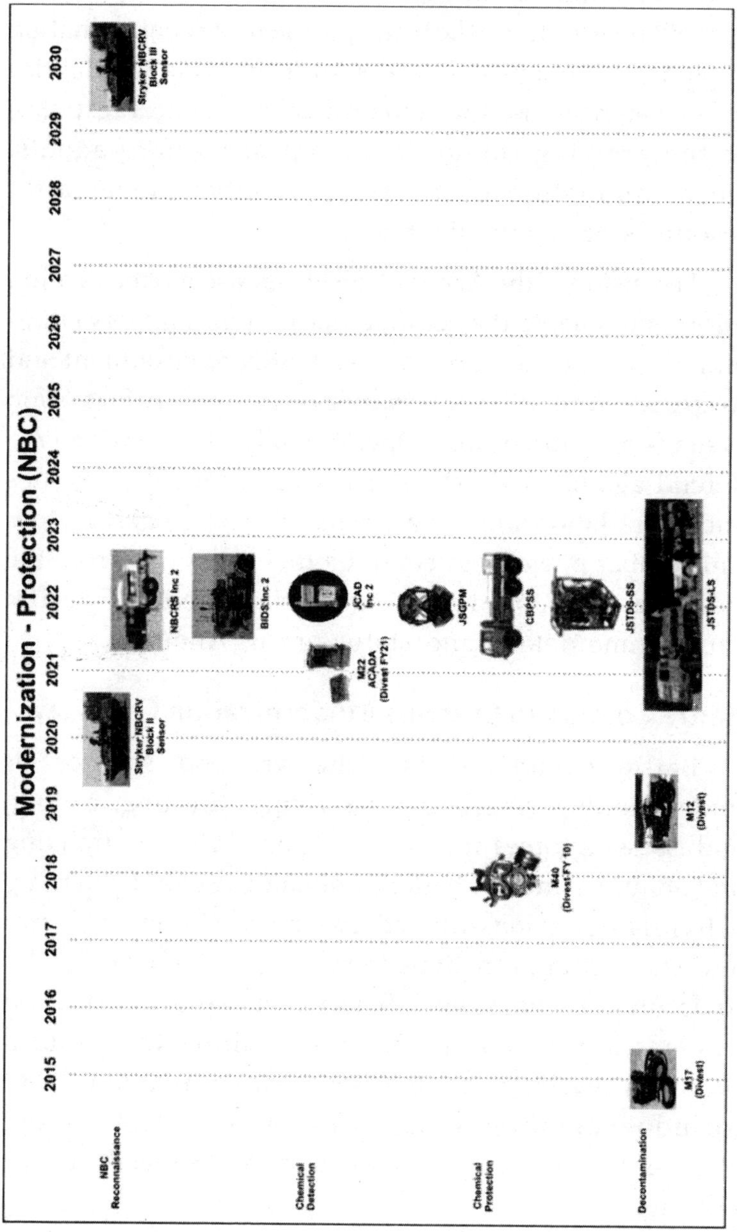

capabilities with specialized chemical units. With their point and standoff detectors, CBRN reconnaissance and surveillance units are the principal means of contamination avoidance. Biological detection units provide capabilities to shorten response times to initiate the medical response to the growing threat of biological warfare agents. Decontamination units restore combat power after resources are contaminated.

The vision of the Army's CBRN defense modernization effort is to enable the commander to minimize casualties and preserve combat power in a CBRN environment and to create information superiority by using C2 information systems and obscurants. Operationally, our mission is to defend against a CBRN attack with minimal casualties and degradation, allowing commanders to quickly restore full combat power and continue their mission across the full spectrum of operating environments. Specific programme details and status are in Annex A.

## Battle Command Systems Modernization Overview

Battle Command is: "the art and science of understanding, visualizing, describing, directing, leading, and assessing forces in operations against a hostile, thinking and adaptive enemy. Battle Command applies leadership to translate decisions into actions—by synchronizing forces and warfighting functions in time, space and purpose—to accomplish missions." Battle Command Information Systems are the equipment and facilities that collect, process, store, display and disseminate information. These include computers—hardware and software—and communications as well as policies and procedures for their use.

## Section 7: Battle Command

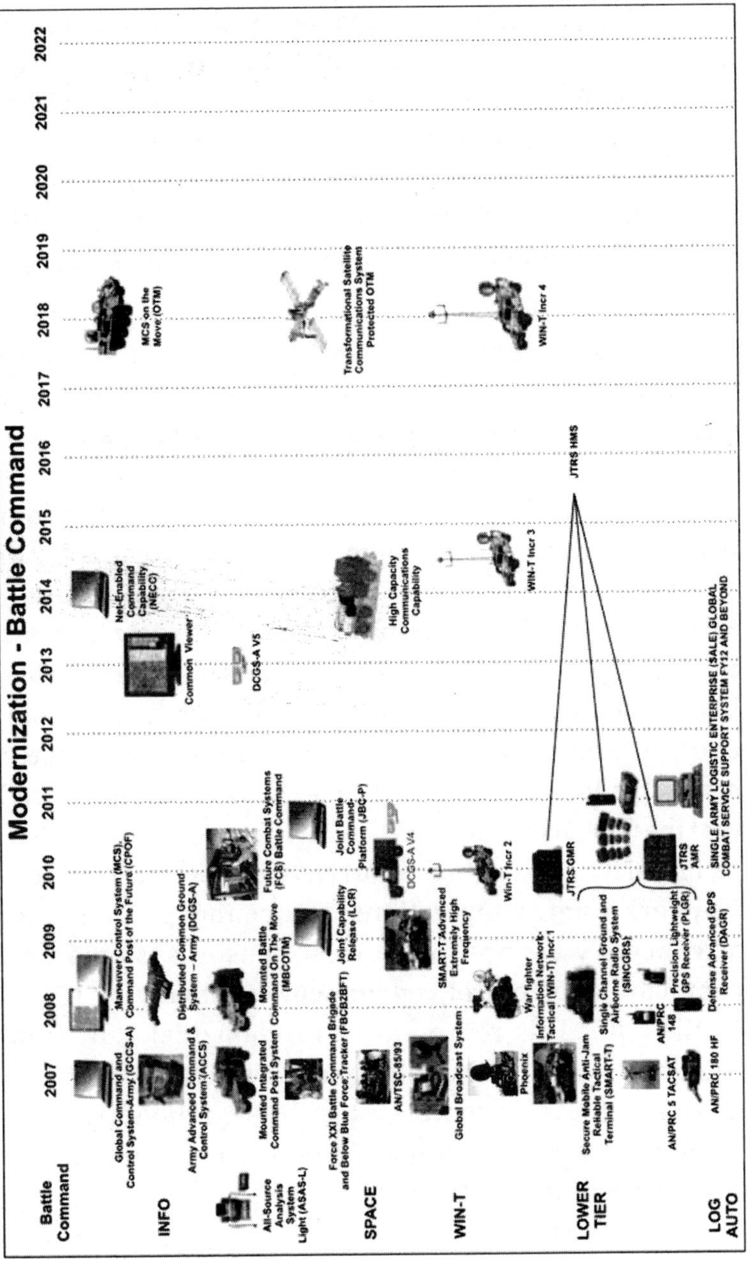

LandWarNet consists of globally interconnected, end to end Army warfighting capabilities, associated process and personnel for collecting, processing, storing, disseminating and managing information on demand to support warfighters, policy makers and support personnel. It enables Battle Command capabilities. Focused on leaders and Soldiers— LandWarNet integrates command and control capabilities to enable leader—centric operations.

Army Battle Command modernization will field integrated information technology and achieve warfighting advantages through the comprehensive networking of informed, geographically dispersed, modular forces. This integrated Battle Command combined with corresponding changes in DOTMLPF will allow our future land forces to remain dominate across the full spectrum of operations. The 2004 National Military Strategy and 2006 Quadrennial Defense Review directed the Services to become more "agile" (rapidly deployable, highly mobile, self-sustained, and full spectrum capable) and "fully networked" (information-based and integrated across the Joint forces). Additionally, DoD has mandated that the Global Information Grid, (GIG) will be the primary technical framework to support Network Centric Warfare/ Network Centric Operations. Under this guidance, all advanced weapons platforms, sensor systems and command and control centers will eventually be linked to the GIG. This represents a fundamental shift from developing separate systems to achieve new or improved capabilities to a "system of systems" integration approach, through massive integration efforts. The following four primary tenets will be used:

- A robustly networked force improves information sharing
- Information sharing enhances the quality of information and shared situational awareness
- Shared situational awareness enables collaboration and self-synchronization, and enhances sustainability and speed of command
- Mission effectiveness is dramatically increased by the above three tenets.

Army Battle Command modernization will incorporate these tenets across all echelons to the individual Soldier as we migrate to our Future Force Battle Command.

We face adaptive enemies who employ a full-range of conventional and asymmetric tactics in complex environments. This challenge highlights a critical need to improve the vertical and horizontal integration and dissemination of Battle Command capabilities rapidly, both within the Army and between Services in the Joint environment as well as between agencies and nations in the Inter-Agency and Multinational environments. We can't afford to have a collection of forces from each Service operating independently in the same geographic area. Interoperability is the ability of systems, units, or forces to provide data, information, material and services to and accept the same from other systems, units or forces and to use it to operate effectively together.

Our Future Force network consists of five layers (Standards, Transport, Services, Applications and Sensors and Platforms) that, when integrated, provide seamless delivery of both data and knowledge. The integration of all five layers is necessary to provide greater situational awareness, sensor fusion and networked fires; transforming our ground forces' ability to dominate in land combat. Key systems being integrated include:

- Common standards and protocols, e.g. Net Centric, waveforms, IP; Common Hardware between the Army Modular Forces and the Joint force
- Net-Ready Transport systems such as Warfighter Information Network-Tactical, Joint Tactical Radio Systems, High Capacity Communications Capability and Transformational Satellite Communications System
- Net-Ready Services will be provided by FCS System of Systems Common Operating Environment, Net Centric Enterprises Services, Win-T, and FCS network management services
- Future applications include FCS Battle Command, Net-Enabled Command Capability, and Distributed Common Ground System – Army
- A wide range of sensors on unmanned ground platforms, unmanned air platforms, and manned platforms networked and fused are critical for greater situational awareness.

Again, integration of all these layers is the key to providing LandWarNet from the dismounted Soldier to mobile command posts and sustaining bases.

The Army supports the DoD vision of net-centricity with the ultimate goal to improve the ability of our systems to work together. Another way to say this is to reduce

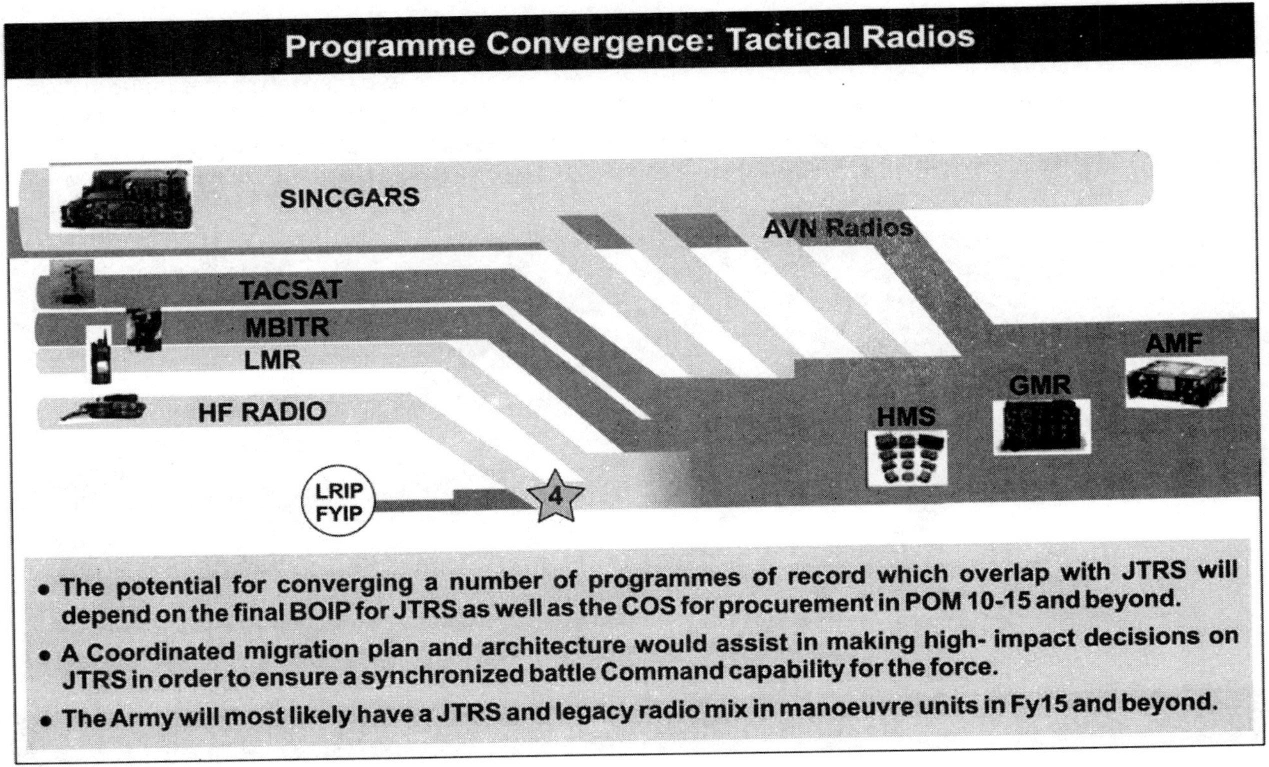
Programme Convergence: Tactical Radios
SINCGARS
AVN Radios
TACSAT
MBITR
LMR
HF RADIO
LRIP
FYIP
4
HMS
GMR
AMF
• The potential for converging a number of programmes of record which overlap with JTRS will depend on the final BOIP for JTRS as well as the COS for procurement in POM 10-15 and beyond.
• A Coordinated migration plan and architecture would assist in making high- impact decisions on JTRS in order to ensure a synchronized battle Command capability for the force.
• The Army will most likely have a JTRS and legacy radio mix in manoeuvre units in Fy15 and beyond.

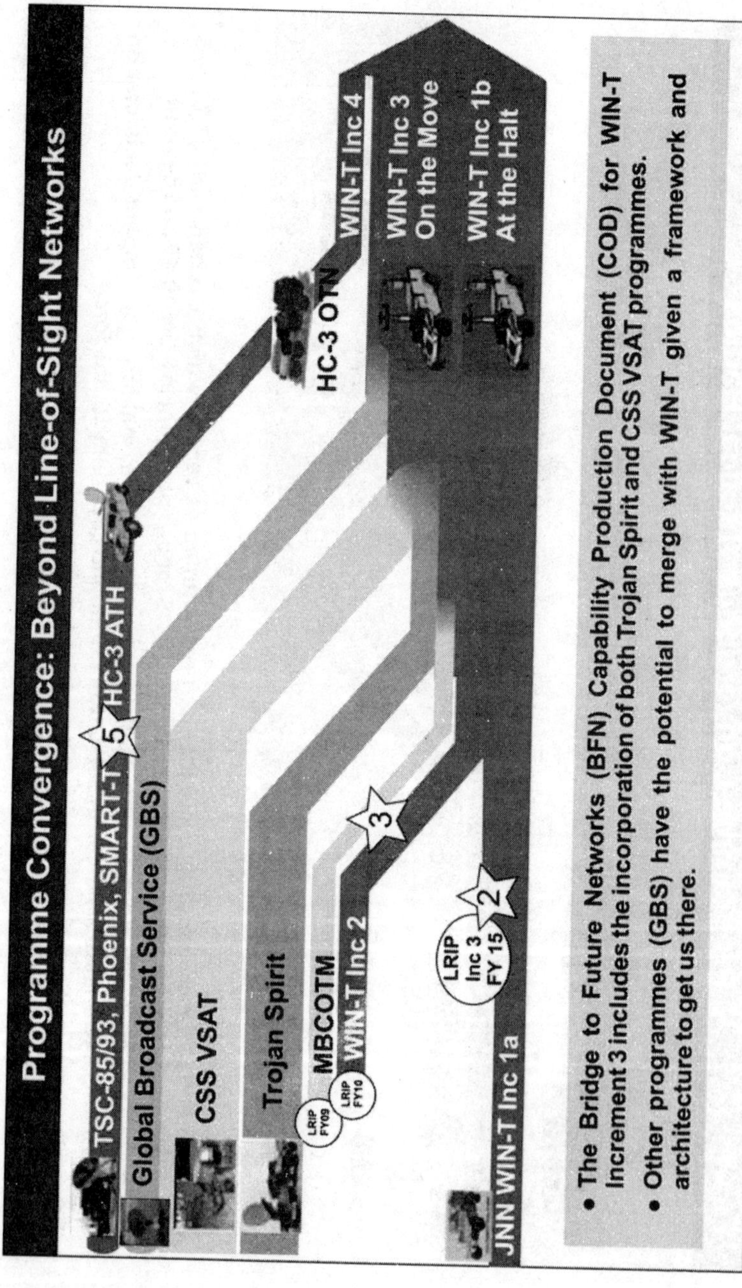
Programme Convergence: Beyond Line-of-Sight Networks
TSC-85/93, Phoenix, SMART-T
5
HC-3 ATH
Global Broadcast Service (GBS)
CSS VSAT
Trojan Spirit
MBCOTM
LRIP FY09
LRIP FY10
WIN-T Inc 2
3
HC-3 OTN
WIN-T Inc 4
WIN-T Inc 3 On the Move
WIN-T Inc 1b At the Halt
JNN WIN-T Inc 1a
LRIP Inc 3 FY 15
2
• The Bridge to Future Networks (BFN) Capability Production Document (COD) for WIN-T Increment 3 includes the incorporation of both Trojan Spirit and CSS VSAT programmes.
• Other programmes (GBS) have the potential to merge with WIN-T given a framework and architecture to get us there.

the number of seams among systems and organizations. Our vision is to develop robust networking solutions that enable commanders, leaders and Soldiers to access critical data and information anywhere, anytime and to create a global environment where Soldiers and leaders have the same look and feel when accessing information from home station, through training bases to deployment. We are accomplishing this by migrating existing systems where possible and developing new Net-Ready programmes to meet the unique challenges of ad hoc networking and command and control of land forces on the move. Early steps in the transition will be accomplished through the fielding of new Battle Command capabilities to the Current Force units in the FCS Spin-outs beginning in 2010.

The following charts outline the convergence strategies for Battle Command equipment. A key part of the Army's overall strategy for Battle Command Systems is to move beyond the era of new stove piped capabilities and to converge on multi-functional, multi-supportive, mainline Army communications systems. On the lower tier, the strategy calls for the convergence of multiple and varied tactical radio systems into the Joint Tactical Radio System (JTRS) family of radios. This convergence will rely on a number of factors, including the final basis of issue for JTRS, radio cost, C4I funding availability and an architecture which seamlessly and successfully converges the radios into JTRS in the fiscal year 2015 to 2020 timeframe.

For Beyond Line-of-Sight Networks, the proliferation of special-purpose, incompatible communications systems on the battlefield creates special problems for support and integration agencies. The Bridge to Future Networks Capability Production Document for Warrior Information

## Section 8: Battlespace Awareness Modernization

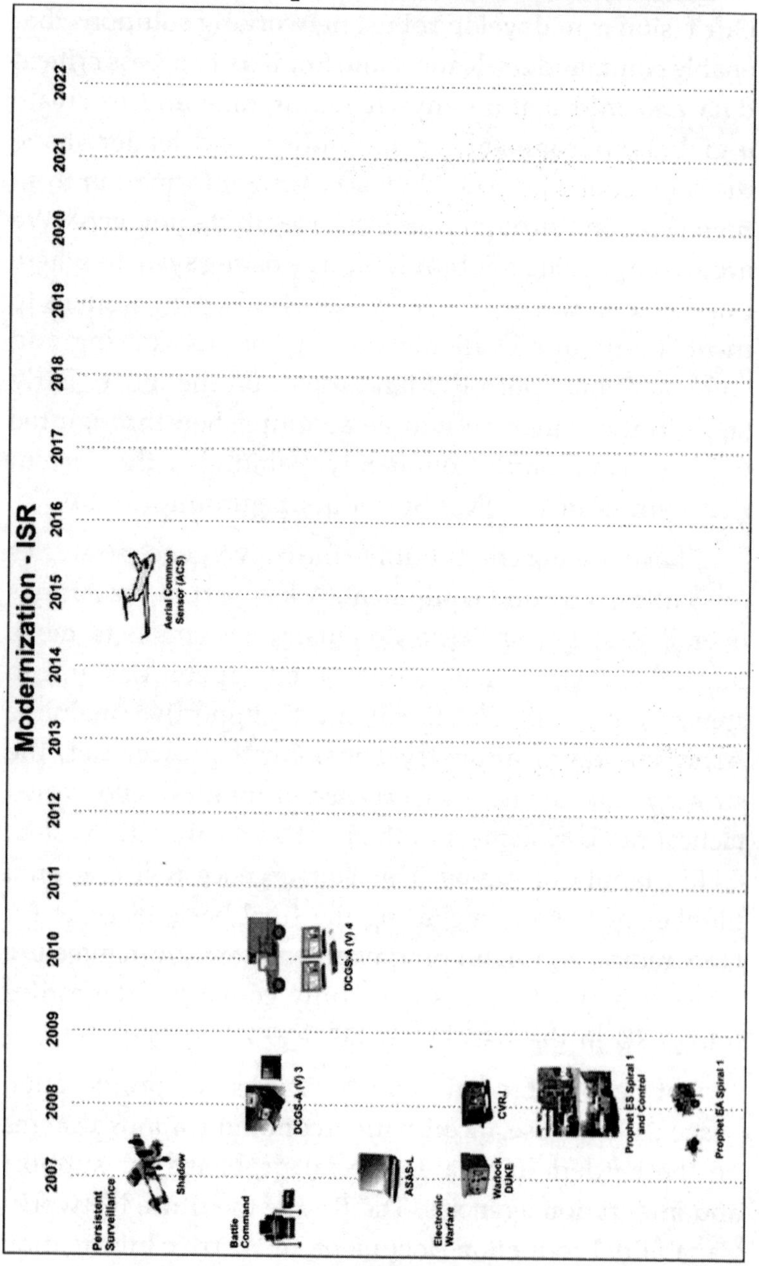

Network-Tactical (WINT) Increment 3 included the incorporation of both the Intelligence community's Trojan Spirit as well as the Logistical community's Combat Service Support Very-Small Aperture Satellite (CSS VSAT) programmes. While this is the immediate challenge for the Army, other special purpose systems such as Mobile Battle Command On the Move (MBCOTM), Global Broadcast Service (GBS) and others present the potential for systems convergence into WIN-T, thereby simplifying support and integration tasks and moving the Army closer to a truly network-centric capability. Specific programme details and status are in Annex A.

## Battlespace Awareness Modernization Overview

Battlespace Awareness (BA) materiel systems collect and disseminate data to support development of situational awareness and situational understanding. BA Programmes require reliable communications to support the collection and dissemination of data. Decision makers require current BA to support decision making, including National-Policy, Strategic Planning, Combat Commanders, operations centers, platforms, and individuals. For the Army, Reconnaissance, Surveillance and Target Acquisition/ Intellignece Surveillence and Recon (RSTA/ISR) is the full spectrum combined arms mission that integrates ground and air capabilities to provide effective, dynamic, timely, accurate and assured combat information and multi-discipline actionable intelligence for lethal and non-lethal effects/decisions in direct support of the ground tactical commander. Command and Control of BA assets, synchronizing RSTA/ISR with operations, tasking and dynamically re-tasking assets, monitoring/tracking assets and activities, planning and assessing operations support the development of situational awareness and situational understanding. Observation and collection of data provides surveillance of broad areas; focuses on targets of interest; finds, identifies and tracks needs and measures and monitors environmental conditions. Critical aspects of BA include identification of enemy courses of action, integrating enemy and friendly data and information on cultures, social issues and resources. BA is critical to support automatic target recognition, employment of human resources, distributed processing, data fusion, analyst collaboration, distributed archives, collaboration between analytic centers, identification of enemy patterns of behaviour and defeating denial and deception. Specific programme details and status are in Annex A.

The Army is transforming while at war to provide enhanced BA capabilities and highly trained Soldiers and civilians in support of Army, Joint, and combined operations worldwide. The current and foreseeable strategic environment in which our Soldiers will operate is an era of persistent conflict. We will continue to fight highly adaptive, smart enemies, who rapidly incorporate off-the shelf technology to conduct asymmetric operations. Joint and multi-national operations will be fought in complex operating environments where the enemy will attempt to maintain anonymity among the population. A 24/7 worldwide media, the global internet, powerful networks, technological innovation, ideological and cultural differences, combined with extended borders and distances, are challenges our warfighting formations will face. This environment will exact an increasing demand on Army Intelligence combat operations in Afghanistan and Iraq, as well as sustained operations in Korea and elsewhere, clearly demonstrating the critical need for increased Military Intelligence (MI) capabilities within brigade combat teams and maneouvre battalion, where the risk is greatest.

Ongoing MI transformation efforts enable Soldiers to fight "among the people" in complex operating environments, integrate advanced fusion and "find, fix, finish, exploit and analyze" capabilities into Battle Command processes at BCT, battalion, and company levels. Aggressive intelligence/operations teaming, a shared common operating picture and the effective employment of MI assets enable timely fusion of all information across a flat network.

Current and projected operational information will be continuously fused by robust knowledge management systems and disseminated to all levels of users through adaptable, flexible, networked, communications systems. Within this flat network, force elements will subscribe to products or data. Software agents will broker data and products, posting some unprocessed information. In this manner, all Joint, Allied and Coalition warfighters will have a synchronized common operating picture of the battlespace with access to common data, within security access and transport layer constraints and the ability to construct their own tailorable, relevant operational pictures resulting in enhanced BA.

Soldiers expect and deserve the best possible intelligence tools and BA capabilities the Nation can provide as they execute challenging missions in unforgiving, complex environments. The Army, as part of the Joint team, is taking aggressive action to meet these challenges in close coordination with Joint, Department of Defense and National Intelligence Community partners.

## Space Capabilities

Space is a significant area of Joint development that supports enhanced BA capabilities, and is the backbone for the National and military ISR architecture, as well as the domain of choice for commercial broad-area sensing enterprises with military utility. Space-based communications provide reach and NLOS connectivity, while space-based ISR and commercial imagery platforms substantially enhance strategic, operational and tactical intelligence collection, processing and dissemination. Space-based assets continuously monitor the globe for foreign missile launches and can be leveraged to detect large infrared events on the ground in near-real time. Soldiers in OEF and OIF use space-based systems to communicate, navigate, target, find and fix the enemy, anticipate weather, receive missile warning, maintain situational awareness across extended areas of operations, avoid fratricide and much more. Army Space Forces are deployed worldwide supporting U.S. efforts to fight and win the GWOT. Army Space Support Teams have provided space products and services to corps, Marine Expeditionary Forces and Joint Task Force headquarters throughout OIF/OEF. Space Support Elements, as part of modular division and corps staffs, have filled a critical space planning and coordination role. Army Space Forces continue to enhance the effective application of spacebased assets and capabilities across the full spectrum of military operations in an interdependent, Joint and multinational environment.

## Role of Space in the Army

Among the Army's formidable capabilities is its global space reach, with assets and operations around the world. Space support to Army operations is divided into four space mission areas: Space Force Enhancement, Space Control, Space Force Application, and Space Support. Army Space Forces execute tasks within the Space Force Enhancement and Space Control mission areas. Space Force Enhancement functions improve the effectiveness of forces across the full-spectrum of operations by providing space-based operational assistance to ground maneouvre force elements. These functions include long-haul and reach back satellite communications spanning multiple frequency domains, environmental monitoring of both terrestrial and space conditions that may impact operations, and space-based intelligence, surveillance and reconnaissance. Other Space Force enhancement functions provide precision position, velocity, navigation, and timing information that is crucial to modern combat operations, theater missile warning and near-real time battlefield characterization.

Space Control operations ensure freedom of action in space for the United States and its allies and, when necessary, deny an adversary freedom of action in space. Space control involves the interrelated objectives of space surveillance, protection, prevention and negation.

## Engineer Construction Modernization Overview

The *Army's Strategic Planning Guidance* calls for a more relevant and ready Engineer force with a Joint and expeditionary mindset. To accomplish this, the Army must retain the best of its current capabilities and attributes

## Section 9: Engineer Equipment

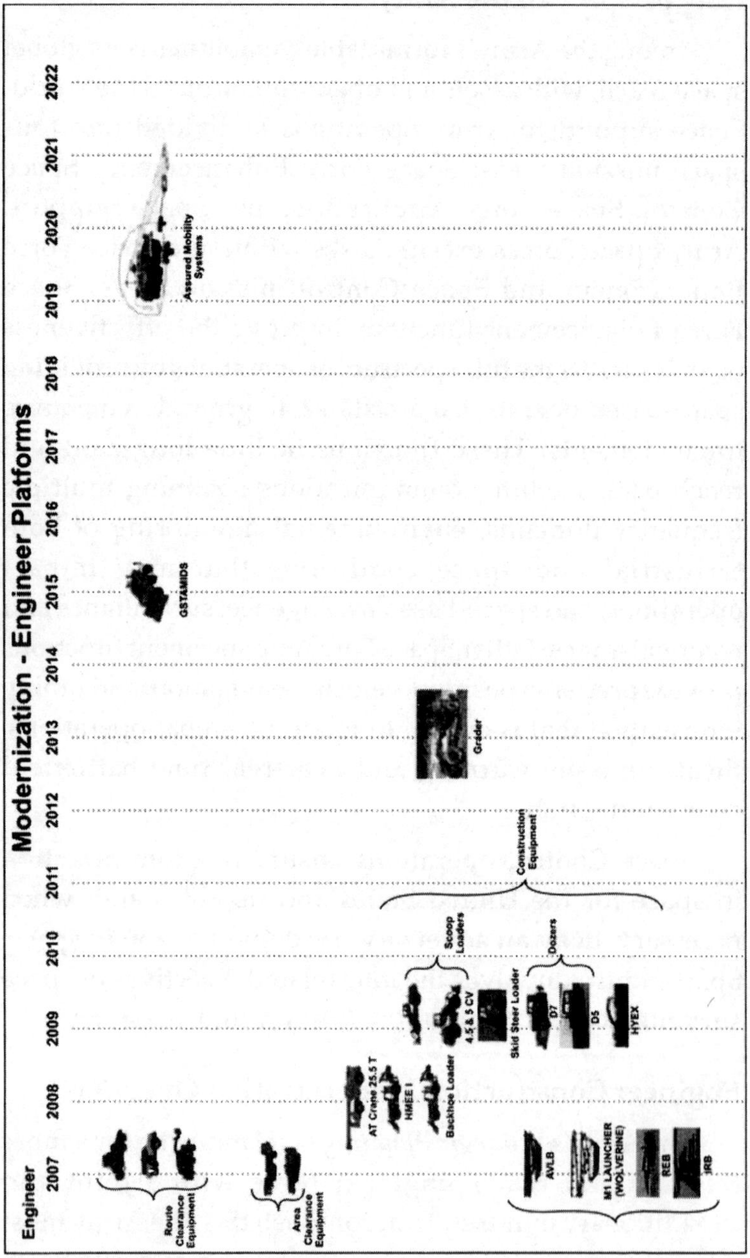

## Section 10: Tactical Wheeled Vehicles Modernization

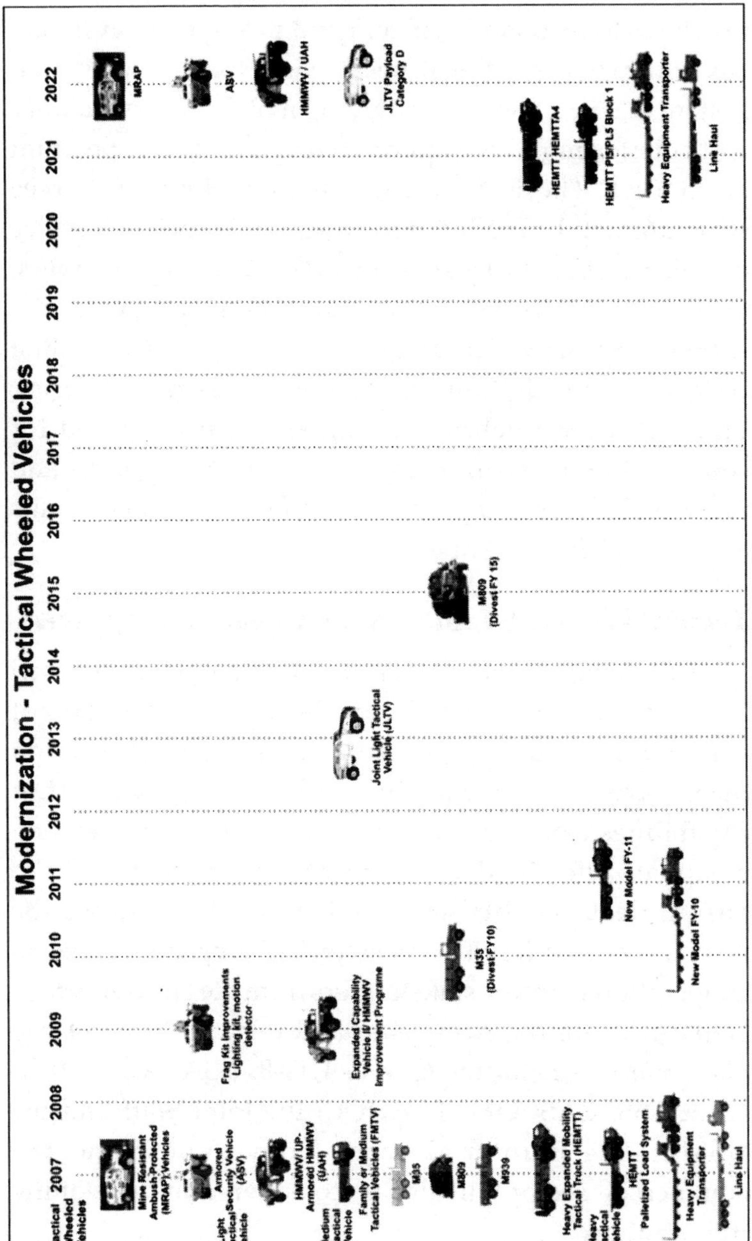

while developing others that increase relevance and readiness to respond in current and projected operational environments. A critical need exists for an excavation system that is capable of providing mobility, survivability and counter mobility support across the entire spectrum of conflict. The Future Construction Engineer Forces structure will be modularized and consist of the families of vehicle such as Dozers, Loaders, Graders, Scrapers, HYEXs and a host of other equipment. A few of the supporting tasks will perform include: preparing and filling craters on airfields, filling in pot holes, clearing/ repairing drainage, lifting debris, loading aggregate required for construction or repair, digging trenches for culverts and rapid repair of existing roads. Specific programme details and status are in Annex A.

## Tactical Wheeled Vehicle Modernization Overview

The Army's Tactical Wheel Vehicle Strategy will achieve the proper balance between a variety of competing factors: support of current operations and fleets, Army transformation, and building future fleet capabilities while optimizing strategies for procurement, recapitalization, and sustainment. The strategy seeks to ensure fleet viability and combat effectiveness for the next three decades. The strategy is being developed in cooperation with key stakeholders from the Headquarters, Department of the Army staff and selected Major Army Commands—including G-3, G-4, G-8, ASA (ALT), PEO-CS & CSS, CASCOM, TRADOC, the Joint Staff and the USMC. The industrial base, Army depots and the commercial sector will also be considered in developing this strategy.

The TWV assessment conducted in fiscal year 2003 indicated the TWV fleet was aging at an accelerated pace because of the current operational environment and low funding levels. Current operations and the Global War on Terrorism have added significant wear and tear to the fleet and revealed major shortcomings in the areas of force protection, mobility, transportability and maintainability. As such, specific recommendations and initiatives are being implemented to address these issues and serve as the foundation of the TWV strategy. A modernization plan is being developed for each category of the TWV fleet: light, medium and heavy wheeled vehicles and trailers.

Modernizing the Army's TWVs is a critical imperative that strives to provide the Soldier with the best protection, payload and performance in each vehicle in the fleet. Rapidly evolving threats and constant improvements in technology require a continuous modernization effort. The success of such an effort depends upon both the ongoing application of evolutionary improvements to current platforms and investment in revolutionary improvements for future platforms.

In the near term, the Army's main modernization focus for its TWVs is to apply the concept of scalable armour across the TWV fleet. This concept involves producing vehicles with armour "A kits/A cabs" and "B kits." The A kits/A cabs consist of armour that is integrated at the time of production at the factory to provide an inherent level of protection and has the ability to accept supplemental armour in the form of a modular B kit. Having scalable armour provides the Army with tactical flexibility to deal with contingencies where armour may, or may not be needed. It also supports continuous improvements in armor capability by allowing the latest armour technology to be applied to a vehicle in the form of a B kit, without replacing the entire vehicle. Fielding began by shipping over 600 armored medium and heavy tactical vehicle kits in support of the surge. This scalable armour concept has been applied to Uparmour HMMWV production since late 2006 and the Army intends to apply it to Medium Tactical Vehicle and Heavy Tactical Vehicle production in late 2008 and beyond. For the MTV fleet, the application of scalable armour involves slight modifications to the existing production of the Family of Medium Tactical Vehicles. Additionally, the FMTV is an ongoing modernization effort that is scheduled to result in the divestiture of all M35 trucks from the Army by the end of 2010 and all M800 series trucks by the end of fiscal year 2015.

In the case of the HTV fleet, the application of scalable armour will be executed in conjunction with the production of new HTV variants, such as the Heavy Expanded Mobility Tactical Truck A4 in 2008, the Palletized Load System Block 1 planned for 2009, and the M915A5 Line Haul also planned for 2009.

Light Tactical Vehicles represent 63% of the total fleet. This plan seeks to improve on the original High Mobility Multi-purpose Wheel Vehicle concept by developing a Joint Light Tactical Vehicle family with increased ballistic and blast protection with assigned category payload, agility, mobility, sustainability, and rotary wing transportability. The procurement of this future force JLTV family, coupled with modernization under the recapitalization programmes, would increase the capability of the current LTV aging fleet.

Taking this longer view into account, the Army continues to develop and assess the JLTV as a possible replacement for an undetermined number of HMMWVs. As currently planned, the JLTV has the potential to provide significant and revolutionary increases in protection, performance and payload capabilities beyond those available in the current HMMWV or up armoured HMMWV (UAH). However, the ability of the JLTV to achieve these capabilities depends in large measure on the maturity of technology and the availability of resources in the coming years.

In the interim, the Army will continue to assess the potential of the HMMWV Improvement Programme designed to use existing technology to improve the UAH's force protection, performance, and payload capabilities. Additionally, the Army is also considering procurement of a next-generation HMMWV as a possible bridge to the JLTV. The decision to procure an interim HMMWV will be based in part on how well the development of the JLTV progresses in the coming years.

The Army envisions this strategy to be a living document and will conduct annual assessments of the TWV fleet at strategic decision points. It will track the progress of this strategy, identify shortcomings and make necessary adjustments during the subsequent Programme Objective Memorandum builds. The continuing use of advanced technologies will ensure enhanced capabilities are provided to support our Soldiers and overall Army requirements. Specific programme details and status are in Annex A.

## Combat Service Support Modernization Overview

Modernizing the Army's Combat Service Support (CSS) equipment is a critical enterprise that provides the Soldier with the latest in capabilities required to sustain and maintain current and future weapon systems. Rapidly evolving threats and developing technologies require continuous employment of evolutionary improvements to most current platforms in the near term and investment in revolutionary improvements to others for the long term.

The development of CSS equipment is imperative to the success of the war fighter. In many cases visibility is lost as to the ramifications of non-modernized CSS equipment and its impact on the fighting force. The ever progressing technology involved in creating more deadly and effective combat platforms is the same technology-base required in the support functions. For example; common progression of Windows based software has dramatic impacts on support equipment to maintain complex weapons hardware.

## Section 11: Combat Service Support

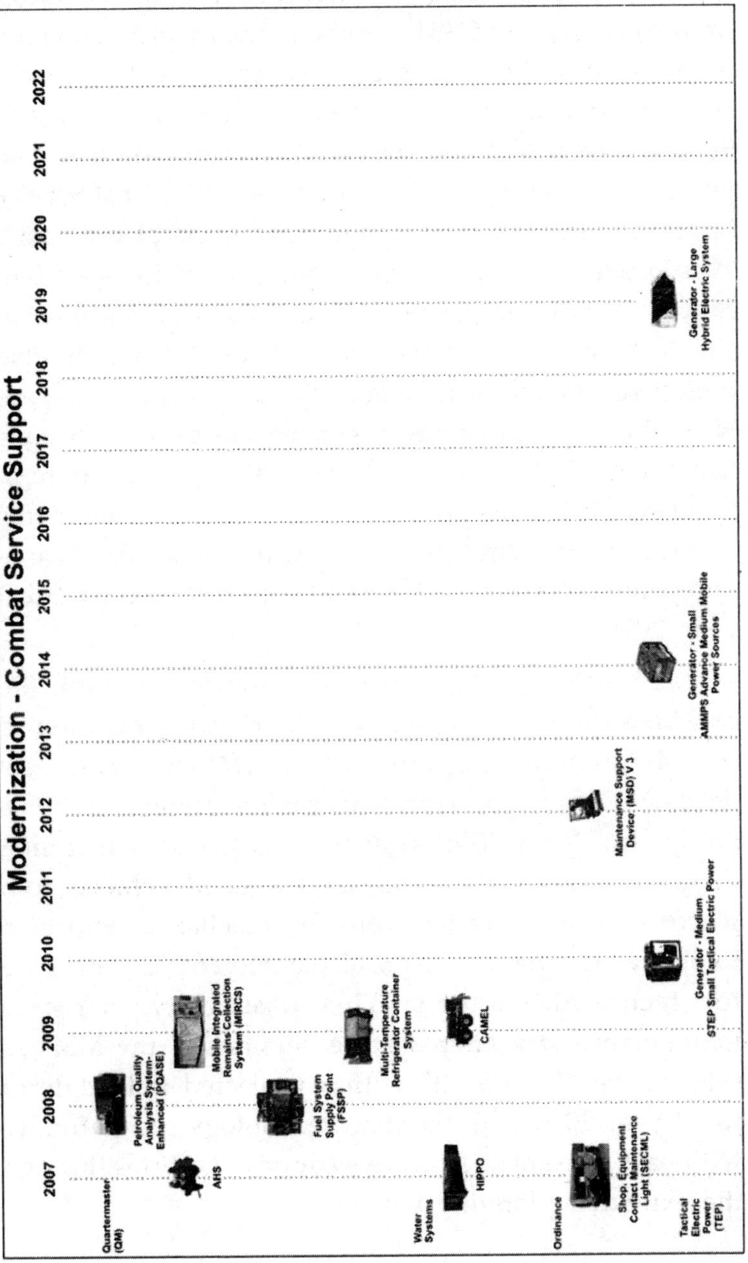

Several programmes are involved in this technology driven evolution of CSS Equipment. Logistics Automation modernization includes the advancement of the current standard tactical army management information systems Standard Tactical Army Management Information System programmes with the adoption of Global Combat Service Support System - Army programme in fiscal year 2011. This programme will consolidate several independent functions into one platform. The spiral development of the Next Generation Automatic Test System is also intended to incorporate advanced technology to keep pace with the steadily increasing progression of weapons technology. With a planned first unit equipped date of fiscal year 2010, this programme through the installments of three increments, is designed to consolidate three independent testing platforms into one by the end of fiscal year 2010.

Maintenance diagnostics is supported through the continual life-cycle-replacement and modernization of the Maintenance Support Device (MSD). Originally designed and procured to replace the aging Soldier Portable on System Repair Tool system, MSD has grown from a diagnostic tool for wheeled and tracked vehicles to a platform heavily relied upon by mechanics and also Explosive Ordnance Disposal technicians as data base for technical manuals. This drastically increases maintenance efficiency. Future versions of the MSD as seen in the "Version 3" with a projected field date of fiscal year 2010 will maintain technology compatibility with past, present and future weapons platforms through the extended planning period.

Power generation is supported through the procurement and advancement of Tactical Electrical Power. A bulk percentage of the current inventory for Power Generation is the Military Standards that do not meet current doctrine requirements in supporting today's Soldier. Introduction of the new Small Tactical Electrical Power in fiscal year 2014 will dramatically reduce fuel consumption and extend usage timelines. Advanced Medium Mobile Sources will begin a progressive replacement of current Medium Generator sets starting in 2010. Advancements are being made to modernize a Hybrid Electric System which will dramatically reduce the Army's power reliance on petroleum based fuels.

Combat Service Support Equipment modernization also includes the evolution of the Petroleum Quality Analysis System. The next generation of this programme is referred to as the PQAS-Enhanced which provides the ability to carry Armor kits and conduct higher levels of Petroleum, Oil & Lubricant testing never before available in the field.

The first major revolution in basic water distribution is taking place with the induction of the Camel which replaces the water trailer. This new Camel brings greater water capacity, the ability to heat and cool its contents, and has more then doubled the available water distribution points on the tank.

Implementation of modularity and transformation has created the absolute need for a smaller logistical footprint and modernization to support the force. This openly implies the need for consolidated support platforms with consolidated capabilities. As the current

## Section 12: Army Watercraft

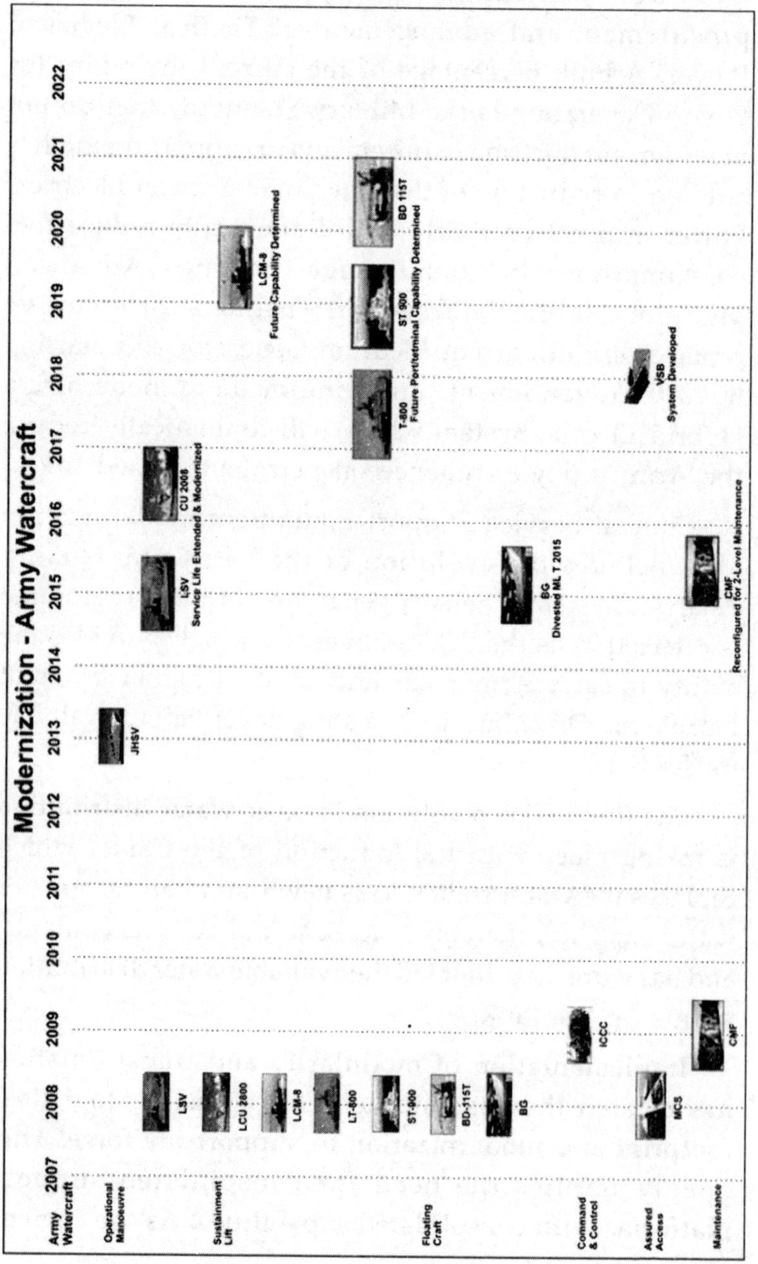

operational environment continues to evolve, so must the inventory of Combat Service Support equipment that supports it. Specific programme details and status are in Annex A.

## Army Watercraft Modernization Overview

The Army Watercraft Fleet has undergone significant change since the Army initiated the *Army Watercraft Restructuring Plan* in 2002. This plan directed the following:

- Divestiture of 135 vessels
- Reallocation of 355 Active Component and 264 Reserve Component spaces
- Implementation of forward-stationing and pre-positioning strategies resulting in cost avoidance of approximately $40M per year through elimination of APS 3 sustainment and deployment costs
- Recognized emergence of a new capability defined by the Joint High Speed Vessel programme.

*The 2008 Fleet Modernization Strategy* builds on earlier work by charting a course for continued modernization of Army watercraft capabilities in the context of future Joint operational requirements. This strategy seeks the balance between fighting a continuing global war while also transitioning to the Army's Future Modular Force, and is built on input from a wide range of stakeholders from across the Army and DoD. The U.S. Army Combined Arms Support Command recently completed a Capabilities-Based Assessment of Army Watercraft. Approved by the Army Capabilities Integration Center on 13 November 2007, this Joint CBA has been translated

## Section 12: Army Watercraft (Continued)

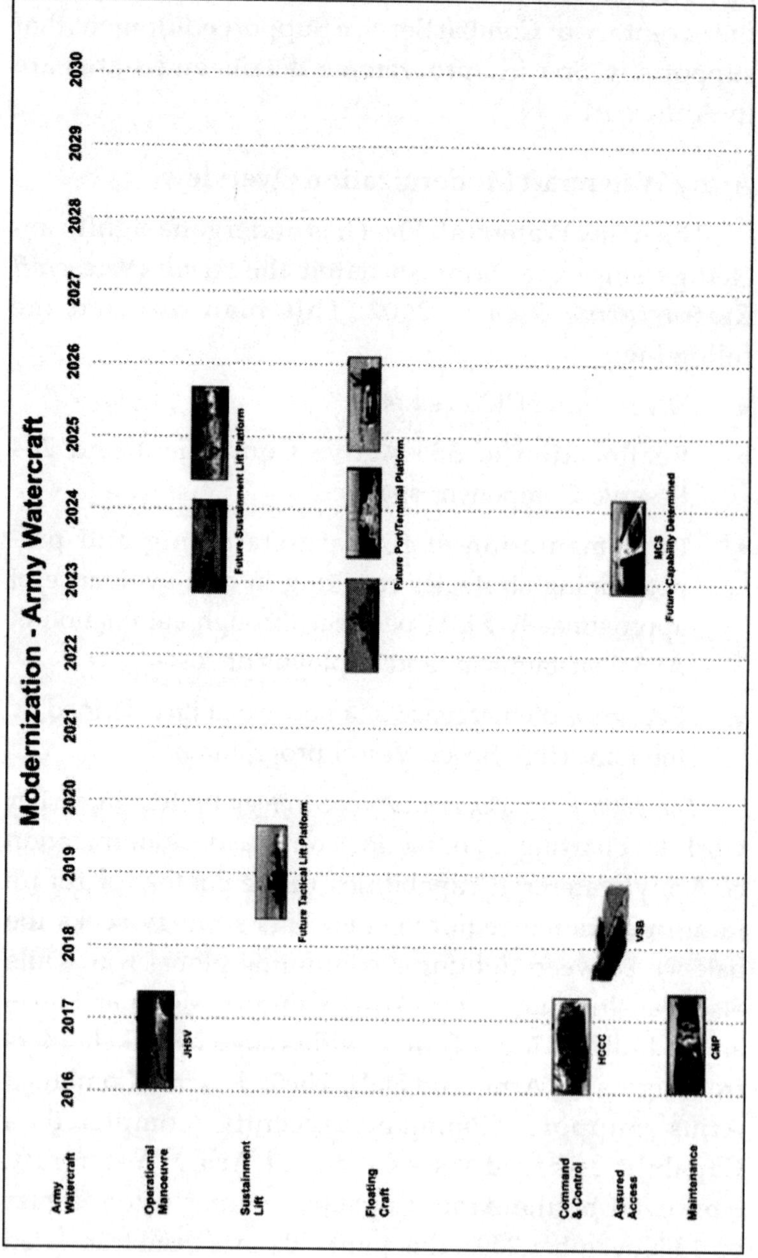

into a modernization strategy detailed in the 2008 *Army Watercraft Master* Plan (Fleet Strategy).

*The 2008 Army Watercraft Fleet Strategy* sets the priorities and describes the actions to take to ensure the fleet possesses capabilities dictated by the Army's Future Modular Force. This modernization strategy focuses on the actions that must take place in the 2008-2014 timeframe to achieve and maintain the minimum operational capabilities needed through 2024: Field Joint High Speed Vessel, Harbormaster Command and Control Center and Vessel-to-Shore Bridging. The JHSV and the HCCC are critical capabilities already under development that fill critical gaps in closing, maneouvring, providing battle space awareness for, and interoperability with Joint and Modular Forces. Further, Vessel-to-Shore Bridging capabilities are a key enabler for the JHSV and current fleet vessels in meeting speed and assured access requirements.

The Future Force needs an Army Watercraft Fleet that possesses a range of lift capabilities. The JHSV helps close new capability gaps in operational and tactical manoeuvre, but the Army will continue to require the heavy sustainment lift provided by the LSV and LCU-2000 fleets. Our strategy will be to maintain our existing LSVs and LCUs, and focus our resources on making the upgrades needed to those vessels' C4ISR and force protection capabilities.

LCM-8 watercraft are rapidly nearing a "dropdead" date beyond which they are not viable due to maintainability costs. The Army places a priority on determining the Future Force requirements for continuing this capability.

Our Joint analysis and fleet assessment indicates the need to integrate Army Watercraft Fleet modernization with emerging terminal operations concepts. Our current floating craft fleet can meet the capabilities the Army requires in the 2015-2024 timeframe.

The CBA identifies the need to develop future sustainment lift capabilities, however, we can meet Future Force sustainment lift requirements by extending the service life and applying appropriate upgrades to the LSV and LCU fleets. The Army is also beginning to explore future platform requirements while executing planned upgrades to the current fleet. We will continue to actively engage and participate in capability development programmes in partnership with other Services and COCOMs that will impact Army Watercraft fleet modernization and potentially lead to future material and non-material development. Specific programme details and status are in Annex A.

# Chapter 4

# New Technologies for Future Combat Systems & Research and Development

## Introduction

The Army recognizes the need to accelerate emerging technologies to improve the capabilities of Soldiers fighting in combat today. Incorporating new technologies derived from Army Science and Technology (S&T) and FCS R&D allows the Army to exploit and leverage R&D efforts sooner with mutually supporting technology enhancements across the force. Through a process known as Spinouts, the Army is leveraging Army S&T and FCS R&D efforts to insert promising new capabilities into the Current Force. FCS core and complementary systems that address current capability gaps are integrated into current formations, or "Spun-out," as they mature. Over the last several years, the

Army demonstrated its adaptability by pushing future capabilities to the Current Force while deployed. Precursors of the Future Combat Systems programme are in combat today in Afghanistan and Iraq. For example, 18 Micro Aerial Vehicles (MAVs) are currently deployed with Navy Explosive Ordnance Disposal units. These FCS Class I UAV precursors are used to locate IEDs and have proven critical to mission accomplishment. A Brigade Combat Team has deployed 36 MAVs to Iraq in mid 2008. Additionally, there are approximately 4,000 robots in theater today. Many of these systems are precursors like the FCS Small Unmanned Ground Vehicle that performs vital IED defeat missions that may otherwise be conducted by Soldiers. Finally, as a result of the Army Science and Technology and FCS efforts, improved fragmentary protection kits for HMMWVs and MRAPs were provided to respond rapidly to an evolving threat.

## Setting the Conditions for Spin-outs

The Army must methodically set the conditions to execute the Spin-out plan while maintaining the flexibility to respond to urgent needs. FCS Spin-outs are based on requirements that are defined in accordance with the Joint Capabilities Integration and Development System. FCS Spin-outs are programmed in the Army's base budget request. The fielding plan adheres to Joint acquisition and force management, doctrine, requirements and metrics. Accordingly, technologies will be demonstrated and deemed mature before the Army commences Low Rate Initial Production of FCS Spin-out systems. The Army has established a programme manager responsible for

FCS Spin-out integration, as well as TRADOC's Future Force Integration Division (FFID) at Fort Bliss, TX to synchronize Spin-out development.

Setting the conditions for Spin-outs requires two essential efforts. First, the Army must address the capability gaps of Current Force vehicles that must host FCS Spin-out technologies. The Army's Spin-out efforts to date demonstrate that Current Force vehicles cannot support the power loads and the internal space required to deliver full FCS capabilities. The Army must aggressively address the challenges and limitations of its current fleets in order to deliver the capability improvements envisioned for Spin-outs. Secondly, the Army must leverage the full capacity of the Army Science and Technology community. This will afford the Army the flexibility to address the Army's needs comprehensively by deriving solutions to diverse problems from the FCS programme and beyond.

## Overcoming the Limitations of Current Platforms

The Army's Spin-out plan recognizes upgrading current systems are a critical component to delivering FCS Spin-out capabilities to the Current Force. Today's Soldiers desperately need the ability to send and receive digitized data in volume while on the move. Capabilities that were once exclusive to static headquarters must be resident in the platforms that deliver Soldiers into combat. Delivering less deprives the Soldier and his leader the situational awareness that is required in a dynamic combat environment. Current Force vehicles lack the power and space available to host many needed technologies without significant upgrades.

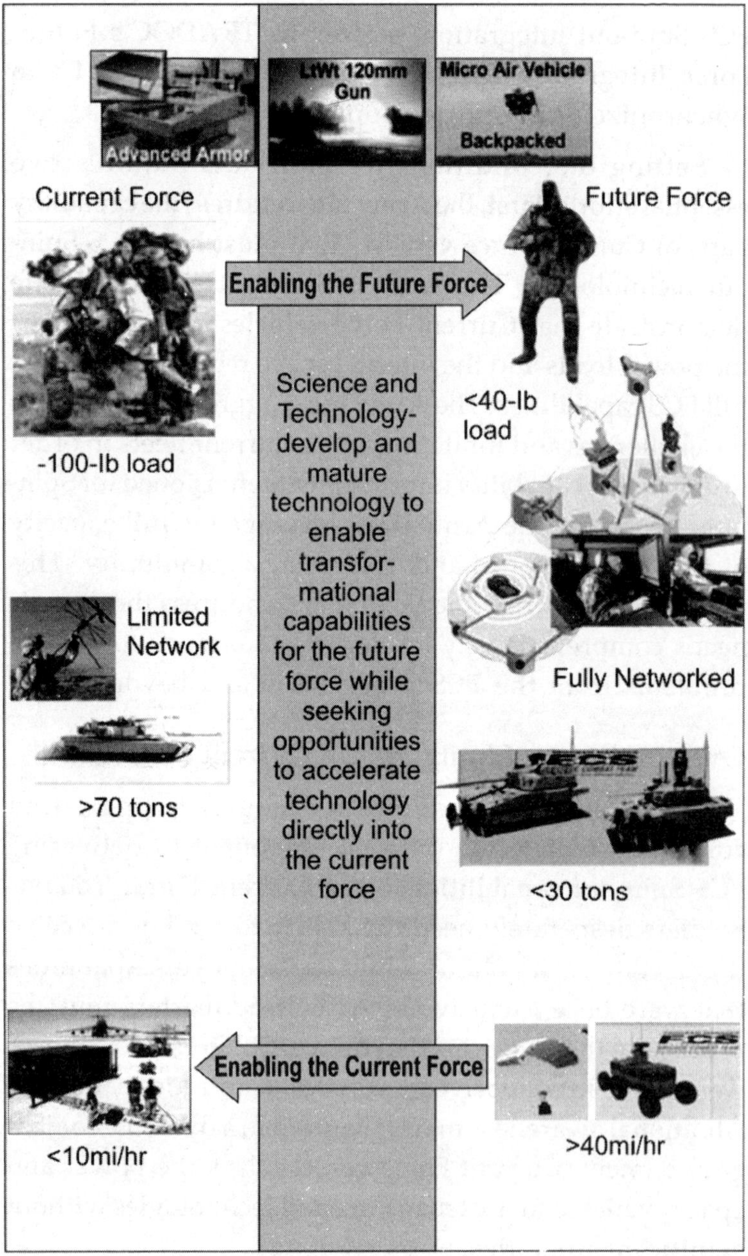
Advanced Armor
LtWt 120mm Gun
Micro Air Vehicle
Backpacked
Current Force
Future Force
Enabling the Future Force
-100-lb load
<40-lb load
Science and Technology-develop and mature technology to enable transformational capabilities for the future force while seeking opportunities to accelerate technology directly into the current force
Limited Network
Fully Networked
>70 tons
FCS
<30 tons
Enabling the Current Force
FCS
<10mi/hr
>40mi/hr

Spin-outs must be fully interoperable with upgrades to current platforms to ensure seamless execution of our Spin-out plan. FCS Spin-out components must compete with other valid claims against the space, and power of our current platforms. Lessons learned in combat are manifested in incremental capability upgrades to our combat platforms. In many cases these new capabilities are derived from new components that add weight and power requirements to our already stressed fleets. The Army recognizes that its modernization strategy is mutually supportive. In this case, the efforts discussed in the previous chapter to upgrade current platforms lay the foundation for incorporating new technologies derived from FCS research and development.

## Leveraging Science and Technology—Enhance the Current Force, Enable the Future Force

The Army is developing technology through investments in the three components of Science & Technology (S&T):

- In the near-term, demonstrating mature technology in relevant operational environments to speed technology transition into acquisition programmes.
- For the mid-term, translating applied research into militarily useful technology applications.
- For the far-term, conducting basic research to create new understanding for technologies that offer paradigm-shifting capabilities.

Army S&T Strategy is to pursue technologies that will enable the Future Force while simultaneously seeking opportunities to enhance the Current Force. These forces require technology solutions from networked capabilities and increased responsiveness through speed and precision lethality. From a strategic perspective, the S&T community supports the GWOT in three ways. First, Soldiers benefit today from technologies that emerged from our past investments. Second, we exploit transition opportunities by accelerating mature technologies from on-going S&T efforts. Third, we leverage the expertise of our scientists and engineers to develop solutions to unforeseen problems encountered during current operations.

The Army's largest S&T investments are for force protection technologies to detect and neutralize Improvised Explosive Devices, mines, rockets, artillery and mortars; to improve Soldier and vehicle survivability and to enhance area/facilities protection.

The Army's S&T invests in a diverse portfolio of technologies and research to provide solutions across a spectrum of enduring capability needs. This portfolio includes C4ISR, lethality, Soldier Systems, unmanned systems, logistics, advanced simulation, medical and manufacturing technologies and basic research.

**C4ISR:** We are developing and demonstrating technologies to speed the ability to collect and disseminate information from sensors through Battle Command software and hardware for current and future C4ISR capabilities.

- Sensor development seeking to provide Soldiers with the means to detect individuals, platforms, and other threats at greater stand-off distances and with more fidelity

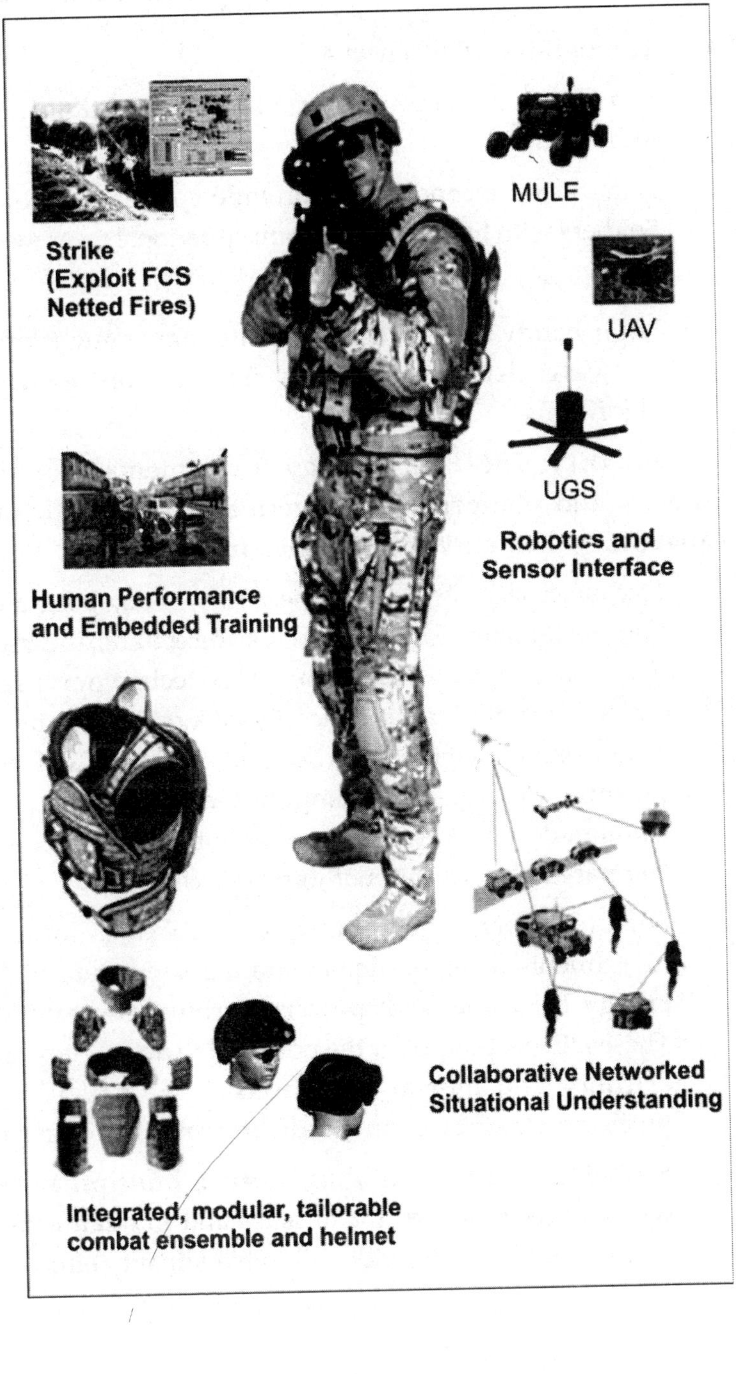
Strike
(Exploit FCS
Netted Fires)
MULE
UAV
UGS
Robotics and
Sensor Interface
Human Performance
and Embedded Training
Collaborative Networked
Situational Understanding
Integrated, modular, tailorable
combat ensemble and helmet

- Through-the-wall sensors
- Sensors for detecting, tracking and "tagging" individuals
- Data fusion technology to provide commanders and Soldiers with timely and relevant situational awareness
- Networked sensors
- High bandwidth directional antennas, networking software, decision tools and information security algorithms.

**Lethality:** These technology investments provide Soldiers and platforms with overmatch against threat capabilities. Lethality technologies include:

- *Electromagnetic (EM) Gun.* The Army is pursuing EM Gun technology for conventional direct and indirect fire cannon (gun) propulsion. This technology uses large electrical currents to accelerate a projectile rather than using conventional propellants. EM Gun has the potential to reduce and simplify the logistics burden through decreased size and weight of these projectiles compared to conventional gun projectiles
- *Directed Energy (DE) weapons.* DE technology investments focus on demonstrating solid state high energy laser and high power microwave weapons. These DE weapons offer the potential to defeat rockets, artillery and mortar munitions while providing precision area protection— reducing collateral damage
- *Scaleable lethality warheads.* Future multipurpose warhead technologies for missiles and gun launched munitions seek to provide tailorable lethality effects

- Novel energetics for increased lethality
- Advanced precision guidance, control and munition seeker components

**Soldier Systems:** S&T investments seek to enable TRADOC's Soldier as a System concept that envisions equipping Soldiers with an integrated modular ensemble (using an open architecture), providing mission tailorable capabilities. Technologies to provide individual Soldiers with platform-like lethality and survivability include:

- Ultra-lightweight materials and nanotechnology to enhance Soldier protection from bullets, fragmentation, blast and other lethal mechanisms
- Lightweight, long-endurance electric power generation and storage

This graphic depicts clockwise from top left:
1) Micro Air Vehicle, 2) Robotic Follower—Stryker, 3) Packbot

- Physiological status and diagnostics as well as reporting and "on the uniform" medical response interventions
- Embedded and immersive training and mission rehearsal environments, as well as cultural awareness and translation tools.

**Unmanned Systems:** The goal of unmanned S&T investments is to provide Soldiers with new capabilities that can unburden them from dangerous, routine and long duration missions that do not require the full dimension of human capabilities. Technologies are being developed for unmanned aerial and ground vehicles, unattended sensors and "intelligent" (automated functioning) munitions. Unmanned systems have already demonstrated their ability to enhance Soldier capabilities in a variety of applications to support the Global War on Terror. The S&T emphasis is pursuing more autonomy in unmanned systems through work to improve perception, mobility and "intelligent" vehicle control with less human supervision. Unmanned systems technologies include:

- Algorithms for real-time object and terrain detection, classification and identification
- Algorithms for increased tactical behaviour enabling unmanned systems to act more independently during tactical manoeuvres
- Passive and active sensor technology along with multispectral and robotic sensor fusion for higher performance systems (speed, autonomous vehicle situational awareness)

- Intelligent agents, adaptive automation, augmented and interactive displays to enable human-unmanned and unmanned-system capabilities.

**Logistics:** Technology investments are focused on increased reliability, durability, and reduced maintenance for all systems and components. Embedded prognostics and diagnostics are being developed for dynamic monitoring of critical vehicle component and system "health" and reporting equipment status before a failure occurs. While pursuing operational and support cost reduction and increased performance, the technology programme is also seeking to reduce fuel consumption. Up to 15 tons precision air-drop delivery technology is being developed that is enabled by GPS guidance, ram-air parachutes and impact absorption landing technologies to provide essential logistics. Logistics technologies include:

- Water recovery and purification systems
- Petroleum fuel reformation technologies
- Prognostics and diagnostics modeling, sensors and signal processing
- High efficiency vehicle power and drive drains for reduced fuel consumption and increased performance
- Technologies for reduced operations and sustainment demands for rotorcraft
- Energy and Power:
- Electric and hybrid electric vehicle technologies have the potential to achieve significant reductions in fossil fuel requirements and the associated logistics burdens.

- Advanced batteries, capacitors, switches, generators, auxiliary power units, fuel cells; and other devices will improve electric power generation, storage and conditioning efficiency to reduce Soldiers' loads and equipment weight.
- Compact pulse power systems will also enable new capabilities such as electromagnetic armor or directed energy weapons.

**Advanced Simulation:** Advanced simulation technology investments seek to provide robust, networked, live, virtual and constructive simulation environments that have the potential to enable revolutionary training, mission rehearsal, leader development and simulation tools for designing and evaluating new technologies. Investments in simulation technology also provide the tools, techniques, and analyses capabilities to enable collaborative, distributed and Joint operational simulations.

**Medical Technology.** Medical technology investments to improve protection (inclusive of blasts from explosive devices), treatment and life-saving interventions for Soldiers. This programme has three components: infectious disease (diagnosis, treatment and preventatives), combat casualty care and military operational medicine under environmentally extreme conditions world-wide.

**Manufacturing Technology:** This programme focuses on improving new technology producibility and affordability by developing reliable manufacturing processes and increasing production yields. This technology seeks cost savings and risk reduction in military-unique manufacturing processes to achieve economic production rates. This

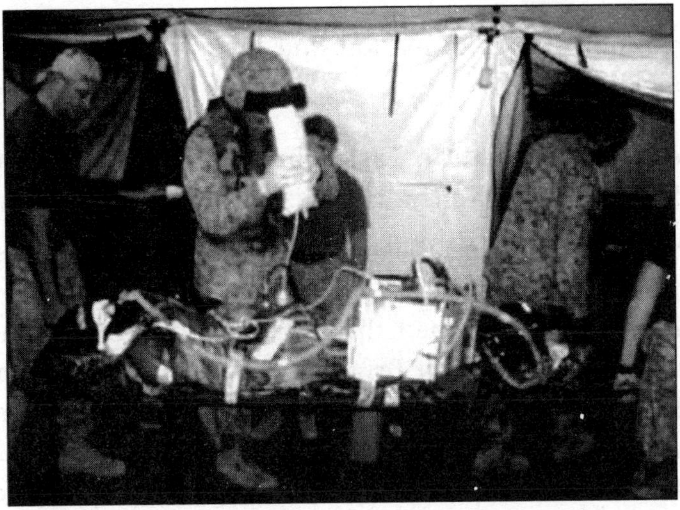

programme also fosters the transfer of new/improved manufacturing technologies to the industrial base.

**Basic Research.** Basic research seeks to provide new understanding in nanomaterials for ballistic protection, biotechnology for improved materials for network sensors, network science to enable next generation, network-centric technologies and immersive simulations for training and mission rehearsal.

The Army's S&T efforts are consistent with the capabilities the FCS programme is developing. By focusing on our broader S&T efforts the Army gains valuable flexibility filling the urgent needs of Soldiers in combat today. The formal Spin-out plan is currently comprised of FCS core and complimentary systems. In these uncertain times the Army is poised to draw from the great reservoir of talent and skill within its S&T community to respond to urgent needs through FCS Spin-outs. This maximizes our opportunities to exploit and leverage R&D efforts sooner.

## The Army Evaluation Task Force (AETF): Evaluating FCS Technology in the Hands of Soldiers

The Army has established the Army Evaluation Task Force at Fort Bliss, Texas, to evaluate and validate new technologies developed through the FCS Programme. Designated as the 5th Brigade, 1st Armored Division (AETF), this unique Army organization supports the evaluation and testing of the FCS Brigade Combat Team designs, operational concepts, war-fighting capabilities and training.

With the AETF providing input, the Army Test and Evaluation Command (ATEC) assesses the performance of FCS Spin-outs technologies as well as the FCS core programmes. The net impact of 5th Brigade, 1st Armored Division (AETF) is to put Soldiers into the design cycle and streamline FCS development for the Army. Soldiers of the AETF, with their relevant combat expertise (over 80% of the leadership are combat veterans), unleash the power of the Future Combat Systems in the desert of Texas and New Mexico, rather than the unforgiving sands of Iraq and Afghanistan.

The AETF was established to provide a dedicated unit and Soldiers to provide feedback for system development and fielding decisions for FCS systems. The unit is manned and equipped, based on tester, material developer and the Training & Doctrine Command and Forces Command review to ensure a complete evaluation of FCS systems. As decisions are made on future Spin-outs, the design and organization of the AETF will be reviewed to ensure it is organized to best support its ongoing mission.

The Future Force Integration Directorate (FFID) is also located at Ft. Bliss. It provides an integrated staff of material developers, modeling and simulation personnel, and capabilities managers and developers to oversee the AETF and provide integrated support and oversight to the FCS programme testing and evaluation. This organization, a

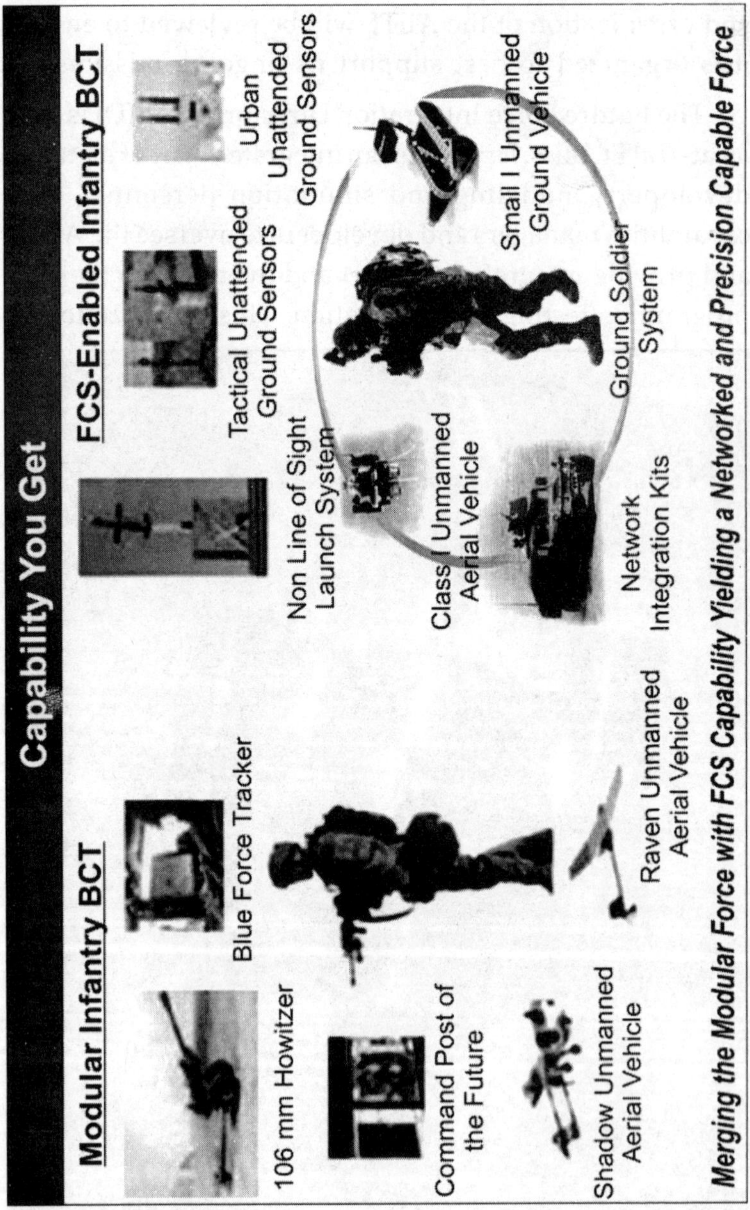
Capability You Get
Modular Infantry BCT
106 mm Howitzer
Blue Force Tracker
Command Post of the Future
Shadow Unmanned Aerial Vehicle
Raven Unmanned Aerial Vehicle
FCS-Enabled Infantry BCT
Non Line of Sight Launch System
Tactical Unattended Ground Sensors
Urban Unattended Ground Sensors
Class I Unmanned Aerial Vehicle
Ground Soldier System
Small I Unmanned Ground Vehicle
Network Integration Kits
Merging the Modular Force with FCS Capability Yielding a Networked and Precision Capable Force

directorate of the Army Capabilities Integration Center (ARCIC) of TRADOC, is key in the identification, design, development and synchronization of capabilities into the Army current Modular Force and the validation of the Spin-out process, ensuring FCS Spin-outs are integrated throughout the domains of Doctrine, Organization, Training, Material, Leader Development, Personnel and Facilities.

## Delivering Spin-outs to Infantry Brigade Combat Teams

The Army recently decided to focus FCS Spin-outs initially on Infantry Brigade Combat Teams (IBCTs). This decision is based on lessons learned from combat. Operational Needs Statements (ONS) from IBCT commanders were almost double the number from Heavy Brigade Combat Team (HBCT) commanders for 2007 and 2008. Additionally, IBCTs have capability gaps not found in our heavy force. Our Infantry Brigade Combat Teams (IBCTs) have been the highest demand in combat operations over the last five years. The Army is growing to meet global requirements and will add six IBCTs to meet the demands of today and tomorrow. The Army has the opportunity to make this adjustment because of the progress of FCS technological development.

The Army's FCS re-sequencing efforts, from the HBCTs to IBCTs, will align the programme with current demands, our new doctrine and shifts of funds to refocus on enhancing the IBCTs first. The Army is deploying enhanced capabilities to the IBCTs first to increase their effectiveness and survivability across the spectrum for today and tomorrow's fight. Greater Soldier and unit effectiveness is essential to readiness.

Starting in July 2008, the FCS equipment will undergo a Preliminary – Limited User Test (P-LUT). The P-LUT is intended to refocus the previously scheduled Heavy BCT Limited User Test. The results from this testing effort will support doctrine, organization, training and material development efforts. The formal LUT scheduled in FY09 had become the basis of the Spin-out 1 acquisition decision. These changes will ensure that all 43 IBCTs are fully equipped with Spin-outs technologies by 2025.

The capabilities being brought to the Current Force from the FCS are ensuring the continued advantages of today's Soldier. The accelerated fielding of FCS technology is already evident in the precursor Class I UAV fielding to current brigades in the fight. The potential for today's units to simultaneously provide real time visual awareness of friendly and enemy forces at the company and platoon level will greatly enhance small unit operations. The unveiling of the FCS Non Line of Sight (NLOS) Cannon technology is a milestone in the integrated network system.

The combination of the Ground Soldier System, Tactical/ Urban Sensors, NLOS Launch System, and integrated network communications on the HMMWV platform will give the IBCT unprecedented ability to see, know, understand, and act first down to platoon level.

# Chapter 5

# Field Future Combat Systems

## Introduction

The Army is transforming into a networked Modular Force that is agile, globally responsive and sustainable. FCS is the core of this effort. FCS is designed to provide the Soldiers and leaders who engage the enemy with the situational awareness required for a decisive advantage in combat. Networked Battle Command and sensors will enhance the ability of platoons and companies to see the enemy and engage with precision. This is accomplished by providing Soldiers with Battle Command and sensor capabilities similar to those currently resident in brigade and division headquarters. The FCS BCT will be an integrated combat formation employing a system of systems approach to deliver the capabilities the Army needs. Fielding FCS will be fulfilling the Army's vision for the future by integrating full spectrum capabilities in its systems.

FCS is the fastest and surest way to transform the Army because it drives R&D, rapid fielding and modernisation programmes. The FCS BCT will be the Army's future tactical warfighting echelon – a dominant ground combat force that complements the Joint team. Although optimized for offensive operations, the FCS BCT will be capable of executing full spectrum operations. The FCS BCT will improve the strategic deployability and operational manoeuvre capability of ground combat formations without sacrificing lethality or survivability. FCS is designed to provide Soldiers with the necessary situational awareness and force protection to defeat adaptive adversaries. FCS embeds an advanced digital network in a family of highly survivable Manned Ground Vehicles. FCS breaks the mold of incremental, evolutionary improvements in favour of revolutionary change.

FCS responds to the critical needs of the Army. Operational Needs Statements confirm that commanders in Iraq and Afghanistan require:

- Increased Lethality
- Improved Survivability
- Increased Intelligence Surveillance and Reconnaissance
- Networked Battle Command
- Enhanced Logistics

The FCS BCT addresses these gaps through three complimentary efforts. These include developing an advanced digital network, enabling precision effects and building a modern platform that meets the needs of 21st Century.

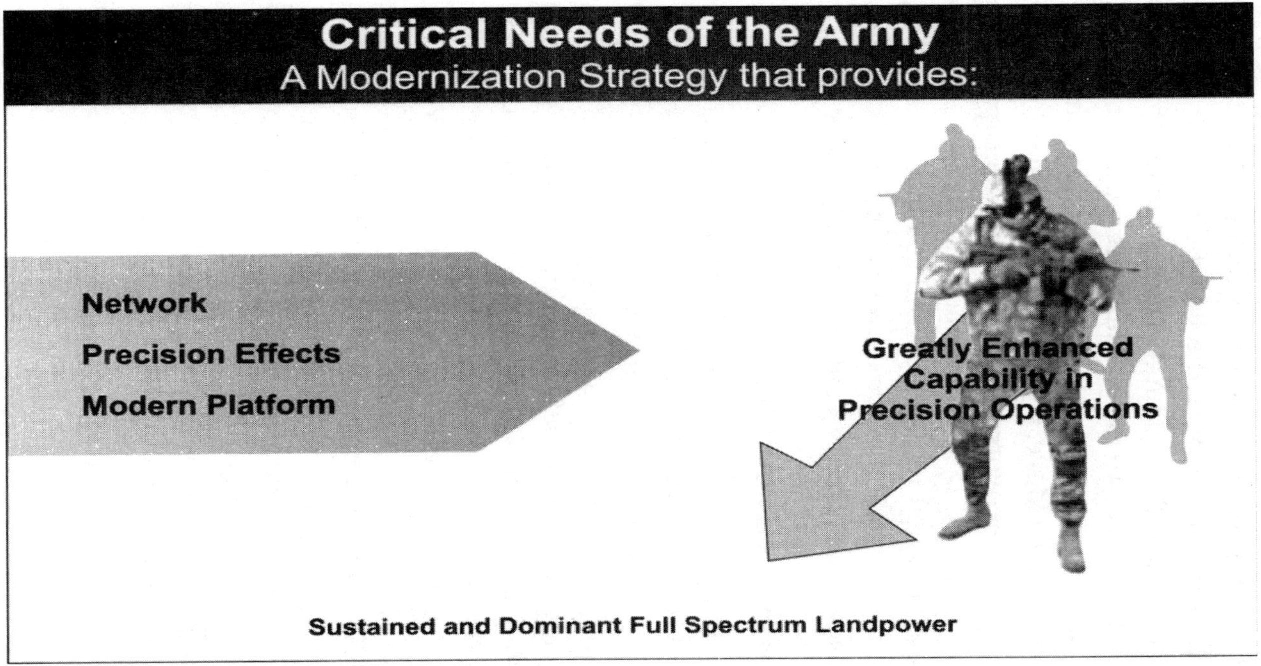


Figure 5-1 – Enhanced capabilities of the soldier by providing an advanced network, and associated precision effects, integrated into a common platform. The result is dominant land power across the full spectrum of operations.

## The Network

Information precision is the key for future land-power. The FCS network affords the FCS BCT the situational awareness and understanding necessary to effectively focus precision effects. Current Force units are severely hindered by the lack of real time situational awareness, and Battle Command on the Move. FCS provides redundant, scalable and tailorable networks on the move. The capabilities currently resident in division and brigade headquarters will be distributed to platoons and companies, allowing for unprecedented situational awareness for the Soldiers and leaders who make contact with the enemy.

## Delivering Precision Effects

The FCS network is the means the Army will leverage to provide precision effects to units in combat. Networked sensors and unmanned vehicles allow companies and platoons to develop the situation with far greater precision before making contact with the enemy. Precision in situational awareness and access to information leads to true precision fires for organic and Joint assets as well as improved force protection. These capabilities are essential in irregular warfare typically fought among the population. Enhanced vehicle prognostics, fault reporting and greater asset visibility enable precision logistics. Greater precision in logistics, coupled with other FCS efficiencies, reduces the numbers of convoys—one of greatest vulnerabilities in current logistics operations.

## The Modern Platform for the 21st Century

The Manned Ground Vehicle is the ground combat platform that will deliver the FCS network and associated precision effects to Soldiers in combat. By incorporating the network into the original design, the MGV will deliver capabilities far beyond the limits of current platforms. Today's vehicles lack the power and space to integrate full FCS technologies. The MGV is designed for the power loads envisioned in the 21st Century. The MGV is the key to a more agile force, by employing a common chassis that is lighter and less logistically dependent. Manned Ground Vehicles create efficiencies that allow double the number of infantrymen in squads (compared to an HBCT)—a key force multiplier in counter-insurgency operations. MGVs offer several advantages to include:

- Advanced power generation and management—essential for network integration
- Embedded network capability to enhance situational awareness, which improves survivability and effectiveness
- Replaceable armour that can be upgraded to meet developing threats as technology advances
- Significantly improved reliability and maintainability as compared to Current Force; 80% of field level maintenance can be done by the crew, reducing requirements for mechanics
- Beyond Line of Sight and Non-Line of Sight precision fires at platoon and company level
- Advances in hybrid power propulsion mean fewer gallons of fuel and petroleum required to sustain operations

- Networked Battle Command
- Enhanced logistics

## Improving Force Protection

FCS Manned Ground Vehicles afford some of the most advanced ballistic technologies available. However, we will never be able to provide enough armour against an adaptive foe. Events in Iraq and Afghanistan have shown that ballistic upgrades are quickly overwhelmed by enemy counteractions. Instead, we must protect Soldiers with a comprehensive approach built on improved situational awareness, enemy detection, threat disruption, and hit avoidance, as well as improved armour.

Future Combat Systems provide a holistic approach to survivability including:

- Signature management and low probability intercept to deny the enemy the ability to detect FCS systems electronically
- Improved situational awareness and threat detection
- Improved protection against Improvised Explosive Devices, Rocket Propelled Grenades, and Anti-tank missiles
- Improved ballistic protection (360°) comprised of upgradeable Active Protection System (APS)
- Improved defence against Chemical, Biological, Radiological, and Nuclear (CBRN) effects, and toxic industrial materials and contaminants.

## Enhanced Capabilities to Soldiers; Dominant Landpower to the Nation

FCS integrates an advanced digital network, and enhanced precision with modern platforms in order to provide greater capabilities for Soldiers. FCS arms the Soldier for today's environments while posturing for future threats and uncertainty. FCS reflects our commitment to fielding trained formations with the best technology available. FCS gives Soldiers knowledge, and through the network, the means to transmit knowledge. FCS drastically improves lethality, survivability, ISR, Battle Command, battlefield awareness, and logistics forming a quantum leap in force effectiveness. The result is dominant landpower to defeat enemies across the full spectrum of conflict.

Maintaining the momentum of this modernization effort is critical to ensuring Soldiers in combat maintain a decisive advantage over current and future adversaries. For immediate impact, the FCS capabilities will "Spin-out" into the Current Forces to exploit opportunities and sustain critical overmatch. As fielding commences, the impact of the modernization programme achieves precision fires, precision tactical awareness and precision logistics—a Joint, revolutionary development in warfare. Army Modernisation, with FCS as the core, represents the Nation's commitment to providing Soldiers with the necessary resources to win the Nation's wars.

## Discussion of Future Combat Systems Material Programmes

The **Soldier** is the integral element of the FCS Brigade Combat Team. The Soldier is connected and integrated to the FCS network and FCS Battle Command. This connectivity provides the Soldier superior situational awareness mounted and dismounted, enabling the Soldier to effectively perform Battle Command functions while maximizing Soldier and force lethality and survivability. Network connectivity also enables the Soldier to more effectively employ and control FCS unmanned ground and aerial systems, and to take full advantage of embedded training, logistics and medical functions.These network-enabled capabilities are executed when mounted via the MGV Common Crew Station, and when dismounted via the Centralized Controller.

The **Sensors and Platforms** Layer is comprised of a distributed and networked array of multi-spectral sensors that provide the FCS (BCT) with the ability to "see first." Intelligence, Surveillance and Reconnaissance sensors will be integrated onto all Manned Ground Vehicles, all unmanned ground vehicles and the two classes of unmanned aerial vehicles within the FCS (BCT). These sensors will be capable of accomplishing a variety of collection missions including Wide Area Surveillance, Reconnaissance, Surveillance, and Target Acquisition,

Mobility and Survivability. In addition to collecting data locally within the FCS (BCT) area of operations, the ISR Layer architecture will facilitate the fusion of Joint, Current Force, and National sensor data into the COP through the Distributed Common Ground System—Army. The sensor data collect from FCS (BCT) internal, Current Force, Joint, and National sensors will provide timely and accurate situational awareness, enhance survivability by avoiding enemy fires, enable precision networked fires and maintain contact throughout an engagement.

To provide warfighters with current, accurate, and actionable information, the data from the various distributed ISR and other external sensor assets are subject to complex data processing, filtering, correlation, aided target recognition, and fusion (level 0 and 1 automated fusion, and levels 2-5 semi-automated fusion). The Sensor Data Management software organizes all the sensor data—

including detection reports— and tracks information as received from the sensor packages.

The FCS (BCT) **Unattended Ground Sensors** (UGS) programme is divided into two major subgroups of sensing systems: Tactical-UGS, which includes Intelligence, Surveillance and Reconnaissance and Chemical,

Radiological and Nuclear (CBRN)-UGS; and Urban-UGS, also known as Urban Military Operations in Urban Terrain Advanced Sensor System (UMASS). An UGS field will include multimode sensors for target detection, location and classification; and an imaging capability for target identification. A sensor field also includes a gateway node to provide sensor fusion and a long-haul interoperable communications capability for transmitting target or situational awareness information to a remote operator, or the common operating picture through the FCS (BCT) JTRS Network. The UGS are used to perform mission tasks such as perimeter defence, surveillance, target acquisition and situational awareness, including Chemical, Radiological, Nuclear and early warning. Urban-Unattended Ground Sensors provide a low cost, network enabled reporting system for situational awareness and force protection in an urban setting, as well as residual protection for cleared areas of Urban Military Operations in Urban Terrain environments. They are hand-employed by Soldiers or delivered on robotic vehicles either inside or outside buildings and structures. Urban UGS support BCT operations by monitoring urban choke points such as corridors and stairwells as well as sewers, culverts, and tunnels. Urban UGS gateways provide the urban situational awareness data interfaced to JTRS networks. Soldiers involved in the testing of the UGS during Spin-out 1 provided invaluable feedback that was incorporated and now in final development and fielding.

The **FCS Network** will provide Soldiers with key situational awareness and communications capability. The network is not only for battlespace awareness, but will also allow Soldiers to receive and transmit a variety of

real-time data, including calls for lethal effects. FCS is the flagship of the Army's advanced network development.

Networks have become part of our daily lives and by extension warfare. Rarely will a person leave home without a cell phone, blackberry, or GPS. It should be no different for a Soldier. Except their capabilities will be fully integrated into a single system e.g., a Soldier should not have to look up an address in a cell phone and enter that address into his GPS. The Network will provide the Soldier this solution - integrating the components is key. Networks have become and will continue to be part of our lives.

The FCS network consists of five layers (Standards, Transport, Services, Applications, and Sensors and

Platforms) that, when combined, provide seamless delivery of both data and knowledge. The integration of all five layers is necessary to provide greater situational awareness, sensor fusion and networked fires; transforming our ground forces' ability to dominate in land combat.

The **Non-Line-of-Sight–Launch System** (NLOS-LS) consists of a platform-independent Container Launch Unit with self-contained tactical fire control electronics and software for remote and unmanned operations. Each Container Launch Unit consists of a computer and communications system and 15 Precision Attack Missiles with a range of .5 to 40 kilometres. The NLOSC provides rapidly deployable and network linked off precision guided munitions launch capability that is currently not available within the Army.

Precision Attack Missiles are modular, multi-mission, guided missiles with two trajectories—a direct-fire fast-attack trajectory, and a boost-glide trajectory. The missile receives target information prior to launch, and can receive and respond to target location updates during flight. The PAM supports laser-designated, laser-anointed and autonomous operation modes and is capable of transmitting near-real-time information in the form of target imagery prior to

impact. PAM is being designed to defeat high payoff light and heavy armoured targets either moving or stationary. The NLOS-LS, which has also successfully completed airdrops from a C-130 is part of Spin-out 1 and will provide superior situational awareness for Soldiers in any field.

The **Class I Unmanned Aerial Vehicle** (UAV) is a platoon level asset that provides the dismounted Soldier with Reconnaissance, Surveillance and Target Acquisition and laser designation. Total system weight (which includes the air vehicle, a control device, and ground support equipment) is less than 51 pounds and is backpackable in two custom MOLLE type carriers. The air vehicle operates in open, rolling, complex and urban terrains with a vertical take-off and landing capability. It is interoperable with selected ground and air platforms and controlled by mounted or dismounted Soldiers. The Class I uses autonomous flight and navigation, but it will interact with the network and Soldier to dynamically update routes and target information. It provides dedicated reconnaissance support and early warning to the smallest echelons of the Brigade Combat Team in environments not suited to larger assets.

The Class I system provides a hover capability that is not currently available in the current Army UAV inventory for urban and route surveillance. The Class I system also fills known gaps that exist in force operations, such as: Protect Force in Counterinsurgency (COIN) Operations, Soldier Protection in COIN environment, Ability to Conduct Joint Urban Operations, Enhanced ISR/RSTA Capabilities, and Hover and Stare operations.

The Class I UAV has entered accelerated evaluation by Soldiers at the Army Evaluation Task Force, where Soldiers have started training on the equipment. These evaluations are set to conclude in the Fall of 2008, when FCS and Army capabilities managers will provide recommendation on whether to field the platforms or continue system development under the core FCS programme.

The **Class IV Unmanned Aerial Vehicle** has a range and endurance appropriate for the brigade mission. It supports the Brigade Combat Team commander with communications relay, long endurance persistent stare and wide area surveillance. Unique missions include

dedicated manned and unmanned teaming with manned aviation; Wide Band Communications Relay; and standoff Chemical, Biological, Radiological, Nuclear detection with on-board processing. Additionally, it has the payload to enhance the Reconnaissance, Surveillance and Target Acquisition capabilities by cross-cueing multiple sensors. The Class IV will be able to land without a dedicated air field. Class IV development is shared with the Navy's Fire Scout programme.

The **Small Unmanned Ground Vehicle** is a lightweight, man portable UGV capable of conducting military operations in urban terrain, tunnels, sewers and caves. The SUGV is an aid in enabling the performance of manpower intensive or high-risk functions (i.e. urban

Intelligence, Sur-veillance and Reconnai-ssance missions, Chemi-cals/Toxic Industrial Mat-erials reconnaissance) without exposing Soldiers directly to the hazard. The SUGV modular design allows multiple payloads to be integrated in a plug-andplay fashion. Weigh-ing less than 30 pounds, it is capable of carrying up to six pounds of payload weight.

The SUGV has entered accelerated evaluation by Soldiers at the Army Evaluation Task Force, where Soldiers have started training on the equipment. These evaluations are set to conclude in Fall 2008, when FCS and Army capabilities managers will provide recommendation on whether to field the platforms or continue system development under the core FCS programme.

The **Mounted Combat System** is part of the Manned Ground Vehicle family that provides Line-of-Sight (LOS) and Beyond-Line-of-Sight ( B L O S ) offensive firepower capability allowing BCTs to close with and destroy enemy forces. The MCS delivers precision fires at a rapid rate to destroy multiple targets at standoff ranges quickly and complements the fires of other systems in the BCT. It is capable of providing direct support to the dismounted infantry in an assault, defeating bunkers and breaching walls during the tactical assault. When employing the Mid-

Range Munition, the MCS also provides BLOS fires to destroy point targets through the integrated sensor network. This capability enhances SoS lethality and significantly increases the options available to the BCT commander for the destruction of point targets through the integrated fires network. MCS shares a common chassis with the other FCS Manned Ground Vehicles and consists of Light Weight 120-millimeter Cannon and an Ammunition Handling System.

The **Infantry Carrier Vehicle** is part of the Manned Ground Vehicles family that consists of four platform versions: a Company Commander; a Platoon Leader; a Rifle Squad; and a Weapons Squad. The Infantry Platoon includes an ICV Platoon Leader variant; three ICV Rifle Squad variants; and an ICV Weapons Squad variant. The ICV Rifle Squad variant and ICV Weapons Squad variant each deliver nine-person infantry squads to a location from which they will conduct a close assault. The ICV effectively employs weapon systems and rapidly manoeuvres during blackout, day and night operations,

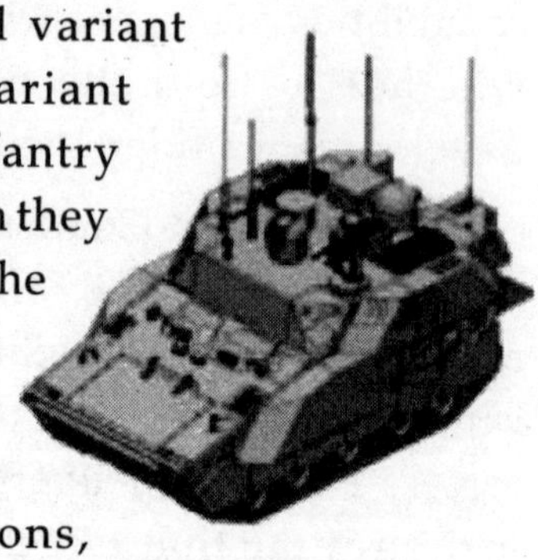

inclement weather and limited visibility periods. The ICV carries the majority of equipment freeing the individual Soldier to focus on mission. The ICV can move, shoot, communicate, detect threats and protect crew and critical components under most land-surface environments. Data transfer with other components of the BCT permits constant update of the common operational picture and rapid identification of targets. The ICV features the MK44 30- millimeter cannon as its primary armament plus a 7.62 machine gun.

The **Non-Line of Sight Cannon** (NLOS-C) is an indirect fire support component of the Manned Ground Vehicle family. The NLOS-C is a self propelled howitzer with a

two men crew. It will provide net-worked, extended range, responsive and sustained precision attack of point and area targets in support of the FCS (BCT). It fires a suite of munitions that include special purpose capabilities to provide a variety of effects on demand including precision guided munitions such as the XM982 Excalibur.

NLOS-C provides close support and destructive fires for tactical standoff engagement during both offensive and defensive operations in concert with line-of-sight, beyond-line-of-sight, other NLOS, external and Joint capabilities in combat scenarios spanning the spectrum of ground combat and threats. It has a 155-millimeter, Zone 4, 38-caliber cannon, fully automated armament system and a high level of commonality with other MGV variants. It incorporates a suite of protection measures to enhance crew and platform survivability.

The NLOS-C is deployable worldwide and can operate in a wide range of natural environmental conditions. The cannon can move rapidly, stop quickly and deliver lethal first round effects on target in record time. The NLOS Cannon has a Multiple Round Simultaneous Impact capability. The MRSI capability, coupled with the NLOS-C superior sustained rate of fire, will provide record effects on target from a smaller number of systems. The cannon, like all MGV variants, can rapidly rearm and refuel and its system weight makes it uniquely deployable. Fully automated handling, loading, and firing is a centerpiece of the NLOS-C. The NLOS-C balances deployability and sustainability with responsiveness, lethality, survivability, agility and versatility. The NLOS-C is designed to minimize its logistic and maintenance footprint in the theater of operation and to employ advanced maintenance approaches to increase availability and to support sustainability.

The **Non-Line of Sight Mortar** is the short-to-midrange indirect fire support component of the Manned Ground Vehicle family. It provides networked, responsive and sustained indirect fire support to the Combined Arms Battalion in the FCS (BCT). It fires a suite of 120-millimeter munitions that includes special purpose capabilities to provide a variety of fires on demand including precision guided munitions. NLOSM provides close support and destructive fires for tactical standoff engagement during both offensive and defensive operations in concert with line-of-sight, beyond-line-of-sight, other NLOS, external

and Joint capabilities in combat scenarios spanning the spectrum of ground combat and threats. The NLOS-M mounts a secondary armament and will incorporate a suite of protection measures to enhance the three person crew's survivability.

The **Reconnaissance and Surveillance Vehicle** is part of the Manned Ground Vehicle family and is the eyes and ears of the battlefield. It features a suite of advanced sensors to detect, locate, track, classify, and automatically identify targets from increased standoff ranges under all climatic conditions, day or night. Included in this suite are a mast-mounted, long-range electro-optic infrared sensor, an emitter mapping sensor for Radio Frequency intercept and direction finding, remote chemical detection and a multifunction RF sensor. The RSV also features the onboard capability to conduct automatic target detection, aided target recognition and level one sensor fusion. To further enhance the scout's capabilities, the RSV is equipped with Unattended Ground Sensors, a Small Unmanned Ground Vehicle and a Class I Unmanned Arial Vehicle system.

The **Command and Control Vehicle** is part of the Manned Ground Vehicle family and the hub of battlefield command and control. The C2V platform provides the tools for commanders to synchronize their knowledge of combat power with the human dimension of leadership. It is located within the headquarters sections at each echelon of the BCT down to the company level, and via mission workstations contain the warfighter machine interface that allows commanders and their staffs to access Battle Command applications that will aid in mission planning and preparation, mission execution and situation understanding.

These applications enable commanders and their staffs to perform tasks such as fusing friendly, enemy, civilian, weather and terrain situations and distributing this information via a Common Operating Picture. Commanders also utilize the C2V's integrated C4ISR suite to receive, analyze and transmit tactical information both inside and outside the BCT. The Command and Control Vehicle can also employ unmanned systems, such as unmanned aerial vehicles to enhance situational awareness throughout the BCT.

The **Medical Vehicles** are part of the Manned Ground Vehicle family and are designed to provide advanced trauma life support to critically injured Soldiers. The Medical Vehicles serve as the primary medical system within the BCT and have two versions: Evacuation and Treatment. The time-sensitive nature of treating critically injured Soldiers requires an immediately responsive force health protection system with an expedient field evacuation system. The Medical Vehicle-Evacuation allows trauma

specialists, manoeuvreing with combat forces, to be closer to the casualty's point-of-injury and is used for casualty evacuation. The Medical Vehicle-Treatment vehicle enhances the ability to provide Advanced Trauma Management/Advanced Trauma Life Support treatments and procedures forward for more rapid casualty interventions and clearance of the battlespace.

Both Medical Vehicle versions will be capable of conducting medical procedures and treatments using installed networked medical information interfaces, with the ability to interface with Medical Communications for Combat Casualty Care. The Theater Medical Information Programme Real-time monitoring/reporting of medical status during medical sustainment operations is another core capability.

The **Recovery and Maintenance Vehicle** is part of the Manned Ground Vehicle family and is a manoeuvre sustainment system, providing recovery and maintenance support within the BCT. Each BCT has a small number of 2-3 man Combat Repair Teams within the organic Brigade

Support Battalion to perform field maintenance beyond the capabilities of the crew chief/crew, more in-depth Battle Damage Assessment Repair and recovery operations. The FRMV's recovery winch and integrated crane will provide maintenance lift capability and recovery of overturned or mired vehicles. The FRMV has a crew of three with additional space for two recovered crew members and carry equipment and spare parts to conduct on-site vehicle repairs. The weapon system for the FRMV is the Close Combat Armament System.

The **Multifunctional Utility/Logistics and Equipment** (MULE) Vehicle is a 2.5-ton Unmanned Ground Vehicle that will support dismounted and air assault operations. The Multifunctional Utility Logistics and Equipment Vehicle is sling-loadable under military rotorcraft. The MULE Vehicle has three variants sharing a common chassis: transport, countermine and the Armed Robotic Vehicle Assault-Light.

The Transport MULE Vehicle will carry 1,900-2,400 pounds of equipment and rucksacks for dismounted infantry squads with the mobility needed to follow squads in complex terrain. The Countermine MULE Vehicle will provide the capability to detect, mark and neutralize anti-tank mines by integrating a mine detection mission equipment package from the Ground Standoff Mine Detection System, FCS (BCT) programme.

The ARV-Assault- Light MULE Vehicle is a mobility platform with an integrated weapons and reconnaissance, surveillance and target acquisition package to support the dismounted infantry's efforts to locate and destroy enemy platforms and positions. The MULE Common

Mobility Platform is the programme's centerpiece providing superior mobility built around the propulsion and articulated suspension system to negotiate complex terrain, obstacles and gaps that a dismounted squad will encounter.

The FCS programme is truly revolutionary, not just an incremental improvement to existing capabilities. Future Combat Systems BCTs will far exceed the capabilities of our current brigades. Soldiers in FCS units will be better protected by better and scalable armour, by using unmanned vehicles and unattended sensors to see and destroy the enemy at safe distances and by using the active protective system to destroy incoming enemy rounds. FCS will save lives as it increases Soldier capability and productivity.

# Chapter 6

# Conclusion

## Risks to Army Modernization

Primary risks to Army modernization involve loss of support by the Administration or Congress. Even small cuts in modernization funding will impact Soldiers in today's fight. Small decrements in FCS funding will impact our ability to provide the benefits of future-related technologies to Soldiers today. The affordability of modernization cannot be placed above risk to Soldiers or the readiness of the Army. There is also concern on the part of some that the needs of the current fight outweigh our commitment to modernize. We cannot mortgage the future to support the current fight. We must restore balance and build readiness through modernization for Soldiers both now and in the future.

A potential drawdown in current operations creates the potential that supplemental dollars could decrease. This would be acceptable if the supplemental only funded contingency costs, but some of programmes funded with supplemental appropriations would require transfer to

the base budget. The Army has procured a large amount of equipment in the last six years for use in the Global War on Terror. While this equipment is used in Iraq and Afghanistan, sustainment of this equipment is funded by supplemental dollars and upon return we anticipate that Reset of this equipment would also be funded in supplementals. Long term sustainment of that equipment, however, would require funding support in the base budget, where dollars did not previously exist. These requirements would all compete for modernization funding.

The Army has moved quickly to properly equip, modernize, and transform our Army with the best available equipment, but we still have much to do. The Army must have continued access to stable and predictable base and supplemental funding. Access to proper funding allows the Army to better manage resources, maintain a stable work force and generate efficiencies with industry. It takes one year to produce a Stryker vehicle and 18 months to recapitalize an Abrams Tank. Predictable funding can cut these production and recapitalization times nearly in half through more timely procurement of necessary parts.

Equipping and modernizing are not just challenges for the Army. Proper equipping, both for today and for the future, have implications for the security of our Nation. Balancing equipping and modernization is a challenge the Army needs to overcome in order to ensure we can defend the Nation today and prepare for the future. This is a matter of National priority, not affordability.

Plan as we may, the actions of the enemy affect the true costs of war. Resource tension will remain a constant as long as we remain engaged in combat operations while continuing to modernize and transform our Army. Adequate funding is essential to on-time equipping and modernization for our Soldiers; this is something we can plan for, and we owe them nothing less. With continued support from the President, the Secretary of Defense, and Congress for our needs, the Army will be able to execute this modernization strategy in order to achieve balance and maintain the readiness of our Army in an era of persistent conflict.

Annexure A

# Modernize the Force

Modernization provides material solutions to improve capabilities that enhance the Army's ability to conduct successful early-entry, full spectrum operations world-wide. Modernization provides the capabilities required to transform to a force that meets the demands of persistent conflict in the 21st Century. We have updated key weapons and equipment since the early days of the current fight and have been steadily working to improve our speed and efficiency in this area. Our improvements are driven by Combatant Commander's assessments, mission requirements and our commitment to Soldier protection.

The Army must continue to prepare its Soldiers to succeed in the current conflict. The best equipment must be supplied adequately and on time. The Army must also continue to provide the technological edge over any future enemy that we face under any conditions. In the near term, the Army is committed to providing Soldiers with overmatch capability to defeat current and future adversaries. The Army faces several challenges in modernizing and equipping the Current Force. High-demand, low-density items such as up-armored tactical wheeled vehicles, Counter-Improvised Explosive Device and route-clearing vehicles are not available in adequate numbers to equip all non-deployed units. The result is that units returning from war require rotational equipment sets to support training. These shortfalls impact the Army's capacity to sustain operations. The Army is mitigating shortfalls in capacity by implementing Army Force Generation and investing in the stocks necessary to equip the force within ARFORGEN. However, the Army must also continue to invest in capability by supporting upgrades to current modular formations and by introducing emerging technologies to the force.

## Programme Budget Review 09-13

Programme Budget Review 09-13 in conjunction with proposed supplemental funding supports the upgrade of the Current Force to include

- Accomplishing two variants of Tanks and Bradley's by fiscal year 2013
- Displacing M113A2s and ambulances, with Strykers by fiscal year 2014
- Accelerating the Network (Warfighter Information Network – Tactical)
- Accomplishing Distributed Common Ground System – Army Version 3 by fiscal year 2010
- Accomplishing Pure Fleet Patriot by fiscal year 2011
- Maintaining Aviation Modernization (Joint Cargo Aircraft)
- Replacing Fox with Nuclear, Biological, and Chemical Reconnaissance Vehicle by fiscal year 2014
- Replacing all M35 Trucks by fiscal year 2010
- Beginning Programme Improvement for Paladin (automotive/ power train)
- Supporting Growth and Rebalance – Grow the Army equipping

## Core Material Programmes Modernization

In the coming years the Nation will invest considerable resources to upgrade the Active and Reserve Component to include the Abrams and Bradley fleets as well as the tactical wheeled vehicles fleet. Aging ambulances; M113 command vehicles; and Nuclear, Biological and Chemical vehicles will be displaced throughout the force by Stryker variants. The plan accelerates aviation modernization efforts, restructures and standardizes attack/lift formations across the force, and upgrades an additional

96 Apache Attack helicopters in the Reserve and National Guard. Lastly, the Army will pure fleet the Patriot missile force transforming 1980s technology to more lethal missile defence systems. All of these efforts contribute to ensuring that our Army is relevant in the 21st Century. A modernization overview of the Army's Core Material Programmes is organized in the following Appendices:

Appendix 1: Combat Platforms – Manoevre

Appendix 2: Soldier as a System

Appendix 3: Aviation Systems

Appendix 4: Air and Missile Defence

Appendix 5: Fire Support

Appendix 6: Chemical, Biological, Radiological and Nuclear Defence

Appendix 7: Battle Command

Appendix 8: Battlespace Awareness

Appendix 9: Engineer Equipment

Appendix 10: Tactical Wheeled Vehicles

Appendix 11: Combat Service Support

Appendix 12: Army Watercraft

Appendix 13: Focused Logistics

# Appendix 1: Combat Platforms–Manoevre

## Discussion of Core Combat Platforms Material Programmes

### *Abrams Tank*

Modernization of the Abrams tank centers around getting the entire force equipped with two variants of the M1 main battle tank by 2013. The two variants, M1A2 SEP V2, and the M1A1 AIM SA provide the lethality and survivability necessary for the Abrams tank to be a viable part of the Army's inventory well into the future. The 120-millimeter main gun, a powerful 1,500-horsepower turbine engine, and special armor combine to make the Abrams tank especially effective against heavy armor forces on future battlefields.

The M1A1 tank modernization programme includes increased armor protection, suspension improvements and a protection system against chemical attacks. An advanced computer system with embedded diagnostics, a second generation thermal sensor and the capability to designate targets from increased distances can be incorporated into existing Abrams tanks. M1A2 tank modernization provides for the following:

- Commander's independent thermal viewer
- Independent commander's weapons station
- Navigation equipment
- Embedded diagnostic systems
- Improved fire control systems

The M1A2 System Enhancement Programme adds second generation thermal sensors and a thermal management system. This programme also includes upgrades to processors, with additional memory to allow the M1A2 to use the Army's Common Command and Control Software - enabling rapid transfer of data that provides additional situation awareness.

Abrams modernization is also responsible for an overall engine rebuild programme, better management of spare parts and a database of all parts to ensure that a complete package of parts in available for any rebuild project or new production.

## Programme Status

The following units have fielded M1A2 SEP tanks:

- The Army Evaluation Task Force
- The 3rd Armored Cavalry Regiment
- The 1st Cavalry Division
- The 4th Infantry Division

By March 2009, 1st Brigade, 1st Armored Division projects fielding of M1A2 SEP tanks, to be shortly followed by remainder of the Brigade Combat Teams in 1st Armored Division. In FY09, 3rd Infantry Division begins fielding M1A1 Tanks with 2nd generation Forward Looking Infrared Radar.

The Army National Guard has added M1A1 Tanks to two of its Heavy Brigade Combat Teams. In August of FY08, the National Guard's 278th Brigade is projected to field M1A1 Tanks with 2nd generation Forward Looking Infrared Radar. All of these variants of the Abrams Tanks improve lethality, survivability and situational awareness.

## Bradley Fighting Vehicle

Bradley Fighting Vehicle recapitalization rebuilds and upgrades Bradleys to the most modernized M2/ M3A3 CM/ED configurations. The A3 version adds the following:

- Two second-generation Forward Looking Infrared Radar – one in the commander's independent viewer and one in the improved Bradley acquisition sight
- A position/navigation system
- Core electronic architecture
- Digital command and control

These upgrades improve crew ability to navigate, pinpoint and identify friendly and enemy positions, and engage two targets nearly simultaneously in both day and night conditions. The digital command and control provides near real-time data links between Bradley Fighting Vehicles and headquarters.

## Programme Status

The following units have fielded M2/M3A3 Bradleys:

- The Army Evaluation Task Force
- The 3rd Armored Cavalry Regiment
- The 1st Cavalry Division
- The 4th Infantry Division

By August 2008, 4th Brigade, 1st Armored Division projects fielding of rebuilt (recapitalized) M2A3 Bradleys, followed by remaining Heavy Brigade Combat Teams in 1st Armored Division. By December 2011, 3rd Infantry Division is scheduled to complete fielding. The Army is currently fielding Bradley ODSE vehicles to engineer companies in Heavy Brigade Combat Teams.

By FY13 National Guard Heavy Brigade Combat Teams begin fielding upgraded M2A2 Bradley Fighting Vehicles with second generation Forward Looking Infrared Radar.

## Stryker Brigade Combat Teams and Stryker Armored Vehicle Modernization

The SBCT is inherently a precision unit. The force design of the SBCT provides the Army with dominant manoeuvre and precision engagement capabilities found in the modular brigade-centric force. Specifically the RSTA squadron, equipped with unmanned aerial vehicles and ground-based HUMINT specialists, provide the commander with unequalled situational understanding. The networked C2 architecture allows the commander to provide the same picture to lower echelons and major combat platforms, such as the Stryker vehicle, thereby establishing a realtime friendly force operational picture for the unit. The SBCT also features organic, ground-based sniper teams – the essence of precision strike and a critical combat requirement.

The SBCT's force application capability is truly global. C-130 transportable, the unit can deploy rapidly to austere environments, thereby overcoming enemy area-denial and anti-access efforts and can quickly mount offensive operations with minimal reception, staging and integration. Although it excels in the midpoint of the operational spectrum, it can fight effectively as a fully committed unit in major engagement and battles with augmentation (such as attack aviation and rocket artillery). With its superior tactical mobility and excellent battlefield situational awareness, the SBCT can also execute difficult security missions such as guard, cover, screen, counter reconnaissance and rear-area combat operations. The superior off-road manoeuvreability of the Stryker vehicle, combined with its dismounted infantry assault capability featuring robust anti-tank weaponry, ensures the SBCT can very effectively engage and destroy enemy armor in close, complex and urban terrain.

The Army is currently benefiting from the capability of the SBCT in operational missions in Iraq. The unit is maximizing the capabilities of this transformational organization in combat operations. Examples are increased speed and survivability provided by the Stryker family of vehicles in the brigade; near-seamless situational awareness down to the combat vehicle crew level allowing quick execution of changing missions; high rate of reliability of the Stryker vehicles; and high confidence in the vehicle and its capabilities by the Soldiers in the brigade.

**Stryker Family of Armored Vehicles**

The Stryker Family of Armored Vehicles is the centerpiece combat and combat support platform for the SBCTs. Ten configurations of the Stryker will be fielded: the Infantry Carrier

Vehicle, Reconnaissance Vehicle, Commander Vehicle, Mortar Carrier, Fire Support Vehicle, Anti-tank Guided Missile Vehicle, Engineer Squad Vehicle, Medical Evacuation Vehicle, Nuclear, Biological and Chemical Reconnaissance Vehicle and the Mobile Gun System. Stryker capabilities include:

- Strategically responsive and deployable on the complete U.S. Air Force family of transport aircraft, C-130 and larger
- Roll-on/roll-off combat capable with minimum preparation
- Superior situational awareness with inter-netted/networked communications
- Survivability enhanced by all-around 14.5- millimeter armor piercing and 152-millimeter artillery airburst protection (add-on armor provides protection against RPG anti-tank weapons)
- Accurate target acquisition with LRAS3 mission package
- Accurate target engagement with Remote Weapon Station (MK19 grenade launcher and M2.50 caliber machine gun)
- Decisive offensive action with dismounted ICV
- Bunker-busting capability with 105-millimeter cannon for roles in immediate fire support of dismounted infantry operations and with TOW missile bunker-buster munitions
- Responsive indirect fires with 120-millimeter mounted mortar
- Anti-tank capability with TOW 2B and Javelin equipped dismounted infantry (ICV)

- Mobility enhanced by mine plow, roller and detector
- Integrated NBC sensor capability

Stryker provides a unique family-of-systems approach that maximizes commonality and integrated capabilities while filling an immediate capabilities gap in the Current Force. Stryker Brigade Combat Teams utilize the unit set fielding approach, which provides a new equipment training package for both operations and maintainers. The Stryker Brigade Combat Team is an infantry-centric, full spectrum combat force that provides division, corps, or Joint task force commanders a unique capability across the spectrum of conflict. The SBCT balances lethality, mobility and survivability against the requirements for rapid strategic deployability. Inherently, the SBCT is a precision unit that can operate in various types of battlespace, to include, some of the most austere locations in the world because of its deployability capabilities.

The force design of the SBCT provides the Army with dominant manoeuvre and precision engagement capabilities not found in any other Army brigade-sized unit. The RSTA squadron, equipped with unmanned aerial systems and ground-based HUMINT specialists, provide the commander with unrivalled situational understanding. The networked command and control architecture allows the commander to provide the same picture to lower echelons and combat platforms, such as the Stryker family of vehicles, thereby establishing a near, real-time friendly force operational picture for the unit. The SBCT also features organic, ground-based sniper teams and robust Stryker Mobile Gun Systems equipped with enhanced optics and firepower—the essence of precision strike and decisive operations meeting critical combat requirements.

## Programme Status

Planned procurement is for 3,324 vehicles consisting of ten variants. This will equip seven brigade-size units including maintenance floats, a strategic pool of ready-to-fight systems, Institutional Training Base, Test Articles, an Equipping Force Pool managed by the Army Material Command, other operational requirements and NBCRVs to fill non-SBCT armored CBRN requirements. The Stryker programme has obtained a FRP decision on eight of the ten configuration variants. The Army has funded, and the Secretary of Defence has authorized, procurement and fielding of seven SBCTs to fulfill the defence strategy and National security requirements.

### Stryker-Nuclear, Biological and Chemical Reconnaissance Vehicle

The Stryker-NBCRV incorporates integrated chemical and biological point detectors that allow on-the-move standoff biological and chemical agent detection. The Chemical Biological Mass Spectrometer improves the detection and identification of liquid chemical agents, while Joint Biological Point Detection System provides a first-time biological agent detection capability to the reconnaissance platform. The sensor suite automatically integrates contamination information with data from onboard navigation and meteorological systems and rapidly transmits contamination hazard and non-contaminated area intelligence to the appropriate operations center. Integration of the common CBRN technical architecture allows for expansion/upgrading of the onboard computers at minimal cost, as well as the command and control of CBRN-sensing UAVs and unmanned ground vehicles in the Future Combat Systems.

### Programme Status

Stryker-NBCRV Milestone C was reached in fourth quarter, FY04, allowing the start of LRIP for 17 NBCRVs. An Extended LRIP was authorized for 95 additional NBCRVs in first quarter FY08. The FRP decision is now scheduled for FY10. The Stryker-NBCRV begin fielding in FY06, will field to HBCTs in late FY10; and planned fielding to chemical companies is thereafter.

### Stryker-Mobile Gun System

The Stryker MGS provides rapid direct supporting fires to assaulting infantry in order to destroy or suppress hardened enemy bunkers, machine gun positions, create breach points in up to double reinforced concrete walls and sniper positions in urban, restricted and open rolling terrain. Its primary weapon system is the M68A1E8, 105-millimeter cannon with an 18-round auto-loader capacity. Additionally it has a coaxial mounted 7.62 millimeter machine gun and a pintal mounted .50 caliber machine gun for the vehicle commander. The main gun is capable of firing current 105-millimeter munitions which include: canister, SABOT, HEAT and HEP rounds.

**Programme Status**

MGS Milestone C was reached in first quarter, FY 04, allowing the start LRIP of 72 MGS Strykers. SBCT 4 fielded 27 MGS in FY 07 and is currently conducting combat operations with the MGS. SBCT 3 and 5 have been fielded with 9 MGS each in third quarter, FY 07. On 22 Dec 07 the DAE authorized the procurement of the long-lead items required to support the FY-08 production quantity of MGS's. The MS III Full Rate Production DAB decision is currently for second quarter, FY 08, for the remaining 199 MGS.

# Appendix 2: The Soldier as a System

## Discussion of Core Soldier as a System Material Programmes

### *Ground Soldier Ensemble*

Ground Soldier Ensemble (GSE) integrates multiple components and leverages emerging technologies to provide overmatching operational capabilities to ground combat Soldiers and small units. The GSE gives infantry Soldiers additional capability above the core Soldier system, specifically oriented to network integration of the individual Soldier, protection, mobility, sustainability, reliability and embedded training. GSE capabilities, based on the predecessor Land Warrior System, are intended to meet the needs of all Soldiers who conduct ground combat and provide the dismounted Soldier component of the Future Combat Systems and of the Brigade Combat Teams. GSE increases capabilities of individual Soldiers to conduct offensive and defensive operations by incorporating the following:

- Network-centric enabled operations at the small unit level
- User defined operating picture
- Improved force protection against threats
- Access to weapons, sensors and external assets formerly available only to higher level units
- Embedded training to enable the Soldier to meet the growth in demand for future skills
- Affordable, supportable, adaptable and highly mobile logistics concept

The GSE is required to be modular to fit within the SaaS architecture, permit tailoring for mission requirements, allow tailoring of the combat load and to streamline maintenance.

### Programme Status

GSE fielding is scheduled to the Army Evaluation Task Force in FY10 and planned to achieve First Unit Equipped in FY12. GSE fielding will be aligned with FCS Spin-out #2 BCTs starting in FY13. GSE is scheduling a milestone B decision in third quarter FY08.

## Air Warrior

Air Warrior (AW) is a Soldier system for helicopter crewmen that provides a new generation of integrated, missiontailorable, life support equipment, body armor, chemical and biological protection equipment with reduced weight/bulk. It is designed to improve aircrew endurance and performance. AW significantly improves flight time in Mission Oriented Protective Posture from 1.6 to 5.3 hours. Components include:

- Microclimate cooling system that includes a microclimate cooling garment and a small microclimate cooling unit that chills water and pumps it through small tubes embedded in the garment
- Survival equipment subsystem that includes a survival gear carrier, soft and hard body armor, thigh holster and survival knife
- Interim Modular Integrated Helmet Display System with laser eye-protection and a night vision device mount
- Over-water survival subsystem that includes a personal flotation device, survival egress air (breathing oxygen) and an inflatable raft that is integrated into the ensemble and worn by the crew member
- Nuclear, biological and chemical protection with modified chemical protective undergarment, M-45 or M-48 protective mask with blower unit, gloves and over boots
- Aviation clothing items that include modified aircrew battle dress uniform and the Aircrew Cold Weather Garment System

Future AW system spiral development improvements focus enhanced components reflecting emerging technologies defined in AW Blocks II and III. Air warrior transitions to Air Soldier under the SaaS concept once the Air Soldier CDD is validated by HQDA in FY08/09.

Block II developmental and production efforts are underway and will add an encrypted Aircraft Wireless Intercom System and the Electronic Data Manager (EDM). AWIS will enhance crew member performance by providing the capability for wireless communications within the aircrew and with ground crew or ramp support personnel such as in a tactical forward area rearm and refueling point. The EDM, in the form of a digital kneeboard, provides a capability to the aircrew to generate, store, display and distribute digital information and will interface with Blue Force Tracking systems.

Block III efforts will increase performance and capabilities by adding a fully compliant MIHDS helmet. The MIHDS helmet will provide, as a baseline, the same safety performance characteristics as the HGU-56/P helmet. The MIHDS will be tailorable and compatible with the Apache helmet-configuration and head tracking technologies and will also provide an improved day/night helmet-mounted display symbology for those aircraft that currently lack this feature. These helmet-mounted displays will be compatible with aircrew prescription spectacles, CB protection, oxygen masks, laser eye protection and nuclear flash protection technologies. CB protection will be donned in-flight without removing the helmet.

### Programme Status

Air Warrior currently is being fielded to the force. Approximately 76 percent of AW Block I equipment and 27 percent of the EDMs have been fielded. The encrypted AWIS is still in development and testing.

### Mounted Soldier System

Mounted Soldier System (MSS) will provide combat vehicle crewmembers and platform commanders with increased mission effectiveness in the areas of command and control, situational awareness, communications, force protection, survivability, mobility and sustainability. MSS provides dismounted and mounted combat crews uninterrupted viewing of their immediate surroundings while remaining connected to onboard platform C4ISR capabilities, providing crews with continuous SA and communications with both mounted and dismounted Soldiers.

MSS also will provide maximum individual protection from Chemical/Biological contamination without reducing individual dexterity, tactility, agility and mobility. The MSS includes a Combat Vehicle Crewman helmet head-mounted display, and improved audio headset and microphone; body gear subsystem, providing cordless communications; crew member over garments; gloves; footwear; ballistic protection; CB protective mask and over garments; ballistic eye protection; and on-the-move hydration; as well as a Vehicle Interface Kit subsystem with components that mount to the vehicle. The MSS equips all Combat Vehicle Crewman and selected Manoevre Support and Manoevre Sustainment Soldiers who perform mounted missions.

### Programme Status

MSS achieved Milestone B on 17 October 2007. MSS programme funding will be initiated in FY09 for System Development and Demonstration. This funding will enable the development of MSS in support of an initial fielding to 13 HBCTs (two heavy divisions) and seven SBCTs.

### Combat Identification

Combat Identification measures enhance Soldier protection and overall combat effectiveness by minimizing fratricide incidents. As a result of lessons learned in OEF and OIF, the Army has fielded thousands of the Joint CID Marking System kits to its forces. The JCIMS kit consists of thermal and infrared marking devices that enable forces equipped with FLIR and night-vision sensors to identify friendly forces based on unique signatures of the JCIMS devices. Combined with the increasing density of GPS systems, BFT systems, FBCB2 and Second Generation FLIR technology, these devices on the battlefield have significantly reduced fratricide incidents through improved ability to locate and identify friendly forces.

An interactive vehicle recognition training device called Recognition of Combat Vehicles is being issued to Soldiers at every level and can be easily downloaded because it comes on a computer disc. Army Combat Training Centers have put in place measures to assess CID and SA during unit rotations and an aggressive programme for capturing, reconciling and leveraging lessons learned from OIF, OEF and CTCs. CID is a major focus area at the Center for Army Lessons Learned.

## Programme Status

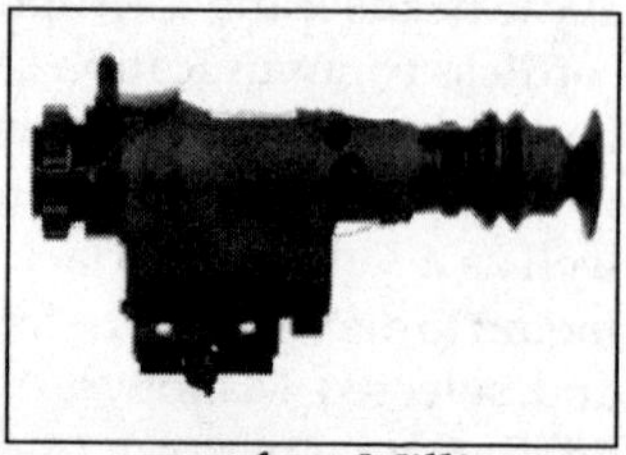

In March 2006, the Army and Marine Corps Board, co-chaired by Army G-8 and the U.S. Marine Corps Assistant Deputy Commandant, Programmes & Resources, conducted a review of CID efforts in the Army and Marine Corps and directed the following: implement a Joint acquisition strategy for a Millimeter Wave cooperative target identification capability; implement a Joint acquisition strategy for Radio Based Combat Identification capability align with AMCB/JFCOM A-G CID study banded investment recommendation of 4 Jan 2006; fully embed and institutionalize Millimeter Wave and RBCI in services' training strategy and programmes; coordinate Joint acquisition strategy within POM 08-13; provide appropriate guidance to service authorities and programme managers to implement Joint acquisition strategy for Millimeter Wave and RBCI; approve the recommended follow-on actions for other assessed technologies. OSD Programme Decision Memorandum II added funds within existing resources for BTID development and maintain option for POM FY10 MS B for the programme of record if full funding requirements are satisfied in POM FY 10 and required resolution of Joint and Coalition Cooperative Target ID-Ground capability strategy at Army/Marine Corps Board with report to DAWG by May 1, 2008; include recommended POM FY 10 funding.

## Thermal Weapon Sights

Thermal Weapon Sights are a family of low-cost, lightweight, man-portable IR imaging devices used for surveillance and fire control of individual and crew served weapons during daylight and darkness, adverse weather and dirty battlefield scenarios. They can also penetrate light foliage, smoke, dust and camouflage. Un-cooled microbolometer technology has evolved to enable the development of advanced TWS II systems. TWS II systems offer increased performance in a smaller, lighter package and employ the use of standard commercial batteries.

**Programme Status**

The TWS programme is in fielding/sustainment, having fielded more than 39,000 light, medium and heavy systems. Fielding will continue to FY13 to meet the Acquisition Objective. The Future Weapon Sight is in early development, intended to further improve situational awareness, interoperability and operational flexibility. LRIP is expected to start in FY12, with full rate production in FY13 and beyond.

**Enhanced Night Vision Goggles**

The next generation of night-vision goggles for the Soldier is the Enhanced Night Vision Goggles. It combines both an un-cooled thermal and an image intensification capability into a single integrated device. ENVG improves Soldier situational awareness by providing the capability to rapidly detect and recognize man-sized targets, while simultaneously maintaining the ability to see detail and to use rifle-mounted aiming lights. The ENVG provides Soldiers the ability to engage and execute close combat in all levels of light, to include the zero-illumination conditions found in caves and underground environments, adverse weather conditions and under battlefield obscurant conditions. This is a system component of the Soldier Warrior programmes.

**Programme Status**

The ENVG completed Operational Testing in June 2007. The first Unit was equipped in February 2008.

**M-4 Carbine**

The M-4 is the Soldier's weapon of choice in Iraq and Afghanistan. It has been a combat proven weapon since its introduction into the force in 1991. The M-4 Carbine is the primary individual combat rifle for the Army's BCTs and ARSOF Soldiers. Lessons learned have shown that the M-4's combination of light weight, manoeuvrability and lethality are clearly preferred by Soldiers and units in the field. It is also easily maintained.

The Army began combat operations in 2001 with a mix of M16A2s, M16A4s and some M-4 Carbines. All M-4s initially issued did not include the full suite of enhancements now available, but

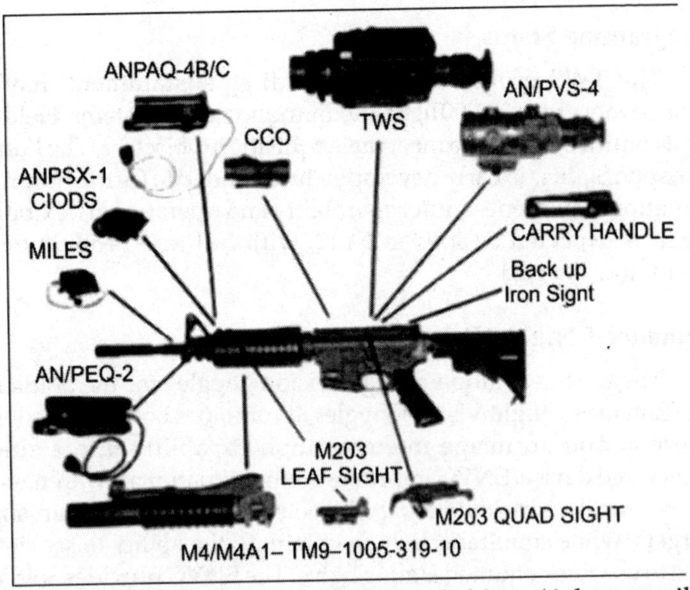


all are now included with current M-4 fielding (Adapter rails, collapsible butt stock, 3-point sling, back-up iron sight, close combat optic and seven new magazines). This gives the M-4 the most current technology available of any mass produced rifle/carbine in general use today by any Army and allows for the weapon to be further enhanced with technology improvements.

### Programme Status

The M-4 is currently in production and fielding.

## *M110 7.62 millimeter Semi-Automatic Sniper System*

The selected replacement for the M24 Sniper Weapons System, the M110 7.62 millimeter Semi-Automatic Sniper System is effective against personnel and light Material targets. Capable of rapid fire/rapid reload, this suppressed sniper rifle exceeds the rate-of-fire and lethality of the M24 Sniper Weapon System. SASS is lighter than the M24 and its anti-personnel ranges are equal to or greater than M24. SASS

includes an enhanced sniper spotting scope, a detachable suppressor, a carrying case and other support equipment.

**Programme Status**

The M110 currently is in production and fielding to Army units preparing to deploy to the current Theater of Operations. The current production rate is 75 weapons systems per month.

## *XM 150 Rifle Combat Optic*

The XM 150 Rifle Combat Optic will improve the capability to recognize and engage targets from zero to 600 meters with the M-4 carbine, M16 Rifle and the M249 SAW. The optic will allow Soldiers to rapidly transition between long and close-quarter engagements without degrading the ability to conduct reflexive fire techniques. The optic can be used to scan an area for acquiring and engaging targets. When a target is acquired, the ranging reticle within the optic can be used to obtain an accurate range to the target. An appropriate aiming point on the reticle can then be selected to accurately engage the target.

**Programme Status**

The Rifle Combat Optic has an approved CPD. The sight is currently being fielded via RFI to units directly involved in the GWOT. Approximately 33,000 RCOs are in use in Iraq and Afghanistan at this time. Type Classification was scheduled for March 2008 with the first Unit being equipped in 4th Qtr FY08.

**Land Warrior/ Mounted Warrior**

Land Warrior, the precursor to what will be the Ground Soldier System, provides small unit leaders with Battle Command and situation awareness capabilities that have proven to be combat multipliers in tactical operations. The Battle Command and situational awareness information shared and displayed among leaders enable greater mobility, speed of execution, flexibility, momentum, coordination and synchronization between mounted and dismounted manoeuvre elements. The visualization of the fight, enabled by Battle Command and situational awareness information, enhances the ability to mass combat power at the right place and time to kill or capture enemy forces, minimize friendly casualties and successfully execute tactical missions, thereby enhancing the small units' lethality and survivability in combat.

Leaders at each level are very positive about the Land Warrior and Mounted Warrior capabilities. For example the digital icon provides an excellent visual reference capability and has proven to be a very useful tactical command and control measure for small units. The ability for small unit leaders to communicate, the situational awareness capabilities in Land Warrior, coupled with the GPS navigation capability have greatly enhanced small unit combat operations.

# Appendix 3: Aviation Systems

## Discussion of Core Aviation Material Programmes

### *AH-64 Apache Attack Helicopter*

The AH-64 Apache is the Army's heavy attack helicopter assigned to armed reconnaissance battalions and regimental aviation squadrons in both the Active and Reserve Components. Apache is a two-pilot, twinengine attack helicopter designed to meet the current mission requirements for reconnaissance and attack worldwide, day or night, under obscured battlefield and adverse weather conditions. The upgraded AH-64D Longbow began fielding in 1998. The AH-64D upgrades, among other improvements, adds a millimeter wave Fire Control Radar, Radar Frequency Interferometer, fire-and-forget radarguided missile and cockpit management and digitization enhancements. The combination of FCR, RFI, and the advanced navigation and avionics suite provides increased SA, lethality, and survivability.

The Apache-focused recapitalization programme integrates a number of related initiatives to produce and retrofit aircraft across the Apache fleet to meet objectives of the Army's recapitalization policy and to address lessons learned from recent combat operations and deployments. This programme applies reliability and safety modifications, increases aircraft life by addressing high-maintenance demand/operating and support cost drivers and incorporating a second generation forward-looking infrared with the Modernized Target Acquisition Designation Sight/ Pilot Night Vision Sensor.

The programme goals are to reduce the overall average airframe age of the fleet to the half-life metric of 10 years by 2010, increase the unscheduled mean time between removal rate by 20 percent for selected recapitalized components, and maximize the return on recapped components by 20 percent.

### Programme Status

Remanufacture of 621 AH-64As to the AH-64D Longbow configuration will be complete in FY10. In January 2007, the first of 120 AH-64A model Apaches was inducted for conversions to D model Longbow configuration. This will continue through FY10. Deliveries will begin in FY08 and end in FY11. The Army has been funded for 32 additional War Replacement Aircraft with three deliveries in FY08, 11 in FY09 and 18 in FY10.

### ARH-70A Arapaho Armed Reconnaissance Helicopter

The mission of ARH-70A helicopter is to provide a robust reconnaissance and security capability for the Joint combined arms air-ground manoeuvre team. The ARH programme was established to correct OH- 58D capability gaps for use in reconnaissance. As a result of Aviation Focus Group analysis, in February 2004, the Army Chief of Staff identified the need for 368 ARH aircraft to replace the existing OH-58D fleet. The requirement has since grown to 512 aircraft. The increase to 512 aircraft is due to the conversion of four AH-64A National Guard Apache battalions to the ARH-70A.

### Programme Status

ARH's first flight occurred on 20 July 2006. A Limited User's Test was conducted in November 2007 with a subsequent LUT expected in February 2009 following its Milestone C decision in June 2008. A Full Rate Production decision review is expected in 1st quarter FY11 with the First Unit Equipped in 4th quarter FY11.

The Lakota is a light, commercially procured helicopter designed to perform a variety of missions – from Joint to non-governmental to homeland security and Force medical evacuation operations. It is the newest aircraft in the Army's inventory. The UH-72A fleet is composed of 18 aircraft as of 21 December 2007. The Army intends to procure and field 322 Lakotas from FY06-15; estimated cost of the LUH programme is $5 billion. LUH is designed to transport two crew and six Soldiers. Additional configurations include two NATO litters with patients and one medical attendant. The aircraft has a hoist for use in emergency evacuations. The ARNG will be the primary user of the LUH, conducting missions in support of homeland security such as civil search and rescue, medical evacuation, and counter-drug operations.

### Programme Status

On 13 February 2006, OSD delegated the LUH Programme to the Army as an Acquisition Category (ACAT) 1C (COTS). UH-72A LUH FUE completed in May 2007. The UH-72A LUH programme received Full-Rate Production decision in August 2007.

## UH-60 Black Hawk Helicopter

With its 28 configurations and mission equipment package variants, the UH-60 Black Hawk is the Army's Current and Future Force utility and MEDEVAC helicopter. The UH-60 Fleet is composed of 1,669 aircraft. There are 949 UH-60A models, which began production in 1977; 671 UH-60L models, which began production in 1989; and 26 UH-60M models, which began production in 2005. The Black Hawk can transport 11 fully equipped combat troops, plus an external load up to 9,000 pounds, depending on the model. The UH-60 provides rapid and agile manoeuvre capability through air assault, general support, airborne C2 and MEDEVAC, providing commanders the ability to initiate, conduct and sustain combat operations by providing internal and external lift of troops, weapon systems, supplies and equipment. In the airborne C2 role it provides full Joint and combined interoperability with other C4ISR elements. The Army will procure the UH-60M/HH-60M to extend fleet capabilities through 2025, incorporate Global Air Traffic Management requirements and extend aircraft life.

### Programme Status

The UH-60M and HH-60M programmes received full rate production decision in June 2007. FUE for UH- 60M is FY08. The accelerated development of new technologies has resulted in an upgrade programme for the UH-60M that will include fly-by-wire Common Avionics Architecture System, Composite Tail cone and Drive shafts and Full-Authority Digital Engine Control. In-process review cut-in decision for these upgrades will occur in late FY08.

### CH-47 Chinook Helicopter

The CH-47 Chinook is a twin-turbine, tandem-rotor, heavy-lift transport helicopter with a useful load of up to 25,000 pounds. Secondary missions include MEDEVAC, aircraft recovery, parachute drops, disaster relief and search and rescue operations. These aircraft are the Army's only heavy-lift aircraft and are fielded to heavy helicopter companies and Special Operations Aviation Regiment.

Key modifications integrate a new-machined airframe, an upgraded T55-GA-714A engine to restore performance capability, Common Avionics Architecture System, Air Warrior, Common Missile Warning System, enhanced air transportability, Digital Automatic Flight Control System and an Extended Range Fuel System II for self-deployment missions. The CH-47F recapitalization programme provides a more reliable, less costly way to operate aircraft compatible with Joint digital connectivity requirements in the Future Force with an extended life of approximately 20 years. The CH-47F is expected to remain the Army's heavy-lift helicopter until at least 2020-2025, ultimately to be replaced by the Joint Heavy Lift Aircraft.

### Programme Status

A total of 452 CH-47F model aircraft are planned for delivery to the Army over the next 12 years. Of these, 120 will be new builds and the remaining 352 "remanufactured" aircraft. The remanufactured aircraft have 97 items that are recapitalized from retired CH-47Ds. With the exception of these items, all other components, including airframes, wiring bundles and hydraulic systems on the remanufactured CH-47Fs are new. FUE was completed on 20 July 2007. Subsequent CH-47F units will be fielded at a rate of two units per year.

## Joint Heavy Lift

The Joint Heavy Lift (JHL) is intended to be the Department of the Army's next-generation heavy lift rotorcraft to support the Army's Mounted Vertical Manoevre concept. The JHL programme calls for an aircraft that can transport up to 29 tons – the currently anticipated weight of a vehicle in the FCS – to a radius of about 500 nautical miles at speeds greater than 250 knots. The need for a JHL solution has been recognized by the Services and documented in the form of a draft JHL Initial Capabilities Document (ICD). However the Army and Air Force are still discussing the final version of the ICD. In FY 05, the Army, in cooperation with its Joint Service and NASA partners, announced the award of five 18 month agreements/contracts for the Concept Design and Analysis (CDA) of a Vertical Takeoff and Landing (VTOL) Joint Heavy Lift (JHL) rotorcraft. In May 07, JHL programme officials unveiled a sketch of a "High Efficiency Tilt Rotor" (HETR) that reduced industry offerings from five to three. The Army strongly advocates the immediate initiation of a Joint Technology Demonstration for JHL to begin in FY 08.

### Programme Status

The FY08 Army budget request included $6 million in FY07 and $3.065 million in FY08 for RDT&E to complete the final Concept Refinement Design Review; complete a preliminary Joint Concepts Analysis of Alternatives; and develop a draft Capabilities Document. The FY08 request also terminates the Future Transport Rotorcraft Programme shown in the FY07 request. An Initial Capabilities Document Adjudication Conference was held on 4 Dec 2007. Currently, the Army and Air Force are working through differences in their positions.

### Fixed-Wing Aircraft

The fixed-wing modernization strategy addresses an aging fleet of 292 aircraft of 21 different models by procuring an Aerial Common Sensor, Joint Cargo Aircraft and a Future Utility Aircraft. Decisions on the movement, retirement and reorganization of the fixed-wing fleet will be based on the fixedwing *Operational and Organizational Plan*. The approved fixed wing O&O Plan addresses Table of Distribution and Allowances to Modified Table of Organization and Equipment reorganization; composition of the fixed-wing fleet; and required capabilities for fixed-wing aircraft in the Future Force.

**Programme Status**

The Army will retain the approved fixed-wing force structure, given recent agreements with the U.S. Air Force on the Joint Cargo Aircraft, and in anticipation of the outcome of the Programme Decision Memorandum II OSA Study, the PDM III FCA/LCA Study, PDM IV Non-Standard Airlift Study and the USAF Intra-theater Airlift Force Mix Analysis. Army senior leadership will review and adjust the final transformation of the fixed-wing fleet at the conclusion of these studies.

**Hellfire Family of Missiles**

Hellfire air-to-ground missiles destroy armored and high-value point targets. Semi-active laser HF tracks laser energy delivered by ground or airborne designators, while Longbow HF uses internal millimeter wave radar frequency for autonomous guidance. AH-64 Apache, ARH, ER/MP and OH- 58D Kiowa Warrior use HF as their primary-air to ground weapon. Joint Air-to-Ground Missile is programmed to be the follow-on to Hellfire. JAGM provides a multi-mode seeker coupled with a multipurpose warhead that provides increased range over Hellfire.

**Programme Status**

The P+ Hellfire missile is scheduled for production in sufficient quantities to support the fielding of the ER/MP UAV from FY09-13. Additional procurements will be addressed in the FY09-13 POM. JAGM is programmed for use on Army Aviation helicopters and UAS, and select USMC and USN helicopters and fixed wing aircraft. Initial fielding is programmed for FY11.

**Unmanned Aircraft Systems**

In Operations Enduring Freedom and Iraqi Freedom, Unmanned Aircraft Systems such as Raven, Shadow 200, Hunter

and Improved GNAT are providing a new dimension to manoeuvre forces. Raven enhances small-unit reconnaissance, surveillance, and target acquisition, and is used for training by deploying units. The Army's first Tactical Unmanned Aircraft System to go FRP is the Shadow 200, fielded to military intelligence companies in manoeuvre brigades. Planned system improvements include engine and airframe upgrades, refined target location error, Tactical Common Data Link and addition of a laser designation into the payload gimble.

Hunter is fielded in the aerial exploitation battalions of the Intelligence and Security Command Theater Military Intelligence Brigades. Hunter is a RSTA/ ISR and battle-damage assessment asset providing ground forces with near real-time imagery via electro-optical/infrared intelligence at ranges up to 200 kilometers. Used extensively as an ISR platform, Hunter UAS has been upgraded to employ Viper Strike munitions; its capability will be sustained until the ER/MP UAS is fielded at the division level as a RSTA/ISR, target attack and command, control, communications and intelligence system.

The Future Combat Systems include two separate and distinct efforts. The Class I UAS provides the ground Soldier with Reconnaissance and Surveillance and Target acquisition. The Class I UAS uses autonomous flight and navigation, but it will interact with the Network and Soldier to dynamically update routes and target information. It provides dedicated reconnaissance support and early warning from the lowest echelon to the Brigade Combat Team in environments not suited for larger assets. The Class I UAS provides a dedicated UAV capability at platoon level, hover and stare capability enabling observation of urban infrastructure, Electro-Optical/Infrared/Laser Designation/Laser Range Finder Sensor capability and a heavy fuel engine propulsion system. The CL IV will be multifunction aerial systems capable of providing reconnaissance, security/early warning, long endurance persistent stare, target acquisition and designation, wide area surveillance and have the capability to team (with Level IV Control) with airground forces throughout the FCS BCT. The aerial systems will provide information from operating altitude and standoff range both day/night and adverse weather. The aerial systems should be capable of acting as a communication relay, detect Chemical, Biological, Radiological, Nuclear materials or high-yield explosive devices and perform meteorological survey for the FCS BCT throughout their area of influence.

## Extended Range/Multi-Purpose Unmanned Aircraft System (ER/MP)

Extended Range/Multi-Purpose is an unmanned aircraft system to conduct continuous operations against moving and stationary targets. The ER/MP system is composed of 12 multi-role air vehicles (six with SATCOM), five ground control stations, two portable ground control stations, five TCDLs ground data terminals, two TCDL portable ground data terminals, one SATCOM system, four automatic takeoff and landing systems, 12 electro-optic/infrared and 12 synthetic aperture radars/moving target indicators.

ER/MP UAS provides division-level and above commanders dedicated mission-configured UAS support to battlefield surveillance brigades and fires brigades, and tactical commanders a realtime responsive capability to conduct an array of missions to include reconnaissance, surveillance and target acquisition, C2, communications relay, signals intelligence and BDA capability. ER/MP equates to a company-size organization and is planned to be fielded as a separate company organic to the combat aviation brigade.

## Programme Status

FUE for ER/MP is planned for FY09 with IOC planned for FY10. Ten companies plus a training base asset are planned.

## Small Unmanned Aircraft System (SUAS)

Small Unmanned Aircraft System is man portable and consists of five basic components: ground control station, remote video terminal, air vehicle (three per system), payload and field repair kit. SUAS provides company- to brigade-level commanders a greater ability to shape over-the-hill operations with dedicated unmanned aerial vehicles.

With a wingspan of 4.5 ft. and a weight of 4.2 lbs, the hand-launched battery-powered AV provides aerial observation, day or night, at line-of-sight ranges up to 10 kilometers and delivers colour or infrared imagery in real time to the GCS and RVT. Flight duration of 90 minutes is possible with organic rechargeable lithium batteries. Assembly, preflight and launch are accomplished in less than five minutes. Hand-launch and auto-land recovery are made in a small area without a prepared site or auxiliary equipment. Both one-man and two-man operations are possible.

### Programme Status

On October 5th, 2006, the Milestone Decision Authority authorized the SUAS programme to enter FRP and exercise options in the SUAS contract for FY07 and beyond to procure the quantity of systems identified in the SUAS Acquisition Plan.

## *Other Aviation Initiatives*

### Aircraft Survivability Equipment (ASE)

The suite of Integrated Infrared Countermeasures will provide an enhanced IR countermeasure capability for aviation, rotary and fixed wing platforms. A component of the SIIRCM is the Common Missile Warning System, with an Improved Countermeasure Munitions Dispenser system with advanced flare countermeasure munitions. The CMWS/ICMD recently has been installed on all deployed rotary wing and limited types of fixed wing aircraft platforms. Efforts now will be directed to installing A/B kits on unit aircraft prior to scheduled deployment with follow on rotations and on aircraft undergoing recapitalization.

In June 2006, the Army validated requirements that endorse placing ASE system A-kits on all Army aircraft platforms while providing system B-kits for all tactical aircraft. Additional procurement for the current aircraft fleet will be considered in the FY10/15 programme planning process. The Army plans to add a Hostile Fire Detection capability to the Aviation fleet.

## Aviation Electronics

Aviation Electronics programmes ensure aviation platforms meet combined arms and Joint requirements for C2, mission planning, communications, navigation (to include worldwide civil airspace) surveillance and information interchange and interoperability. Major avionics initiatives include the future fielding of the JTRS in modernized aviation platforms. Delays in JTRS have necessitated the procurement of an interim radio suite known as Alternate Communications, which provides significant increases in capabilities to include data exchange and SATCOM. Other advancements in avionics include migration of the Aviation Mission Planning Systems to a Joint Mission Planning System, which will provide significant increases in mission planning capabilities including an enhanced mission rehearsal capability; upgrades to the Improved Data Modem as the centerpiece to digitization; GPS equipment for improved navigation accuracy; GATM equipment mandated when flying in civil airspace; and development of the Joint Precision Approach and Landing Systems, which provides a Joint common instrument approach system for fixed base, tactical field sites and shipboard procedures.

## Air Traffic Services / Airspace Command and Control (ATS/AC2)

ATS provide the full range of air traffic services supporting disaster relief, peacekeeping missions, homeland security and military operations from contingency operations through major combat operations. ATS remains the Army's core enabler for Joint, Interagency and Multi-national airspace command and control, ensuring synchronized access into diverse and the increasingly congested airspace systems. ATS modernization fields smaller, lighter, more efficient, more robust, digitally connected terminal and en route communications, tracking and precision navigation systems for tactical and fixed-base operations. Major programmes include the Tactical Airspace Integration System, the Air Traffic Navigation, Integration, and Coordination System, Mobile Tower System, and JPALS; plus a variety of fixed equipment at locations throughout CONUS, Korea, Europe, the Balkans, Honduras, Iraq, and Kuwait.

## Aviation Ground Support Equipment (AGSE)

The goal of AGSE modernization is to reduce logistical support requirements by pursuing common ground support equipment that is mission configurable, enabling flexible capabilities while improving aircraft operational readiness. Initiatives focus on improved automation, modularity, sustainability and integration of seamless logistics management through automation systems; and replacement of aging ground support equipment. Specific improvements include a new towing tractor, a life extension programme for the Aviation Ground Power unit and recognition that AGSE is fielded based on G-3 GWOT priorities.

## Aircraft Component Improvement Programme (ACIP)

ACIP sustains engineering efforts to investigate, identify, and address user identified safety and reliability related deficiencies. ACIP inserts emerging technology, extends service life, drives down O&S costs and improves readiness by keeping components operationally ready longer. ACIP also reduces Safety Risk Assessments thereby improving aircraft safety; reduces maintenance, inspections and spare parts procurement.

## Training Aids, Devices, Simulators and Simulations (TADSS)

Aviation TADSS will leverage technology to provide effective and affordable combined arms/Joint training and mission planning and rehearsal simulators that are current with the aircraft/systems they replicate. Major initiatives include simulator concurrency, fidelity and combined arms tactical and mission rehearsal simulators/simulations that network virtual, constructive and live simulation systems.

# Appendix 4: Air and Missile Defence

## Discussion of Core Air and Missile Defence Material Programmes

### *Patriot/Medium Extended Air Defence System Combined Aggregate Programme*

Patriot is an echelon-above-corps AMD system that can simultaneously engage and destroy multiple air and missile threats at varying ranges and altitudes. It is the world's only battle-proven theater AMD system and will be a key AMD element for the next two decades, providing Combatant Commanders with modular, scalable, mission-tailored capabilities to dominate, enable and exploit the third-dimension battle-space and contribute to operational force protection in support of the Joint team.

The Patriot recapitalization programme improves operational capability by bringing existing Patriot assets to a "like-new" state; thereby achieving OSD's Set the Force objectives and enabling the Army to meet future Combatant Commander requirements. The recapitalization programme is planned and fully funded in fiscal years 2007 and 2008, and funding shortfalls for fiscal years 2009-13 are being addressed by Headquarters, Department of the Army.

MEADS will provide Joint and coalition forces critical asset and defended area protection against multiple and simultaneous attacks by short to medium range ballistic missiles, cruise missiles, unmanned aerial vehicles and tactical air-to-surface missiles. MEADS will have a netted and distributed architecture with modular components to increase survivability and exibility of employment in a number of operational congurations. MEADS implements the plug and ght capability to support exible interoperability in support of AMD Task Force requirements. It comprises a Battle Manager capable of integrating into Army and Joint SoS Battle Command architectures using Link-16 and wide-band networking capabilities to provide maximum protection of supported forces by engaging at longer ranges with distributed system operations and BLOS engagements.

**Programme Status**

COCOMs require 15 battalions of PAC-3 capability to meet current threat. The PAC-3 Pure Fleet and Grow the Army initiatives are intended to result in 15 Patriot PAC-3 tactical battalions. These initiatives are synchronized with the separately funded Patriot Recapitalization Programme. PAC-3 Pure Fleet was fully funded in the FY07 Omnibus Reprogramming ($212 million) and the FY08 Budget ($208 million). The first pure fleet battalion fields early FY09 and remaining two pure fleet battalions field in FY10.

Patriot GTA was intended to add 2 additional PAC-3 Battalions in FY11 via a split FY08 and FY09 funding strategy. However, Congress funded the Patriot GTA FY08 request at only $147.5 million, half of the FY08 GTA request of $294.5 million. As a result of the FY08 GTA funding decrement, the FY09 cost to complete GTA will grow to approximately $500 million (planned $309 million plus $187 million - $147 million cut plus at least $40 million for lost efficiencies) thus delaying by a year the fielding of the 15th battalion until FY12.

## Terminal High Altitude Area Defence (THAAD)

Terminal High Altitude Area Defence is a mobile, ground-based missile defence system designed to protect forward-deployed military forces, population centers and high value civilian assets from short, medium and intermediate-range ballistic missiles. As an element of the Missile Defence Agency's terminal defence segment, THAAD will provide the opportunity to intercept and destroy enemy ballistic missiles, both outside and inside the earth's atmosphere, that were not destroyed earlier by another anti-missile system. That is, THAAD protects against missiles which were not destroyed in the boost phase or midcourse phases of flight by other Ballistic Missile Defence System elements, such as Aegis or the Ground-Based Midcourse Defence System Interceptor.

A THAAD unit consists of a command and control/ battle management element, truck-mounted missile launchers, missile interceptors encased in canisters and mounted on the trucks, an X-band radar and ground support equipment. The THAAD missile interceptor is comprised of a single-stage booster and a kinetic kill vehicle, which destroys enemy warheads through hit-to-kill collisions. The THAAD radar is a solid-state, phased-array, X-band radar that performs search, track, target discrimination and other fire control functions. The THAAD radar also sends updated target information to the kill vehicle while in flight.

### Programme Status

The Missile Defence Agency is developing THAAD in incremental, capabilities-based blocks. Having achieved seven successful flight tests which began in FY06 as part of an extensive test and evaluation programme the capability continues to be demonstrated. The THAAD acquisition strategy will rely on test programme results to make future acquisition decisions. Although currently funded by the Missile Defence Agency, the THAAD programme will produce and deliver a weapon system manned and operated by the Army. Four THAAD units are planned for fielding beginning in FY09 and concluding in FY13.

## Surface-Launched Advanced Medium-Range Air-to-Air Missile (SLAMRAAM)

Surface-Launched Advanced Medium-Range Air-to- Air Missile is the Army's only medium range weapon system designed to protect

designated critical assets and manoeuvre forces from the emerging, stressing cruise missile and UAV threat. SLAMRAAM is a key component of the AMD Composite Battalion and will complement the PAC-3 and MEADS systems in cruise missile and other air-breather defence missions. Without SLAMRAAM, the Army and Joint force will not have a dedicated, lethal capability against stressing cruise missiles, UAVs and other air-breather threats. SLAMRAAM is a lightweight, day-or-night, and adverse-weather, NLOS weapon system with engagement capabilities in excess of 18 kilometers. The system is comprised of: a HMMWV mounted launcher with common Joint launch rails, launcher electronics, onboard C4 components and four to six AIM-120 Advanced Medium-Range Air-to- Air Missiles; an Integrated Fire Control Shelter to command and control its sensor and launchers; and the Sentinel Enhanced Target Range Acquisition Classification radar to provide surveillance and fire control data. The system will also be capable of receiving data from other Joint and Army external sensors when available. SLAMRAAM is critical to the successful development and fielding of the IAMD SoS.

### Programme Status

The SLAMRAAM entered the SDD phase in Sep 2003. It is funded to meet a Milestone C decision in FY10 and to field to the first unit equipped of a battery in FY11. FUE will equal IOC.

### Ground-Based Midcourse Defence (GMD)

Ground-Based Midcourse Defence is a fixed site, land-based system designed to provide protection to the United States against an intercontinental ballistic missile attack. The capability is limited in scope to providing an effective defence against accidental, unauthorized, or authorized limited launch of ballistic missiles. The GMD uses a System of Systems approach. Its architecture is comprised of the following components: the GMD Communications Network, the GMD Fire Control, In-Flight Interceptor Communications devices, the Ground-Based Interceptors and a series of new and existing radars which not only detect and track targets but also guide the interceptor to an incoming missile. The GMD SoS radars include several Upgraded Early Warning Radars, the AN/TPY-2 (Forward Based) Radar, the Aegis Ballistic Missile Defence Radar and the Sea Based X-Band Radar. The GMD SoS also receives target data from the Space-Based Infrared System and its Defence Support Programme predecessor.

## Programme Status

The GMD, as an element of the MDA's broader Ballistic Missile Defence System, is a capabilities-based developmental acquisition programme utilizing a block approach. That is, capabilities are fielded as they are developed. The system is in a constant state of evolution. The Army has served as lead Service for the GMD, minus acquisition since 1999 and today has focused its efforts on providing installation support, facilities, resources, force protection and operational personnel in support of the deployed capability which also serves as a developmental test bed. Currently, the GMD meets the National

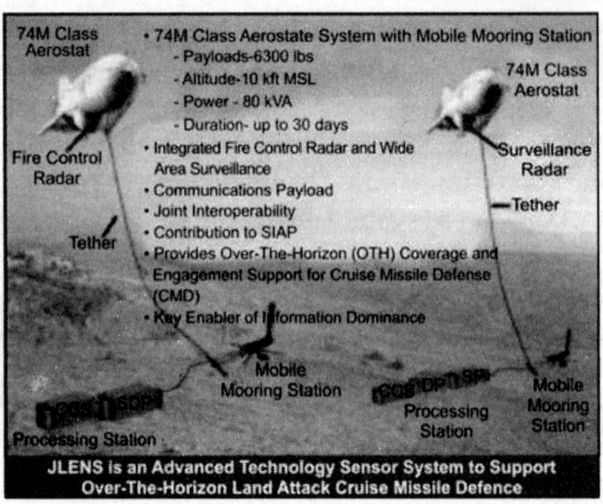


JLENS is an Advanced Technology Sensor System to Support Over-The-Horizon Land Attack Cruise Missile Defence

Command Authority's directive of providing a fielded limited operational capability against ballistic missile threats. System improvements are ongoing, and the scope of defence may be expanded to include protection of friends and allies against long-range ballistic missile attack.

## Joint Land Attack Cruise Missile Defence Elevated Netted Sensor System (JLENS)

Joint Land Attack Cruise Missile Defence Elevated Netted Sensor System is the only persistent, elevated, wide area surveillance and fire control sensor system currently under development for the Department of Defence. It is a critical component of both the Army AMD Future Force and the Joint force CMD kill chain. Without JLENS, the Army and Joint force will not have an elevated sensor capable of providing persistent surveillance cuing and fire control quality data to ground-based shooters in order to protect the force against stressing cruise missiles at extended ranges.

JLENS uses advanced sensor and networking technologies to provide 360-degree Wide Area Surveillance and Fire Control capability against the emerging, stressing land attack cruise missile threat as well as other air-breathing threats to include UAVs, UCAVs and rotary and fixed wing platforms. It will also provide surface moving target data and TBM boost launch warning to the Joint force and can also serve as a long-endurance communications relay. JLENS enables Joint and Army Integrated Air Missile Defence to conduct beyond LOS and NLOS engagements against aerial targets out to each respective interceptor's maximum effective kinematic range. JLENS directly supports all facets of Joint theater AMD active air defence and contributes to offensive counter air/attack operations and C4I through multi-link dynamic data distribution. This system supports the JTAMD mission set execution by providing surveillance and supporting integrated fire control, and aerial CID activities. JLENS is a major contributor to the JTAMD Capstone Requirements Document objectives of SIAP and CID, providing precision tracking and measurement information. As a key element of the SIAP, JLENS correlates organic tracks/measurements with

Identification Friend or Foe and Precise Participant Location Identification Data. The correlated data is then placed on the external networks. JLENS can stay aloft for up to 30 days, providing 24-hour battlespace coverage over extended areas. JLENS is an Army-led, Joint interest programme.

## Programme Status

JLENS is being developed, demonstrated and procured using an evolutionary acquisition strategy consisting of spirals and increments that lead to the fulfillment of ORD requirements. Block I consists of two spirals, with Spiral 2 meeting Block I requirements. Each spiral is being constructed to support air directed surface-to-air missile engagements, SIAP and CID capabilities. Block II will provide increased fire control and wide area surveillance capability with each sensor hosted on a non-tethered platform. Block III provides an increased system capability with sensors hosted on a single non-tethered platform for high mobility. JLENS Block 1 successfully completed its Milestone B in FY05 and is currently in SDD. It is an ACAT 1D programme with a FUE of one battery in FY11 with IOC in FY13. Milestone C decision is scheduled for FY 11.

## Sentinel Enhanced Target and Classification System

The Sentinel radar employs a modern phased array antenna that automatically detects, tracks, classifies and identifies CMs, UAVs, helicopters and fixedwing aircraft to cue Manoevre Air and Missile Defence weapons systems. The Sentinel is comprised of a radar-based sensor system with its HMMWV prime mover, power, IFF and command and control interfaces. The antenna/ transceiver group has an advanced 3rd dimensional battlefield air defence radar housed aboard a light tactical trailer chassis. Targets can be hovering or fast moving, from nap of the earth to the maximum engagement altitude of MAMD weapon systems. The radar operates in the X-band, transmitting 1,100 pencil beams per rotation. It rotates at 30 rpm. Sentinel, with ETRAC, improves operations in a Joint environment to detect smaller cross section targets and is critical for airspace SA/SU, deconfliction and advanced threat early warning. ETRAC upgrades add 20 rpm rotation and staring capability to enhance the detection and tracking of CMs. The instrumented range and altitude are 40 kilometers and four kilometers, respectively. The Sentinel utilizes the SINCGARS and EPLRS radios to provide a track file of more than 60 targets. Sensor data is passed through the FAAD-C2 system to ADA weapon systems. Sentinels will be organic to the multi-functional ADA battalions, providing 360-degree surveillance to counter CMs, UAVs and other ABTs, enabling Avenger today and SLAMRAAM in the future to defeat those threats.

**Programme Status**

The programme completed its primary Sentinel procurement in FY01 and is currently undergoing preplanned product improvement to improve surveillance and tracking capabilities. Additional upgrades and system modifications are currently scheduled through FY19 for many AC and RC units to improve target identification, increase Joint combat ID capabilities and reduce the potential for fratricide. ETRAC modifications will be applied to 76 radars by FY13. The ETRAC modifications consist of two upgrades: Phase 1A improves the radar detection range against low-observable and stealthy targets; Phase 1B improves the radar classification of low-observable and stealthy targets at extended ranges. The Phase 1B capability for target airframe classification will support the Joint identification and target classification function that allows manoeuvre weapons to operate at maximum effectiveness. Although modularity decisions removed Sentinels from the corps, division, and brigades, strong consideration is being made to reintegrate Sentinel in the division headquarters. The Sentinel radar is the ground manoeuvre commander's sensor designed to provide Joint low altitude air coverage and is critical for airspace deconfliction and advanced early warning.

## Forward Area Air Defence–Command and Control (FAAD-C2)

The Forward Area Air Defence–Command and Control system digitally processes and disseminates real-time target cueing and tracking information, the common tactical air picture, and command, control and intelligence information to ADA battalions Avenger weapon systems and Counter Rocket Artillery and Mortar (CRAM). The FAAD-C2 system enables Engagement Operations (EO) through the integration with the Multifunctional Information Distribution System, the Joint Tactical Terminal, Single Channel Ground and Airborne Radio System, Enhanced Position Location Reporting System, Global Positioning System, the Airborne Warning and Control Systems, the Sentinel radar and the ABCS architecture. The FAADC2 primary system is an EO workshop (WS). The EO WS is used to process and exchange Sentinel air track data between the air battle management operations center and Sentinel radars in the sensor network, external track sources via a JDN and intra-AMD EO/ FO data. The EO WS digitally processes, develops and disseminates a real-time air picture to the ADSI. The EO WS processes airspace control measures, rules of engagement and air defence warnings. The EO WS can provide third-dimensional situational awareness to ADA Battalions Avenger weapon systems and CRAM if assigned/ attached to the division/ sector to provide low altitude air defence/ CRAM.

## Programme Status

FAAD-C2 is an ACAT II programme with an Aug 95 approved ORD. The FY10-15 programme plan funds FAAD-C2 Common Hardware Systems upgrades to the ARNG ADA Battalions Avenger weapon systems. FAAD-C2 programme funding will provide FAAD-C2 EO WS in 92 ADAM Cells.

## Air And Missile Defence Planning And Control System (AMDPCS)

The Air and Missile Defence Planning and Control System integrates Air and Missile Defence operations for Army Air and Missile Defence Command Headquarters, Air Defence Artillery Brigade Headquarter, Air Defence Airspace Management Cells, and Joint command and control elements. As a part of the ADA Transformation Plan, the ADA force is modernizing its C2 by standardizing AMDPCS configurations at the AAMDCs and ADA Brigades. The AMDPCS-AAMDC and ADA Brigade systems will comprise of a set of modular, re-configurable and standardized automated data processing equipment packaged in the ADAM system, AN/TSQ-253 and the Command Post Platform, AN/TSQ-232.

The AMDPCS-A system will be employed at the AAMDC Headquarters in the following Command Post configurations: TAC includes one each ADAM system, AN/TSQ-253; MAIN includes one each AN/TSQ-252 shelter, one each CPP shelter; and the REAR includes one each AN/TSQ-252 shelter, one each CPP shelter. The AMDPCS-B system will be employed at the ADA Brigade Headquarters in the following Command Post configurations: Jump TOC includes one each ADAM system, AN/TSQ-253; and the MAIN includes one each AN/TSQ-252 shelter, one each CPP shelter. Working in concert with the Army's transformation to the Battle Command as a Weapon System concept, the AAMDC and ADA Brigade incorporates two of the BCAWS enablers–ADAM system and the CPP shelter, thereby creating the initial plugs necessary to receive Army's modernization to the Functional Support Brigades.

## The AMDPCS ADAM System

AMPDPCS ADAM provides the Manoevre Commander with a modular, scalable cell, consisting of air defence and aviation personnel/equipment, capable of providing airspace management, air defence and airspace planning and coordination utilizing third dimensional situational awareness/situational understanding obtained from organic sensors or the Joint Data Network. The ADAM system is organic in the corps and division, manoeuvre BCTs, CABs and multi-functional support brigades. Additionally, the ADAM system will now be organic to the AAMDC and ADA functional Support Brigades equipped with AMDPCS and FAAD-C2 systems manned by air defence personnel. AMDPCS component includes an AMDWS and an ADSI workstation. The FAAD-C2 component includes an Engagement Operations Work Shop with an intelligence processor. Additionally, the ADAM system is equipped with the TAIS AWS, and at the SBCTs-it includes an Aviation Mission Planning WS, both WSs manned by Aviation personnel.

## Programme Status

Current funding will procure 160 ADAM Cells; upgrade one AAMDC, eight ADA Brigades to meet the Army Modular Force MTOE authorizations. To date, the Army has fielded 76 ADAM Cells and will field an additional 84 in fiscal years 2010-13.

## Joint Tactical Ground Station Multi-Mission Mobile Processor (JTAGS M3P)

The Multi-Mission Mobile Processor is a P3I of the current, operationally proven Joint Tactical Ground System. M3P's will be acquired as part of the mobile ground segment for the Space-

Based Infrared System; the successor to the Defence Support programme. M3P is a transportable missile warning and communications system that will receive and process direct down linked raw data from DSP satellites and the follow-on SBIRS sensors. The three forward deployed systems support simultaneous operations in multiple theaters and provide the theater Combatant Commander with in-theater tactical ballistic missile warning, alerting and cueing data. In addition, the M3P with the SBIRS sensors will provide battlespace characterization data for situational awareness. M3P will provide warning and situational awareness data down to the tactical command level. An M3P detachment's equipment will include a 42-foot van, two 100-KW generators, three 5-ton cargo trucks, one 5-ton tractor, three triband antennas and one HMMWV.

### Programme Status

The Army plans to replace the five fielded JTAGS with the M3P systems, of which three are permanently forward deployed, beginning in fiscal years 2012-13. The Joint Requirement Oversight Council approved Operational Requirements Document calls for a total of seven M3P systems. The transition to M3P is expected to occur as the SBIRS Geosynchronous satellites are launched and assume operational capability. The current M3P baseline programme has not been approved on the SBIRS programme. While the Air Force is reassessing the need for mobile systems in their strategic warning mission, the Army plans to move forward with the acquisition of M3Ps. In fiscal year 2013, M3P is anticipated to begin incorporation of data from the technologies developed by the Missile Defence Agency and their development efforts with the Space Tracking and Surveillance System. MDA is currently conducting technology demonstrations that will lead to a Low Earth Orbit constellation in support of theater tactical missile warning.

## Joint Tactical Ground Station (JTAGS)

Joint Tactical Ground Station is DoD's transportable in theater, direct downlink missile warning and communications system. JTAGS receives and processes space based infrared sensor data and then disseminates threat missile data to forward units via multiple theater communication networks, enhancing theater missions for missile warning, missile defence and situational awareness. JTAGS receives data from Geosynchronous Earth Orbit Defence Support Programme Infrared satellite sensors. JTAGS' forward deployed systems provide continuous and simultaneous operations in multiple theaters, providing Combatant Commanders assured warning for deployed forces and allies.

**Programme Status**

JTAGS is undergoing a phased P3I programme to align with advancing communication networks and theater missile warning architectures and sensors. JTAGS ongoing phase I P3I fiscal year 2008-09 enhances the system with numerous communications upgrades and adapts to receive an additional space based data source from the Space Based Infrared Systems Highly Elliptical Orbit sensor. JTAGS P3I Phase II (fiscal years 2010-12) includes interfacing with SBIRS GEO satellites along with dismounting from the JTAGS shelter, the use of commercial antennas and evolving to a net centric architecture for message dissemination.

### Army Integrated Air and Missile Defence Battle Management Command, Control, Communications, Computers and Intelligence

The proliferation of increasingly sophisticated ballistic missile, cruise missile and unmanned aerial vehicle threats force the development of air and missile defence capabilities that are able to defend against the full spectrum of threats. The Army continues working to increase interoperability and integration among the various current and future Army AMD weapon, sensor and communications platforms to achieve significant increases in operational effectiveness and efficiency. The development and fielding of common AIAMD BMC4I assets will allow the employment of scalable, modular "plug and play" AMD capabilities against the full spectrum of threats throughout the battlespace to support the Army and Joint Current and Future Force.

### Programme Status

Development of a common AIAMD BMC4I is being undertaken in three major increments. The first increment, which is close to completion, is primarily DOTMLPF focused with minimal Material development or fielding. The second increment will use a variety of hardware and software solutions to enable an Army integrated net-centric common AMD Battle Command and integrated fire control capability. The third increment aims at realizing the full capabilities of an Army common IAMD BMC4I, including 360 degree extended range active protection against TBM threats while positioning the Army to become fully integrated with FCS. The effort is on track for a MS B decision in FY07 and a MS C decision in FY10.

### Counter-Rocket, Artillery and Mortar (C-RAM)

During 2007, mortar and rocket attacks in Iraq and Afghanistan have forced American and Allied forces to reassess their abilities to counter these indirect fire threats. The Counter-Rocket, Artillery and Mortar effort is a holistic, multi-Service approach for providing integrated, modular and scalable capability to counter rocket, artillery and mortar attacks against friendly forces. The C-RAM initiative is built upon seven functional areas: Shape, Sense, Warn, Intercept, Respond, Protect and C4 to provide the Current Force

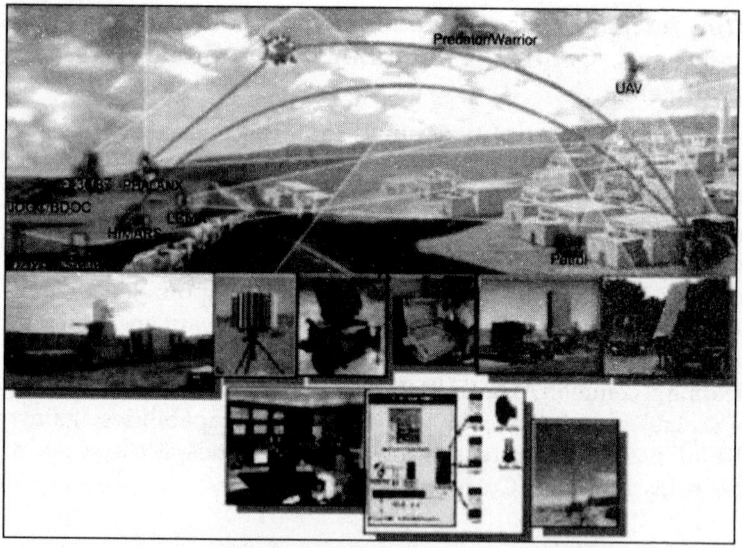


with present, near-term and future early warning, intercept, and rapid response protection against rockets, artillery and mortars. It highlights the operational concept shift from a "system-centric" focus to a network-centric component "plug and fight" architecture capable of operating within the Army and Joint digital architectures. Several agencies within the Army are an integral part of the Joint C-RAM solution including the TRADOC Futures Center, Fires Center of Excellence, Air and Missile Defence Battle Lab, other TRADOC schools, and the Manoevre Support Center, the Counterstrike Task Force, the Engineer Research and Development Center, the Rapid Equipping Force and various material developers.

## Programme Status

The current operational need to protect friendly forces from indirect fire attacks in support of the global war on terrorism serves as a catalyst for continued interest in C-RAM development. Already, the Army has deployed 16 integrated Shape, Sense, Warn and Respond capabilities utilizing a variety of systems including the Land-based Phalanx Weapon System, Forward Area Air Defence-Command and Control, Lightweight Counter Mortar Radar, Firefinder Radar, Sentinel Radar, Wireless Audio Visual Emergency

System, Rapid Aerostat Initial Deployment, and Air and Missile Defence Workstation and Artillery Tactical Data System. Deployment of more robust Shape, Sense, Warn, Intercept and Respond capability to support the ongoing war on terrorism is planned. HQDA and TRADOC are working to determine what the C-RAM capability requirements are for the Future Force and how best to bring these capabilities to the Army and Joint force. Future capabilities being explored include improved kinetic energy and potentially directed energy solutions to support the improved intercept functions and integration of base defence security through integrated sensor suites, information sharing and improved Battle Command to support the Sense, Warn, Shape, Respond and C4 functions.

# Appendix 5: Fires Support Modernization

## Discussion of Core Fire Support Material Programmes

### *High Mobility Artillery Rocket System (HIMARS)*

The M142 High Mobility Artillery Rocket System provides Joint early entry forces, SOF and BCTs with an indirect fire launch platform that provides extremely lethal, responsive, continuous and all-weather, precision medium to long-range rocket and missile res to a depth of 300 kilometers. Highly tactically deployable, the HIMARS launchers have been very successfully employed in both OIF and

OEF, providing exceed-ingly accurate and devastating res. HIMARS units are organic to modular res brigades that provide integral re support for BCTs. HIMARS lls the gap in range between direct-resystems, short range artillery systems and longer range air systems. Mounted on a Family of Medium Tactical Vehicles chassis, the HIMARS is C-130 transportable and provides full Multiple Launch Rocket System family of munitions capability, yet requires 70 percent fewer airlift resources to transport than the current M270 A1 MLRS launchers. When firing GMLRS-Unitary precision rockets, HIMARS can support to a range of 70 kilometers with low-collateral damage enabling danger-close res in support of friendly troops in contact, as well as engaging high valued point targets in open, urban and complex environments. When employing ATACMS Unitary, HIMARS can extend low-collateral lethal precision attack to 300 kilometers.

## Programme Status

HIMARS is in Full Rate Production with three battalions fielded to date. HIMARS is fielded to both Active and Army National Guard units replacing select M270 and towed M198 cannon battalions.

## Lightweight Laser Designator Range Finder (LLDR)

The Lightweight Laser Designator Range Finder is a man-portable, thirty-five pound, long-range fire support targeting sensor that significantly improves the commander's ability to shape the battlefield through use of indirect and precision fires. LLDR can accurately locate, identify, range, self-locate, determine azimuth, vertical angle and designate hard or soft, stationary or moving targets. LLDR replaces the Ground/Vehicular Laser Locator Designator and associated first generation night sight with a state of- the-art lightweight targeting system. The LLDR provides Light, Interim and Heavy Forces with ability to locate, identify and designate during day and night to provide combat overmatch in symmetrical and asymmetrical environments

## Programme Status

The Lightweight Laser Designator Rangefinder began low-rate initial production and fielding in 2003. LLDR production is now at 28 systems per month, with maximum capacity of 40/month being reached by 2nd Quarter FY 2009. LLDR AAO is 3,113 systems and will complete Army wide fieldings in 2013. To date, the Army has fielded 305 systems.

## Meteorological Measuring Set-Profiler

Profiler, AN/TMQ-52 provides a modernized, real time meteorological capability for a wide range of deep fire weapons and munitions over 60 kilometer battlespace with potential to extend coverage to 500 kilometers of battlespace. Profiler replaces

the Army's Meteorological Measuring Set, AN/TMQ- 41 currently nearing obsolescence. Profiler gives the artillery the capability of applying MET data from the firing platform to the target area; target area MET is critical in the selection of the proper munition and for calculating the aim point for "smart munitions".

**Programme Status**

Full rate production and fielding to modular BCTs initiated in FY06 and will continue through FY08.

## M777A2 Lightweight 155-Millimeter Howitzer

The Army has a requirement for an advanced, towed, lightweight 155-millimeter howitzer, with selflocating and aiming capability, that meets increased operational thresholds for mobility, survivability, deployability and sustainability. A Joint USMC/ Army programme, the M777A2 will provide accurate, reliable, responsive, on-demand, 24-hour, all -weather and all-terrain close support fires to manoeuvre forces.

**Programme Status**

A four-year production contract was awarded 22 March 2005. Full Material Release for the M777A1 version was achieved in January 2007, and fielding to Army and USMC artillery units is currently underway. The first Army unit fielded was 2-11 FA. Development of upgraded software which integrates the Excalibur precision guided munition capability was completed with Full Material Release of the Excalibur capable M777A2 in June 2007. The M777A1 version fielded to 2-11 FA have been upgraded, and the first Army unit to be fielded the M777A2 version was 3-321 FA, 18th Fires Battalion. Additional software upgrades are being developed to give the M777A2 more capabilities, and will be incorporated into future fieldings.

## M119A2 Lightweight 105-Millimeter Towed Howitzer

The M119A2 has been in service since 1989, and is used by the Army's light forces to fulfill direct support artillery mission within those units. Decisions to pursue modularity and convert the ARNG to a pure fleet of M119A2s have roughly doubled the Authorized Acquisition Objective for M119A2s to 814 systems. This requirement has driven the need to re-enter production and produce 400 additional M119A2s.

**Programme Status**

Funding to restart the M119A2 program and initiate production was received in the FY05 and FY06 Supplementals. A make/buy decision was made to produce the howitzers at Rock Island Arsenal. Using fiscal years 2005 and 2006. Supplemental funding, long-lead materials have been placed on order and manufacturing activities to produce the initial year's order quantity of 35 weapons have begun. The first delivery of a complete new production M119A2 was completed in April 2007. After production testing is complete, Material release is expected by the end of third quarter FY08 with fieldings commencing in third quarter FY08.

## M109A6, PALADIN

The M109A6 155-millimeter howitzer was fielded in 1993. It is the most technological advanced selfpropelled cannon system in the Army. The Paladin has state-of-the-art components to achieve dramatic improvements in survivability in shoot and scoot tactics; improved ballistic and NBC protection. It is capable of firing within 45 seconds from a complete stop with on-board communications, remote travel lock, and automated cannon slew capability. Paladin achieves accurate fires from its on-board position navigator and technical fire control system. It has an extended range of 30 kilometers with HE, rocket assisted projectile and also fires the Excalibur precision-guided munitions with Portable Excalibur Fire Control System.

**Programme Status**

Paladin Integrated Management programme will rebuild platforms, apply current Modification Work Order's, and deliver a ready, relevant, and sustainable platform. The objective of the Paladin PIM programme is to modernize and sustain the Paladin fleet to fight side-by-side with NLOS-C in the HBCT formations well into the 21st Century.

**M1200 Armored Knight Fire Support Vehicle**

The M1200 Armored Knight provides precision strike capability by locating and designating targets for both ground and air-delivered laser-guided ordnance and conventional munitions. It replaces the M707 Knight and M981 Fire Support Team Vehicles used by Combat Observation Lasing Teams in both Heavy and Infantry BCTs. Prior to 2005, Knight was delivered on unarmored HMMWV M1025 chassis configured with the Fire Support Sensor System. Up-armored HMMWVs with Knight MEP are approximately one ton over gross vehicle weight, and unable to accommodate user requirements for additional survivability, mobility, space and power. FY07 procures Armored Knight vehicles configured with the Armored Security Vehicle M1117 chassis. This will enable Armored Knight to meet Army's modularity requirements with FS3 objective sensor, improved survivability, mobility, mission payload, gross vehicle weight, and growth potential not attainable with HMMWV.

Armored Knight operates as an integral part of the brigade reconnaissance element, providing COLT and fire support mission planning and execution. Specifically, Armored Knight provides fire support planning, direction, control, target designation and night observation in a highly manoeuvreable platform, and acquires, processes and transmits target information directly into the AFATDS fire support network. It has the ability to self-locate, determine range, azimuth and vertical angle to target, target destination and night observation. This capability provides terminal guidance for any munitions requiring reflected laser energy.

Armored Knight's secondary mission is gathering intelligence through AOR surveillance and reconnaissance. Armored Knight utilizes an M1117 ASV hull and provides full 360-degree, continuous armored cupola coverage and the fully integrated Knight Mission Equipment Package common with the M7 BFIST/ M707 Knight and Stryker FSV.

### Programme Status

The M1200 Armored Knight, began fielding with an urgent material release in 2007. Current FY07 funding supports procurement of 107 M1200 Armored Knights to be delivered beginning March 2008. The programme is currently funded to meet a modularity end-state of 342 systems.

## Lightweight Counter Mortar Radar (LCMR)

The Lightweight Counter Mortar Radar, AN/TPQ-48 is a developmental, lightweight, man-portable weapons location sensor that provides continuous 360-degree accurate mortar location up to a range of 5 kilometers. LCMR was originally developed for the U.S. Special Operations Command in response to 1999 MNS described by the 75th Ranger Regiment for automatic location of indirect fire weapons, with emphasis on mortars. The MNS also identified the requirement for a sensor with 360 degrees of azimuth coverage that was small and light

enough to be inserted with airborne troops and transported on the ground by two persons. Enhancements in the AN/TPQ-48 were implemented to refine the design and to address feedback received from users during both testing and operational use in OIF/OEF. A developmental effort for the AN/TPQ-48 system and delivery of 13 prototypes has been initiated to provide improved operational and physical functionality over the existing LCMR and radar systems, to have increased accuracy and range, to be highly mobile and two-man transportable, have improved emplacement capabilities and be a ruggedized battlefield radar system.

**Programme Status**

LCMR AN/TPQ-48 (Version 2) continues to be fielded to the Army, USMC, C-RAM and various Foreign Military Sales coalition countries. A long-term contract for LCMR Version 3, with extended range and target detection capability, is under development and is projected to begin fielding in FY2010.

**Enhanced AN/TPQ-36**

The Enhanced AN/TPQ-36 radar is a replacement for the aging AN/TPQ 36 and AN/TPQ-37 counter fire radar systems. The EQ-36 is a system technology upgrade that provides a 360-degree capability with improved range and accuracy in a clutter environment.

**Programme Status**

The EQ-36 will be produced in two increments based on two tiers of technical threshold requirements. Increment I requirements will incorporate 360-degree coverage, improved 90-degree range and accuracy, single C-130 sortie capability and AFATDS interoperability. Increment II will incorporate improved 90- and

360-degree range and accuracy capabilities. Enhancements include increased performance in high-clutter, improved accuracy from .65 percent of range to .30 percent of range, and improved range from 14.5 kilometers to 32 kilometers for cannon and 24 kilometers to 50 kilometers for rockets. Crew size will be reduced from six to four for Q-36, and from 12 to four for Q-37. Programmed funding fully funds RDTE for increments I and II, provides for five radar systems for integration and testing, and procures 204 production systems at the most economical production rate.

# Appendix 6: Chemical, Biological, Radiological, Nuclear (CBRN) Defence

## Discussion of Core CBRN Defence Material Programmes

### *M31A1/M31E2 Biological Integrated Detection System (BIDS)*

M31A1/M31E2 Biological Integrated Detection System is a shelter-mounted system on a dedicated vehicle, and equipped with a biological detection suite employing complementary technologies to detect large-area biological attacks. The M31E2 BIDS is capable of detecting all types of biological agents in less than 10 minutes, and identifying any 10 agents simultaneously in less than 30 minutes.

#### Programme Status

The M31A1 and M31E2 versions of the BIDS are currently fielded. All new activating units will receive the M31E2 version.

### STRYKER-Nuclear, Biological and Chemical Reconnaissance Vehicle (NBCRV)

The STRYKER-Nuclear, Biological and Chemical Reconnaissance Vehicle incorporates integrated chemical and biological point detectors that allow on-the-move standoff biological and chemical agent detection. The Chemical Biological Mass Spectrometer improves the detection and identification of liquid chemical agents, while Joint Biological Point Detection System provides a first-time biological agent detection capability to the reconnaissance platform. The sensor suite automatically integrates contamination information with data from onboard navigation and meteorological systems and rapidly transmits contamination hazard and non-contaminated area intelligence to the appropriate operations center. Integration of the common CBRN technical architecture allows for expansion/ upgrading of the onboard computers at minimal cost, as well as the command and control of CBRN sensing UAVs and unmanned ground vehicles in the Future Force.

## Programme Status

Stryker-NBCRV Milestone C was reached in fourth quarter, FY04, allowing the start of LRIP for 21 NBCRVs. An Extended LRIP was authorized for 95 additional NBCRVs in the first quarter FY 08. The FRP decision is scheduled for FY10. The Stryker- NBCRV began fielding in FY06, will field to HBCTs in FY10 and fielding is planned for chemical companies thereafter.

## Monitoring and Survey Hazardous Response (MSHR) CBRN Set, Kit and Outfits

The Monitoring and Survey Hazardous Response CBRN Set, Kit and Outfits is a developmental system containing CBRN sensors specifically designed for dismounted use during the assessment of sensitive sites that are inaccessible by mounted CBRN reconnaissance vehicles. The MSHR CBRN provides the warfighter with handheld chemical, biological, radiological and nuclear sensors and individual protective equipment incorporated on a specialized HMMWV trailer that can be used to assess hazardous materials incorporated into weapons or that are produced by industry.

## Programme Status

The MSHR CBRN is expected to begin fielding by FY11. It will be issued to CBRN recon platoons assigned to IBCTs, heavy chemical companies, Special Forces chemical response decon units, and potentially to hazardous response decon platoons.

## M56 Wheeled Smoke System

The M56 Wheeled Smoke System, COYOTE provides large-area, multi-spectral screening for manoeuvre and support forces from the M1113 HMMWV, and can generate large-area obscurants throughout the battlespace to counter enemy reconnaissance, surveillance and target acquisition systems. Missions include providing static and mobile visual, IR screening in the form of a haze, blanket and curtain. Major components include a turbine smoke generating system. It has the capability of providing continuous visual smoke for up to 90 minutes and 30 minutes of IR screening smoke. A proposed P3I can add a 30-minute millimeter wave obscuring capability to defeat enemy radar RSTA/ISR devices and weapon systems. A two-person crew operates the M56 and has the capability to counter the threat arising from the wide proliferation of advanced visual and IR sensors.

### Programme Status

Fielding of the M56 is complete. Limited production of six M56E1 systems is expected NLT FY08. The PM is currently exploring options to improve system survivability. The Army Acquisition Objective of 265 has been met.

### M7 Vehicle Obscuration Smoke Systems

M7 Vehicle Obscuration Smoke Systems provide an immediate smoke screen that can obscure threat surveillance, target acquisitions, and weapon guidance systems in the visual through infrared spectrum. The system provides approximately 20-120 seconds of obscuration, which enables the vehicle to manoeuvre out of the immediate threat area. The M7 Light Vehicle Obscuration Smoke System provides this capability for up-armored HMMWVs. The M7 system utilizes 66-millimeter grenades and a launcher configuration of four tubes. Multiple launcher systems are utilized to provide all-around screening capability.

### Programme Status

The M7 programme is currently funded.

### Chemical Biological Protective Shelter System (CBPSS)

The Chemical Biological Protective Shelter System is a self contained highly mobile, rapidly deployable chemically protected shelter system designed for emergency medical use in the forward battle areas. The shelter consists of an air beam supported soft shelter offering 300 square feet of working space, power systems and environmental control equipment. The foldable shelter, power system and environmental control equipment is housed on a lightweight multipurpose shelter, mounted on an expanded capacity vehicle with a modified 1-1/4-ton, high-mobility trailer which has a permanently mounted tactical quiet generator set.

### Programme Status

CBPSS programme currently is reviewing design options to convert the existing CBPSS from an unarmored HMMWV to an up-armored Medium Tactical Vehicle platform. CBPSS fieldings will continue through FY13.

## Chemically Protected Deployable Medical System (CP DEPMEDS)

The Chemically Protected Deployable Medical System is a containerized collective protection system that provides U.S. Army Deployable Medical System Combat Support Hospitals the capability to sustain medical operations in a CBRN environment for 72 hours. The system consists of modular M28 chemical/ biological protective liner sections, 200 hermetically sealed filter canisters, recirculation filters, pressurized protective entrances, additional power generation, a CBRN-protected water system, low-pressure alarms, and CBRN protected latrine facilities for patients and staff.

### Programme Status

CP DEPMEDS AAO specifies 23 systems. The Joint Operational Requirements Document was updated in October 2003 to reflect the Medical Reengineering Initiative configuration, which allows for smaller, split-base hospital operations and can deploy incrementally to protect a 44-bed early

entry hospital, an 84-bed hospital company, a 164-bed increment, or a fullup 248 bed CSH.

### Joint Chemical Agent Detector (JCAD)

Joint Chemical Agent Detector will be a combined portable monitoring and small point chemical agent detector for individual Soldier applications. This handheld, pocket-sized detector will be designed to automatically detect, identify and quantify chemical agents. The primary function of the JCAD is as a chemical weapon agent point detector that can be used to detect, identify, quantify, and warn personnel of the presence of vapour chemical agents. Follow-on increment will also detect specified toxic industrial chemicals.

#### Programme Status

Testing of a candidate system is underway at Edgewood Chemical Biological Center. Increment I fielding was scheduled for third quarter, FY08. Increment II is scheduled for FY10.

### Joint Chemical, Biological, and Radiological Agent Water Monitor (JCBRAWM)

Joint Chemical, Biological, and Radiological Agent Water Monitor will provide the warfighter the capability to detect, identify and quantify the presence of CBR contamination in water. The ICD describes the need for monitoring to protect the warfighter from drinking or using contaminated water. The JCBRAWM will detect and identify CBR agents during three water-monitoring missions: source site selection, treatment verification and quality assurance of stored and distributed water.

#### Programme Status

The system is pre-milestone B and will potentially be fielded as incremental capabilities for each separate threat.

### Joint Warning and Reporting Network (JWARN)

Joint Warning and Reporting Network provides standard integration and analysis of NBC detection information with command, control, communications, computers, information and

intelligence on the battlefield. JWARN automates the NBC warning and reporting processes now performed manually throughout the Services. It will provide additional data processing, production of plans and reports and access to specific NBC information to improve the efficiency of NBC personnel. JWARN will be integrated on MCS and GCCS-A in the near term and FBCB2 in the out years.

**Programme Status**

JWARN will be distributed as a module of the MCS (software block 9/11) and GCCS-A systems. IOC will be achieved when JWARN is fielded to initial units and training bases, unit personnel are trained, training base is established and a maintenance system is in place.

**Joint Effects Model (JEM)**

Joint Effects Model will provide commanders with advanced modeling and simulation capability to forecast and display the effects of CBRN events, including toxic industrial hazardous, based on inputs from JWARN-networked sensors, intelligence and other units. JEM supports force protection and operational deployment planning by providing critical CBRN/TIH planning and defensive information.

**Programme Status**

JEM Increment-I is currently in the SDD acquisition phase and will be included as a module of the MCS (software block 9-11).

**Joint Service Transportation Decontamination System (JSTDS)**

This mobile system provides the capability to conduct operational and thorough decontamination of medium-to-large mobile or fixed equipment, aircraft, facilities, shelters, surface areas and terrain. The small-scale Joint Service Transportation Decontamination System replaces the M17 LDS and M12A1s in non-chemical units. The large-scale system will be integrated into or mounted on a dedicated vehicle/system. The large-scale system replaces the M12A1 in chemical units. Specifically, this will be a cross-spectrum system designed to support Current and Future Forces, or homeland security operations. It will be capable of decontaminating fixed sites, terrain, large aircraft and seaports of debarkation and aerial ports of debarkation.

### Programme Status

JSTDS-SS IOC is scheduled for FY10. FOC is scheduled for FY12. IOC of 350 JSTDS-LS is scheduled for FY13. FOC is scheduled for FY15.

## Joint Service Personnel/Skin Decontamination System (JSPDS)

Joint Service Personnel/Skin Decontamination System replaces the M291 SDK and will decontaminate the skin, individual equipment and individual weapons. IOC is scheduled for FY10 and will be achieved when JSPDS is fielded to forward-deployed units, rapid deployment units, unit personnel are trained; a training base is established; and a maintenance system is in place.

### Programme Status

IOC is scheduled for FY10. FOC is scheduled for FY13 and will be achieved when the JSPDS AAO is reached and all authorizations are filled. Total number of systems is 2,285,451.

## Joint Platform Interior Decontamination System (JPID)

Joint Platform Interior Decontamination System will consist of a decontaminant and an applicator for use primarily in immediate and operational decontamination operations. The target items for decontamination will be small non-sensitive equipment and key areas on large non-sensitive equipment. The JPID will decontaminate threat agents to lower levels than current portable systems used for these operations.

### Programme Status

The IOC for this system is projected in FY10, with FOC planned for FY13.

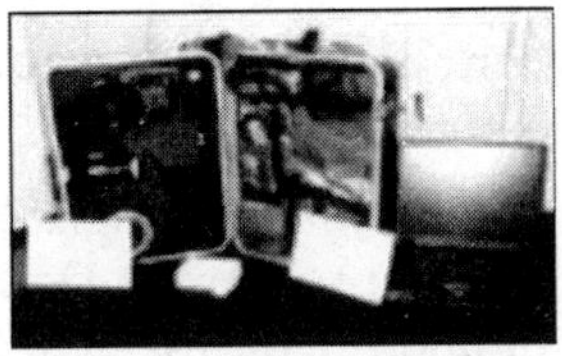

### Joint Service Sensitive Equipment Decontamination System (JSPDS)

Joint Service Sensitive Equipment Decontamination System provides a first-ever capability to decontaminate chemical and biological warfare agents and toxins from sensitive electronic, avionics, and electro-optic equipment. Its use will be compatible with and not degrade sensitive materials or equipment. It will be operator safe and offer protection from off–gassing and direct liquid exposure during decontamination.

### Programme Status

IOC for this system is projected in FY10, with FOC planned for FY13.

### Joint Service General Purpose Mask

The XM50 and XM51 are two new protective masks that make up the Joint Service General Purpose Mask lightweight mask system. The XM50 mask replaces the existing M-40 individual mask, and the XM51 replaces the M-42 crew member mask. Each mask consists of a faceblank assembly, front module cover, mesh-type head harness assembly, self-sealing valve, inlet/ outlet valve, internal and external drink tubes, carrier, waterproof bag, canteen cap, dust cover, laser outsert, primary filters, operator cards and accessories as required. The masks allow intelligible voice transmissions.

### Programme Status

FRP memo was signed in September 2007. Fielding is scheduled to continue beyond FY15. The program is funded for the Total Service Requirement of the Army, Air Force, Marine Corps and Navy.

## Joint Biological Agent Identification and Diagnostics System (JBAIDS)

The Joint Biological Agent Identification and Diagnostics System program is DoD's initial effort to develop and field a common medical test equipment platform amongst all the Services. JBAIDS is an evolutionary, three-block, reusable, portable and modifiable biological agent identification and diagnostic system capable of simultaneous reliable identification of multiple biological agents of operational concern and other pathogens of clinical significance. JBAIDS Block I tests a variety of environmental samples and clinical specimens for non-diagnostic purposes, and performs confirmatory testing of samples collected by existing and future biological detection systems. Block II focuses on the militarization and hardening of critical toxin identification technologies based on a COTS/NDI candidate system. JBAIDS Block III is planned to be a handheld, FDA-approved device capable of providing the full range of biological agent identification and diagnostics.

### Programme Status

Block II development is scheduled for FY08.

# Appendix 7: Battle Command

## Discussion of Core Battle Command Material Programmes

### *Global Command and Control System – Army/Net-Enabled Command Capability (GCCS)*

Global Command and Control System–Army is the Army's strategic, theater and tactical command and control system providing seamless operational information and data from the strategic GCCS-Joint to Army theater elements and below. The system provides an interface between Joint/Combined Forces (Joint GCCS) and Tactical Army Battle Command Systems (ABCS). GCCS-A is an integral component of the GCCS-FoS programme and provides a robust and seamless command and control capability to senior military leaders and decision makers. Net-Enabled Command Capability replaces GCCSA and is the DoD's principal command and control capability that will be accessible in a net-centric environment and focused on providing the commander with the data and information needed to make timely, effective and informed decisions. The NECC draws from the C2 community to evolve current and provide new C2 capabilities into a fully integrated, interoperable, collaborative Joint solution. Warfighters can rapidly adapt to changing mission needs by defining and tailoring their information environment and drawing on capabilities that enable the efficient, timely and effective command of forces and control of engagements.

### Programme Status

NECC programme has not yet received MS B approval. An APB will be established to document this programme when approved. Army funding addressed in this WSR for NECC is a part of the Joint NECC programme and will be covered in the NECC APB.

### Battle Command Common Services (BCCS)

Battle Command Common Services (BCCS) is a suite of standardized and configured servers that provide a tactical infrastructure of server and service capabilities that extends the

NECC and NCES environment to tactical echelons from battalion to Army Service Component Command. This infrastructure enables Army Battle Command System interoperability and data management, supports modularity and provides for enterprise services. Enterprise services consist of commercial products that are integrated and standardized to provide the current tactical infrastructure and will migrate to become the key component of the Net Centric Environment. These services include Windows Service Configuration and user management (Active Directory, Domain Name Service and Windows Server), e-mail (Microsoft Exchange), Web Portal (Microsoft SharePoint) for Knowledge Management, security and virus protection, backup, failover and restoration services. Battle Command system interoperability is enabled currently with a Publish and Subscribe Service that is evolving to a Data Dissemination Service compliant with the NECC and NCES environment. PASS and DDS are used by multiple Army systems and support data exchanges and dissemination throughout the unit. BCCS also supports ongoing Joint convergence efforts with the Marine Corps by providing a data exchange gateway that allows the direct exchange of COP data between Joint Services.

## Mounted Battle Command on the Move (MBCOTM)

The Mounted Battle Command on the Move system is a set of Command, Control, Communications, and Computers mission equipment integrated into a Bradley (ODS, M2A3, M3A3), Stryker Commander's Vehicle and the future light tactical vehicle for use by Commanders and selected Battle Staff personnel.

The focus of MBCOTM is to facilitate commander execution-centric operations versus command postcentric operations. MBCOTM provides for Battle Command by providing a commander situational awareness in the form of a digital common operating picture, enabling a commander to maintain situational understanding while moving and physically

separated from fixed command posts. MBCOTM will be able to host Army Future Combat Systems Battle Command Technology as it is developed and will provide the integration necessary to enable Battle Command for Tactical Command and Control On The Move.

**Programme Status**

Updated CPD JROC approved, followed by MSC/ LRIP ADM in 2QFY07. FUE is scheduled for 1/2QFY09.

**Manoevre Control System (MCS)**

Manoevre Control System is the mission critical command and control system that allows Commanders and their staffs to visualize the battlespace and synchronize the elements of combat power for successful execution of combat operations. The MCS provides a software capability that has transformed the way the manoeuvre commander, from battalion task force through corps, collaboratively creates and manages critical information to include location of friendly units, enemy units, targets, plans and orders, as well as operational graphics. MCS is used to improve and shorten the decision making process, enhance planning operations, and supervise the execution of operations. MCS provides tools and displays that collect and process information from various sources as desired by the tactical commander and various battle staff users. MCS is the heart of the Army's Battle Command System, the "system of systems" for Battle Command. Using formats and templates that are familiar to users, the MCS system can quickly develop and distribute battle plans and orders. Its automated features provide commanders the capability they need to conduct multi-node collaborative planning sessions to execute the battle plan, and coordinate forces for precision engagement. MCS as part of ABCS, is the Combined Arms Commander's tool for visualization of the battlefield.

In this capacity, MCS receives critical Battle Command information and data from each ABCS Battle Field Functional Area and displays that information on the COP display as required by commanders and their staffs. MCS also provides critical COP information to each BFA as required for execution of their functional area. These information and data exchanges are completed directly via military messaging, data exchanges, email, hosting client applications, or indirectly using the ABCS Publish and Subscribe Service capability and web-based services.

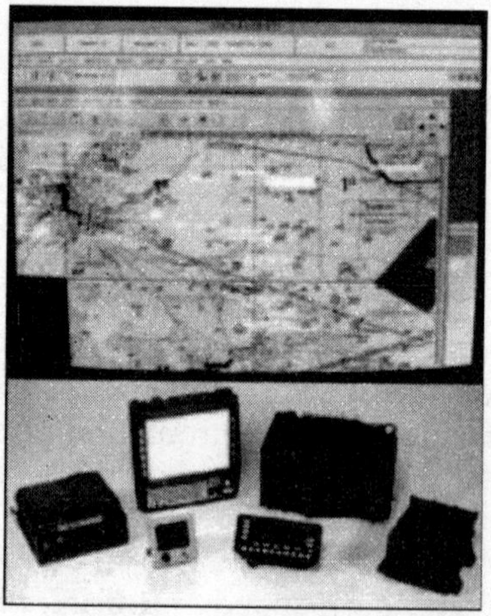

MCS also provides the enterprise services necessary to support Battle Command functions and for the system to operate across the battlespace and seamlessly integrate with ABCS, other battle command enablers, Net Centric Enterprise Services and the Global Information Grid. MCS will use resident enterprise services to integrate information within the battlespace and through NCES, bring information from beyond the battlespace to the commander on the ground.

## Programme Status

MCS 6.4 Milestone III (FRP)–29 June 2005. MCS capabilities are being transitioned as services and will become part of the Joint Convergence effort. Command Post of the Future capabilities will also be added to MCS as a technical insertion.

## Command Post of the Future (CPOF)

The Command Post of the Future is the commander's executive level decision support system, providing situational awareness and collaborative tools for tactical decision making, planning, rehearsal and execution management from Army Service Component Command to battalion level. CPOF supports visualization, information analysis, and collaboration in a single, integrated environment. Through the technological insertion of CPOF into the MCS programme, commanders and key staff have an executive level decision support capability with enhanced real-time collaborative tools. These capabilities provide critical contributions to the commander's warfighting capabilities by enhancing his/her situational awareness and supporting an execution-focused Battle Command process. CPOF operators interactively collaborate, sharing thoughts, workspace and plans to analyze information, and evaluate courses of action with real-time feedback for an immediate and comprehensive view of the battlefield. CPOF creates a commander-centric software environment that can be tailored to fit specific visualizations. This custom view supports distributed and collaborative operations that allow the commander to command anywhere on the battlefield. CPOF is designed to enable deep cohesion of thought processes between the commander and his staff. Users are able to selectively and dynamically generate and transmit their evolving analysis, plans and execution. CPOF is a comprehensible collaborative environment from the moment the system is turned on. Users just need drag and drop a visualization product into the "shared products" region, and it is instantly shared with all registered users.

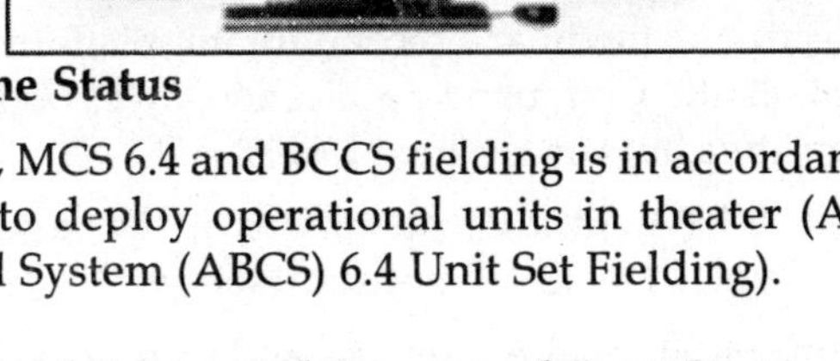

**Programme Status**

CPOF, MCS 6.4 and BCCS fielding is in accordance with G3 priorities to deploy operational units in theater (Army Battle Command System (ABCS) 6.4 Unit Set Fielding).

**Standardized Integrated Command Post System (SICPS)**

Standardized Integrated Command Post System is primarily a non-developmental effort that consists of the integration of

approved and fielded C2 and other C4ISR systems technology into platforms supporting the operational needs of battalion through echelon above corps command posts. SICPS consists of various systems, specifically the SICPS Command Post Platform, which includes: Command Post Communications System, an intercom, the Command Center System and the Trailer Mounted Support System. SICPS provides:

- Standardized CP Infrastructure allows commanders and staffs to digitally plan, prepare and execute operations
- Systematic integration of Army tactical communications systems, Battle Command systems, and supporting systems into standard platforms
- Standardized / modular / reconfigurable platforms, enabling multiple Battle Command applications over both classified and Sensitive but Unclassified LANs
- Supports NET-Centric CP operations on the move and at the long and quick halt C-130 transportability
- Real-time Situational Awareness and Common Operational Picture in Command Information Center with CCS
- TMSS (comprised of tents, environmental conditioning, and infrastructure) to support collaborative staff operations

## Programme Status

SICPS is an ACAT II programme, currently in Low Rate Initial Production. SICPS fieldings continuing IAW Unit Set Fielding schedule. Implementation of VCSA Command Post standardization directives is on-going.

## Force XXI Battle Command Brigade and Below (FBCB2)

Force XXI Battle Command Brigade and Below is a Joint interoperable, digital, Battle Command information system for brigade level and below. FBCB2 is designed to provide mounted and dismounted combat elements with near real-time, integrated SA and C2 functionality. FBCB2 enhances the ability of tactical commanders to better synchronize their forces, achieve agility and gain a sense of the battlespace through improved SA and better combat awareness reporting while on the move. FBCB2 is a key component of ABCS.

FBCB2 operates over both terrestrial communications networks and SATCOM networks. The system consists of a ruggedized computer with a touch screen and keyboard in which the Soldier sees either a digital map or satellite imagery overlaid with icons representing the vehicle's location, other FBCB2 Blue Force Tracking (BFT) vehicles, known enemy units and objects such as minefields and bridges. FBCB2/ BFT was expeditiously fielded in reduced quantities to every Army Command, Army Service Component Command, and Direct Reporting Unit, as well as the USMC and United Kingdom forces participating in OEF and OIF. In theater BFT has been fielded on 50 percent of all Up-Armored HMWVVs, and 100 percent of ASVs. The Army is currently fielding BFT on 100 percent of its MRAPs. Completion of fieldings for the Modular Force is scheduled for FY10.

## Programme Status

FBCB2 is currently funded to continue improvements in the Network Operations Center re-architecture, synchronization of software releases, satellite architecture and waveform redesign to reduce latency caused by increased system demands, Type 1 encryption, beacon capability development, logistics product development and Internet Protocol V6 development.

## ISYSCON V4 Tactical Internet Management System (TIMS)

The ISYSCON (V) 4/Tactical Internet Management System is a software system that resides on the FBCB2 system located in the S6/G6 sections of the digitized force architecture. The ISYSCON (V)4/ TIMS uses FBCB2 software as a foundation and adds developmental and commercial off-the-shelf software to plan, configure, initialize and monitor the Tactical Internet. The ISYSCON (V) 4/TIMS enhances the FBCB2 system management capability, and provides the Signal Officer, G6/S6, with a network management tool that allows him/her to plan, disseminate, configure, initialize, monitor and troubleshoot the Tactical Internet as well as the Tactical Operation Center and Command Post Local Area Networks.

### Programme Status

The programme is currently providing ABCS and network system management hardware/software tools to deploying forces in accordance with the *Army Campaign Plan*.

## COBRA-Based Blue Force Tracking Systems and Supporting Architecture

The MTX is the current DoD BFT system that leverages existing National Space Infrastructure/ National Technical Means (NTM).These devices give commanders the ability to track and receive position location information (PLI) and short brevity codes, in near real-time, from friendly forces requiring a extremely secure, low probability of intercept/low probability of detection (LPI/ LPD) C2 link. These systems substantially enhance security and reliability through the use of LPI/LPD COBRA (collection of broadcasts from remote assets) waveforms, encryption certified by the National Security Agency and military GPS. SMDC/ ARSTRAT's BFT Mission Management Center (MMC) supports MTX use of the existing COBRA architecture by coordinating with National system managers and warfighting units to help collect, process and disseminate warfighter BFT data.

Due to the security advantages, SOF used the COBRA based BFT systems during OEF and OIF while Coalition Forces Land Component Command main formations used FBCB2. Post-OIF I, has developed a capability to successfully integrate disparate BFT systems used by different units and Services into the COCOM's TOP COP, deliver these devices' PLI data via the Integrated Broadcast Service and maintain special mission "discrete" BFT data feeds to those users requiring significant security. These BFT systems, the MMC and the NTM architecture give operational-level commanders a substantially enhanced COP to date by increasing their situational awareness.

### Programme Status

Approximately 6,000 MTX systems have been produced and fielded to USSOCOM components (e.g., every USAF Special Operations airframe and deployed ground team in support of OEF/OIF has an MTX), other Government Agencies (OGAs), and all other services who have a specialized requirement for secure/LPI/LPD BFT support. The MTX and the MMC were developed and fielded as a result of supplemental appropriations and budget additions, but have since been accepted as critical and indispensable support systems to the GWOT. The NRO has also invested heavily in upgrading and expanding the COBRA support architecture to make it mission ready for DoD and OGA requirements.

## Single Channel Ground and Airborne Radio System (SINCGARS)

Single Channel Ground and Airborne Radio System provides commanders with a highly reliable, secure, easily maintained combat net radio that has both voice and data handling capability in support of C2 operations. SINCGARS, with the Internet controller, provides the communications link for the digitized force. The Advanced System Improvement Programme models are of a reduced size and weight, providing further enhancements to operational capability in the Tactical Internet environment.

### Programme Status

SINCGARS continues to be the workhorse in the Army. FM Combat Net Radio in OIF/OEF is being fielded to Active, ARNG and Reserve forces in current operations as well as supporting Army transformation.

## Global Positioning System (GPS)

Global Positioning System is a space-based radio POS/NAV system that provides extremely accurate, continuous, all-weather, common-grid, worldwide navigation and three-dimensional positioning, velocity and timing information to land, sea, air and space users. These components are the space, ground control and user equipment segments.

## Programme Status

The Defence Advanced GPS Receiver (DAGR) began replacing the current Precision Lightweight GPS Receiver in 1QFY05. The DAGR includes the Selective Availability Anti-Spoofing Module and other significant improvements including size, weight and battery requirements. The PLGR will be cascaded from units fielding the DAGR to fill authorized requirements in other units. The DAGR is projected to be replaced starting in FY13 by an improved Military (M)-Code capable handheld GPS device when the associated M-Code satellite constellation and ground control stations have reached FOC.

## Bridge-to-the-Future Networks (BFN)

Bridge-to-the-Future Networks is the Army's bridging strategy to deliver increasing net-centric capabilities into the Current Force today, and will be followed by the initial transition to the Warfighter Information Network–Tactical capability. Capability enhancements within the Army's BFN strategy are increased voice, data and video services that are Joint network ready and supports the Army's modular designs. The BFN provides the Current Force with a state-of-the-art COTS communications backbone network (high-speed and high-capacity) that will enable them to exchange information (voice, data, and video) throughout the tactical corps and into the sustaining base.

The objective of the BFN is to incrementally insert increased capability, COTS solutions to the Army's Current Force to satisfy existing capability gaps. BFN capability increments build off the recapitalization of the current Multi Subscriber Equipment (MSE) and Tri-Services Tactical Communications (TRI-TAC) systems. The Army's BFN CPD fuses the Army's Joint Network Node, connect the Logistician–CSS, and intelligence Trojan Spirit initiatives into a single strategy to deliver increased capabilities to the warfighter today. The BFN capability increments build off of the existing *Area Common User System Modernization Plan* and recapitalization of the current MSE and TRI-TAC systems.

## Warfighter Information Network–Tactical (WIN-T)

Warfighter Information Network–Tactical is designed to provide the backbone of the tactical network, continuous and full communications-on-the move (users and network infrastructure) capability at all echelons, Joint and coalition voice and data services to all command posts, a flexible and dynamic task reorganization capability, and a more survivable and less complex network.

WIN-T's single integrated network will provide multi-level classified Joint and coalition voice and data services to all command posts. Conceptually, this is intended to eliminate the need for stovepipe (CSS-VSAT, Trojan Spirit) communications systems. As an integral component of the FCS network, WIN-T is a critical element in the Army's transition to robust network based operations. WIN-T provides the key capability for on-the-move communications through a threetiered architecture (ground, airborne and space) that enables continuous network connectivity. The ground layer will equip Soldiers, sensors, platforms, command posts, and access nodes (signal shelters) with integrated transmission (radio) systems, switching, and routing capabilities that will serve as WIN-T points of presence. The airborne layer will serve as an access node and relay by positioning transmission, switching and routing capabilities onto airborne

platforms. The space layer will serve as an access node and relay by leveraging the transmission, switching and routing capabilities provided on the satellite.

**Programme Status**

The Army has restructured the WIN-T Programme to absorb the former Joint Network Node Network programme. The restructured WIN-T programme will consist of four Increments:

- Increment 1: Networking at-the-Halt
- Increment 1a: Extended Networking at-the-Halt - the former JNN programme with Ka military satellite communications capability
- Increment 1b: Enhanced Networking at-the-Halt - the former JNN Programme with Net Centric Waveform and Colorless Core Capability
- Increment 2: Initial Networking on-the-Move
- Research, Development, Test & Engineering for Soldier Network Extensions and High-capacity Network Radios, Tactical Communications Nodes, Points of Presence and other associated Configuration Items
- Procurement of limited numbers of SNEs, HNRs, TCNs, POPs and other associated CIs
- Increment 3: Full Networking on-the-Move
- Full mobility to include Future Combat Systems support
- Increment 4: Protected Satellite Communications (SATCOM) on-the-Move
- Enhanced capability for protected SATCOM through tech insertions from High Capacity Communication Capability

The Army has combined the former JNN programmes funding and WIN-T funding into a single funding profile that clearly identifies funding for each increment. The Army will procure Increment 1 equipment to complete fielding to about 199 Army units; and will procure Increment 2 equipment for about 37 Army units, based on affordability through fiscal year 2013.

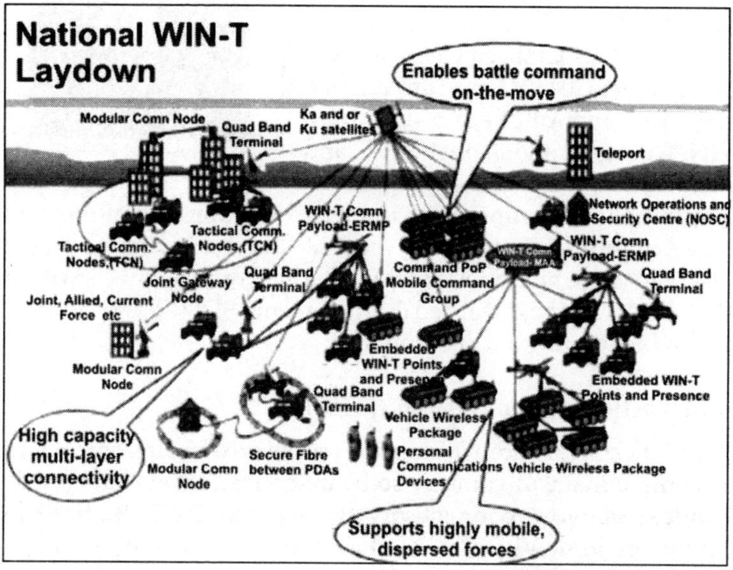

In FY 2008, the Army will provide Increments 3 and 4 content description, cost, schedule and affordability details. Also in FY08, the Army will finalize its plan on realigning the former JNN programme assets (if needed, depending on whether FY08 supplemental funding is provided), from manoeuvre brigade combat teams to those sustainment, engineer and battlefield surveillance brigade units, which require only communications at-the-halt capability.

The Joint Requirements Oversight Council approved WIN-T Capability Development Document will be used as the foundational requirement document for the restructured WIN-T programme and its increments. The JROC validated the former JNN programme Annexure of the Bridge to Future Networks CPD, which will provide the capabilities for WIN-T Increment 1a. The Army will develop a CPD for Increment 1b and any additional increments of the restructured WIN-T program. The PM will establish a formal agreement with the FCS program office to establish final performance requirements by WIN-T Increment 3

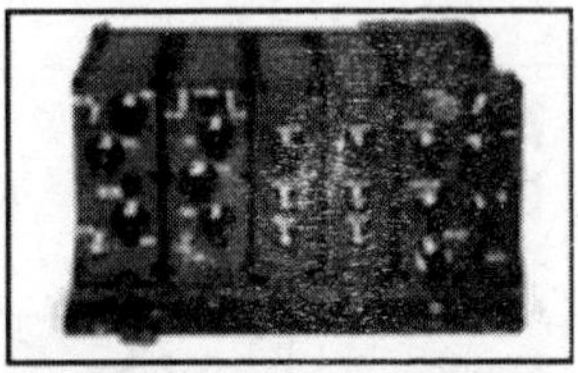

Preliminary Design Review that includes Size, Weight and Power-Cooling (SWaP-C) specifications for CIs to be provided to FCS, based on balanced trade. Increment 1 of the restructured WIN-T programme is post-MS C and is authorized the procurement of Low Rate Initial Production units to meet operational requirements of the Army. Increment 2 is now a post-MS B procurement. Increment 3 is post- MS B, but the APB will be broken out from the existing APB. WIN-T PM has awarded the Increment 3 SDD Phase 3 contract and to begin work on Increment 2.

## Joint Tactical Radio System (JTRS)

Joint Tactical Radio System is a family (ground, airborne, and maritime domains) of common software-defined radios that provide seamless network connectivity throughout the battlefield in support of Joint Vision 2020 objectives. JTRS is the military's affordable, mobile, high-capacity, lightweight, multi-band radio system providing simultaneous voice, data and video communications. JTRS will be a key component of the Tactical Internet and GIG using a family of network waveform applications. The Army is the executive agent for the JTRS programme requirements, and the Navy is the executive agent for JTRS acquisition. The Army is responsible for two (Ground Mobile Radio (GMR) and Handheld, Manpack, Small Form Fit (HMS) of the four primary product lines (GMR, JEM, HMS, and AMF). GMR is developing the ground vehicular radio, AMF is developing an airborne radio for Army rotary wing aviation platforms, and HMS

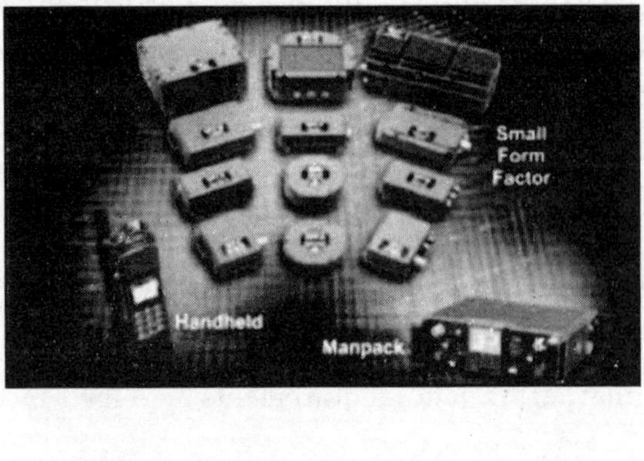

is developing the handheld, manpack and small form fit radios. In order to support the Spin-out of FCS capabilities into the Current Force that begins in 2010, an initial "slice" of the GMR capabilities will be included in the early Spin-out fielding. As the JTRS programme continues through its development milestones, the capability within the FCS network will be enhanced.

### Programme Status

The JTRS Joint Programme Executive Office has restructured its programme to ensure the GMR, HMS and AMF product managers deliver Increment 1 capability. Both GMR and HMS are in the SDD phase. Increment 1 Low Rate Initial Production (LRIP) for GMR is anticipated to begin in 2QFY11 and LRIP for the various HMS products ranges from 4QFY10 to 2QFY11. AMF is in the Pre-SDD phase and LRIP for the rotary wing radio is projected to begin in 4QFY11.

### Joint Network Management Systems (JNMS)

Joint Network Management Systems provides a common, automated tool for network planning and management that will support the Combatant Commanders and their deployments. It consists of primarily commercial off-the-shelf software modules/ capabilities to accomplish its mission. JNMS includes the following capabilities:

- High level planning, to include creation/ editing and/or loading of data bases; definition of network sites and units; assignment of responsibilities and schedules; and generation and distribution of planning data (Commander's Evaluation Request, Annexure K to the Operations Plan, Joint Communications-Electronics Operating Instruction, Communications Service Requests.
- Detailed planning and engineering, activation and modification, to include planning and engineering for circuit switches, Asynchronous Transfer Mode, Defence Message System, commercial and military satellite communications systems, data networks, message switches, transmission systems, and single channel networks, generation and distribution of planning and engineering data, and link and network activation and gateways between networks.

- Monitoring, to include collection of data from equipment and networks, data analysis, display, data base updates and generation and distribution of reports.
- Control and reconfiguration, to include network device configuration, processing of incoming data, generation and evaluation of alternative responses and implementation of appropriate responses.
- Spectrum planning and management, to include information management, spectrum engineering; allotment/assignment of frequencies, deconfliction, electromagnetic compatibility and electromagnetic interference analysis.
- Security, to include formulating network security requirements, physical security, user security, information assurance and Communications Security/Electronic Protection.

## Programme Status

JNMS ORD Rev 3 Approved 12 Jun 06. Fielding ongoing for–11 full JNMS systems (planning & JNN based management/Help Desk) with 27 additional JNMS Network Planning Systems to be fielding to Signal Brigades, Corps, Echelons Above Corps Signal and SOF Commands.

## Cryptographic Modernization Programme

Cryptographic security is an integral part of LandWarNet, the Army's portion of the GIG. It is necessary to provide the high assurance and robust technology required to protect and secure our National Security Information and National Security Systems from Nation States intent on gaining access to critical command and control systems. Cryptographic

Modernization is a DoD initiative. The National Security Agency and Services have a collaborative partnership that plans for the incremental replacement of an aging cryptographic equipment inventory that is rapidly approaching functional obsolescence. The current inventory of cryptographic devices is not net-centric (GIG Compliant), no longer in production and whose components are no longer logistically or economically supportable. Cryptographic Modernization provides highly assured, technologically advanced, robust cryptographic solutions that are adaptive to evolving network architectures. The improved capabilities may be in the form of improved algorithms, expanded functionality, or the integration of new and emerging technologies. Cryptographic Modernization is inextricably linked to NSA's migration from Electronic Key Management Systems to Key Management Infrastructure which will facilitate over the network keying and downloadable and reprogrammable algorithms. The overarching efforts of CryptoMod are to provide cryptographic solutions that support the following tenants:

- Programmable/Downloadable Algorithms
- Embeddable Solutions (Whenever Possible)
- Scalable Components (Software Upgradeable)
- EKMS/KMI Compliant (Over-the-Network Keying)
- Network-Ready (Network Awareness, Plug and Play)
- Joint Interoperability

**Programme Status**

Currently the programme is procuring and fielding the latest, available technologically advanced network security devices to support warfighter demands for more bandwidth capable solutions to support information sharing, video and the extension of SIPRnet connectivity down to battalion and company levels. Devices such as the KIV-7M/KIV-19Ms, the INEs, the voice over IP secure phone and KSV-21 STE card will be integrated into the Current Force via technology refresh initiatives. The KSV 21 is an NSA directed replacement initiatives for the KOV 14 STE card currently in used. The KIV-7M is a converged technology solution that combines the dual functionality of the link encryptor family and a trunk encryptor family in the same form factor. The KIV 7M will be integrated into the Joint Network Node (JNN), HUB sites (collocated with Teleport reach back), the Single Shelter Switch and other new and modernizing Army programmes beginning in FY08. The KMI Capabilities Increment (CI) 2 contract was awarded on 31 July 2007. The newer INEs incorporate High Assurance Internet Protocol Interoperability Standards (HAIPIS) scalability and both Suite A and B algorithms. The suite B solutions support allied and coalition interoperability. The secure IP phones will support the migration to everything over IP.

# Appendix 8: Battlespace Awareness Modernization

## Discussion of Core Battlespace Awareness Material Programmes

### *Space Support Enhancement Toolset (SSET)*

The Space Support Enhancement Toolset is a COTS/ GOTS prototype capability supporting Army Space Support Teams and Space Support Elements in current theater of operations. It provides ARSST and SSE specialized tools and software to maintain situational awareness of all space assets, monitor satellite status, and produce specialized products from space-based assets, as well as providing the capability to maintain continuous communications with National and Joint space organizations in CONUS. SSET is a mission essential item of equipment for both ARSST, augmenting corps, and JTF headquarters and other Services and Joint, Interagency and Multinational headquarters as military and strategic situations call for; and SSE, organic to modular division, corps,and select Army headquarters. It provides capabilities needed by ARSSTs and SSEs to conduct space operations planning, integration and coordination and the production of enhanced space products.

Originally SSET was developed through the efforts of the Space and Missile Defence Battle Lab. The SSET has been combat-tested in OEF and OIF, where spacebased products provided by SSET-equipped teams provided enhance C2 and situational awareness for land force commanders. The complete SSET consists of a communications suite, four workstations and ancillary equipment housed in a V5 rigid-walled shelter, mounted on an M1113 HMMWV. Modular Force designs incorporate a four-person SSE at division level, a five-person SSE at corps level and a six-person SSE at army level, each equipped with an appropriate version of SSET.

### Programme Status

SSET is an emerging requirement funded in fiscal years 2008-13 program funding. The Army Acquisition Executive assigned

SSET system lifecycle management responsibilities to the Programme Executive Office Intelligence, Electronic Warfare and Sensors (PEO-IEWS). Consequently, the PEOIEWS directed that responsible programme offices and the TRADOC Capabilities Manager to: determine ARSST and SSE capability, functionality and communications requirements to support OIF/OEF; whether those requirements can only be provided by Space Operations System boxes; the SSET capability current fielded in OIF and any shortfalls; identify any unique SSET capabilities that could be incorporated into the Distributed Common Ground System–Army CDD; and assess the cost and schedule impacts to incorporate these unique SSET capabilities into the DCGS-A programme.

### Distributed Common Ground System-Army (DCGS-A)

Distributed Common Ground System-Army is the Army's contribution to the DoD DCGS programme. Its core functions are ISR integration, fusion of sensor information and direction and distribution of sensor information. DCGS-A will draw information from a wide variety of automated and manual sources, space platforms, unattended air and ground vehicles, existing and new ISR capabilities and an assortment of databases. The system enhances the capabilities of Current and Future Force commanders to execute Battle Command, synchronize fires and effects, rapidly shift battle focus, achieve situational awareness and protect the force. It does so by providing tactical and operational commanders access to advanced ISR capabilities and allows them to synchronize ISR collection, exploitation, processing and distribution of information, while operating in a multi-level security network. DCGS-A provides access to National, theater and Joint Services intelligence databases. DCGS-A is a complementary system to FCS and will affect all levels of the Army by providing fixed systems at theater MI brigades, mobile systems at battalion to Army Service Component command levels, and embedded software to provide ISR data and access to ISR systems to Soldiers operating non-ISR, non-intelligence systems.

### Programme Status

The Army is leveraging its successful integration of Joint Intelligence Operations Capability-Iraq into the DCGS-A programme to accelerate the introduction of advanced DCGS-A capabilities to the Current Force. The Multi-National Corps-Iraq has requested that Army employ DCGS-A (V)3 software intheater. In response, in 2QFY08, Army will begin upgrading DCGS-A Theater Provided Equipment in Iraq with DCGS-A(V)3. Simultaneously, Army will begin increasing the capability of the All Source Analysis System systems in next deploying OIF and OEF units with DCGS-A(V)3 software. By the end of FY10, Army intends to have a DCGS-A base capability in all Active, National Guard, and Army Reserve units. Advanced software, DCGS-A Software Baseline 1.0 will undergo an operational evaluation in 2QFY09 with the Army's Software Block 2+. The Army will incorporate DSB 1.0 into existing Programme of Record systems, ASAS, Tactical Exploitation System-Forward, Common Ground System and Digital Topographic Support System to "Spin-out" advanced DCGS-A capabilities to the Current Force in FY10. DCGS-A will undergo a Limited Users Test in 2QFY10 with DSB 2.0 and fully up-armored platforms. This will lead to a Low Rate Initial procurement decision in 4QFY10 and an Initial Operational Test and Evaluation in 3QFY12. Army anticipates beginning Full Rate Production in FY13. Army intends to continue DCGS-A development, primarily software development, through the 10-15 POM. These efforts will meet objective requirements and keep

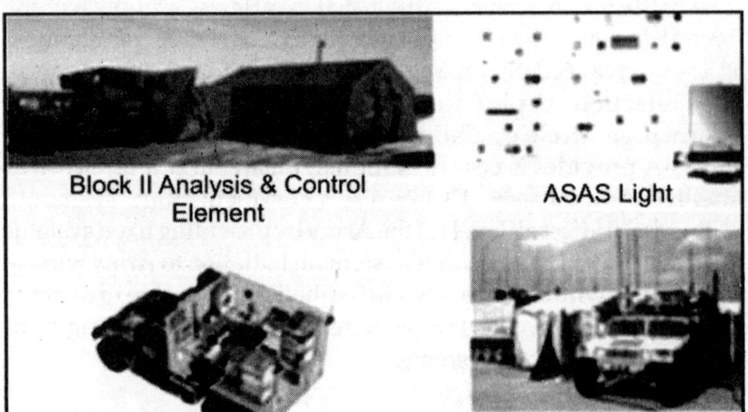

DCGS-A relevant as advanced sensors and other advanced technologies are introduced through the next decade.

### All Source Analysis System (ASAS)

The All Source Analysis System is the Army's primary intelligence fusion programme. ASAS automates the planning and management of intelligence, counterintelligence and electronic warfare operations; intelligence collection management; the processing and analysis of intelligence and combat information; and the dissemination of intelligence and combat information products to tactical and operational commanders.

ASAS provides an automated interface to the Army Battle Command System and the Joint Global Command and Control System. These interfaces provide battlefield commanders with enhanced situational awareness and timely intelligence on enemy force deployments, capabilities and potential courses of action, as part of the COP. In turn, the Army intelligence community receives current information on blue force locations, activities and plans.

An ASAS system is authorized in all combat and combat support units and designated combat service support units at all Army echelons from battalion to field Army. Because of its ubiquitous presence and the fact that substantial ASAS software capabilities were incorporated into DCGS-A(V)3, Army decided to upgrade the ASAS Family of Systems with DCGSA( V)3 software to accelerate the introduction of DCGS-A capabilities into the Current Force. The initial DCGS-A Enabled ASAS systems were fielded in 4QFY07 and Army intends to equip all units deploying in FY08 with DCGS-A Enabled ASAS. By the end of FY10, all authorized Active, National Guard and Army Reserve units will be equipped with DCGS-A Enabled ASAS systems. This will provide the Current Force a base DCGS-A capability that will be the foundation of transforming the Intelligence, Surveillance and Reconnaissance capabilities of the Current Force into Future Force capabilities.

### Programme Status

ASAS Block II is in FRP. In Oct 07, the Project Director for Intelligence Fusion in the ASAS program office came under the operational control of PM DCGSA. All ASAS systems produced in FY08 and FY09 will meet DCGS-A specifications and be fielded as integral components of the Army's initial DCGSA capability. The programme to upgrade currently fielded ASAS equipment to this configuration began in1QFY08. By end of FY09, ASAS will be totally merged into the DCGS-A programme and will cease to exist as a separate entity.

## Grenadier Brat (GB) and Mini-transmitter (MTX) Blue Force Tracking (BFT) Systems and Supporting Architecture

GB and the MTX are two separate and distinct current DoD BFT systems that leverage and take advantage of the existing National space infrastructure National Technical Means. These devices give commanders the ability to track and receive position location information of dismounted teams and vehicles equipped with the devices. The systems are monitored and disseminated by the Mission Management Center, which supports GB/MTX use of the existing COBRA architecture by coordinating with National system managers and warfighting units to help collect, process and disseminate operational BFT data. These BFT systems, the MMC and the NTM architecture give operational-level commanders a COP which substantially increases their situational awareness.

### Programme Status

GB was acquired as a Warfighter Rapid Acquisition Programme and currently 500 systems are fielded with U.S. Army Special Operations Command, U.S. Central Command and U.S. Army South. No further systems will be procured and the programme will be de-fielded by first quarter, FY08 due to architecture updates. There are approximately 5,500 MTX systems produced and fielded to all services, USSOCOM components and other Government agencies that have a specialized requirement for secure/LPI/LPD BFT support and will continue to be available as a lightweight man portable BFT device.

## Aerial Common Sensor (ACS)

Aerial Common Sensor is an Airborne Reconnaissance, Surveillance and Target Acquisition/Intelligence, Surveillance, and Reconnaissance capability directly supporting Battlespace Awareness for tactical commanders. Specifically, ACS will provide real-time, persistent, precision, networked, wide-area, high capacity, multi-sensor, intelligence collection capability throughout the Joint operating environment. ACS will quickly produce actionable intelligence that provides commanders and Soldiers critical shared situational understanding delivered with the speed, accuracy, and timeliness necessary to conduct successful and when necessary, lethal Joint operations. ACS will support focused Intelligence Preparation of the Battlespace, Indications and Warnings, precision targeting, battle damage assessment, situational development, Battle Command and Force Protection. Each of these will be synchronized with operations in order to develop and maintain situational awareness and reduce clutter in the manoeuvre environment. ACS will be a manned, high performance fixed-wing aircraft capable of rapid worldwide deployment carrying multiple sensor payloads and intelligence processing, appropriate air/ground/satellite data links and air crew. The RSTA/ISR payload will consist of a suite of modular, scaleable signal intelligence and imagery intelligence sensors and processors that can operate alone or simultaneously in combination with each other.

The intelligence processing suite onboard ACS and in the ground station, provided by the Distributed Common Ground System-Army, will integrate the products from all ACS Sensor payloads as well as the sensor feeds from other Joint force sensors, including manned/unmanned teaming with Army Unmanned Aircraft Systems, to provide a correlated near-realtime picture of the tactical operational environment with the greatest degree of granularity possible. Onboard communications will consist of a robust set of line-of-sight and satellite communications datalinks that will enable direct linkage to Brigade Combat Teams, Manned-Unmanned teaming with Army UAS, wideband/worldwide connectivity to DCGS-A, the Global Information Grid, and interoperability with other Army, Joint and National RSTA/ISR assets. ACS will be a critical and integral component of the Future Force.

### Programme Status

The ACS Programme is in pre-Milestone B status. The Army is currently on track for a MS B decision during 2QFY09 and System Development and Demonstration contract award in 3QFY09.

## Tactical Exploitation System (TES)

The Tactical Exploitation System Family of Systems is the Army's Tactical Exploitation of National Capabilities system that tasks directly, receives through direct downlinks or relays, processes, exploits and disseminates electronic intelligence, communications intelligence externals, Imagery and MTI data from satellites, USAF (U-2, Global Hawk, Predator & JSTARS), Navy (P-3, Maritime Global Hawk & SHARP) aircraft/ sensors and from direct downlinks and other fixed and mobile ground stations. TES is embedded in the corps and division force structures is providing vital space-based and airborne imagery, signals intelligence, blue force tracking and communications reach to and from deployed units for OIF. The TES family of systems is a key part of the emerging DCGS architecture with TES variants in Army, USN, USMC, limited USAF units and selected National and Joint agencies/ headquarters. TES software and middleware are the basis for DCGS-A fixed systems.

The TES programme combines the intelligence functions of four previously stovepiped ISR collection systems into an integrated downsized, open, scalable, modular and network-centric architecture with all elements fully transportable by C-130 aircraft. TES generates timely information, intelligence, and precision targeting data. TES also is capable of limited MASINT processing and analysis. TES receives space-based blue force tracking data and provides it to the GCCS–Army. TES has a direct digital/ network interface with the AFATDS, Automated Deep Operations Coordination System and the Joint Intelligence Operations capability in Iraq/ Afghanistan. TES performs preprocessor, processor, analytical functions for the ASAS, Common Ground Station, JIOC-I/A and Digital Topographic Support System.

## Programme Status

TES-Main and TES-Forward systems have been fielded to III, V, XVIII Airborne corps and 513th MI Brigade. As the Army transforms to its new structure, the TES-Main will support the theater as a component of the Theater Intelligence Brigade and the TES-Forward will be organic in both the Corps and selected TIBs. The first TES Main moved to a TIB from XVIII Airborne Corps in FY06 as the corps started its transformation to a Modular Configuration. Division-TES have been fielded to all Active divisions. The TES-Forward (minus) was fielded to the 501st MI Brigade and to I Corps in FY06. Thirteen of 21 TES-Lite systems were fielded to I Corps, SOF units, Korea, and selected TIBs in FY06. An additional eight will be fielded to XVIII Airborne and III Corps, SOF units and selected ARNG units on a rotating bases to support OIF/OEF deployments in FY07.

The JIOC I has been fielded to Multinational Forces- Iraq command center. The TES Remote Interface System that provides expanded direct database access between TES/DTES and ASAS has been fielded to XVIII Airborne Corps, along with III Corps, V Corps, 4th ID and as stay-behind equipment in support of Multinational Corps-Iraq. A number of TES systems continue to be deployed in OEF and OIF and judged in after-action reviews as being very supportive of high OPTEMPO, ISR, and dynamic targeting demands. TES systems have remained the primary source of theater and National near real-time imagery and SIGINT data for MNC-I and divisions. TES systems will be in the force structure until the objective DCGS-A system is fully fielded, sometime after 2012. Significant TES components will be re-designated as DCGS-A components over the next three to four years.

## Trojan Special Purpose Integrated Remote Intelligence Terminal (SPIRIT)

Trojan SPIRIT provides assured Top Secret/ Special Compartmented Information satellite communications to deployed warfighters from brigade to EAC. It provides critical intelligence reach to strategic, operational and tactical Army and Joint formations. Trojan SPIRIT was born as a quick-reaction capability during Operations Desert Shield/Storm, as commanders needed a way to receive time-sensitive TS and Secret imagery and intelligence data at high data rates. From those beginnings, the system became a programme of record in 1993, designated the Trojan SPIRIT II, with initial fieldings to separate brigade/ACR, division, corps, and EAC units. Trojan SPIRIT II fielding ended in 1998, but the advent of the Stryker brigade brought the system back to life with a new variant, the Trojan SPIRIT Lightweight Integrated Telecommunications Equipment. There are three versions of the Trojan SPIRIT LITE: a transit case version, in use by SOF, and HMMWV-mounted wheeled versions used at the BCT through EAC levels. All feature a 2.4 meter satellite dish that provides up to T-1 (1.544 mbps) bandwidth throughput using the C or Ku frequency bands. Each Stryker brigade receives two V2 and one V3 Trojan SPIRIT LITE. Under the Modular Force design, each BCT receives one V3 system, a significant increase in Trojan SPIRIT density across the force. The Modular Divisional Headquarters retains the two Trojan SPIRIT II systems formerly in the division MI battalion, with fielding of a third system in FY08-10 to provide TS/SCI bandwidth for the Tactical Command Post. As part of Grow the Army, each Battlefield Surveillance Brigade Headquarters will also receive a Trojan SPIRIT LITE V3.

### Programme Status

Trojan SPIRIT is an interim solution for assured TS/SCI satellite communications until the fielding of WIN-T. The program is beyond Milestone III. LITE V2 production ceased after fielding of Stryker Brigade 7. LITE V3 and V1 production and fielding will continue through FY12 as the Army resources all Modular Force brigades and ARNG division headquarters with the system and as Army Special Forces Groups increase in size.

### Prophet

Prophet provides an all-weather, 24/7 near-real-time view of the BCT/ACR/SBCT/BfSB AOR through the use of SIGINT sensors, to include the capability to detect, identify and electronically attack selected enemy emitters. It is the BCT Commander's only organic, ground SIGINT capability allowing him to visually depict and understand his Battlespace, now and in the future. The Prophet programme has migrated from a block acquisition strategy to a spiral acquisition strategy. Prophet

Electronic Attack Spiral 1 provides a modern EA capability that assists the Brigade and Division Commander in overwhelming the enemy, shaping the Battlespace, and protecting friendly operations. Prophet Electronic Support Spiral 1 provides the brigade with the improved ISR capabilities across a broader range of missions. The spiral enhancements capitalize on Commercial off-the- Shelf/Government off-the-Shelf solutions and Technology Insertion capabilities. Prophet can operate on-the-move, mounted on a HMMWV, or stationary in a mounted or dismounted configuration.

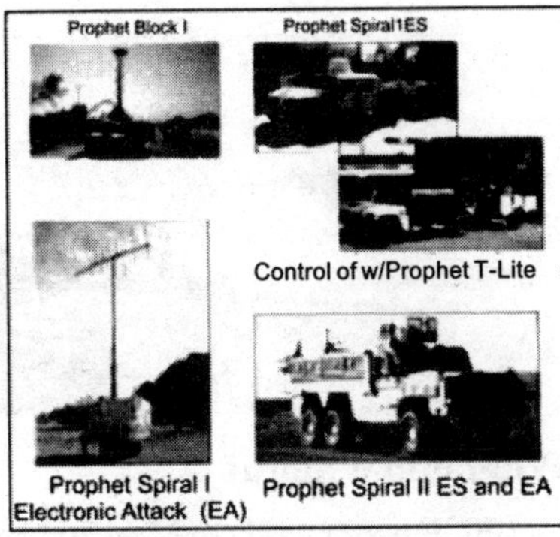


**Programme Status**

The Prophet ES Spiral 1 system began fielding in FY08. The Prophet EA Spiral 1 Initial Operational Test and Evaluation was conducted in 4QFY08 with fielding beginning in FY09.

**Tactical Unmanned Aircraft Vehicle (TUAV) Shadow 200**

The RQ-7A Shadow 200 TUAV provides the manoeuvre commander with a near real-time, highly accurate, sustainable capability for over-the-horizon RSTA/ISR and BDA. Each Shadow 200 TUAV system consists of four Shadow 200 aircraft, two HMMWV mounted GCS, one portable GCS and four remote video terminals that can provide near real-time video to commanders on the ground. The Shadow 200 TUAV has an onboard electro-optical/IR sensor payload. Future planned improvements include a Laser Designator, Tactical Common Data Link for secure, jam-resistant data forwarding, and an upgrade of the engine to gain reliability improvements. The threshold range is 50 kilometers with an objective range of 200 kilometers and an on-station endurance of four hours. The threshold payload is 60 pounds with an objective capacity of 100 pounds. OPTEMPO requires a threshold of 12 hours per 24-hour period and an objective of 18 hours per 24-hour period.

**Programme Status**

FUE was 1/4 ID in May 2002 and IOC was achieved in October 2002. The TUAV programme was revalidated by JROC in 2004. Production and fielding continues to meet the HQDA approved procurement objective of 115 systems.

## Counterintelligence Human Intelligence Automated Reporting and Collection System (CHARCS)

During January 2007 the PEO IEW&S chartered a Counterintelligence Human Intelligence Automated Reporting and Collection Systems Product Director to manage the future development process for Human Intelligence team member, Counterintelligence investigator, interrogation collection and reporting systems and tools. The PD CHARCS provides focused development support for the collection and reporting elements of the CI and HUMINT architecture. Specifically, the PD CHARCS has development responsibilities for the collection and reporting components; source and mission management; DOCEX and language translation; biometrics; interrogation management tools, media forensics and counter human deception detection devices and was the initial developer of the Tactical HUMINT Team Kitbag that is in wide use throughout OIF and OEF. Additionally, CHARCS systems support both Army Special Operations Command and INSCOM with CHARCS system variants tailored for their specific mission requirements. Due to an evolving threat, new systems and upgrades are required to maintain relevancy. The latest increment is referred to as CREW 2.1.

Two systems, the AN/PYQ-8 Individual Tactical Reporting Tool and AN/PYQ-3 CI/HUMINT Automated Tool Set are the centerpieces of CHARCS collection and reporting capability and have been fielded to CI and HUMINT intelligence units worldwide. CREW production has been completed. Production of CREW 2.1 is ongoing and theater fielding began in March 2008.

## Programme Status

CHARCS Increment 1 is Type Classified Standard and has Full Material Release. Components are currently being fielded to the Reserve Component and to deploying units. Full fielding is expected in 2011. The CHARCS Increment 2 Capability Development Document, which is presently in Army staffing, provides the requirements foundation for the next generation of collection and reporting systems and tools. CHARCS is the next evolution for CI and HUMINT collection and reporting addressing the lessons learned from the over 2,000 ITRT and CHATS fielded through FY06 to Army units in support of GWOT. New software and hardware components being designed under CHARCS FY07 through FY10 will aggressively leverage the open architecture framework defined by DCGS-A and provide flexible, modularized human intelligence collection and reporting solutions. Enhancements will provide smaller, lighter and mobile modularized collection and reporting tools with simplified software baselines and improved communications capability.

## Sequoyah Foreign Language Translation System

Military, contract and host nation linguists provide a critical capability that is unavailable in sufficient numbers to satisfy the language translation needs of the Services, Joint and National agencies. The Sequoyah Foreign Language Translation System addresses this capability gap by enabling nonlinguists with two-way automated speech and text cross-lingual communication capabilities on demand. S-FLTS will provide commanders an organic capability to rapidly perform two-way speech and text cross-lingual operations at all echelons and in all environments where linguist support is minimal or unavailable. S-FLTS interoperable design will enable it to be embedded on diverse platforms throughout the Joint community which includes, but is not limited to, the BCS, GSS, FCS and the DCGS. S-FLTS capabilities will be available via a browser, and as downloadable modules for systems that are not always linked to the network.

**Programme Status**

The Army has been designated as the lead Service for S-FLTS with JROC interest designation. Joint Forces Command, in response to an Urgent Need Statements provided by the Multi-National Security Transition Command-Iraq, 25th Infantry Division, USCENTCOM, USPACOM and USSOCOM is providing the initial speech to speech capability by leveraging DARPA's tactical translation programme. DARPA's Global Autonomous Language Exploitation programme is being leveraged to provide the Text to Text capabilities. SFLTS Capability Development Document has been approved by the Army Requirements Oversight Council and funding programmed in FY09-13. FY08 funding is being reprogrammed to S-FLTS to initiate documentation preparation to support a 1QFY09 Milestone B Review.

**Counter Radio Controlled Improvised Explosive Device Electronic Warfare Increment 2 (CREW-2)**

The original Counter Radio Controlled Improvised Explosive Device Electronic Warfare Increment 2 was a response to Operational Needs Statements for a capability to prevent and defeat Radio Controlled Improvised Explosive Device detonation ambushes that are a pervasive threat throughout Operations Iraqi Freedom and Enduring Freedom theaters of operation. CREW is a family of radio frequency jammers that target cell phones, beepers, garage door openers and like systems. It provides frequency coverage against many known RCIED threats, increased protection range, ease of programmability, reduced size/weight and power required, and a built-in capacity for future growth, CREW-2 is providing significant support to forces who must deal with counterinsurgents.

**Programme Status**

CREW transitioned to a Programme of Record. CREW-2 CPD was AROC/JROC approved on 12 March 2007.

**Biometrics Automated Toolset (BAT)**

Biometrics Automated Toolset is a multi-modal biometric collection system originally designed for the Counterintelligence/

Human Intelligence community to collect, store, match and share Red Force and grey Force biometric data in current theaters of operation. Red Force biometric and identity information is a critical type of associated intelligence data used to identify detainees, enemy combatants, enemy prisoners of war, or persons of interest. Grey Force biometric and identity information is essential because it facilitates the vetting of locally employed persons on U. S. Military bases across the world and can be used to control access to those bases. BAT provides biometric and identity identification, tracking, dissemination and situational awareness capability which can enhance the CI/HUMINT, Military Police and Military/ Civilian Intelligence community's ability to monitor, assess, and react to the unique threat environments that are being encountered throughout the world, now and in the future.

**Programme Status**

Initially an Advanced Concept Technology Demonstration, BAT was approved for Programme of Record status in Nov 2006. The BAT CPD is under review by TRADOC. Hundreds of BAT systems have been issued to deployed units to support current operations.

# Appendix 9: Core Engineer Material Programmes

## Discussion of Core Battlespace Awareness Material Programmes

### *Family of Dozers*

The Army is replacing its 30 year old D7 dozer fleet with a new model that will have the ability to add on armor as required, and be joystick controlled. A new D5 dozer will be placed in the Engineer Support Companies which will give them more capability to perform their mission.

### Programme Status

Programme strategy is to procure all Dozers by FY15. Capability Production Document approved in FY06.

### Family of Loaders

The new procurement of Skid Steer loaders, Backhoe loaders and type I HMEEs are embedded into the SBCT, IBCT, HBCT and will be an added capability to these units. This gives the Army the capability to repair and expand operating capacities of Ports of Embarkation, Intermediate Staging Bases/Forward Operating Bases, Ports of Debarkation, entry points and opening of temporary lines of communication.

### Programme Status

Procurement began in FY08. Capability Production Document was approved in FY06.

### Family of Graders

The Army is replacing its 25 year-old fleet of Graders with a new model that will be capable of adding on armor as required. The Heavy Road Grader is a diesel engine, pneumatic tired, 6x4

front steer with articulated frame steer type. The Grader provides capability for grading, shaping, bank sloping, ditching, scarifying and general construction and maintenance of roads/airfields and other horizontal construction projects.

## Programme Status

Begin fielding graders FY10, planned completion of fielding FY15. All CPDs are approved.

## Family of Scrapers

The Army is upgrading its scraper fleet which will make them add on armor capable. The scraper is a self-propelled open bowl, pneumatic, two-axle, single diesel engine driven, articulated frame steer vehicle. Its capacity is 14 cubic yards assisted by a pusher tractor during loading, but can self-load. The scraper provides a self-loading, hauling and dumping capability to perform efficient earthmoving tasks in support of earthmoving projects. It can excavate 56-72 cubic yards per lift.

## Programme Status

All CPDs are approved and fielding of the loader will be completed by FY10.

## Improved Ribbon Bridge (IRB)

The Improved Ribbon Bridge, fielded to multirole bridge companies, provides a dependable roadway or raft capable of crossing assault vehicles or tactical vehicles over non-fordable wet gaps. This system is capable of a military load classification of 100 wheeled and MLC 80 tracked. The bridge sections are transported by Common Bridge Transporters (CBT), which are modified HEMTT LHS providing enhanced, multipurpose transportation capabilities. Each MRBC will be capable of emplacing 210 meters of bridging. The system is external airlift transportable by CH-47 and CH-53 helicopters. The bridge bays are air transportable, partially disassembled, in C- 130s. The

IRB has enhanced capabilities of operation in swifter water speeds up to 10.3 feet per second and over 2.1 meter banks. It provides a 4.5 meterwide roadway, improved hydrostatic capabilities and various other design improvements.

**Programme Status**

This multi-year contract started in FY00, will field 23 MRBCs with the IRB. Eleven units are fielded to date, with the remaining units to be fielded by FY11.

**Dry Support Bridge (DSB)**

Dry Support Bridge is a modular bridge assigned to the MRBC that can span a 40 meter gap and can be emplaced in 90 minutes by eight Soldiers. One bridge set provides either a 40 meter or two 20 meter bridges. The bridge will cross MLC 96W/70T traffic and will allow crossing of a heavy-equipment transporter carrying a combat-loaded M1 tank. DSB consists of a launcher permanently mounted on a Palletized load System (PLS), three CBTs and four PLS trailers that carry the modular components as palletized loads. A bridge set consists of six M1077 flat-rack loads of bridge components, one M1077 flat-rack load of launch beams and a launcher vehicle. To transport and launch one complete DSB system requires the launcher, three CBTs and four PLS trailers.

**Programme Status**

A multi-year production APO of 92 systems. Fielding initiated FY03 with final fielding programmed to be completed in FY11.

## Rapidly Emplaced Bridge System (REBS)

REBS is a wheeled, vehicle-launched, bridge system providing a four-meter roadway width, MLC 30 tracked (T) and wheeled (W) normal and MLC 40(T) (W) gap crossing capability up to 13 meters. Transported on a CBT, each SBCT will have four REBS. This system is transportable by C-130 aircraft. The assembled bridge is externally slinglift- transportable by CH-47 and CH-53 helicopters. Two Soldiers can deploy the REBS in the daytime, within 10 minutes, with little or no site preparation.

### Programme Status.

7 SBCTS was fielded in FY07.

## Assured Mobility Capabilities

The Engineer Future Force will be organized, manned, equipped and trained to be more strategically responsive, deployable, agile, versatile, lethal, survivable and sustainable across the full spectrum of military operations. Future Engineer Force structure will be comprised of modular, scalable, and flexible organizations for prompt and sustained land operations capable of quickly transitioning between changes in task, purpose and directions.

Assured mobility capabilities support force application by manoeuvre forces as well as focused logistics by sustainment forces. Current operations in OEF and OIF highlight the enduring importance of systems that provide ground forces the capability of detecting, defeating and emplacing minefields and other obstacle effects, allowing unparalleled freedom of manoeuvre and force sustainment. This capability is critical to gaining the positional advantage needed to retain the initiative and enhance Joint precision fires as well as ensuring sustainment force movement remains effective across the distributed battlefield environment.

## Ground Stand-off Minefield Detection System (GSTAMIDS)

Ground Stand-off Minefield Detection System is a time-phased developmental programme designed to provide the warfighter a capability to execute on-route countermine missions for the FCS.

GSTAMIDS will be employed on an overpass-capable countermine Multifunctional Utility/Logistics and Equipment Vehicle (MULE) variant UGV. The system will employ future improvements that will automatically detect, mark and neutralize all metallic and nonmetallic Anti-Tank mines.

**Programme Status**

GSTAMIDS is currently in SDD and preparing for fourth quarter, FY08 Preliminary Design Review. GSTAMIDS is planning for a Milestone C and production in FY12.

**Airborne Surveillance, Target Acquisition, and Minefield Detection System (ASTAMIDS)**

Airborne Surveillance, Target Acquisition, and Minefield Detection System is an FCS Tier 1 Complementary Programme. ASTAMIDS is an FCS Class IV Fire Scout UAV sensor payload that provides near-real time detection of surface and recently buried minefields and obstacles in day and night conditions. Minefield and Obstacle information is used to update the COP/SA of the unit. ASTAMIDS also performs an FCS BCT Class IV Fire Scout UAV RSTA/ISR and Laser Designation mission and function in addition to its countermine mission.

**Programme Status**

ASTAMIDS is in the SDD phase of acquisition. The programme completed its Preliminary Design Review during April-May 2006. Contractor Functional and Qualification Testing is planned throughout FY07. An MS C/LRIP decision is planned during second quarter, FY09.

**Route Clearance Vehicles**

Route Clearance Vehicles consist of a family of mine-protected vehicles employed by Combat Engineers in route clearance operations. The three vehicles include the Buffalo Mine Protected Clearance Vehicle (MPCV), the Interim Vehicle Mounted Mine

Detector (IVMMD), and the Medium Mine Protected Vehicle (MMPV). The systems are employed within a route clearance team with 1-2 MMPVs serving as a command and control vehicle and providing local security to the team. The IVMMD is then employed to detect the mine or IED hazards so that the MPCV can investigate suspicious items with its articulated arm. All three vehicles provide the crew protection from explosive blasts and small-arms fire, and each is designed for rapid repair after an explosive incident. All three vehicles are NDIs that have proven effective in war time operations.

**Programme Status.**

The Route Clearance Vehicles have been fielded in support of OEF and OIF. The MPCV and MMPV have AROC approved CPD and the IVMMD CPD is pending approval. MS C is expected in FY07 pending funding and completion of full material release actions.

# Appendix 10: Tactical Wheeled Vehicles Modernization

## Discussion of Core Tactical Wheeled Vehicles Material Programmes

### *Family of Medium Tactical Vehicles (FMTV)*

The Family of Medium Tactical Vehicles is built around a common chassis and drive train, featuring over 80 percent commonality of parts and components between models and weight classes. Operating worldwide in all weather and terrain conditions, the FMTV provides unit mobility, re-supply and transportation at all organizational levels. It serves as the weapon systems platform for HIMARS and the support vehicle for Patriot. FMTV enhances crew survivability through use of hardened cabs, three-point seat belts, central tire inflation and machine gun ring-mount capability. It provides enhanced tactical mobility and is strategically deployable in C-5, C-17 and C- 130 aircraft. FMTV reduces the Army's logistics footprint by providing commonality of parts and components, reducing mainte-nance downtime, and lowering operation and support costs that older trucks require.

### Programme Status

FMTV is in full production with over 28,000 trucks and 6,100 trailers fielded to date. A competitive requirements contract will be awarded starting in FY09. The new contract will include the 10-ton Dump Truck. The FMTV-Load Handling System is currently being fielded, initially to medical units. The Expansible Van started fielding to all units in early FY08. Current fielding supports modular transformation and modernization of infantry, heavy, Stryker, sustainment and fires brigade teams.

## High-Mobility Multipurpose Wheeled Vehicle (HMMWV)

High Mobility Multipurpose Wheeled Vehicle is a light, highly mobile, diesel-powered, four-wheeldrive vehicle with common chassis. Using common components and kits, it can be configured as a troop, armament, TOW, shelter carrier or ambulance. It is a multi-Service programme that also provides vehicles that satisfy USMC, USN, USAF and foreign military sales requirements. When armor is added, the M1151A1 has up-armored HMMWV-like protection with a greater payload and incorporates operational lessons learned from OEF and OIF. An enhanced troop, cargo, shelter carrier M1152A1 entered production in February 2006. The useful life of existing HMMWVs is being extended through an ongoing recapitalization programme.

### Programme Status

There are 21,000 Up-Armored HMMWVs (UAHs) currently in U.S. Central Command's area of responsibility AOR supporting Operational Force protection requirements. Near-term production of HMMWVs will support theater requirements as well as system interchange requirements for platforms such as Trojan SPIRIT, Tactical Operations Centers, Secure Mobile Anti-Jam Reliable Tactical Terminal and Tactical Unmanned Aerial Vehicle. Over 23,000 recapitalized HMMWVs are in the fielding process in CONUS, including modularly converted units and SBCTs. Continued HMMWV deliveries will support modularizing units in the near future.

## Heavy Expanded Mobility Tactical Truck (HEMTT)

The Heavy Expanded Mobility Tactical Truck Family of Vehicles provides all-weather, rapidly deployable transport capabilities for re-supply of combat vehicles and weapon systems. There are six primary variants of the HEMTT series trucks: M977/ M985 cargo truck with Material Handling Crane, M978 2,500-

gal fuel tanker, M984 wrecker, M983 light equipment transport and the M1120 HEMTT-Load Handling System. A self-recovery winch is also available on certain models. HEMTT-LHS provides the Soldier with an efficient and economical forward area distribution system. The HEMTT A4 Product Improvement Programme/Long-Term Armor Strategy will be in full production starting June 2008 and will have a modern power train consisting of a 550 hp C- 15 engine which offers 55 horse power more than the HEMTT A2, air-ride suspension, updated electrical system, anti-lock brakes traction control, common cab with the Palletized Load System, integrated mounting for GPK and machine gun mount and A kit and B kit armor. HEMTT series trucks were built for cross-country missions carrying payloads up to 11 tons, and are designated an FCS-complementary system and a key enabler to achieving a distribution-based logistics system.

## Programme Status

The M978 Tanker, M983 LET, M984 Wrecker and M1120 LHS Truck are currently in production. The FY07-13 fielding schedule includes COMPO 1 SBCTs 4-7, 1/1 AD HBCT, 2/1 AD HBCT, modular infantry and heavy BCTs, 43 SUS BDE, 507TH SUS BDE and fires brigades and OIF combat-loss replacements. COMPO 2 371/67/38/40/369 sustainment brigades as well as COMPO 3 requirements include vehicles for 162/474/164 sustainment brigades, 263 AAMDC and 16/35 engineer brigades.

## Palletized Load System (PLS)

Palletized Load System is a 16.5 ton payload prime mover with an onboard load handling system and removable flat racks. The vehicle can also be equipped with Material Handling Equipment and winch. Its mission is to rapidly move combat configured loads of all classes of supply, either containerized or non-containerized. The system also includes a PLS trailer, a PLS Container Handling Unit for transporting 20′ ISO containers, an M3 Container roll-in/Out Platform, and M1 Flatracks.

## Programme Status

The PLS Block 1 Product Improvement Programme will be in full production in 2009 and will include a modern power train (CAT C-15 600 hp Engine, Allison 4500SP Transmission, larger cooling system, 2004 EPA Compliant), independent front suspension, updated electrical system, ABS & traction control, climate control and a common cab w/HEMTT A4 & LTAS compliant. The M3 CROP is currently in production, whereas the M1077 and M1 flatracks are no longer in production. Note, the M1077 flatracks are incorporated into the Forward Repair System and the M1 flatracks are used in support of engineer systems. FY07-13 fielding schedule includes AC and USAR engineer mission modules, APS and OIF combat-loss replacements. Funding supports ARNG requirements for the 371/38/67/40 369/162/ 474 Sustain-ment Brigades.

## M1070 Heavy Equipment Transport (HET) with M1000 70 Ton Trailer

The M1070 Heavy Equipment Transport System consists of the M1070 Truck Tractor and the M1000 Heavy Equipment Transporter Semi-trailer. The HET transports payloads up to 70 tons–primarily Abrams tanks. The M1070 also transports fighting and recovery vehicles, self-propelled howitzers and construction equipment. It operates on highways worldwide, secondary and cross-country roads. The HET has a number of features that significantly improve the mobility and overall performance of the system in a tactical environment. The M1070 tractor has front- and rear-axle steering, a central tire-inflation system and cab space for six personnel to accommodate the two HET operators and four tank crewmen. The M1000 semi-trailer has automatically steerable axels and a load-leveling hydraulic suspension. The 25-ton loading winches are fitted as standard together with an auxiliary winch to handle cables and for general utility purposes. Despite its bulk the M1070 heavy equipment transporter can be airlifted.

**Programme Status**

The M1070 HET is a powerful tractor truck with an 8 x 8 drive configuration and advanced features such as an electronic engine control system to ensure maximum efficiency at all times, and an 'air ride' rear suspension to ensure all axles remain in contact with the ground at all times while smoothing out the worst round-terrain shocks to the chassis frame. To assist traction further, across rough terrain, another standard feature is a central tire inflation system. The HET's payload is 140,000 pounds and has a 500- horsepower Detroit Diesel and a 5-speed automatic transmission. The HET can travel up to 40-45 mph on highway (25-30 mph with 70 ton payload) and has a range of 300 miles. The HET can be transported using the C-5A and C-17 Cargo Aircraft. The M1070 HET is currently not in production; however, Project Manager, Heavy Tactical Vehicle is currently working on a new HET Truck & Trailer with production starting in 4QTR FY09/FY10.

## M915 Family of Vehicles

The M915 Family of Vehicles refers to three variants that share body components, drive train design and logistics support. Each of the three serves a unique tactical mission. All three are manufactured under a FY00 Requirements-Type contract with Freightliner LLC that has been extended into an eighth year. The three models are the M915A3 6X4 Line Haul Tractor, M916A3 6X6 Light Equipment Transporter, and the M917A2 6X6 20-ton Dump Truck. The M915 primary wartime mission is to provide a means for highspeed line haul transport of all classes of supply from port to division. It is found in Medium Truck Transportation Companies throughout the Active and Reserve Components.

With its 2-inch kingpin compatible 5th wheel it is the prime mover for the M872 Series 34-ton flatbed and M1062 7500-Gallon Tanker. It is also interoperable with other existing semitrailers that includes the M871 Series 22.5-ton flatbed, M900 Series 5000-

Gallon Tanker, M127A1 and M129-Series Van semitrailers. The M916A3 LET and M917 Dump Truck share a chassis and drive train. The M916A3 is a tractor equipped with a 3.5-inch kingpin compatible 5th wheel and a 56,000 pound hydraulic rear winch. It is the prime mover for the M870-Series 40-ton low bed semitrailer used by Engineer units. The M917A2 20 ton Dump Truck is also found in Engineer units and supports construction and quarry missions.

**Programme Status**

The M915A3 and M916A3 will continue to be in full production in 2008. M915A3 production will support an approved ONS from the MNF-I Theater Transportation Mission. Prior to overseas transport these trucks will receive add-on-armor kits installed by depot teams. Scheduled 2008 M916A3 production was funded by 2007 Main Supplemental. These trucks will be used to support AC/RC shortages that exist due to left-behind equipment, a growing Army Acquisition Objective and washout of over-aged M916s and M920s. ARNG NGREA funds received to date will acquire additional M916A3 and M917A2s. Awarding new delivery orders are pending approval of a second Family of Vehicles contract extension. The extension will also include FY08 PA funded M916A3s. The M917A2 has not had a budget line since 2003. The only M917A2s ordered since that time has been through receipt of National Guard and Reserve Equipment Appropriation funds.

Numerous product improvements have been incorporated in the M915A3s on the current contract in response to the changing mission threat resulting from the GWOT. The location of U.S. forces in combat zones, with the associated increase in their mission readiness has caused these forces to adopt an OPTEMPO far in excess of normal peacetime requirements. As a result they are experiencing battle damage and accelerated wear and tear. To address these issues additional design improvements have been proposed that would improve survivability, safety, reliability and add new capabilities.

## Tactical Wheeled Vehicle (TWV) Force Protection

The Army has continued its aggressive approach to upgrading tactical wheeled vehicle protection as an important part of the Army's responsibility to sustain the Joint force with equipment able to survive on the modern battlefield. The highest priority is to provide such protection to our forces involved in ongoing operations in Iraq and Afghanistan. At the same time, the Army has developed and is implementing a long-term armoring strategy that will integrate effective armoring and other protection initiatives that will enable TWV to better survive on future battlefields. Currently, the Army has two distinct levels of armor protection on TWVs. The first, "level I", refers to fully integrated armor installed during production and retrofit. The second, "level II", includes officially approved and centrally manufactured add-on armor kits that can be installed on vehicles anywhere. Concurrently, the Army is assessing and testing other technological improvements to ensure that all TWVs involved in operational missions are equipped with the best protection available.

Armoring of the TWV fleet has been an enormous effort for the Army since late 2003. This endeavor was challenging because it required the design, testing, production, and installation of armor components on TWVs that were never designed to accept armor. In spite of the challenge, the Army met theater requirements for AoA kits by September 2006, with over 26,000 TWVs outfitted. However, AoA kits were never envisioned as long-term armor solutions for TWVs. The Army's long-term armoring strategy for TWV consists of a combination of an "A cab" and "B" armor kit. The "A cab", manufactured into the vehicle, provides the framework upon which the armor "B kit" is mounted. The B kit can be installed or removed to meet mission requirements. The Army will begin fielding medium and heavy "A cab/ B kit" vehicles in FY 08. In addition to protecting TWVs with AoA kits, the Army is also providing enhancements to the factory-installed armor on the M1151 up-armored HMMWVs. Started in early 2006, these fragmentation protection kits add armor to protect such areas as the door edge, rocker panel, front wheel wells and doors. Armored TWVs remain a critical component of the Army leadership's highest priority, protecting our Nation's military force.

In addition to the essential Material solutions to these operational requirements today, the Army is also fully involved in pursuing nonmaterial measures that can directly improve the sustainment and protection of the Joint force. These steps include the work of the Joint Improvised Explosive Device Defeat Task Force, which is working across the interagency and international spectrum on material and nonmaterial solutions to defeat this threat. Tangible results include effective countermeasures, fielding systems that increase detection and enhance detonation, and training solutions that increase awareness and incorporate lessons learned. In the end, this is and will remain the highest-priority task for the Army and one that is fully integrated into equipping and operational requirements and responses.

## Armored Security Vehicle (ASV)

The Armored Security Vehicle is an armored all-wheel drive vehicle with 360 degree armor protection against armor-piercing, high-explosive fragmentation, and anti-tank mines under the wheels and under the hull. The ASV has a crew of three plus one passenger; vehicle intercom system with combat vehicle crewman helmets. The armament suite consists of a MK19 grenade machine gun and M-48MG. It has the collective NBC protection system as well as a digitization package which includes FBCB2, Blue Force Tracking, and SINCGARS. The ASV provides essential protection to Combat Support units in highly exposed threat environments. Increased lethality is provided via both point/area weapons (M-48/MK19) in the same turret. The ability to reload under armor adds to crew survivability. The ASV survivability and lethality increase the military police capability to conduct operations throughout the spectrum of conflict to include convoy escort; area and route reconnaissance and surveillance; counter-incursion reaction force roles; and security of critical assets, key personnel and lines of communication. Vehicle capabilities have been so successfully demonstrated that it has been diverted to CCP use.

### Programme Status

Currently, 2,776 ASVs, the Army Acquisition Objective, are funded and theater requirements have been met. Fielding of ASVs to CONUS based units began in August 2007 and is scheduled to continue through FY 22.

### Mine Resistant Ambush Protected Vehicles (MRAP)

The Army, Air Force, Navy, Special Operations Forces, and USMC are procuring Mine Resistant Ambush Protected vehicles to fill requirements from theater for better armor protected vehicles. The MRAP family of vehicles will provide operating forces multiple, mission-role platforms capable of defeating and mitigating the effects of IEDs and other casualtyproducing threats currently seen in theater. Due to the potential increase in vehicle size and weight

which may be necessary to defeat these threats, the MRAP vehicles may not be capable of executing all the mission requirements currently executed by uparmored HMMWVs. As such, it is the

Army's intent to replace some; but not all, up armored HMMWV's in theater. There are three categories of MRAP: CAT 1 comprises Mine Resistant Utility Vehicle/Urban Combat Operations, and can accommodate six or more personnel. CAT 2 comprises Multi-Mission (convoy escort, troop transport, ambulance, EOD, combat engineer) and can accommodate ten or more personnel. CAT 3 comprises Mine/IED Clearance Operations (Buffalo) and can accommodate six or more personnel.

### Programme Status

This is a Joint Services acquisition with the Navy as the Executive Agent. A Joint Marine Corps/Army request for proposal was issued 9 November 2006 for up to 4,060 MRAP vehicles with awards granted 26 January 2007. Since then, accelerated testing of candidate vehicles was conducted at Aberdeen Test Center, and the Army placed production orders on 5 variants of MRAPs. Fielding to Army units in theater began in November 2007. Theater Combatant Commanders will provide an Operational Assessment in February 2008. This assessment will define the final number of MRAP vehicles required. In addition to the essential material solutions to these operational requirements today, the Army is also fully involved in pursuing nonmaterial measures that can directly improve the sustainment and protection of the Joint force. These steps include the work of the JIEDD TF, which is working across the interagency and international spectrum on material and nonmaterial solutions to defeat this threat. Tangible results include effective countermeasures, fielding systems that increase detection and enhance detonation, and training solutions that increase awareness and incorporate lessons learned. In the end, this is and will remain a high-priority task for the Army and one that is fully integrated into equipping and operational requirements and responses.

# Appendix 11: Combat Service Support

## Discussion of Core Combat Support Material Programmes

### *Joint Precision Airdrop Systems (JPADS)*

The Joint Precision Airdrop System is a high altitude capable, autonomously operated airdrop capability with significantly increased accuracy to a ground location. The system consists of a family of differently sized, high glide canopies, allowing airdrop of various weight categories. Currently a 2,000 pound and a 10,000 pound programme are being pursued. A lower weight category is desired by USMC and SOF, and an Army Technology Objective has also demonstrated a 30,000 pound capability. JPADS is not totally wind dependent and is releasable from altitudes up to approximately 25,000 feet Mean Sea Level. Based on winds and release altitude, 25 kilometer standoff distances are also possible. On aircraft Mission Planning capability, an Autonomous Guidance Unit (AGU) and space-based GPS technology provides for aerial navigation and manoeuverability of the Air Vehicle throughout descent; steering into the wind as necessary, and permitting highly accurate ground touchdown locations. JPADS is a critical logistics transformation enabler that facilitates dedicated aerial sustainment, helps achieve full distribution-based logistics, and serves as a force protection measure for delivery aircraft, ground recipients and the IED threat to ground transportation.

**Programme Status**

The 2,000 pound programme is preparing for Developmental Test and is fully funded to meet Army Acquisition Objectives. Rapid Fielding Initiatives have placed prototype capability in the AOR. As possible, Urgent Material Release will be examined to satisfy COCOM requirements. The 10,000 pound variant was the subject of ACTD. ACTD was successfully transitioned to programme in Nov 07, and will commence in progression to the 2,000 pound programme. The 10,000 pound programme is also funded. The 30,000 pound variant is an ATO, and currently unfunded. Requirements for this weight capability are being examined.

## M100A1 Advanced Aviation Forward Area Refueling System (AAFARS)

M100A1 Advanced Aviation Forward Area Refueling System is a modular, four-point refueling system. The principal components are engine, pump, filter and control modules, along with hoses, nozzles, couplings, defueling pump, fuel blivets, fire-suppression equipment, fuel spill containment berms, nozzles and fuel test kit. AAFARS is transported inter-theater in three specialized shipping containers.

### Programme Status

There have been 244 systems fielded. Current production and fielding schedules is four per month through August 2009.

## Petroleum Quality Analysis System (PQAS)

Petroleum Quality Analysis System is a complete petroleum quality surveillance laboratory capable of conducting B-level testing in accordance with MILSTD-3004 on kerosene-based, e.g., jet propellants and diesel military mobility fuels.

### Programme Status

PQAS is being redesigned to meet the Full Armor solution with system integration of the HMMWV Shelter Based Laboratory, FUE FY09, into the FMTV International Standardization Organization Shelter Based Laboratory. The selected for use in the new design is the Standard Automotive Tool Set shelter used by PM-SKOT.

## Tactical Electric Power (TEP)

Tactical Electric Power are all-mobile, diesel-fueled, electric power generating sources, 840KW and smaller, which are skid mounted, trailer mounted, or man portable. TEPs are capable of independently producing electric power when operating on diesel, JP-8, or other fuel sources. Included are followon power sources such as fuel cells, hybrid electric systems, renewable energy systems, alternative energy systems, and thermoelectric devices. These mobile, tactical generators provide quality power to operate DoD systems away from a fixed power grid and are found in nearly every organization in the Army. They directly support all field electrical systems such as C4ISR, medical, maintenance, fire direction and controls, target acquisition, life support, sustainment and illumination.

## Programme Status

TEP Tactical Quiet Generators are currently in production and being fielded. The next generation of TEP generators, the Advanced Medium Mobile Power Sources (5-60K), reached MS B in November 2003 and begins production in FY10. To date, 75 percent of the older MILSTD generators have been replaced by TQGs and 15,000 remain to be replaced by TQGs and AMMPS. Current FY08 fielding strategy is to support procurement to fill critical shortages for deploying units. Funding supports procurement and fielding of over 30,000 AMMPS generators and Power Distribution Illumination Systems Electrical. Funding will modernize 30 percent of all Army Component's power generation requirements.

## Standard Automotive Tool Set (SATS)

The Standard Automotive Tool Set system is a base tool set of the most frequently required automotive maintenance tools that can be augmented by modular packages that are tailored to suit unit mission requirements and organizational design. SATS eliminates obsolete tools, eliminates unneeded redundancy and inefficient in tool proliferation, increases tool quality, improves transportability and improves tool accountability. The most significant advantage gained through use of SATS is its minimization of the logistics footprint. This is achieved through standardization and modernization, which eliminates the need for four 5-ton cargo trucks and accompanying trailers.

SATS is a modular, flexible, standardized automotive maintenance shop system that will replace the most numerous types of field level shop sets. SATS enables a modular, expeditionary, campaign-quality force and supports the Army transformation to a two-level maintenance system. The SATS consists of a transportable, International Standardization Organization 8x8x20 container with an integrated governmentfurnished, electric power generator and Environmental Control Unit. The container includes secure storage space for a complete base set of COTS and government-furnished industrial-quality tools and equipment needed to perform field-level maintenance of military vehicles and ground-support equipment.

### Programme Status

SATS is in full production with over 175 sets fielded to date. SATS is programmed for fielding FY08-13 with 126 deliveries in FY08, 139 in FY09, 144 in FY10, 117 in FY11, 41 in FY12 and 56 in FY13.

## Containerized Kitchen (CK)

Containerized Kitchen integrates standard and commercial kitchen equipment into an expandable 8x8x20 foot ISO container. CK has onboard refrigeration and uses the improved modern burner unit. It has a running water system and the interior is environmentally controlled. CK can feed three meals a day to 800 Soldiers. Its efficiencies over the Mobile Kitchen Trailers include overall decreased footprint and manpower requirements.

### Programme Status

More than 300 CK systems have been produced and fielded and have been in continuous production since FY02. Production continues at the rate of four per month from FY07 through FY13.

## Camel Unit Water Pod System

The Camel system consists of an 800-900 gallon storage capacity tank, heater/chiller unit, government-furnished M1095 medium tactical vehicle trailer, and contractor developed components mounted to or carried by the trailer. Under the SBCT concept, Camel will provide a manoeuvre company operating in a temperate environment two or more days of supply of water at a minimum sustaining consumption rate. It will have provisions for at least six retail dispensing points, and be fully capable of stand-alone operation. Camel will be capable of transporting both full and partial loads of water by C-130 and larger aircraft, external-lift helicopter, and lowvelocity, air-droppable means. Camel replaces the M107, M149 and M1112 series water trailers.

### Programme Status

Four prototypes have been procured with Product Qualification Testing began early 2007, contract award FY08 and the first unit equipped FY09.

## Load Handling System Compatible Water Tank Rack System

Hippo consists of a 2,000 gallon, ISO-framed, potable water tank rack. Hippo has an organic 125-GPM water pump, filling stand, 70 foot hose reel for both bulk suction and discharge and retail distribution. Hippo will enhance water distribution by providing one system that enables both hard wall bulk water transportation and unit retail water support. It will allow for water transport directly from water purification points to supported manoeuvre elements and can be used as a water distribution point.

### Programme Status

Hippo will replace the Semi-trailer Mounted Fabric Tank and the majority of the Forward Area Water Point Supply System. Fielding of the Hippo began in first quarter, FY07.

## 1,500-GPH Tactical Water Purification System

The Tactical Water Purification System supports Army's mission to provide life and mission sustaining water to front line and remote units in tactical environments. It is capable of supplying 1,500 GPH of potable water for division and brigade ground units within remote areas. In addition, it provides quality water support to civilian agencies or host nations for disaster relief, humanitarian efforts and peace keeping missions.

### Programme Status

The Army requirement is for 221 systems. All units should be fully fielded by FY09.

### Container/Material Handling Equipment (C/MHE)

The Container/Material Handling Equipment includes all container and material handling equipment required to support the deployment of unit equipment and the distribution of sustainment items. The primary tactical C/MHE includes the Rough Terrain Container Handler and the All-Terrain Lifter Army System. The RTCH is the primary capability for handling 20 and 40 foot-long containers weighing up to 53,000 pounds. RTCH is deployable by air, operates on all types of terrain and is capable of stacking containers up to three high. ATLAS has a 10,000 pound capacity and is capable of handling fully loaded 463L Air Force pallets, has a variable reach boom for removing items from 20-foot containers and is capable of deploying by air.

### Programme Status

The RTCH programme was terminated in FY04 with 346 of the 627 systems fielded. Production for Army requirements will restart again in FY08 and continue through FY12, and reach approximately 85 percent of the AAO. The initial contract production for ATLAS I ended in FY05 with 1,809 of 2,500 systems fielded. Funding currently is provided through FY10 that will procure additional systems to reach the entire AAO.

### Next Generation Automatic Test System (NGATS)

The Next Generation Automatic Test System is a highly mobile, rapidly deployable, generalpurpose, reconfigurable automatic test system which directly supports testing and screening of Army weapon systems to maintain their readiness to shoot, move, and communicate. This system will utilize spiral development leveraging the Joint ARGCS ACTD to provide capabilities to incrementally replace DSESTS, the Army standard IFTE BSTF(V)3, and the electro-optical testing capabilities of the BSTF (V)5. NGATS will be a reconfigurable ATS housed in an ISO Shelter and be transported by a HEMTT LHS. NGATS will be 100% compatible for use with all Test Programme Sets currently employed by Army off-platform automatic test equipment. It will have full sustainment level diagnostic maintenance capability on the full spectrum of current and future Army weapon systems. A key feature of NGATS is that it will use Joint service developed test technologies and move DoD closer to its stated goal of a common ATS architecture capable of cross-service weapons system testing.

**Programme Status**

NGATS is currently in the RDT&E phase. Two prototypes have been built. Distribution will be in accordance with current Army doctrine to support the Modular Force. Full Rate Production is currently scheduled to begin FY10.

## Maintenance Support Device (MSD) Version 2

As the replacement for the Soldier Portable, On-System Repair Tool and Maintenance Support Device is a lightweight, rugged, compact, man-portable, generalpurpose automatic tester used to verify the operational status of systems, both electronic and automotive, and to isolate faulty components for immediate replacement. MSD is also used as a software uploader/verifier to restore or provide new software to weapon systems, and supports testing requirements of current and FCS. The MSD is in wide use throughout the Army's ground combat and CSS vehicle, as well as aviation fleets.

**Programme Status**

MSD is currently being fielded. A recent change in the basis of issue will provide the MSD to fieldlevel maintainers at a ratio of 1:3 per maintainer occupational skill. MSD AAO is 35,000, of which 50 percent have been fielded/modernized with MSD/MSD-

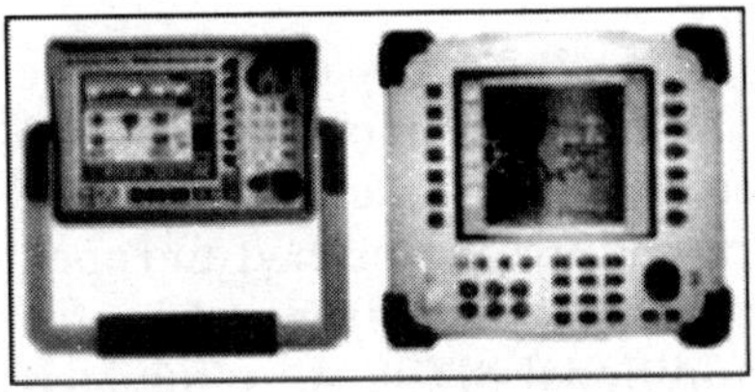

V2. No projected buy-out of MSD as it is a recurring modernization effort driven by the development of new weapons technology. Current platform runs on Windows XP based software maintaining operability with new FMTV production vehicles and Paladin upgrades. Expired MSD/SPORT platforms run on older versions of Microsoft Windows and are not compatible with new FMTV production vehicles and Paladin upgrades. Approximately 6,000 MSD-V2 Kits have been produced and fielded.

## General Purpose Electronic Test Equipment (GPETE)

General Purpose Electronic Test Equipment products are COTS/NDI consisting of lightweight, man-portable, general-purpose, electronic test equipment used to test, maintain, and calibrate Army current and future systems. Examples include the oscilloscope, spectrum analyzer, data communication analyzer, frequency counter, multi-meter, signal generator, radio test sets and radar test sets. GPETE modernization efforts continue to improve Army weapon system readiness, minimize GPETE proliferation and obsolescence, and reduce operations and support costs.

## Programme Status

Current GPETE modernization efforts include the AN/PRM-35 Radio Test Set, AN/GRM-123 Radio Test Set, SG-1364/U Signal Generator and Function Generator. There are 36 other GPETE candidates for the Test Equipment Modernization programme. These candidates will be sequentially modernized by priority as documented in the Army G-3 approved GPETE Identification and Replacement Prioritization List.

## Man-Transportable Robotic System (MTRS)

Man-Transportable Robotic System provides a two person, portable, lightweight robotic system. Current operations have shown a need for smaller, portable robotic systems. Lack of this capability requires EOD and Combat Engineer Soldiers to

physically approach explosive devices and manually perform reconnaissance and render safe procedures in confined and open spaces. Requirements for additional MTRS were initiated and validated in response to the increased number and sophistication of potential threats.

**Programme Status**

The new MTRS AAO of 461 incorporates additional requirements resulting from lessons learned in OIF and OEF. These requirements are included in the programme plan through FY10 and are currently undergoing reform based on 06 approved FDU.

**Forward Repair System (FRS)**

Forward Repair System is a high-mobility maintenance system designed to support forces in the battle area. FRS includes a crane and maintenance enclosure mounted on a component flat-rack. The crane has a 5.5-ton lift capacity with a 14 foot radius capable of removing and replacing major components, including full-up power packs of all models of military vehicles. The maintenance enclosure includes a 35KW generator; air compressor; welding equipment including arc; and industrial-quality air and electrical power tools ranging from 3/8- to 1-in drive with associated tool cabinets.

**Programme Status**

FRS is currently in full production and fielding. Projected procurement/fielding of AAO by FY12 to include GTA.

# Appendix 12: Army Watercraft

## Discussion of Core Army Watercraft Material Programmes

### *Joint High Speed Vessel (JHSV)*

The Joint High Speed Vessel is the Army's next generation self-deploying watercraft. JHSV will maximize intra-theater lift from an offshore or out of sector staging base, or within littoral waters to provide warfighters the capability to maneuver combat ready forces into forward areas. It can also provide follow-on sustainment through minor and degraded ports. Leveraging technology as it is developed, the JHSV will be faster, more capable and have greater survivability than current generation watercraft.

#### Programme Status

Since JHSV is a documented programme of record with an approved ICD and Capability Development Document, the CBA validates the JCIDS actions already under way. The Army is procuring five JHSVs.

### Harbormaster Command and Control Center (HCCC)

Harbormaster Command and Control Center is the mission critical material system required by Harbormaster Detachments. HCCC provides command and control tools, sensors, technical connectivity, and physical configuration to properly manage Army watercraft assets to ensure that watercraft-delivered sustainment is responsive to warfighter requirements. HCCC will have interoperable C4ISR systems and be able to send and receive information classified up to SECRET.

#### Programme Status

Currently under development, the HCCC is a documented Acquisition Category III programme of record with an approved CDD and a funding line in the current POM. CASCOM and TCM-

Trans are currently working closely with the Programme Manager –Tactical Operations Centers to finalize the Capability Production Document, and support production of the prototype system in FY08. The current plan is to complete integration and field the eight operational systems and training packages.

### Vessel-to-Shore Bridging

The Vessel-to-Shore Bridging capabilities encompass lightweight floating bridging that can be carried on current and future watercraft with little space and weight requirement. Easily and quickly employed to allow vessels access to austere and bare-beach littoral access points they could otherwise not reach, VSB provides a causeway-like platform for the offload of wheeled and tracked vehicles, as well as containerized cargo. Existing systems–the Army's Modular Causeway System and the Improved Navy Lighter System–can only be delivered by major shipping, thereby negating the speed advantage of future vessels like the JHSV, and require a large investment in time and manpower, thus defeating the goal to reduce or eliminate logistics footprint.

### Programme Status

VSB capabilities are still under development, however, feasibility and military utility is scheduled for demonstration in 2008 by one of the key elements of the Joint Enable Theater Access–Sea Ports of Debarkation Advanced Concept Technology Demonstration. CASCOM is currently completing work on an Initial Capabilities Document that will define required VSB capabilities, support analysis of alternative approaches, and development of material systems. The strategy is to continue to pursue development of capabilities and document VSB requirements IAW JCIDS with the goal of fielding a system by 2011.

### Logistic Support Vessel (LSV)

The Logistic Support Vessel is a world-wide deployable vessel that provides transport of combat vehicles and sustainment cargo in the theater zone. It provides intra-theater line haul of large quantities of cargo and equipment. Tactical resupply missions can be performed to remote underdeveloped coastlines and inland

waterways. It is also ideally suited for the discharge or back load of sealift, including Roll-on/Roll-off (RO/RO) vessels, such as a large medium-speed RO/RO. Because of its shallow draft, the LSV can carry cargo from deepdraft ships to shore ports or areas too shallow for larger ships. The LSV is ideally suited to execute cargo operations along coastal LOCs.

## Programme Status

The Army will continue to require the capability provided by the LSV, a fielded acquisition category 3 programme. It is the Army's workhorse with regard to moving large amounts of sustainment cargo and equipment within a theater of operations. The current platforms, however, are aging and the first vessel in class will reach the end of its projected life cycle–the economic useful life in 2013. The initial LSV modernization plan will be implemented to upgrade critical systems to extend the LSV's service life and provide the minimum capabilities needed to 2024. The LSV's lack of speed will remain an issue, but the planned upgrades will allow the fleet to maintain its "amber" capability level.

## Landing Craft Utility

The Landing Craft Utility-2000 provides transport of combat vehicles and sustainment cargo. It provides intra-theater movement of cargo and equipment. Tactical resupply missions can be performed to remote, underdeveloped coastlines and inland waterways. This includes missions in LOTS operations in remote areas with austere shore facilities or unimproved beaches. It is also ideally suited for the discharge or back load of sealift, including RO/RO vessels such as an LMSR.

## Programme Status

The LCU-2000 is a fielded Acquisition Category III programme. Lift capability provided by the current platform will continue to be required for the foreseeable future. It is the medium sized vessel used to move containers and outsized cargo. Immediate modernization of the on-board C4I suite will extend the utility of the current vessels for a number of years. A service life extension programme must be developed and implemented within the next three-five years to ensure this capability is available through year 2024.

## Landing Craft Mechanized

The Landing craft Mechanized transports cargo, troops, and vehicles from ship to shore or in retrograde movements. It is also utilized in lighterage and utility work in harbors. It is designed for use in rough or exposed waters and is capable of operating through breakers and grounding on a beach. The bow ramp permits RO/RO operations with wheeled and tracked vehicles. Its small size facilitates its use in confined areas.

## Programme Status

A fully-fielded Acquisition Category III programme, the design of the current platform is 70 years old and the platforms themselves are approaching 40 years of age. Extending the service life of this platform for a third time would not be prudent given the cost. This coupled with the platforms lack of speed and utility for current and emerging missions lead to the need for a new platform.

## Large Tug, LT-800 Series

The 128-foot Series 800 Large Tug is used for ocean and coastal towing operations. It has a secondary mission of accomplishing general-purpose harbor duties, such as positioning floating cranes. The LT can perform firefighting duties, a significant capability, particularly where ammunition ships are deployed.

### Programme Status

LT-800 is an Acquisition Category III programme that is currently being modified to eliminate its fielded stability problems. All modifications are scheduled to be completed by the end of fiscal year 2008. Although the LT 800 will be retained for the foreseeable future, preliminary work should be performed to position a replacement if resources become available.

### Small Tug

The Series-900 Small Tug can move cargo barges and lighters of various types within a harbor, port, or LOTS anchorage. It can also assist larger tugs with utility work, such as docking and undocking of ships of all sizes, movement of floating cranes, and line-handling duties.

### Programme Status

The ST900 is an Acquisition Category III programme designed and built to replace the 65 foot small tug as well as move ammunition LASH barges. Due to this change, these vessels are currently being utilized in port support roles.

### Barge Derrick, 115-Ton

The Barge Derrick can load and discharge heavy lift cargo that is beyond the capacity of ships' gear. It provides the lift and reach needed to discharge the heaviest of projected Army cargo from LMSRs, as well as commercial container ships, to accomplish strategic deployment. It is capable of lifting a 75-ton main battle tank from the centerline of a non-self-sustaining ship.

### Programme Status

This platform, an Acquisition Category III programme, was designed and built to provide the capability to lift an M1A2 main battle tank from the centerline of the Fast Sealift Ship. Because the M1 MBT will be in the inventory for the foreseeable future, the uniqueness of this capability, the uncertainty of commercial availability and it is prudent to retain these platforms.

## Modular Causeway System (MCS)

The Modular Causeway System is made up of four primary modular components that are used to create four systems: the Floating Causeway, the Causeway Ferry, the RO/RO discharge facility and the Modular Warping Tug. MCS is designed to provide the ability to establish logistics sites from remote and austere bare beach environments.

### Programme Status

The MCS is an Army Acquisition Category III programme. Currently, the Army and Navy each employ a different, Service-specific system for providing causeway capabilities to support JLOTS operations: the Army's MCS and the Navy's Improved Naval Lighterage System. The two systems are not interoperable, thus the Army and Navy are currently maintaining two distinct systems.

## Containerized Maintenance Facility (CMF)

The Containerized Maintenance Facility is a combination of tactical rigid wall shelters and a standard ISO container grouped together into a system that, when completely fielded, will be the principal support maintenance for Army watercraft deployed worldwide in improved and unimproved ports. The CMF has its own power generation/distribution system and is capable of using local commercial power sources when available.

### Programme Status

The CMF, an Army Acquisition Category III programme, was developed in 1997 as the principal item of equipment found in the Floating Craft Maintenance Company, and two were fielded in 2007 to the two companies currently in the force structure. Two are currently programmed for procurement for prepositioned assets in fiscal years 2010-2011. As part of the concept to move watercraft maintenance toward two-level maintenance, consideration must be given to the utility of the current CMF.

# Appendix 13: Additional Modernization Initiatives in Focused Logistics

## Logistics Modernization: (Near term)

The Army leadership prioritizes adaptable and responsive near and longer-term technology options that enable the Modular Force Logistics Concept, the longer-term concepts for the Future Modular Force, and ensure that our logistics capabilities are as rapid, precise and agile as the warfighters we support. For logistics, these options are focused on enhancing strategic response, reducing the demand for consumables such as fuel and water, production of consumables closer to the point of use, precision airdrop, prognostics and diagnostics for operational availability and condition-based maintenance, tactical wheeled vehicle fleet modernization, intermodal distribution systems, robotics and decision support tools that provide predictive, anticipatory and effectsbased approaches to logistics. Concepts and enabling technologies are applied against the framework of bandwidth, computing power, sensors and data integration that supports the acceleration of the logistics decision cycle and its synchronization, from strategic to operational to tactical levels, with the operational tempo of the warfighter.

An Army Watercraft fleet has been identified to provide lift assets to an expeditionary focused force to meet deployment goals, provide for assured access, decrease predictability and dwell time and quickly deliver combat sets inter theater and intra theater in order to build and sustain combat power.

To sustain warfighters, logisticians must be able to anticipate and confirm operational requirements and then provide the right capabilities at the optimum place and time. The approved Modular Force Logistics Concept relies on synergies achieved by fielding not only material and technology solutions, but also organizational, leadership and education, doctrinal and policy changes. The FCS BCT will further enhance logistics capabilities by fully integrating Logistics C2 within the FCS Battle Command Network, and by designing systems with dramatically improved reliability, availability and maintainability. This operational transformation, combined with our institutional business process transformation and enhanced by technology insertion is the basis of the Army's logistics transformation, with the ultimate measure of effectiveness being the outcome we are expected to deliver-enhanced and sustained logistics readiness. Select enabling modernization capabilities to achieve these requirements are identified below:

### Unity of Effort Modernization

Global Combat Support System-Army. Battle Command Sustainment Support System and Medical Communications for Combat Casualty Care System.

### Domain-Wide Visibility Modernization

Movement Tracking System, Property Book Unit Supply Enhanced and the Standard Army Maintenance System.

### Rapid and Precise Response Modernization

Joint High Speed Vessel and Joint Precision Airdrop Systems, Family of Medium Tactical Vehicles, High Mobility Multipurpose Wheeled Vehicle, Joint Light Tactical Vehicle and Heavy Expanded Mobility Tactical Truck.

### Command and Control

Command and control describes mission planning and execution, and includes: Army Battle Command System, Common Operational Picture, Joint C2, communications and computer environment, information collection, Army Battle Command System, Manoevre Control System, Logistics Decision Support System, Logistics Data Management System and Platform Soldiers Mission Readiness System.

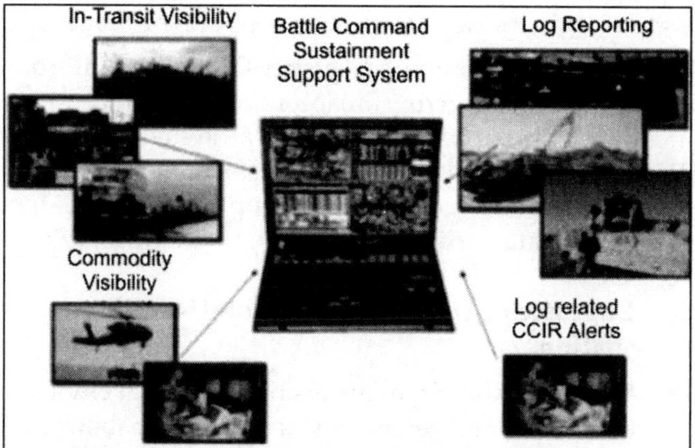

Actionable Logisitics information to Support the Warfighter

## Net-Centric

Net-centric capabilities help provide universal access to all relevant authorities, assets and capabilities, enabling commanders to effectively coordinate battlefield effects and maintain full spectrum dominance and decision superiority. Net-centric capabilities include integrated information systems and supporting information infrastructure. Combat Service Support Satellite Communications Global Positioning System, War fighter Information Network-Tactical, Joint Network Node, and Joint Network Management System.

## Army Logistics Information Technology Modernization

Army Logistics Information Technology is the critical enabler for managing the Army's complex logistics processes. In FY 08, the Logistics Domain will support the Current Force with our current IT structure, while modernizing for the future. Army logistics is transitioning from numerous independent IT systems to an end-to-end, web-based enterprise environment that will link to the platform based tools in the BCTs that are equipped with the FCS capabilities. The core building block of this plan is the Single Army Logistics Enterprise which will provide information superiority through real-time visibility of personnel, equipment and supplies anywhere in the distribution pipeline and within the battlespace. To guide the development and synchronization these programmes, the Logistics Domain will use the Army Integrated Logistics Architecture to support the SALE effort.

In addition, the Common Logistics Operating Environment will be employed by the Army to capture, store, retrieve and utilize logistics data from battlefield operating systems. It will integrate logistics and command and control information systems that automatically produce, consume and propagate logistics-focused near-real-time data—from "the foxhole to the factory."

## Army Logistics Domain Information Technology Transformation

The Army Logistics Domain Vision is a digital environment that builds, sustains, and generates warfighting capability through a fully integrated logistics enterprise based on collaborative planning, knowledge management and best business practices. The Army is enabling this vision through the development of the Single Army Logistics Enterprise and the alignment of Army distribution architectures with Joint distribution processes.

## Logistics Domain Transition Strategy

Army logistics is transitioning from numerous independent and standalone IT systems to an integrated end-to-end system operating in a netcentric environment. Today the Army is developing a comprehensive view of all logistics IT systems and applications as it centralizes existing and future requirements across the Logistics, and other Army Domains. The end state will be a results-oriented logistics capability in support of the Warfighter. To achieve this end state Army Logistics Domain strategy is to:

- Continue to meet Warfighter requirements with current IT systems
- Bridge to enhanced, near term capabilities as necessary
- Deliberately move to a Single Army Logistics Enterprise, taking advantage of modernized enterprise resource planning capabilities

## Support Current IT Systems

Today's current logistics IT systems were acceptable in the 1980's; but are limited at best in keeping pace with today's new, immediate and critical warfighting requirements such as near real time property accountability, total asset visibility and in-transit visibility. Data integration requirements of Army Force Generation, integration of logistics command and control into Battle Command, and increasing information assurance requirements also seriously limit the ability of our current IT. Within the limits of current IT systems, Standard Army Management Information Systems have been refreshed to meet these changing requirements and deliver maximum capabilities. Existing IT systems are identified as either permanent or migrating investments as functionalities are systematically absorbed, replaced or remain consistent with the Army Logistics Vision. Critical modifications to existing logistics IT systems are only made on a case-by-case basis with impact to the warfighter, cost and performance as the basis for these decisions.

### Bridge to Enhanced Near Term Capabilities

The process of transitioning to future IT systems requires the implementation of a bridging strategy that overcomes limitations in our current IT and meets new wartime requirements. Bridging also gives the Army an opportunity to consolidate/retire systems, which provides the opportunity to reduce the complexity of data migration to the modernized systems. Enhancements to bridging systems will be controlled via logistics governance processes, well documented, scrutinized in budgets and tracked with appropriate metrics for performance to meet stringent guidelines of Army leaders and the Planning, Programming, Budgeting and Execution process. Bridging systems cannot significantly expand the scope or burden the current Army logistics IT systems targeted in our plans. They must provide a substantial near term benefit in support of current operations and establish migration plans for consolidation under the SALE.

### Deliberate Move to the SALE–Modernized ERP Capabilities

SALE is the core building block of this plan that will provide information superiority through realtime visibility of personnel, equipment and supplies anywhere in the distribution pipeline and within the battlespace. The SALE will deliver standard enterprise capabilities, assure minimal interfaces and data

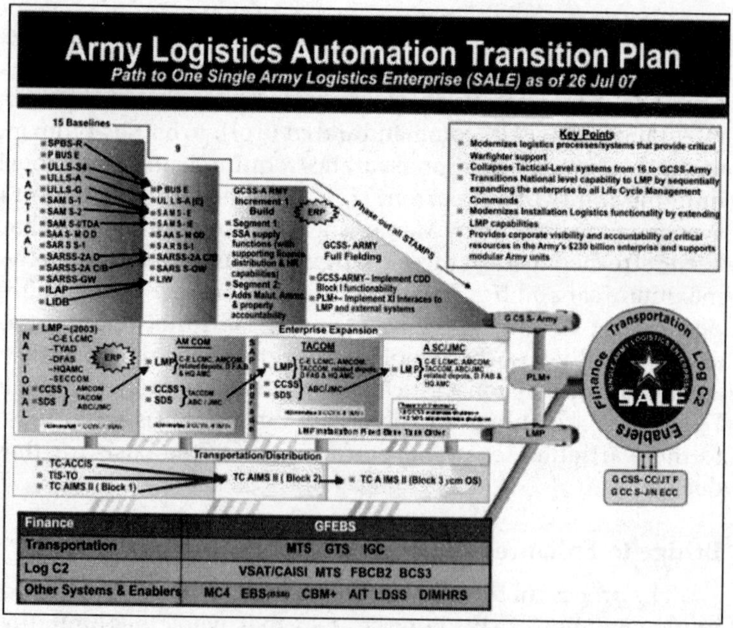


reconciliation, and provide commanders access to authoritative data. These capabilities will satisfy Joint strategic objectives, meet Department of Defence enterprise transition compliance standards and comply with the Business Enterprise Architecture. The SALE end state will be an integrated enterprise solution that enables material readiness, provides asset management and accountability, architecture, acquisition compliancy and financial transparency from factory to foxhole.

The transformation of Army Logistics IT Domain systems is a collaborative effort that will, when completed, move and translate data into meaningful information from multiple sources including individual vehicle platforms to the tactical and national levels. Architecture efforts must be defined and integrated end-to-end in order to establish the required global visibility both within the Logistics Domain and within the larger Army and Joint environments. To guide this effort, the Logistics Domain has identified the Army Integrated Logistics Architecture as the Army G-4's overarching logistics architecture. The AILA informs, guides, and supports decisions for the SALE and assists the Army logistics community in achieving integration and interoperability in the

Business Mission Area and Warfighter Mission Area. The AILA assists the SALE effort by identifying architectures and users of logistics information that is necessary in this effort to eliminate redundant and stovepipe IT investments.

## Managing the Transition

As the Current Force transitions to the Future Combat System, logistics IT systems must be developed to support interoperable forces and move critical sustainment information between logisticians and commanders. The Army G-4 will establish a Logistics Process Integration Laboratory federated with the Central Test Support Facility so that all Logistics Domain capabilities are integrated and tested with the CTSF in accordance with the integrated architecture. The Logistics Innovation Agency's Logistics Process Center will be used to model, test, and simulate modernization proposals across the logistics enterprise for all classes of supplies and logistics functions. It will also assess research and development initiatives to achieve real world, integrated solutions for implementation and integrate data exchanged across the logistics enterprise to achieve interoperability among the generations of forces from the Current Force to the Future Force.

Graphic for Logistics Modernization, Near-Term, page 90, near Language that talks about "Logistics Decision Making"

## Strategic Objective 1

Support today's logistics information technology requirements in support of Combatant Commanders and Joint operations.

Logistics information systems play a key enabling role to ensure the Combatant Commander's forces are successful. The increasing demand placed on these systems requires that they be maintained and improved to provide uninterrupted support while new systems are developed and fielded. To be successful, the Army strategy must meet today's operational requirements, while bridging the gap to tomorrow's Future Force and requirements.

The Army's bridging strategy will continue to enhance current logistics support while allowing the Army time to acquire resources. This will allow the transition to a modernized, enterprise wide management capability, described as the SALE. To support this strategy, the Army will:

- Complete PBUSE fielding
- Continue to field SAMS-E
- Continue to field ULLS-A
- Field FCS BCT with integrated logistics

We will continue to improve our tactical and strategic logistics communications capability by continuing to field Combat Service Support Satellite Communications Automated Information System Interface/Very Small Aperture Terminal capabilities. Command and control of logistics is essential to the warfighting. Further improvements must be made to enable today's Joint warfighters to track and redirect units, equipment, and supplies, to include ammunition, while in route efficiently, and provide the ability to deliver tailored logistics and sustainment packages directly to the warfighter.

To support the way ahead and today's field operations the Army will:

- Continue fielding BCS3 and integrate LOG C2 into the larger Army effort
- Continue fielding the TC-AIMS II Blocks II and begin fielding Block III
- Continue to develop the Business Intelligence tool using the Logistics Integrated Warehouse data as the initial roll out of the Product Lifecycle Management and Master Data Management capabilities of the SALE
- Field the Standard Army Ammunition System, Ammunition Transfer Handling Point

**Strategic Objective 2**

Provide progressive logistics automation capabilities, business processes, and practices necessary for continuous Army Transformation.

The Army's logistics IT transition efforts are enabling best business practices and processes while providing the necessary capabilities to logisticians and warfighters. The Army must develop and share logistics data and requirements across the full spectrum of logistics organizations from the tactical to the National level, across Active and Reserve Components, inside the Army to include Defence Logistics Agency, United States Transportation Command and other Domains and components. The Army Logistics Domain is planning and synchronizing emerging requirements, which will result in an Enterprise solution.

A transformed logistics capability is needed to provide sustained competitive advantage for the Army, the other Services, Defence Agencies and its allies in current and future operations. To support the way ahead the Army will:

- Continue to reduce redundant and stovepipe IT investments
- Enforce the Logistics Domain IT governance process
- Build and use the AILA to inform, guide, and support decisions made in the implementation of the SALE The Army must continue working cross-domain integration issues to achieve a more fully integrated ERP environment
- Business Mission Area. To support the way ahead the Army will collaborate with the Joint community to identify capability gaps and redundancies

To achieve the SALE end state, the Army must define, plan, and field capabilities that integrate logistics processes from "factory to foxhole". This will allow the Army to efficiently and effectively manage its full inventory of assets, provide critical information to commanders in the operational environment and enable the Reset of returning forces. For continuous logistics transformation, the Army will:

- Continue to field LMP (to include Army Installations)
- Plan for and field GCSS-Army (F/T)
- Plan for and field GCSS-Army (PLM+)
- Define and develop an integrated Industrial Base Modernization Solution that consolidates all industrial base IT initiatives

Logistics automation modernization is essential for both operational and business transformation of the Army. Current logistics systems are not able to effectively or efficiently sustain the Army of the future. Modernization is not an option but a necessity.

**Logistics Modernization: (Mid to Long Term)**

The future operating environment will likely present logisticians with the most complex set of challenges yet faced by any force. Army logistics modernization is guided by the requirement to build capabilities that meet the challenges inherent in persistent conflict. These capabilities must support a Joint full spectrum capable land force and will be achieved through the upgrade and modernization of existing systems as well as the insertion of new technologies that improve strategic force projection, intra theater operational manoeuvre and logistics, force protection, modular, scalable and tailorable logistics command and control.

Our focus is on 360-degree readiness, completing the transformation effort, and funding and fielding logistics automation. Building and sustaining combat power is paramount to the Army's success. Our success in future campaigns relies on a Joint-capable, expeditionary logistics community that maintains domain-wide visibility over requirements, resources, and priorities; anticipates and delivers capability with speed and precision to meet operational needs of the Joint force commander; and acts with unity of effort to plan and execute logistics across the Joint operations area. The transformation of logistics automation, current and Future Force, will be synchronized and balanced with the interdependent Department of Defence Logistics Enterprise, and the emerging Army Modular Force structure designed to improve operational readiness, agile sustained capability, efficiency and effectiveness.

Within the tactical BCTs, the integration of logistics into the overall Battle Command suite will be accomplished using FCS capabilities. Not only will this ensure that the commanders consider logistics capabilities and constraints in their mission planning, but that the enterprise logistics environment will directly support BCT mission operations. Combined with the improved diagnostic and prognostic capabilities made available through the FCS logistics automation products, the tactical user logistics requirements will be more accurately generated and automatically linked to the logistics enterprise environment through the GCSS-A.

Logistics automation assures sustainment is delivered with the speed and precision necessary to meet the needs of the Joint force commander via a well defined enterprise architecture that synergizes global assets and unity of effort throughout the planning and execution phases of logistics support across the interdependent logistics spectrum. The objective is to assure expeditionary and campaign quality logistics by maintaining a 360 degree view of equipment readiness, improving and implementing the logistics concepts of support while continuing the execution and implementation of an aggressive Joint-capable logistics strategy that assures domain-wide visibility of requirements, priorities and resources.

## Science and Technology

Future logistics concepts and enabling technologies will support the achievement of operational effects through adaptive planning and execution monitoring, a robust end-to-end information grid and infrastructure and 100 per cent visibility that assures readiness and reduces mission risk. The focused application of technology solutions will reduce demands on manpower, improve the efficiency and effectiveness of logistics support and improve reliability, maintainability, sustainability and operational readiness. Concepts and enabling technologies will be applied against the framework of bandwidth, computing power, sensors and data integration that supports the acceleration of the logistics decision cycle and its synchronization, from strategic to operational to tactical levels, with the operational tempo of the warfighter. New approaches to logistics will enable the Joint capable concept of support and encompass capabilities spanning command and control, organizations, doctrine, tactics, techniques and procedures, with the ultimate measure of effectiveness being the outcome we are expected to deliver - enhanced and sustained logistics readiness.

The Army, as a component of Joint forces, will accomplish operational and tactical missions at higher tempos while distributed across much larger operational areas. With each insertion of the FCS capabilities and tools into the Current Force BCTs, logistics Command and Control will become an integral element of the Battle Command suite ensuring that commanders will be informed of logistics capabilities and constraints when formulating and executing tactical plans. Existing, or projected, Logistics command and control systems necessary to enable the Army as the theater's sustainment provider, must be built to support this tempo, force distribution and notion of interdependence. Characteristics should include improved information processing, automated updating and distribution, filtering, fusion, decision-making and course of action development across functions and levels that help ensure that the volume of information does not overwhelm commanders and staffs. It should also accelerate the logistics military decision making process provide for COA development under rapidly changing conditions, and more effectively link logistics actions to commanders' intent.

A future logistics C2 strategy must be centered upon achieving a life-cycle driven end-to-end logistics enterprise that supports the application of integrated capabilities across the full spectrum of military operations. These capabilities will be characterized by comprehensive physical and virtual connections, enabling collaboration and ability to share information across the Joint force unhindered by distance, terrain, weather or hostile activity. It must meet the Army's objectives in its strategy for Unified Battle Command and must provide logistics C2 that is integrated into a single Battle Command network such as that being developed by the FCS. Logistics C2 will be applied within the operational environment regardless of echelon, and incorporate key elements of battlespace awareness, command and control and net-centric operation Joint functional areas. It will be developed with a capability to counter threat capabilities through a combination of redundant, multi-layered systems that eliminate single points of failure. Self-healing qualities will automatically adjust and reconfigure the network, reroute information flows and execute immediate action measures to thwart enemy actions. Defences against computer network attack, deception, electronic intrusion and monitoring and effects of electromagnetic pulse will be embedded to support operational and tactical manoeuvre.

These capabilities will be enabled by radically advanced data collection, transmission, pattern development, analysis and discovery of links and relationships normally hidden in vast quantities of data scattered throughout multiple global data bases. Logistics C2 will be integrated, tailored, mobile and networked to connect to any other element across the self-forming, global networking grid. This network dynamically adjusts to support the commanders' intent, mission, and op tempo, systemically predisposed for the swift fight.

## Common Logistics Operating Environment (CLOE)

Common Logistics Operating Environment is the *Army Campaign Plan* initiative to synchronize logistics concepts, organizational approaches, information and a new generation of technologies into a single operational and technical architecture for Current and Future Force structures. The ultimate goal is to enable warfighters and logisticians at all levels to have total situational awareness within a Common Operating Picture for all aspects of logistics, from factory to foxhole. At the same time, warfighters and logisticians will have a single set of interfaces to "business" processes such as calls for support, requisitioning an item from supply, in-transit visibility and domain wide total asset visibility that supports unity of effort and enables rapid, precise response across a wide range of military operations.

At the National level, CLOE enabled data flows will enable fleet trending and analysis, reliability growth, adjustments to maintenance programmes and true prognostic capabilities that will leverage information resources to provide substantially better and more costeffective logistics support. The data will also support configuration management and failure analysis, as well as adjustments to stock levels and consumable requirements. Additionally, CLOE enabled capabilities will assist Performance Based Logistics by providing contractors the information necessary to optimize system readiness.

The integration of logistics services into the FCS Battle Command Network will achieve this for the FCS BCT. The FCS program has three Logistics software services:

- Platform Soldier Mission Readiness System

- The Logistics Decision Support System
- The Logistics Data Management Service.

PS-MRS provides the platform centric portion of the embedded diagnostic and prognostic system. PS-MRS also determines the current and predicted platform readiness, functional capabilities, re-supply needs, and maintenance requirements. LDSS supports the overall sustainment concept for the FCS Equipped BCT by providing logistics operation planning and execution. LDMS provides the Product Support Integrators the status and location of national level assets of FCS spares and repair parts. LDMS enables the collection, reporting and collaboration of logistics data on customer demands received from the DOD, STAMIS and ERPs.

CLOE is an ambitious collaborative initiative to synchronize multiple programmes so that emerging logistics transformation concepts and processes work seamlessly, end-to-end. The technologies that comprise the common logistics operating environment mark a step change in sustainment processes. These enablers have the potential to substantially improve agility and effectiveness and provide major increases in the commander's situational awareness and unit combat power. Using tests, demonstrations, simulations, user assessments and proofs of enablers, CLOE has provided the data needed to design a robust logistics operating environment. CLOE will also validate the integrated logistics architecture; demonstrate the capabilities required to implement the operating environment across the logistics domain and to identify the resources, schedule drivers, and integration needed for Army-wide implementation.

## Army Integrated Logistics Architecture (AILA)

In order to establish the required global visibility of logistics information within the Logistics Domain and within the larger Army and Joint environments, an end-to-end architecture must be defined and integrated. The AILA is the Army's designated overarching logistics architecture and provides the means to move and translate data into meaningful information from multiple sources. The AILA spans from the tactical through strategic echelons and supports a Joint integrated environment.

The AILA informs, guides and supports decisions for the Single Army Logistics Enterprise and assists the Army logistics community in achieving integration and interoperability in the Logistics and Warfighter domains. The AILA is compliant with the Department of Defence Architecture Framework and focuses on current and future concepts, their associated concepts of operations, Service Concepts, Army doctrine and transformation of the Total Force. The AILA supports Army modularity and provides the framework for implementing net-centric warfare principles in the logistics domain. The AILA has been developed in a collaborative effort and continues to evolve. The Army has integrated logistics architecture to establish operational framework and baseline technical standards to enable an end-to-end, common logistics information enterprise. The AILA is the TRADOC approved logistics architecture for the Current Modular Force and will be updated with the CMF model library.

This effort continues to perform research and analysis of evolving Army/Joint operating, functional and integrating concepts and doctrine to collect, organize, correlate and store source data required to meet the purpose and objectives of the architecture. In doing so, this effort is producing the Army's Common Logistics Operating Environment to provide an Army/Joint methodology that defines the Focused Logistics Vision and synchronizes individual embedded diagnostic and prognostics efforts into a common architecture. This architecture effort synchronizes programmes and enables them to work within a common framework to clearly defined logistics processes and share awareness across the logistics domain for both logistics managers and operational commanders. The AILA provides the Army with the capability to link the platform, the lowest level of the Army's logistics network, with the enterprise necessary to provide net-centric logistics, and more importantly the larger migration to DOD's future Net- Enabled Command Capability, the next generation command and control system, Net-Enabled Battle Command and the Army's component of NECC.

## Army-USMC Logistics Interoperability

The Army and USMC logistics communities are collaborating on logistics interoperability issues. A multi-phased plan to promote

Joint Logistics Interoperability commenced in August 2006. A demonstration planned for first quarter 2009 will serve as a test bed for emerging technologies and programmes to advance Joint logistics automation, integration, interoperability and build a foundation for Army and Marine interoperability that enables web-based inter-service support in Joint tactical operations. The demonstration will produce a number of products including Interface Design Documents, Service-Oriented Architecture enabling software and an Implementation Plan that will be provided to Combat Developers, Programme Managers and other organizations to serve as a guide for implement tactical logistics interoperability.

## Adaptive Logistics (AL)

The Adaptive Logistics initiative demonstrates the use of intelligent agent technology and cognitive decision support tools to improve situational understanding by monitoring and synthesizing large volumes of data from disparate sources and rapidly providing courses of action to facilitate decision-making. Intelligent agents have the capability to change the way logisticians do business.

The objectives of Adaptive Logistics (AL) are:

- Achieve asset and event visibility throughout the enterprise from the point of need to the strategic base
- Achieve data standardization by leveraging Common Logistics Operating Environment standards
- Employ Non-Standard Equipment or high technology developmental products to bind logistic decisions with operations plans/execution and achieve Joint collaboration and command and control.

Intelligent agents have the capability to mine and fuse data from disparate sources within minutes, creating an initial analysis of the data to provide courses of action to facilitate decision-making. AL lays the foundation for an effects-based, and ultimately a "predict and pre-empt," environment where Army and Joint data are fused to provide a complete picture to all personnel in the operating environment. This capability has the potential to better synchronize logistics support within the larger military decision support process, enable logisticians and customers to see operational requirements in real-time, and sustain the Joint force commander at the point of need.

The chart below illustrates how intelligent agent technology can be used at a Theater Sustainment Command to create a dynamic Theater Distribution Network to support action officer/decision makers with actionable information and Courses of Action relating to theater distribution planning, execution and monitoring.

**Intelligent Agent Technology Used at a Theater Sustainment Command**

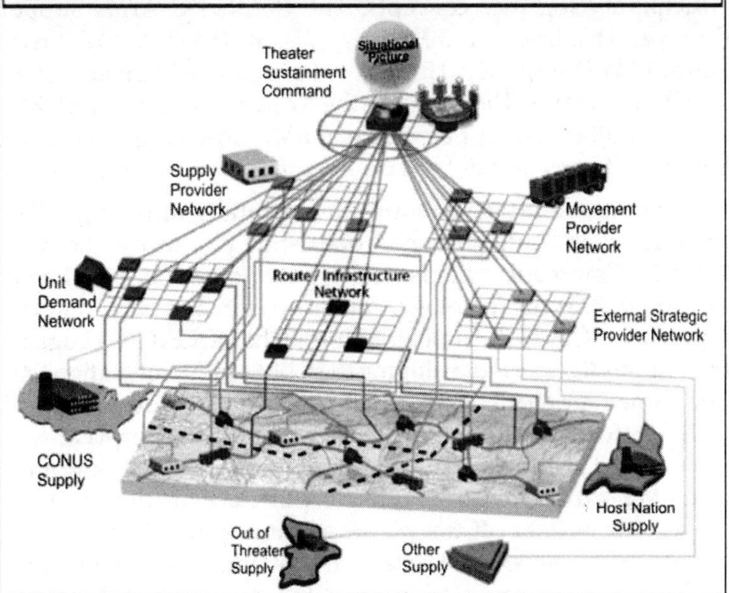


## Condition-Based Maintenance Plus (CBM+)

CBM is a DoD mandated proactive equipment maintenance capability that is enabled by a Common Logistics Operating Environment and uses system health indications to predict functional failure ahead of the event and take appropriate action. "CBM+" consists of a set of rigorously defined maintenance tasks derived from Reliability Centered Maintenance analysis. The tasks can be scheduled in response to accumulation of specified calendar time intervals or operating hours or mileage, or they can be dynamically scheduled, based on the detection of a specified deterioration or operating condition. The goal of CBM+ is to improve the availability of weapons systems throughout their life cycle and reduce cost.

Essentially, CBM+ enables a substantial reduction in equipment downtime, while also providing a dynamic new visibility of equipment health status to operating units. CBM+ will improve maintenance productivity, reduce the deployed footprint required to provide maintenance services to combat units, and provide visibility of equipment status needed to implement anticipatory logistics concepts. The Combined Arms Support Command has inserted CBM+ language into the TRADOC Writers Guide IAW DoD policy. This will ensure Future Combat Systems are CBM+ capable. The challenge the Army faces today with CBM+ is the simultaneous application of CBM+ capabilities to Current Force platforms and enterprise infrastructure and systems.

Programme Managers are incrementally applying CBM+ capabilities to limited numbers of existing platforms. The Army Material Command's Logistics Support Activity is establishing the Army CBM+ data ontology, Combined Arms Support Command is preparing CBM+ documentation, and the ODCS, G-4's Logistics Innovation Agency is developing the CBM+ Implementation Plan. The immediate challenge is that the Army must resource multiple CBM+ efforts simultaneously to achieve an enterprise wide capability. The fundamental building blocks in the development of CBM+ capability are: collection of data on the platform, movement of data off the platform, storing the data in a data warehouse, analyzing the data, and acting on the data. Given these expansive areas of interest the Army must develop a comprehensive resource strategy across Programme Manager lines, life-cycle managers and data storage activities to achieve the desired end state. The CBM+ implementation strategy requires a comprehensive synchronization of multiple system and platform programmes to reach a threshold objective capability within the current FYDP2010-2015. Basic planning will be complete within the next two years, to align ongoing investment programmes and to support complementary resource requests in the POM2012-2017 exercise. The objective CBM+ capability will be realized with a fully integrated and interoperable force consisting of Current Force and Future Combat Systems capabilities.

**Low-Cost/Low-Altitude Aerial Delivery (LCLA)**

Low Cost/Low Altitude is an effective and efficient enabler for aerial delivery of small quantities of supplies at altitudes up to 500 feet above ground level, to units operating in remote, austere and hard-to-reach locations with very limited or no material handling equipment and no viable airstrips. LCLA consists of a family of five parachute systems, which support various weight ranges up to 300 pounds. A subsystem of LCLA currently in development is the Free-drop Packaging Concept Project. The objective of the FPCP is a low-cost package (less than $100), containing 50 to 350 pounds, that can be dropped from an aircraft moving at 65 to 130 knots from an altitude of 50 to 100 feet AGL.

Other objectives include 100% survivability of supplies and recovery and distribution of supplies by two Soldiers without material handling equipment in less than two minutes per package. The free-drop method of re-supply requires an innovative packaging concept where supplies are free-dropped without any decelerator material from a very low altitude and land at the desired location without any damage and in a condition that facilitates recovery and distribution. LCLA and FPCP are two of several key Integrated Logistics Aerial Re-supply Delivery Systems that the Army and Joint communities are developing in synchronization with surface distribution operations to provide the Combatant Commander with alternative capabilities required to meet operational missions. For LCLA, PM FSS is in the process of implementing Indefinite Delivery/ Indefinite Quantity contracts for the manufacture of LCLA parachutes to meet the growing demand from theater.

As of February 2008, forces have conducted over 1600 LCLA airdrops, accounting for over 1.5 million pounds of supplies in support of Operation Enduring Freedom operations and mission requirements. Based on the successful results of FPCP Event 1, further testing was conducted through May, 2008, ranging from static to aircraft airdrops. A final assessment was expected in

March, 2009. LCLA and the FPCP substantially contribute to the agility, effectiveness, efficiency and interoperability of the Joint distribution system. LCLA and FPCP have applicability to Army Special Operations Forces, Airborne Forces, Stryker and Infantry Brigade Combat Teams. Both initiatives support the DCS, G-4's campaign objective of enhanced logistics readiness through the identification, demonstration and transition of technology options that support both the Current Force and the longer-term Future Modular Force.

**Micro Electrical Mechanical System (MEMS)**

Micro Electrical Mechanical Systems are technologies that combine modern electronics with mechanical systems on a small scale to sense, control and act on changing events. MEMS sensors trigger proactive alerts for items that exceed temperature, humidity, vibration, shock and light thresholds. When integrated with active RFID technology, they track and monitor shelf-life and environmental factors affecting assets. MEMS RFID devices improve the ability to preserve material in storage and in-transit, for readiness and timeliness of Soldier support.

To demonstrate MEMS RFID capability, the U.S. Army Logistics Innovation Agency led two sensor pilot demonstrations targeting high pay-off areas. First, long-term storage condition monitoring of assets in Deployable Medical Systems at Sierra Army Depot, CA, in collaboration with Headquarters, Army Material Command, U.S. Army Tank-Automotive and Armaments Command, and U.S. Army Medical Material Agency; and second, in-transit nodal condition monitoring of medical sets, kits and outfits shipped from the U.S. Army Medical Material Center–Europe to customer destinations in the United States Central Command area of operations. This demonstration was conducted in partnership with Product Manager Joint–Automatic Identification Technology. The demonstrations validated that sensor technology is well-suited for long-term storage and in-transit visibility condition monitoring. The sensor data were more accurate and actionable than data from indicators currently in use today for long-term storage. Alerts received via Radio Frequency In- Transit Visibility or e-mail, while assets were in-transit, provided actionable information about the material before it was received downrange.

PM J-AIT is working to fully integrate MEMS RFID technology into RF-ITV. The medical community is exploring further uses of sensors and associated alert capabilities for monitoring medical chemical defence material, and is collaborating with PM J-AIT, the Office of the Army Deputy Chief of Staff, G-4, USCENTCOM and other stakeholders to identify requirements for fielding, sustainment and user training. HQ AMC is working with PM J-AIT to implement sensor security tags in all DEPMEDS at SIAD. Although the demonstrations focused on specific medical assets as high-payoff applications, MEMS RFID benefits extend to all classes of supply and logistics processes, across all Services.

It is clear that these capabilities are particularly appropriate for shelf life or life-limited assets such as medical and food assets; but the applications are many and varied, and each application must be evaluated based on individual merit. Key considerations include examination of business rules, with corresponding changes to and integration of supporting automated information systems, establishment of policies and standards, and training in the school houses. As sensor, RFID and satellite-based location and tracking systems become more interoperable, these networks will help improve the quality, integrity and safety of products in storage and while moving through the supply chain, with improved knowledge for life-cycle tracking.

## Next Generation Wireless Communications (NGWC) for Logistics Applications

NGWC is a NS-E technology integration effort focused on developing and integrating technologies to significantly enhance visibility of Army and DoD assets in both time and space. NGWC encompasses a suite of mesh network-enabled, information assurance compliant, sensor devices that will collect vital logistics visibility data and route that visibility data to the Radio Frequency In-Transit Visibility server via interfaces with existing backhaul communications capabilities already in existence throughout the distribution pipeline. The NGWC effort is characterized as follows:

- Requirements based developmental effort
- Open architecture, standards-based methodology
- Leverages ad hoc mobile mesh network technology as the framework communications architecture
- NS-E sensor-enabled (based on customer requirements)
- DoD Information Assurance compliant
- Mesh functionality designed to support logistics business processes
- Asset visibility in transit, storage and processing
- Logistics operational resource visibility
- Under NGWC, the Army will demonstrate the initial functioning spiral of mesh network technology in late summer of 2008. Additional spirals of mesh network technology will focus on mesh design to support specific logistics business processes. The Army is collaborating with the United States Transportation Command and the United States Joint Forces Command to ensure service and joint requirements are addressed in the overall NGWC asset visibility solution.

## Robotics

Robotics technologies are man-made devices that are capable of sensing and interacting with the environment. The technology is capable of performing functions that are normally performed by human operators. Robotic systems are made up of mechanical components, computers, sensors and other specialized devices. Current robotics applications, with some exceptions, are geared towards performing repetitive, dangerous, or difficult work that humans cannot perform well or would not want to perform.

Applications within the Army, with some exceptions can be sorted into two broad categories: Unmanned Ground Vehicles and Unmanned Aircraft Systems. Based on current and planned unmanned robotics capabilities, the U.S. Army Logistics Innovation Agency developed a Robotics Assessment (August, 2006) that identifies expected robotics capabilities and frames them against potential logistics policy and doctrinal implications. With rapid improvements in robotic technologies, new opportunities are emerging in the application of robotic systems to provide improved logistics support, especially in higher risk operations.

In support of robotics logistics systems development, LIA recently conducted initial analysis that outlines near term, high pay-off logistics applications of robotics technologies (November, 2007). This analysis lays the groundwork for further experimentation with robotics capabilities to improve logistics speed and minimize exposure to dangerous operations.

## Focused Logistics Modernization

The following Programmes and initiatives are the prime modernization efforts of Focused Logistics–not in priority order:

## Science and Technology Capabilities Gap Filler

Convoy Active Safety Technologies (CAST) supports requirements to improve Soldier protection and increase the ability to sustain the force by increasing distribution capability. CAST is a low cost, Leader/ Follower capability for the Current Force tactical wheeled vehicle fleet and uses Future Force autonomous navigation technologies with a Current Force vehicle application. The system demonstrates potential to improve driver safety by increasing situational awareness, reducing collisions and fatigue, as well as improve convoy integrity. Additionally, the system benefits the ability to sustain the force by increasing distribution throughput. This program supports Army Gaps and Shortfalls outlined in the Current Gap Assessment VI, Capability Needs Assessment 10-15, and FY09 Technology Shortfalls Analysis as well as USMC gaps.

## Focused Logistics: Wearable Energetically Autonomous Robotics- Personal Combat Vehicle (WEAR-PCV)

Logistics Variant, formerly known as Exoskeleton, is a robotic augmentation for an individual Soldier that increases Soldier strength and endurance. With the ability to be worn and used in all Soldier work environments, the logistics variant WEAR-PCV is an agile, dexterous, compact and self-powered physical enhancement with potential to significantly reduce workload and fatigue for Soldiers performing logistics repetitive, heavy lifting/moving tasks. This system supports developmental efforts towards a Combat Infantry variant requirement outlined in the Ground Soldier System Capability Development Document. Additionally, the WEAR-PCV could fill low-weight Material Handling Equipment shortfalls as well as supports gaps outlined in the current gap.

## Assessment VI, Capability Needs Assessment 10-15.

Streamlining and improving the turn-around of the BOIP process from product development approval from the PM/PdM to the field. Could this process be automated to make initial allocations and the process for revision quicker and less involved as the Army transforms and modernizes?

## Force Provider

Force Provider is known as the Army's premier deployable base camp capability. Although initially intended to support Reception, Staging and Onward Integration as well as Rest and Recuperation missions, over time it has evolved to being used to support disaster relief, Forward Operating Bases and even relocated with Provisional Reconstruction Teams. In order to meet these missions, the latest configuration Force Provider

Expeditionary remains a 600 person module, but is packaged into four 150 person capability increments. By reconfiguring the modules with air-beam tents and Triple Container based kitchens, laundries, showers, and latrines, a single 150 person increment can deploy on one C-17 and can be operational in less than six hours. The Army is developing, with input from the other Services, a Joint Capability Production Document which incorporates both the core and additional add-on capabilities that the warfighter has requested for Force Provider / base camp support. One of the capabilities that will significantly reduce bulk water resupply requirements is a Shower Water Reuse system, which leverages the Army's Tactical Water Purification System technology. Other add-on capabilities include water bottling, ice production, a Modular Ballistic Protection System for tents, patient care containers and a capability to reduce the vast quantity of solid waste that must be backhauled for disposal. Although these capabilities increase the procurement cost of a module, they quickly pay for themselves by keeping trucks off the road. The Army medical community has provided significant input to the CPD as they intend to leverage many of the Force Provider Expeditionary subsystems for their Combat Support Hospitals. Force Provider Expeditionary and its subsystems are on the way to becoming the Joint solution to support the deployed warfighter.

## Field Feeding

The Army is about to begin fielding the Assault Kitchen, which provides a heat-on-the-move capability to prepare the Unitized Group Ration Heat & Serve and, with the retention of selected items from the Kitchen Company Level Field Feeding, provides units the capability to prepare the UGR-A when appropriate. Through an engineering change to the current Containerized Kitchen, we will provide the cook with thermostatic control of the kitchen appliances and improved work environment, while still retaining the 10KW Tactical Quiet Generator. The recently completed Army Food Programme Capabilities Based Assessment identified the need for a full service kitchen to replace the Mobile Kitchen Trailer which has been in the field since 1975. That effort will be the Battlefield Kitchen and is anticipated to be made available to the field in the 2015 time period after the CK completes fielding. Until then, the Army will continue to reset MKTs as they will continue to be in use for at least another 20 years.

In order to meet the directives of "no stocks on the ground" and Brigade Combat Teams must be three days self sustaining and in conjunction with the implementation of the Configured Loads concept; the Army developed and will soon field the Multi-Temperature Refrigerated Container System. The MTRCS will be fielded to field feeding sections across the force as one per CK/MKT and to subsistence platoons which will enable the movement of frozen and refrigerated items in the same container. The complete MTRCS configuration includes a HEMTT-LHS, PLS Trailer, a Flatrack and the MTRCS refrigerated container, thus providing the ability to support up to 800 personnel with operational rations for three days.

## Aerial Delivery Goals and Direction

Current cargo airdrop equipment is vintage 1940's technology which was designed for delivery from aircraft three times removed from the inventory and from altitudes inconsiderate of current threat capabilities. We must modernize ADE to retain and revive the uniqueness of the airdrop method, to make airdrop relevant to current and Future Modular Force operations, and to have it perform as a viable supply and re-supply method based on theater needs and mission requirements. The goal is to provide a "mix" of airdrop options or a menu of alternative material systems to provide the right capability to accomplish the mission. These capabilities include necessary high tech solutions such as the Joint Precision Air Drop System, as well as low tech solutions like the Low Cost Low Altitude Airdrop System. These systems provide: flexibility in type of aerial delivery platforms, increased air carrier survivability via altitude/horizontal offset, improved ground accuracy which increases load survivability and provides lower cost alternatives that meet performance requirements while moving toward "throwaway" status or a reduced need to be recovered.

Current sling-load operations and equipment are outdated. Material solutions to satisfy gaps here include slings and netting that are stronger, lighter, non-abrasive and less expensive. A nondestructive test capability for these items is necessary; as is the capability for better weighing prepared loads for "handoff" to the aircrews. An automatic/automated capability is being explored that removes ground personnel from the task of having to physically ground the aircraft and then affix the prime sling leg upon the aircraft hook which allows an automatic "hook-up" to loads. Historically, rotorcrafts conduct air-land operations via internal cargo transport and sling-load operations. However, rotorcraft is a viable airdrop platform, to include free drop platforms and should be used in this manner to further reduce blade time. This will also increase air carrier survivability and provide greater flexibility as an aerial delivery platform.

In a broader sense, our goal is to increase the use of aerial delivery platforms as a routine transportation mode for distributing and sustaining troops on the ground. As a result of enemy tactics, techniques and procedures we are left reliant upon a fragile, resource intensive, frequently unreliable and unresponsive Ground Line of Communication. The driving mission for all of us is to sustain the force, wherever they may be located, in a responsive manner. When critical, there is a great difference in customer wait times of hours as opposed to days. The customer is not interested in the transportation mode used or the price paid to transport the supply requirements; they want their items at the right time, in the right place in usable condition.

## Water Distribution Modernization

The delivery of potable water on the battlefield accounts for a significant portion of the distribution footprint. This large footprint translates into increased risk for Soldiers and civilians involved in delivering and protecting those delivering this commodity. One of our goals is to significantly reduce the distribution requirements for potable water by purifying/generating and packaging as far forward as possible. Two efforts that support the reduction of the distribution footprint for potable drinking water are in development:

## The Expeditionary Water Packaging System (EWPS)

The Expeditionary Water Packaging System is a complete water packaging system that consists of a blow molding machine,; work station, plastic preforms stock bin, conveyor system, two ultraviolet sanitizing units, bottle capping machine, bottle labeler, 6 KW air conditioning unit, diesel engine driven generator, banding machine, and shrink wrap machine. The system allows the bottling of ROWPU purified water within or near the battle space of consuming organizations eliminating the need to transport bottled water from regionally available sources or CONUS.

### The Gator, Self Filling Camel (GSFC)

The Gator Self Filling Camel uses water from air technology to generate water at or near the point of consumption. This technology uses a series of proprietary processes to extract and treat water from atmospheric air and dispense pure water on demand. It will operate over a wide range of climatic conditions and provide drinking water in a variety of tactical situations.

### Test Measurement & Diagnostic Equipment (TMDE)

Modernization General Purpose Electronic Test Equipment: GPETE, formally known as the Army's Test Equipment Modernization Program, was chartered in 1983 with goals of: improving the material readiness of weapon systems; reducing TMDE proliferation; as well as obsolescence and support costs. GPETE is a funded program which utilizes commercial off-the-shelf test equipment acquisition to streamline the normal life cycle process. The Programme Director for TMDE acquires TMDE identified by the GPETE Joint Working Group which annually convenes to select and prioritize GPETE requirements. The Department of the Army G-3 is responsible for approving the GPETE Prioritization List. The benefits of the GPETE Programme are: it continues to provide support of weapon systems requiring TMDE, it further reduces the TMDE redundancy and obsolescence in the field, allows for maintenance personnel to have the most current TMDE to perform alignment, calibration or repair tasks and it reduces support cost with limited models of TMDE in the field.

### Container/Material Handling Equipment (C/MHE)

Container/Material Handling Equipment modernization is occurring through the following three programmes:

a. CASCOM requested HQDA approval to transition from the Army's over-age 4,000 pound, rough terrain forklift fleet and adopt the USMC 5,000 pound Light Capability Rough Terrain forklift. In addition to a Joint Army/USMC 5K forklift, enhancements include: increased lift capacity, an extendable boom to assist installing Armor Kits on all vehicles, and a fork mounted pintle attachment to position trailers.

b. CASCOM's approved ORD for the 10,000 pound All-Terrain Lifter Army System has six TACOM contract prototypes at Aberdeen Test Center under-going production Validation Testing for a projected FUE in 2Q FY08. ATLAS II enhancements include: increased reliability, lifetime lubricated axles, EPA approved tier II engine, Addon armor for operator protection and Interactive Electronic Technical Manuals to compress diagnostic and repair times.

c. CASCOM's on-going material handling Capabilities Based Assessment contract will research the Army's future concept needs for all TOE forklift, container handlers and cranes (2015–2025). Deliverables by 1 Oct 08 include four JCIDS documents TRADOC ARCIC will use to grant permission to write new CDD/CPD's incorporating technology for modernizing future forklifts and container handlers.

## Test Measurement & Diagnostic Equipment

Modernization Next Generation Automatic Test System: The NGATS is the Army's latest Automatic Test System within the Integrated Family of Test Equipment. It will serve as the Army's designated off-system diagnostic set providing a balance of support for both aviation and ground platforms which includes Abrams, Bradley, MLRS and Kiowa Warrior. NGATS is designed to replace existing offsystem testers currently fielded and experiencing obsolescence. It has also been identified as the Army's ATS for the Joint Agile Rapid Global Combat Support Advance Concept Technology Demonstration.

The benefit for modernizing IFTE with NGATS is that it complies with the Joint/Department of Defence/NxTest open architecture enabling all services to leverage off each other's diagnostic systems. In addition, NGATS is designed for continued modernization utilizing commercial industry technological standards. NGATS will be C-130 air transportable and self contained allowing for versatility with mission requirements. Potentially, NGATS could perform diagnostics on multi service platforms.

### Advanced Bomb Suit

The Advanced Bomb Suit continues to be updated to increase survivability while maintaining mobility. The second generation EOD 9 helmet provides better ventilation, external lighting and better blast protection than earlier models. As of 2007 all CENTCOM EOD units were issued the latest version of helmet. In response to an Operational Needs Statement, the Army is developing a night vision visor system to allow EOD Soldiers to operate at night without white lights, making themselves less vulnerable to sniper attacks.

Annexure B

# Modernization Advancements in DOTMLPF

Modernization is not just about equipping and upgrading material. Advancements in Army Doctrine, Organizations, Training, Material, Leadership and Education, Personnel and Facilities (DOTMLPF) are supporting the Soldier now and in the future by providing integrated solutions which improve capabilities in how the Army is organized, trained, and led in accordance with new doctrine that forms the basis for conducting full spectrum operations. New personnel Programmes, including significantly increased assistance to Wounded Warriors and Families, have been recently instituted to lower stress and fully address the needs of an All Volunteer Force at war. The installation management community continues to meet the challenge of providing quality, mission-ready installations. This Annexure will outline advancements in DOTMLPF.

## Doctrine and the Army

The Army is a learning organization. Its doctrine cannot remain static. It is continuously revised based on the Joint operational environment, lessons learned and concepts that are validated through Joint and Army experimentation and developed through the Joint Capabilities Integration and Developments System.

Army operations will continue to be based on doctrine and training standards that have proven effective over time. Doctrine forms the basis for how to conduct full spectrum operations, and provides the foundation for training and leader development. Holistically doctrine, leader development, and training support Army readiness. Doctrine facilitates communication among Soldiers – no matter where they serve – and contributes to a shared professional culture that serves as a baseline for curricula in the Army's Training and Education System. Army doctrine consists of principles, tactics, techniques and procedures, terms, graphics and symbols. It is detailed enough to guide operations, yet flexible enough to allow commanders to exercise initiative when dealing with specific situations. To be effective, doctrine must be well known, vetted, accurate, acceptable and commonly understood. Doctrine must also be integrated and consistent with Joint doctrine, and describe the Army's approach to applying dominant land power in Joint operations. The Army's two capstone doctrinal manuals are: *FM 1, The Army;* and *FM 3-0, Operations*. FM 1 contains the Army's vision. FM 3-0 provides the principles for conducting full spectrum operations and describes the operational role of linking tactical operations to strategic aims. It details how Army forces conduct operations in unified action. These two doctrinal publications establish the foundation in preparing the Army to dominate land warfare in Joint operations.

## Sustaining a Doctrine-based Army

Doctrine of the future must enable core warfighting capabilities while increasing strategic responsiveness and land dominance over an expanded range of missions and threats. Our doctrine must encourage relentless pursuit of the initiative in all military operations. It must address the importance of the Army's ability to control land, resources and people through a sustained presence as part of a Joint force.

Doctrine has to support an Army that is a hybrid force that is transforming from the current to the Future Force – and embrace both. Throughout the spectrum of conflict, Army doctrine must emphasize Army contributions to supporting the Joint force commander.

Doctrine cannot predict exact types of asymmetric engagement. It can however, forecast the types of knowledge and information, and the organizational qualities necessary for victory. The Army is applying its cognitive and physical resources to refine its doctrine by incorporating lessons learned from current operations, and experimentation results based on Joint and Army concepts. Doctrinal revisions are to address full spectrum operations—including offensive, defensive and stability operations against potential enemies that may deliberately avoid predictable operating patterns and are likely to use a combination of traditional, irregular, disruptive and catastrophic means to achieve their ends.

The *Army Campaign Plan* directs the comprehensive strategic change of the operational and generating forces, including development of future concepts and doctrine to guide force development and employment of the Army Modular Force. Specific guidance includes the publication of Army's capstone concept, *The Army in Joint Operations: The Army's Future Force Capstone Concept, 2015-2024*. Operating concepts, functional concepts, and concept capability plans within the Army Concept Strategy. Joint and Army concepts provide the conceptual basis for Joint and Army experimentation and the development of future capabilities through DOTMLPF solutions via the Joint Capabilities Integration and Development System.

In the near term, U.S. Army Training and Doctrine Command and other non-TRADOC doctrine proponents will revise key Army doctrine to address current and future operations in the Joint, interagency, intergovernmental, and multinational environments. The recent publishing of FM 3-0, *Operations* (dated 27 February 2008), will drive the revision/ update of several keystone and supporting doctrinal publications. TRADOC will focus on the development of Joint and Army doctrine that maximizes the capability for the current Modular Force to conduct full spectrum operations.

TRADOC continues to explore systems that have the potential to be important enablers to providing routine access to the Army's doctrine knowledge base for the Soldier, the trainer and for the doctrine developer. Technology and publishing standards have evolved to allow for a more logical and efficient way to capture and exchange Army publications information and knowledge. TRADOC continues to evaluate the feasibility of applying this technology to develop doctrine as stand-alone objects. The intent of this theory is to provide an enterprise solution that allows Soldiers to gain immediate access to the latest FMs, and provide doctrine developers with the improved business processes (technologically enhanced) to rapidly update and develop FMs as needed. This concept has the potential to improve content search results, automate workflow to enable efficient business processes, provide a centralized content repository to facilitate content reuse, and support common authoring tools with a standardized taxonomy, schema, and meta-data.

## The Army Doctrine Hierarchy

TRADOC continues to shape the Army doctrine hierarchy to match the Joint doctrine hierarchy as closely as possible. The Army's FM numbering system, which mirrors the Joint system, aligns and shows linkage of Army doctrinal publications with Joint doctrine. The Army's warfighting doctrine is structured into a two-tiered hierarchy to provide for development and operational relationships for implementation/execution. Tier I is the highest level, with the majority of the field manuals directly linked to Joint doctrine. The publications offer broad perspectives on doctrine principles and focus on Army operations in Joint campaigns. The highest level Tier II publications are designated as capstone or keystone FMs. Tier 2 doctrine captures the bulk of proponent's lower-level organizational FMs, most of which are narrower in scope than Tier II FMs, and address subjects in varying levels of detail, depending on the subject, type of force and echelon. These publications provide a variety of tactics, techniques, procedures, terms, symbols and graphics for specific functions, units, multi-Service operations and the employment of Soldiers and systems, as well as references for basic soldiering skills.

## Doctrine to Support a Nation at War and a Transforming Army

As we engage an enemy whose unconventional means force us to respond to a non-traditional threat, the Center for Army Lessons Learned (CALL) continues to deploy teams into theater to capture lessons learned and best practices. Appropriate information is validated and incorporated into doctrinal publications and/or CALL publications that shape and drive training. Topics of particular interest for lessons learned continue to include convoy operations, detainee operations, improvised explosive device defeat, cordon and search and counterinsurgency operations.

CALL will continue to be the primary source of observations, insights, and lessons (OIL) for the Army as it modernizes. CALL collects, analyzes, disseminates, integrates and archives Army and Joint, Interagency, Intergovernmental and Multinational OIL and tactics, techniques and procedures to support full spectrum military operations. CALL deploys Collection and Analysis Teams to both CONUS locations and into theater to collect OIL and TTP relevant to the operational, institutional and Future Force. CALL currently supports the Army through an integrated network or lessons learned specialists located at TRADOC schools, CTCs, divisions, corps with more informal linkages with Joint organizations, and interagency and intergovernmental institutions, to include disaster relief and homeland security. CALL plans to expand the L2I network to Joint, interagency, and intergovernmental partners in the near future. CALL will continue to augment current Army transformation efforts, including the Future Combat Systems, with actual operations and Combat Training Center OIL and TTP.

The centerpiece of the modular Army is the Brigade Combat Team, which has three designs: heavy, infantry, and Stryker. Simultaneously, Army higher echelon headquarters (corps and divisions) have been restructured into modular designs. As the Army continues to transform to these modular organizations, so must the Army continue to revise its doctrine on how to employ and fight these organizations.

The Future Combat Systems – equipped Brigade Combat Team is the Army's primary Future Modular Force Programme initiative. Through the JCIDS and supporting DOTMLPF analysis, TRADOC identified a series of doctrinal publications required to support experimentation, testing, and fielding of the Army's FCS-equipped brigade combat team. These draft publications will be used as a foundation to support evaluation, training, employment, warfighting and identification of necessary changes for the FCS equipped Brigade Combat Team prior to production. Doctrinal publications identified to support employment of the FCS are:

- FMI 3-55.10, FBCT Intelligence, Surveillance and Reconnaissance (ISR)
- FMI 3-04.154, FBCT Manned/Unmanned Teaming Operations
- FMI 3-09.45, FBCT Fires and Effects
- FMI 3-20.82, FBCT Gunnery and Marksmanship Training
- FMI 4-01.01, FBCT Manoevre Support Operations
- FMI 3-90.8, FBCT Manoevre
- FMI 3-90.9, FBCT Operations
- FMI 4-90.9, FBCT Manoevre Sustainment Operations
- FMI 6-0.1, FBCT Battle Command
- FMI 7-11, FBCT Embedded Training

FM 3-90.9 is the FCS keystone pub and is the first of these publications drafted, which sets the foundation to develop the other supporting FCS publications. Along with other draft FCS FMs, it will be used initially to support the Army Evaluation Task Force experimentations and evaluations. They will be continuously updated based on lessons learned from testing. TRADOC and non-TRADOC proponents involved in Rapid Equipping Force and FCS Spin-out initiatives to the current Modular Force are analyzing current and emerging Modular Force doctrine at all echelons to ensure employment of these systems are doctrinally sound and standardized throughout the Army and to maximize capabilities of the Joint force.

### The Army Doctrine Literature Master Plan and Modernization

The Army will continue to use the Doctrine Literature Master Plan (DLMP) as a tool to manage and forecast resources for future development and sustainment of all doctrinal publications. The DLMP provides a snapshot on the status/readiness of Army doctrinal publications and reflects man-hour resources required per fiscal year for doctrine development. It lists all Army, Joint, multi-Service and multinational doctrinal publications for which TRADOC and non-TRADOC doctrine agencies are proponent and/or primary/ technical review authority. It contains a listing of current relevant publications, new developments, revisions, future developments and proposed publications for consolidation. Because doctrine development is decentralized across Army agencies, the DLMP establishes planning standards and consistency and serves to institutionalize a methodology used to sustain the lifecycle of FMs and determine and articulate doctrine resource requirements for the execution, budget and POM planning years.

## Future of the Army Doctrine and Doctrinal Process

The TRADOC Knowledge Management and Information Management Study will drive development of enterprise level recommendations and an implementation plan that will address the basic idea of the Army as a knowledge-based institution and how the Army can improve and progress in the functional areas of information and knowledge management. From a doctrine development and distribution viewpoint the Study results will have a significant impact on how the Army gathers operational information, how the Army gains knowledge or how the Army learns and subsequently how that knowledge and learning is reflected in doctrine products and enablers used by Soldiers, leaders and units in training or when deployed.

TRADOC continues to evaluate the feasibility of applying this technology to develop doctrine as stand alone objects. The intent of this theory is to provide an enterprise solution that allows Soldiers to gain immediate access to the latest FMs, and provide doctrine developers with the improved business processes (technologically enhanced) to rapidly update and develop FMs as needed. This concept has the potential to improve content search results, automate workflow to enable efficient business processes, provide a centralized content repository to facilitate content reuse and support common authoring tools with a standardized taxonomy, schema and meta-data.

## Organizations–Status of the Army Modular Force

The Army is pursuing the most comprehensive transformation of its forces since the early years of World War II. This transformation is intended to produce evolutionary and revolutionary changes which improve both Army and Joint force capabilities to meet current and future full spectrum challenges. Over the past four years, we have accelerated change throughout the Army to better enable it to fight the current fight and be more capable of conducting sustained operations in an environment

of continuously evolving persistent conflict. During fiscal year 2008, the Army will see a great deal of progress in the Army's efforts to transform from a division based to a brigade based force. In addition to developing and executing Army-wide change processes, we are executing several other initiatives that will dramatically shape our future, to include the *Quadrennial Defence Review, Base Realignment and Closure, Guidance for the Development of the Force, and the Integrated Global Presence and Basing Strategy.*

We continue to aggressively reshape the force to become a campaign quality Army with Joint and expeditionary capabilities—transforming to win the war today while simultaneously positioning ourselves to meet future challenges. Army general-purpose forces are proving to be the primary military instrument for creating favorable and enduring security conditions in crisis regions around the world. However, strategic and operational requirements compel the Army to reconcile staying power, durability and adaptability with expeditionary agility and responsiveness. Not only must the Army sustain decisive operations for as long as necessary to win the current fight and achieve politically favorable resolution, Army forces must also continuously adapt to changes across the spectrum of conflict. There is no doubt the Army must remain a learning, transforming organization in the face of adaptive adversaries.

The Army is transforming to meet the challenges of the new security environment characterized by an era of persistent conflict with adaptive enemies in complex environments. Army transformation improves the capabilities of Soldiers engaged in a long war against terrorism. Army transformation improves the capability of units to conduct full spectrum operations and meet traditional, irregular, catastrophic and disruptive challenges. Army transformation improves the capability of the Joint force to defend the homeland, deter conflict in critical regions, respond promptly to small-scale contingencies and swiftly defeat the enemy in major combat operations.

The Army Modular Force reorganizes the operational Army into modular theater armies, theater support structure, corps and division headquarters, brigade combat teams, and multi-functional and functional support brigades based on standardized organizational designs for the AC and RC. The Army is addressing several priorities as a result of this effort: the size of the Army to meet strategic requirements; the wartime costs of equipment Reset and unit readiness; the need to transform and modernize the force; and taking care of Soldiers and their Families.

The Army views transformation as the continuous evolution of capabilities over time from the Current to Future Force. Army transformation produces the optimum mix of land capabilities for the Joint force, manages risk prudently, and is both affordable and essential for the Nation to win the war today and prepare for an uncertain future.

To maximize force effectiveness and strategic flexibility, the Army is reorganizing to a modular, brigade-based force to achieve three primary goals:

- Increase the number of available brigade combat teams to meet operational commitments while maintaining combat effectiveness that is equal to or better than that of previous divisional brigades
- Create brigade-based combat and support formations of common organizational designs that can be easily tailored to meet the varied demands of the geographic Combatant Commanders – reducing Joint planning and execution complexities
- Redesign organizations to perform as integral parts of the Joint force – making them more effective across the spectrum of conflict and enhancing their ability to contribute to Joint, interagency, and multinational efforts
- At the end of fiscal year 2007 the Army accomplished the following transformation activities associated with modular conversion of its forces:
- The AC had a total of 35 BCTs converted and another four BCTs converting and the ARNG had 26 BCTs undergoing modular conversion
- The Army had converted a total of 92 functional brigades (AC – 28/ARNG – 30/USAR – 34) and 52 multifunctional support brigades (AC – 29/ ARNG – 19/USAR – 4)

- The training base continued to transform to perform Service Title 10 and executive agent functions more efficiently. Work continued on determining the requisite size of the institutional Army required to generate, train, and sustain the operational force
- Continued initial implementation of Army Force Generation (ARFORGEN) processes to provide a steady flow of trained and ready forces to Combatant Commanders while ensuring greater stability and deployment predictability for Soldiers and their Families
- By the end of fiscal year 2008, the Army will accomplish the following transformation activities associated with modular conversion of its forces:
- The AC will have a total of 38 BCTs converted and another two BCTs converting and the ARNG will have 28 BCTs undergoing modular conversion, 16 functional support brigades (AC – 7/ ARNG – 6/USAR – 3) and 27 multifunctional support brigades (AC – 4/ARNG – 18/USAR – 5)
- Continued execution of Army Force Generation
- Identification and initial implementation of substantial structural changes to the institutional base of the Army as part of the Total Army Analysis 2010-2015

Despite these transformation activities, the Army will remain challenged to meet anticipated requirements. The Army is out of balance. The demand for forces exceeds the sustainable supply. In January 2007, the President approved a growth in ground forces which increased the Army End Strength by 74,200; a growth of 65,000 in the Active Component (AC), 8,200 in the Army National Guard (ARNG), and 1,000 in the United States Army Reserve (USAR). This plan will build six additional AC BCTs, 15 (8 AC, 5 ARNG, and 2 USAR) support units and associated Combat Support and Combat Service Support units, and culminate in a total of 76 BCTs and approximately 227 Support Brigades across all three components by 2013. In September 2007, the Secretary of Defence approved the Chief of Staff of the Army initiative to accelerate the AC and ARNG End Strength growth to fiscal year 2010 and to accelerate the growth of the sixth additional AC BCT, completing BCT modular conversion and assisting in the restoration of balance in the force by 30 September 2011. Although all units will be under a modular design by fiscal year 2013, full fielding of some items of equipment will take longer. Under the current equipping plan, the fielding of Programmemed items will not be completed until 2015 for BCTs and 2019 for support brigades.

The growth will better posture the Army to build strategic and operational depth across all three components to enable the strategy and meet COCOM requirements; will provide 76 BCTs and over 227 support brigades with essential logistics and sustainment enablers to mitigate persistent shortfalls; and will begin to build Institutional Army capability to generate and sustain the force by the end of the Programme years.

## Adapt the Reserve Components

The Active Component/Reserve Component AC/RC rebalance initiative is an incremental, ongoing process that has evolved over time to hasten the transformation of a post cold war Army into a force capable of effectively addressing war fighting requirements in the new strategic environment. The major tenets of this initiative include: Increasing capabilities to relieve stress on units with persistent shortfalls; the elimination of demand for Reserve Component forces during the initial phase of an operational deployment; and rebalancing structure to maximize readiness and rotational availability while preserving Homeland Defence/Homeland Security capabilities. With the increased emphasis by the Secretary of Defence to reduce the impact on RC structure, AC/RC Rebalance has become an integral part of force management in aligning resources across all three components. The Army is also addressing the imbalance of its key force multiplier capabilities by creating a balanced AC/RC structure in organizations that deploy and sustain the force. This includes the ability to expand certain activities through commercial contracting to ease over reliance on RC assets, provide surge ability for contingency operations, and maintaining routine peacetime operations at strategic nodes and Power Generation Platforms.

The Army began addressing AC/RC Rebalance in Programme Objective Memorandum 2004-2009 with adjustments of approximately 25,000 spaces to restructure the force in a post September 11, 2001 security posture. Following the Secretary of Defence guidance in July 2003, the Army rebalanced an additional

10,000 spaces of structure to reduce RC mobilization and reliance on RC capabilities in the initial phase of an operational deployment. Concurrent implementation of the Chief of Staff, Army Focus Areas effected change in over 90,000 spaces of structure to include the elimination of AC units at Authorized Levels of Organization at less than 100 percent; the reduction of persistent shortfall units in the AC; and elimination of over structure, and establishment of individuals accounts in the RC. For fiscal year 2003-2011 the Army had Programmemed for more than 125,000 spaces of change. In fiscal year 2006 the Army incorporated Office of the Secretary of Defence Guidance on reporting skill set rebalance and the elimination of over structure in the Reserve Components. By the close of fiscal year 2007 the Army had completed the rebalance of more than 53,564 spaces of structure.

With the rebalancing efforts that resulted from decisions made in Quadrennial Defence Review 2006, and the Grow the Army Plan the Army has moved into a new phase of the AC/RC rebalance initiative. This phase added an additional 74,200 spaces of force structure across all three components to meet increasing strategic demands and relive stress on persistent shortfall capabilities. In addition, it completed the reduction of force structure above authorized end strength levels and rite-sized the individual accounts in the RC. In fiscal year 2008-2013 the Army is Programmemed to rebalance an additional 88,712 spaces bringing the Army total to 142,276 spaces.

The AC/RC rebalance initiative is on track. The Army continuously reviews force balance and makes adjustments where necessary in order to distribute deployment burdens across all three components. In the Total Army Analysis cycle supporting POM 2010-2015, the force structure balance will continue to adjust to address force capabilities required by the Army Force Generation (ARFORGEN) model that support Secretary of Defence mobilization and rotation policy, relieve stress on emerging persistent shortfalls, and eliminate the reliance on Reserve Component capabilities in the initial days of an operational deployment.

The AC/RC rebalance initiative is an integral force management tool that provides holistic analysis of Army structure across all three components. As the Army continues to transform the Reserve Component into an "Operational Reserve" this initiative will ensure that force capabilities are balanced in accordance with Secretary of Defence guidance while meeting Combatant Commander requirements.

**Summary of ACP Modular Conversion**
(Reflects GTA Plan)
**Depicts Total Converted/Converting Brigades**

| | Capability | FY07 | FY08 | FY09 | FY10 | FY11 | FY12 | FY13 |
|---|---|---|---|---|---|---|---|---|
| AC | Brigade Combat Teams | 39 | 40 | 42 | 44 | 48 | 48 | 48 |
| | Multi-functional Support Brigades | 29 | 33 | 35 | 37 | 38 | 38 | 39 |
| | Functional Support Brigades | 28 | 35 | 41 | 42 | 44 | 44 | 44 |
| | **Subtotal** | **96** | **108** | **118** | **123** | **130** | **130** | **131** |
| | | **73%** | **82%** | **90%** | **94%** | **99%** | **99%** | **100%** |
| ARNG | Brigade Combat Teams | 29 | 28 | 28 | 28 | 28 | 28 | 28 |
| | Multi-functional Support Brigades | 19 | 37 | 40 | 42 | 46 | 46 | 46 |
| | Functional Support Brigades | 30 | 36 | 36 | 36 | 38 | 38 | 38 |
| | **Subtotal** | **75** | **101** | **104** | **108** | **112** | **112** | **112** |
| | | **67%** | **90%** | **93%** | **95%** | **100%** | **100%** | **100%** |
| USAR | Multi-functional Support Brigades | 4 | 9 | 10 | 10 | 10 | 10 | 12 |
| | Functional Support Brigades | 34 | 37 | 38 | 38 | 48 | 48 | 48 |
| | **Subtotal** | **38** | **46** | **48** | **48** | **58** | **58** | **60** |
| | | **63%** | **77%** | **80%** | **80%** | **97%** | **97%** | **100%** |
| Army | Brigade Combat Teams | 65 | 68 | 70 | 72 | 76 | 76 | 76 |
| | Multi-functional Support Brigades | 52 | 79 | 85 | 89 | 94 | 94 | 97 |
| | Functional Support Brigades | 92 | 108 | 115 | 116 | 130 | 130 | 130 |
| | ***Total*** | *209* | ***255*** | ***270*** | ***277*** | ***300*** | ***300*** | *303* |
| | | **69%** | **84%** | **89%** | **91%** | **99%** | **99%** | **100%** |

**Through FY 07, 209 of 303 programmed units reached E-date (69%) ...E-dates only BEGIN the process of becoming a Modular Force**

- Chart shows ACP progress [Activations/conversions] (Legacy structure is omitted) of modular transformation.
- BCT transformation occurs within 12 months of E-Date for AC HBCTs and IBCTs; 24 months for AC SBCTs; and 48 months for all ARNG BCTs
- Functional Brigades include non-modular legacy structure that will remain in the prgramme force as modularity is completed
- 100% fielding of some equipment items for these units will be an on-going process well their EDATE. Under the current equipping plan, the fielding of programmed items will not be completed unit 2015 for BCT's & 2019 for SPT BDEs.
- Reflects status as of 30 September for each FY

*Source: 20 Sep 07 SAMAS (Includes 1 Nov 07 Acceleration Initiative)*

Figure B-1 Modular Conversion

## The Army Campaign Plan

Army modular reorganization and overall transformation is directed under the Army Campaign Plan (ACP). The ACP directs the planning, preparation, and execution of Army Operations and Army Transformation within the context of ongoing strategic commitments, to include Base Realignment and Closure actions, Global Re-posturing Actions and 2006 QDR recommendations. The Army published ACP change five on 5 April 2007. This change incorporated Base Realignment and Closure actions, global reposturing actions, and 2006 QDR recommendations.

Modular conversion enables Army forces to operate more effectively within a Joint warfight. This year, the ACP establishes mapping of Army organizational capabilities to Joint Functional Concepts that the Department of Defence is using to integrate transformation efforts across services. The decisive operation within the ACP remains the modular conversion of all AC and RC Manoevre brigades. Also, modular conversion will occur in AC and RC division headquarters; select combat, logistics, and sustainment units will convert to modular support brigades; as well as AC and RC echelons division and above logistics, and sustainment structure. The conversion sequence for Army operating forces to modular designs is synchronized with projected operational requirements and should be completed by fiscal year 2013 for the AC, ARNG, and Army Reserve. (The Army's Modular Force conversion sequence is shown in Figure B–1 Modular Conversion, on this page.) Transformation and Modular Brugade Conversion information (schedule, component and end state #'s) are based on the September 2007 Force File. Army structure decisions made...

## Army Special Operations Forces

The Army Special Operations Command (USASOC) modernization strategy is based upon a vision to provide Warriors, who are properly organized, trained, equipped and postured to face a future of potentially persistent conflict. Army Special Operations Forces (ARSOF) provide the regional Combatant Commanders with the specialized direct and indirect skills to address these non-traditional threats. The *U.S. Army Special Operations Command Master Plan* provides the command strategy to balance near-term requirements while developing long-term capabilities

The Master Plan outlines the command strategy along three distinct lines of operation. The first line of operation focuses on the development and employment of immediate capabilities that ensure the success of ARSOF in the Global War on Terror. The second line of operation supports the development of capabilities for USASOC Soldiers in the near-term. A guiding concept for this period is a "presence for purpose" construct which maximizes the expeditionary aspects of ARSOF. The third and final line of operation focuses on developing ARSOF capabilities for the far-term, out to fiscal year 2027. ARSOF development in this phase will be focused through a series of relevant JCIDS studies and other critical analysis.

The complex environments and myriad of threats facing ARSOF requires that the U.S. Army continue to recruit and train Soldiers and leaders who possess higher levels of maturity and the mental and physical toughness to operate under adverse and uncertain conditions. ARSOF training continues to emphasize their specialized skills and reflects the needs of the global Combatant Commanders with the flexibility to meet emerging threats. Likewise, ARSOF equipment and mobility platforms are tailored to support the diverse, often austere operating environments, in which they may have to operate. All the while, ARSOF must maintain and develop the capacity to contribute at the major regional conflict level, if required.

## Organizational Changes

**ARSOF Transformation Initiatives:** Today, over 4,500 Army Special Operations Soldiers are actively engaged in over 40 countries. Present and projected estimates on commitments equate to the near total commitment of specific segments of Active Component and Reserve Component Army Special Operations Forces. Special Forces (SF), Civil Affairs (CA), Psychological Operations (PSYOPS), Special Operations Aviation Regiment (SOAR), Rangers, and Sustainment Brigade (Special Operations) restructuring remains an essential component in USASOC efforts to provide enduring rotational and expeditionary capable forces.

**U.S. Army Special Forces Command** continues to grow in order to provide enhanced and adaptive Special Forces capabilities. Special Forces Group Band III and the QDR growth added an additional Special Forces battalion to each Special Forces Group beginning in fiscal year 2008 through fiscal year 2012. These increases better posture Special Forces to conduct a long-duration, often global, unconventional warfare campaign. Special Forces Groups remain regionally focused and provide the skills that support partner nations and erode areas of likely terrorist support. Likewise, the addition of five Group Support Battalions, provides the organic logistical capabilities that allow Special Forces to support a Combined Joint Special Operations Task Forces with little augmentation. The growth in each Special Forces Group headquarters provides them with additional battle staff for improved command and control planning and synchronization capabilities. Collectively, these increases transform SF into an organization of greater depth and self-sufficiency that is better able to apply their direct and indirect capabilities.

**Civil Affairs** transformation provides a more robust force structure in support of ARSOF requirements by creating an AC Civil Affairs brigade with four regionally oriented AC Civil Affairs battalions. The 95th Civil Affairs Brigade provides enhanced capabilities such as additional Civil Affairs Teams, an organic and deployable Civil-Military Operations Center, organic planning teams, and an organic civil information management cell capable of integrating and fusing the civil situation into the Joint force commander's Common Operational Picture. These capabilities support efforts to assist key host nations at crucial crossroads, and assist the efforts of other U.S. governmental agencies and teams.

**The Psychological Operations** forces redesign continues to emphasize their capability to deliver regionally-focused products that influence and shape diverse operating environments. This growth creates additional tactical Psychological Operations forces that support regional plans to deter passive support to terrorists and enable partner nations. Included in the redesign are new capabilities such as enhanced tactical PSYOP companies equipped with organic print capability, AC-only enhanced Regional PSYOP battalions capable of forming the core of PSYOP Task Forces. AC dissemination forces have improved reachback technologies to ensure the rapid development and production of products, and the fielding of "state of the art" product dissemination technologies (radio, TV, and print) for advanced distribution capabilities.

**The Ranger Regiment** redesign, "Ranger Regiment XXI" (RRXXI) concept, provides a more adaptive and self-sustaining force to meet future requirements. This force growth enhances the 75th Ranger Regiment's lethality and flexibility, by providing a more Modular Force that remains strategically responsive. RRXXI highlights include the addition of a rifle company per battalion, a Ranger Reconnaissance Company at the battalion and regimental levels, growth of an additional Fire Direction Center in the mortar platoons, and the addition of a support company to each battalion. Likewise, the new Regimental Special Troops Battalion is comprised of a support operations detachment; and reconnaissance, MI, signal and operations companies. These formations directly support the Ranger battalions, thereby validating the modular capability of the overall force design.

**Army Special Operations Aviation (ARSOA)** transformation created a more robust force structure for the 160th Special Operations Aviation Regiment (Airborne) to help meet the Special Operations rotary-wing demands of Army, Navy and other Joint SOF elements. This ARSOA force structure realized in 2012 is going to be modular in design with three identical battalions that will support the five major Theaters and their Special Operations Forces (SOF) with expeditionary aviation forces that are flexible and mission tailored. Once completely resourced, these battalions will each have a heavy-lift (MH-47G) and medium-assault (MH-60M) capability that can be deployed as a modular Special Operations Aviation Expeditionary Detachments throughout the world. The remaining battalion is comprised of A/MH-6M and MH-60 aircraft and supports other SOF throughout the operational spectrum. Future organizational changes support the Army modularity concept with the inclusion of an organic Unmanned

Aircraft System capability as well as a Joint Cargo Aircraft capability. ARSOA can best meet the varied demands of GCCs and the Army Special Operations Forces that support them, by creating modular organizations.

**Sustainment Brigade (Airborne)** has the mission to coordinate and monitor Army common and Special Operations-Peculiar Combat Service Support and Force Health Protection; to plan for and provide Force Health Protection and to train, resource, and deploy Special Operations-peculiar signal support in support of ARSOF operations. They also have the capability to deploy and C2 Army logistics and sustainment units deployed in support of Special Operations Forces.

**United States Army John F. Kennedy Special Warfare Center and School (USAJFKSWCS)** continues to provide the challenging hands-on training required to qualify ARSOF Soldiers in their Branch or MOS. To support the growth of Special Forces, Psychological Operations and Civil Affairs officer and enlisted ranks, USAJFKSWCS has supported the activation of a Special Operations Recruiting Battalion and assisted USAREC by manning it with the very best ARSOF officers and NCOs. The result has been an increase in Soldiers recruited and qualified to support Band III and QDR growth. In response to the creation of an Active Civil Affairs component and additional AC and RC Tactical Psychological Operations Companies, the USAJFKSWCS has transformed the initial entry and reclassification pipelines for Psychological Operations and Civil Affairs training to make them more challenging, relevant and efficient.

The Complex environments and threats facing ARSOF require that Soldiers and leaders possess higher levels of maturity and the mental and physical toughness to operate under adverse conditions. USAJFKSWCS training continues to emphasize hands on training in real world scenarios. End of course field training exercises for all branch/MOS pipelines are continually updated to ensure the specialized skills required of ARSOF Warriors are available to the geographic Combatant Commander and his subordinate operational commands.

# Training Modernization

## Overview of the Army Training and Leader Development Strategy

A key component of the *Army Campaign Plan* is the development of an overarching strategy to guide our efforts to train the Army and grow adaptive leaders. *The Army Training and Leader Development Strategy* describes the ends, ways and means required to adapt Army training and leader development Programmes to an era of persistent conflict, to prepare units and leaders for full spectrum operations, and to rebuild strategic depth over the short-term and the FY 2010-2015 POM years. Based on the fundamental assumption that we will be engaged in a decade or more of persistent conflict against networked, adaptive, asymmetrically capable and equipped adversaries, the AT&LDS provides a common vision and guides the allocation of resources across the Army. The strategy nests within *The Army Plan* and is structured to support the Army Vision and the Army Mission. It provides the strategy to support development of full spectrum operational capability, through the ARFORGEN process, across the spectrum of conflict and operational themes as described in FM 3-0.

The ATLDS is structured on foundational principles that set the conditions for sustaining the current fight and building strategic depth for the future. These principles are (1) sustain the concept that Soldiers are the centerpiece; (2) generate cohesive, trained and ready units that can dominate across the spectrum of conflict; (3) train Soldiers and leaders to prevail in the uncertain and volatile contemporary operational environment; (4) responsively adapt our training and leader development in order to defeat our adversary's changing strategies and tactics; (5) train Soldiers and develop leaders across multiple and interconnected domains; and (6) retain our values and bedrock principles.

## The Training Aimpoint

The Army must generate cohesive, trained and ready forces that can dominate at any point on the spectrum of conflict, in any environment, and under all conditions. In an era of Persistent Conflict, we will execute full spectrum operations (a combination of Offence, Defence and Stability or Civil Support Operations) in all Army operations—the amount of each type of operation will vary based on the type of operation and the conditions under which those operations are executed.

While we maintain our readiness for major offensive and defensive operations in Major Combat operations, the projected operational environment and our operational concept (FM 3-0) require that in addition, we train for stability operations, whether we are driven by a Core Mission Essential Task List or a Directed Mission Essential Task List. This will cause us to add training which emphasizes civil security, civil (population) control, provision of essential services, governance and support for economic and infrastructure development. Whether CMETL or DMETL driven, training must include all types of operations under realistic conditions.

We can only achieve full spectrum capability with full spectrum training. The location of the Aimpoint on the spectrum of conflict will be periodically updated by HQDA to provide direction for Army leaders to adjust training conditions as our assessment of strategic conditions dictate. Standardized CMETL and focused training conditions support rapid assembly of force packages, and minimize required additional training for the most probable directed missions. Maintaining a CMETL training focus, absent a Directed Mission, provides the Nation the strategic depth required to execute the National Military Strategy

**ARFORGEN** is the process we use to man, equip and train units to meet Combatant Commander requirements. The focused ARFORGEN process produces increased readiness over time, in predictable periods of availability of trained, ready, and cohesive units prepared for operational deployments. It is designed to focus training and other resources to prepare units to enter the available pool. The basis for this training is a unit's CMETL which focuses a unit on its "as designed" MTOE mission—which will be full spectrum tasks executed under a focused set of full spectrum operations training conditions as portrayed in Figure B-2.

Within the ARFORGEN process, units will shift from CMETL to DMETL at any point in the process. While CMETL training is focused on training for the most likely requirements, DMETL training must prepare units and battle staffs to operate at any

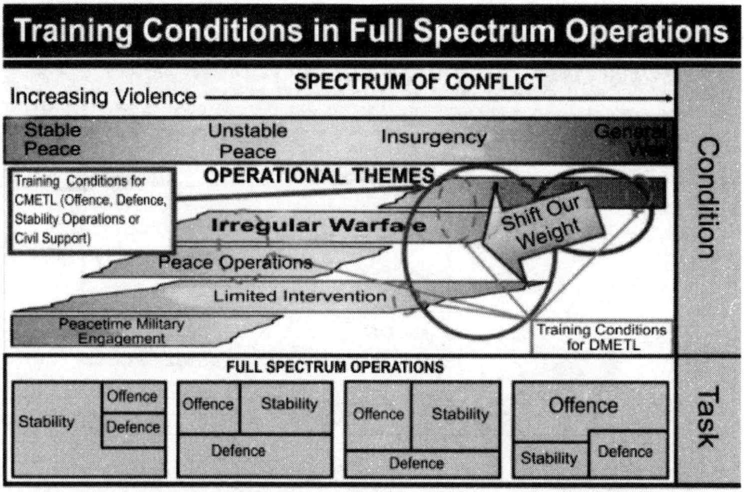


Figure B-2: Training Condition in Full Spectrum Operations

point on the spectrum of conflict. We must be ready for the current operational environment and prepared for the future operational environment.

Our strategy for training units for full spectrum operations has two major parts, as described in Figure B–3 on next page:

**CMETL** Unit training will focus on assigned CMETL throughout the ARFORGEN cycle, until the unit is directed to shift focus to a DMETL. The CMETL is based on the unit's "as designed" MTOE mission, and consists of tasks which support execution of FSO (Offense, Defence, and Stability or Civil Support Operations). Standardized CMETL and focused training conditions support rapid assembly of force packages, and minimize required additional training for the most probable directed missions.

**DMETL** Upon assignment of a directed mission as part of a Contingency Expeditionary Force (CEF) or Deployment Expeditionary Force (DEF), commanders will develop their mission-specific DMETL. The focus of unit training adjusts, at the appropriate point in time, from CMETL to DMETL tasks and conditions which support executing FSO under conditions which realistically portray the specific threat and mission conditions for the theater the unit will deploy into. Since a directed mission may be assigned at any point in the ARFORGEN cycle, training

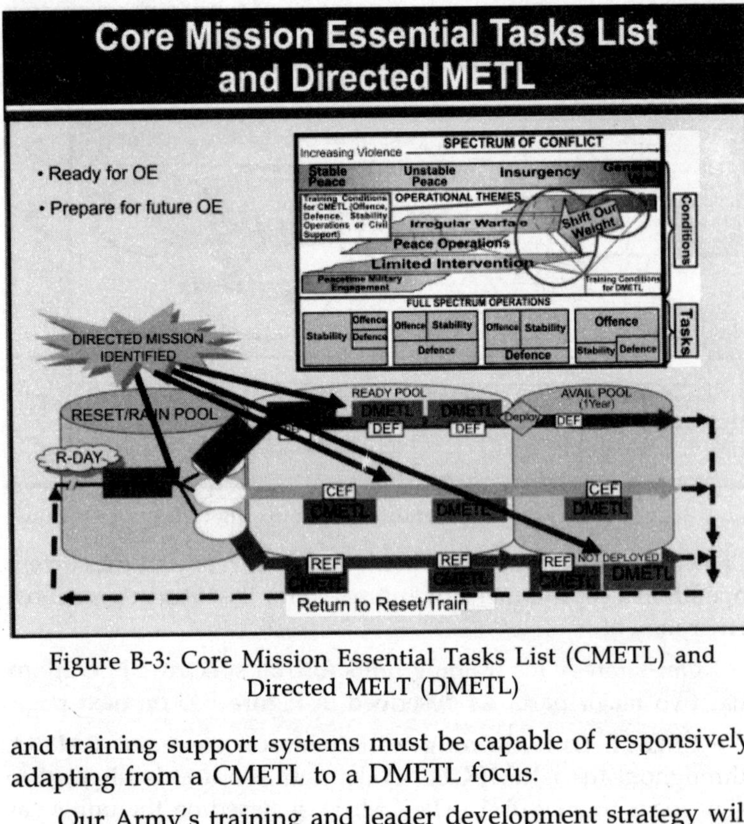


Figure B-3: Core Mission Essential Tasks List (CMETL) and Directed MELT (DMETL)

and training support systems must be capable of responsively adapting from a CMETL to a DMETL focus.

Our Army's training and leader development strategy will produce trained and adaptive Soldiers and leaders, competent in full spectrum operations with our Joint, inter-agency, and multinational operations partners, to support the National Security Strategy. Consequently, a flexible ARFORGEN process produces units trained and ready for their assigned or anticipated missions, supported by agile and adaptive training enablers. Successful training will achieve, sustain, and improve individual and unit readiness to train, alert, deploy and employ forces for prompt and sustained full spectrum operations.

For all members of the Army team—Soldiers, leaders, and Army civilians of the Active and Reserve Components—this will require effective training and education under rigorous and relevant conditions to execute core missions, build the strategic depth to confront unforeseen challenges, and to prepare for anticipated challenges in the future. Fundamentally, no Soldier or leader should be confronted with a task in combat that was not previously trained to standard. We will train for certainty and educate for uncertainty.

In support of this collective training effort, the Army will sustain and improve the Combat Training Center (CTC) capability to realistically portray the ever-changing operational environment, while simultaneously integrating Joint, inter-agency and multinational partners into training. Likewise, home station and deployed training capabilities will be enhanced to portray a more robust operational environment and Joint environment in order to build and sustain critical skills. Our Training Support System will keep pace with the requirements of the operational and institutional domains. TSS must realistically portray training conditions reflecting the operational environment by fielding integrated live, virtual and constructive (LVC) enablers that link to the Joint training environment. Finally, our overall training strategy will continue to be driven by the ARFORGEN process, mission essential tasks and deployment timelines.

## Training Support System

We can only achieve a full spectrum capability with full-spectrum training. To that end, we must create the training conditions that realistically portray the Contemporary Operating Environment. Goal 7 of the AT&LDS defines the Army's Training Support System and objectives required to support both the current and future training environments. This goal directly supports the Imperatives Prepare and Transform. The TSS mission is to deliver training support system products (instrumentation and training aids, devices, simulations and simulators (TADSS), services (training support operations and manpower), and facilities (ranges, simulation centers, training support centers) that are required to create the conditions to realistically portray the operational environment and enable Army training strategies focused on CMETL training, and can be adapted to support DMETL training. These "training enablers" underpin the Army's Combined Arms Training Strategies, Battle Command Training Strategy, weapons training strategies and School POIs by providing commanders the fundamental capabilities to execute Soldier, leader, battle staff and unit collective training to standard at homestation, the CTCs, TRADOC Schools, Centers of Excellence and while deployed.

## Training Support System Objectives

*Objective 7a.* **Use consistent metrics to field TSS capabilities (Non-Systems TADSS, TSS operations, TSS facilities, sustainment and management) IAW the ACP to support CMETL, and as required, adapt to DMETL, training for the ARFORGEN and mission rehearsal for units and battle staffs, as well as institutional training for Soldiers and leaders by fiscal year 2016.** Priority 1 for the Training Support System is to maintain current and near term capabilities in support of Army training at homestation and TRADOC schools/Centers of Excellence. The TSS Master Plan describes the training enablers required at each installation to support Soldier, leaders, battlestaff and unit collective training at each of the homestation. The Master Plan's Mission Essential Requirements provide the metrics for each installation training facilities, training support operations, and TADSS based on the installation's training mission profile (number of type units, type equipment, Soldier density and force generation platform requirements). The MERs are aligned with the *Army Campaign Plan* schedule to ensure the TSS capabilities meet Army Transformation requirements.

*Objective 7b.* **Field a Live, Virtual and Constructive Integrated Training Environment (LVC ITE) capable of supporting BCT level training at Ft Bliss, TX by the end of fiscal year 2010, and on demand at selected locations by fiscal year 2016.** Live training, virtual training and constructive training have been employed for years to successfully train units and Soldiers for combat. However, the net centric environment is expanding the unit's battlespace beyond the physical land boundaries of most homestation training areas. Achieving DoD and Army training transformation goals and objectives requires TADSS to be designed and developed for interoperability across the LVC environments. Operational systems and LVC training systems must now be integrated together to create a training environment that approximates the operational environment. The initial prototype of this Live, Virtual, Constructive Integrated Training Environment (LVCITE) is being developed with existing training systems at Ft Bliss/WSMR to support BCT level training by fiscal year 2010. Where it makes sense, it will also be used by the AETF to support their training and testing requirements. Follow-on LVC-ITE efforts will be field to selected locations by fiscal year 2016.

*Objective 7c.* **Develop, field and sustain LVC training systems to improve fidelity of the I/TADSS and Facilities pillars at the CTCs, including ETC, by 2013.** The Army must continue to sustain and modernize the CTCs training capabilities to realistically portray the ever-changing operational environment, improve JIIM context to support the Joint National Training Capability, while simultaneously integrating new combat systems into the CTC training environment. We must transform these premier training venues to reflect the complexity of modern battlefields while providing an Exportable Training Capability to support the ARFORGEN training cycles. A major capital investment must be made in CTC modernization to replace older training systems, adapt to enable full spectrum training, and realistically portray the operational environment.

*Objective 7d.* **Improve TSS management and the deliver of TSS services in the context of Decision Point 91.** TSS services provide installations the manpower and services that are required to provide the day-to-day operations and support for range operations and Integrated Training Area Management, Battle Command Training Capability, operations for training simulations and simulators and Training Support Center operations and TADSS support. These installation training functions are essential for supporting the execution of homestation training strategies and enabling units to maintain the pace of the ARFORGEN cycle.

*Objective 7e.* **Improve the acquisition process to integrate weapons system specific LVC training aids, devices, simulators and simulations (TADSS), including FCS embedded TADSS, training systems and spinout requirements, into TSS capabilities and LVC ITE.** Achieving Department of Defence Training

Transformation requires TADSS that are developed for interoperability across the live, virtual and constructive training environments. Our weapons systems platforms and Battle Command systems must be interoperable and linked to the LVC training network to support seamless transition from home station training, through mission rehearsal, to mission execution with minimal reconfiguration. The Army's goal is to field TADSS and material systems as a total package, thereby ensuring the fielding of a trainable, logistically supportable and fully operational capability to the force.

*Objective 7f.* **Explore, by the end of fiscal year 2009, gaming technology as a means for providing low-cost, effective training solutions, and institutionalize those solutions under a strategy encompassing all Army gaming capabilities for training starting in fiscal year 2010 and completed by fiscal year 2013.** Implement and refresh continuously after fiscal year 2013. Gaming capabilities have potential to support individual, collective, and multi-echelon training to increase readiness prior to, or during deployment, at home station, at institution or through self-development. Game applications are a low cost training solution that leverages commercial and government off-the-shelf games and advanced simulation technology. They address the need to augment and improve individual, collective and multi-echelon training and fill training capability gaps caused by limited availability, capability and resources of training aids, devices, simulators and simulations and live training opportunities.

For fiscal year 2008 TPO Gaming has developed a Gaming Capabilities Production Document as part of the Joint Capabilities Integration Development System acquisition process. Once approved, the CPD becomes a formal Army requirement. Given this formal requirement, the material developer can begin to look for material solutions to provide this capability (fiscal years 2008-2009).

In fiscal year 2010, TPO Gaming anticipates that the material developer will field a Gaming toolkit comprised of many different applications, genres and Programmes, each with unique characteristics that lend themselves to augment, improve an existing training capability or fill training capability gaps.

*Objective 7g.* **Integrate training and testing LVC solutions where feasible and where economies are achieved starting in fiscal year 2008.** The testing and training communities utilize similar or like-type technologies to meet mission requirements. These technologies include LVC TADSS, instrumentation systems, target systems and targetry, threat simulators and emulators, tactical engagement simulations and other forms of models and simulations. Given these similarities, the Army's goal is to achieve and maintain efficiency by leveraging and integrating testing and training support requirements wherever and whenever it makes sense from a business perspective and does not negatively impact either domain's mission.

*Objective 7h.* **Improve Army training capability within the OSD JNTC construct by strategically focusing requirements based on the CMETL training Aimpoint.** Army forces will train to operate as a Joint team and Army training will be seamlessly nested in Joint training to build mutual trust and confidence and increase understanding of Joint capabilities. A key lever available to support Army training is the Training Transformation (T2) effort, co-sponsored with OSD and the Joint Staff. Nesting Army training with T2 offers a significant opportunity to fully realize the Joint training requirements inherent with the concept of Joint interdependence. T2 will provide the Army way ahead to fully integrate Inter-Agency participation in our training in all domains, but particularly in collective training at our CTCs.

*Objective 7i.* Identify Army Science and Technology Programme investment areas that can address TSS capabilities and LVC ITE gaps starting in fiscal year 2008.

**Training Support System Programmes:** The Training Support System is managed through four major Programmes, each of which provides development and delivery of training products and services to installations and units in the training domains of operation, institution, and self development. These Programmes are:

1. Sustainable Range Programme
2. Battle Command Training Support Programme
3. Combat Training Center Modernization Programme
4. Soldier Training Support Programme

## Sustainable Range Programme

The following are the major Sustainable Range Programme modernization Programmes currently Programmemed, planned and/or being developed. These Programmes (with exception of ADA Targets) are funded through Other Procurement Army under the category of Research, Development, and Acquisition.

**Army Targetry Systems** provide non-instrumented or automated live-fire ranges incorporating stationary and moving infantry/armor targets to meet both individual and crew qualification and collective training for weapons gunnery incorporating realistic threat target scenarios under simulated battlefield conditions. Army Tank and Automotive Command, headquartered at Rock Island, Illinois, is the material provider for the ATS Programme.

**The Air Defence Artillery Target Programme** ensures unit and crew readiness by providing targets and ancillary devices for mandatory live-fire crew weapon system qualification and training events. The ADA Target Programme funds aerial targetry/ scoring hardware and support services to train more than 372 Avenger and MANPAD Stinger crews for qualification and live-fire training prior to deployment, upon entering Reset, and to support homeland Defence in the Nation Capital Region.

**Digital Range Training Systems** includes the Digital Multi-purpose Training Range, Digital Multipurpose Range Complex, Battle Area Complex and Digital Air Ground Integration Range. This Programme provides new and modern ranges capable of training, evaluating and stressing Soldiers and equipment with a realistic, train-as-you-fight environment. These training systems will replace obsolete training methods and equipment to stimulate new weapon systems, and provide enhanced training data collection and After Action Review capabilities. DRTS ranges are part of the Live Training Transformation-Family of Training Systems and have been Programmemed for those major installations with Heavy Brigade Combat Teams. In fiscal year 2008, instrumentation for a Digital Multi-purpose Training Range and a Digital Multi-purpose Range Complex will be installed. PM-TRADE is the acquisition agency responsible for fielding digital range instrumentation.

**Integrated Military Operations on Urban Terrain Training System** provides training range instrumentation in support of the Urban Operations suite of ranges as established by TC 90-1, Training for Urban Operations. Instrumentation

of the Urban Assault Course, "Shoothouse," and Combined Arms Collective Training Facility leverages existing technologies to comply with Common Training Instrumentation Architecture. IMTS provides technology integration for home station, deployed, and CTCs into a single effort, ensuring the capability to train units in a complex terrain environment. The Programme will leverage existing Military Operations on Urban Terrain Training System instrumentation systems and technologies to ensure follow on systems are in accordance with the CTIA. The basis of issue and fielding strategy envisions 33 CACTFs, 40 Urban Assault Courses, and 37 Live-fire "Shoothouses". In fiscal year 2008, five CACTFs and three Urban Assault Courses will be instrumented.

**Aerial Weapons Scoring System** is an integrated group of computer-controlled sensors used to score live-fire helicopter gunnery. It provides near real-time objective scoring results for attack helicopters firing .50-caliber, 7.62-, 20- and 30-millimeter projectiles, and 2.75-inch training rockets. AWSS can objectively score simulated Hellfire missile engagements. Block II

improvements will enable AWSS to provide scoring for Digital Air Ground Integration Range. Six new systems have now been fielded, four in CONUS, one in Germany, and one in Korea. AWSS currently is undergoing a Block II Programme upgrade scheduled for fiscal year 2008 delivery, and will include a data link upgrade and integration of the Smart Onboard Data Interface Module with the AWSS Control Station.

Deployable Range Packages provide deploying units the capability to conduct live-fire training in theater, and can be used as Training Augmentation Range Packages for Army Commands, the Installation Management Command and Theaters.

## Battle Command Training Support Programmes

**Battle Command Training Support Programme** provides virtual and constructive training support systems required by Army Training System. Virtual simulators support graduated training strategies by providing commanders tools to practice collective tasks prior to conducting live training. Constructive simulations give commanders the capability to train their leaders and battle staffs on Mission Essential Tasks List through simulation. Virtual simulators and constructive simulations have been used extensively by leaders to conduct mission rehearsal exercises to prepare for deployment after unit operational equipment has been shipped. The Army is expanding BCTSP to meet training needs from brigade to corps, including multifunctional support brigades and select functional support brigades. The Army's gateway to Joint, Service and Combatant Commander Live-Virtual-Constructive training, LVC-Integrated Architecture is the Army's integrating modeling and simulation architecture for creating its integrated training environment, and is required for LVC training systems to interoperate within an integrated LVC training environment. By enabling distributed LVC interoperability and simulating and stimulating command and control systems, commanders, Soldiers and units can train as they fight using operational equipment and systems. This environment provides common protocols and interfaces to link disparate Army Live instrumentation systems and simulators, enabling a Battle Command Training Capability at home station.

The following are the major BCTSP modernization Programmes currently Programmemed, planned and/or being developed:

**Constructive Simulation** uses computer models and simulations to exercise command and staff functions from platoon through Joint task force. CS permits multiple echelons of command and staff to execute their normal warfighting tasks in an extensive exercise without the resource constraints of large bodies of troops, and is used extensively by deploying units in conduct of Mission

Rehearsal Exercise to provide versatile, cost-effective training environment that trains leaders to visualize battle space and make tactical decisions in a time-constrained, digitized environment. It also provides the "wraparound" for LVC-integrated events, extending battle space to provide more realistic scenarios.

**Joint Land Component Constructive Training Capability** consists of current and projected simulations and supporting applications and hardware to address training needs of the Joint Force Land Component Commander and Army Title X requirements across the full spectrum of conflict. JLCCTC is a federation of simulations/models and associated software required to compose, operate, and maintain a synthetic operational environment to support collective command and staff training. Constructive models in the JLCCTC include: Tactical Simulation, Joint Conflict and Tactical Simulation, Warfighter's Simulation, Joint Non-kinetic Effects Model, the Joint Deployment Logistics Model, Independent Stimulation Model, EADSIM, Virtual Reality Scene Generator/Mapping, Charting, Geodesy Utility Software Environment, Fires Simulation and One Semi-Automated Forces. Joint Land Component Constructive Training Capability provides critical support/enablers for collective digital Battle Command training and Mission Rehearsal, providing only viable Common Operating Environment (short of actual insertion into theater) for training. JLCCTC also supports Modular Force conversion and training transformation by providing realistic modeling of new brigade structures and Tactics, Techniques and Procedures to properly stimulate training, and by providing composable training simulation architectures to maximize efficiency and cost effectiveness

**Intelligence Electronic Warfare Tactical Proficiency Trainer** is a constructive training simulation capability being fielded to the Army to support Military Intelligence units at corps and below, thereby enabling realistic Battle Command training through simulation of Joint and Army intelligence capabilities and stimulating the MI collection system with scenarios that replicate battlefield situations. This puts MI Soldiers in the training loop using operational equipment and providing required reports and data to Combatant Commanders.

**Common Battle Command Simulation Equipment** is commercial-off-the-shelf hardware, operating system and data base software, workstations and servers, networks, and other peripherals used to run JLCCTC software. The Programme provides fielding of technical control suites and network to host the JLCCTC software, and includes workstation computers that provide user interface within Battle Command Training Centers. The Common Battle Command Simulation Equipment technical control suite requires server and COTS software upgrades and additions to support each new version of JLCCTC. CBCSE workstations require replacement every three to five years to maintain relevancy. All sites will be at 90 percent or better by fiscal year 2012. Work station refresh commenced in fiscal year 2008.

**One Semi-Automated Forces** is a tailorable and composable next generation computer generated force, representing a full range of operations, systems and control processes up to brigade level, having variable levels of fidelity and supporting all model and simulation domain applications in both man-in-the-loop and closed-loop modes. It will represent the physical environment, including urban operations, and its effect on simulated activities and behaviors. One SAF may be the future entity-level brigade and below constructive simulation, will be a component of the JLCCTC, and be used in battle labs and research, development and engineering centers.

**Battle Command Training Center**—Equipment Support provides the network and equipment that supports integration of C2 systems and simulations, expands communications from the BCTC to units not hard-wired to training facilities, and significantly improves command and staff ability to build and maintain a digital Common Operational Picture. BCTC-ES is the enabling link in the BCTC that supports stimulation of Army Battle Command System through JLCCTC, and consists of network gear, Battle Sight, radio-to-wire communications interfaces, virtual Unmanned Aerial Systems data and video feeds and Sim-to-Command, Control, Communications, Computer, Intelligence, Surveillance and Reconnaissance systems integration. Currently only the SBCT sites are fielded the full complement of BCTC-ES enhancing capabilities. Enhanced network and Sim-to-C4ISR integration will be delivered by the CBCSE Programme to 14 sites as a part of their JLCCTC update. In fiscal years 2008-15, fourteen new MCA BCTC sites are to receive the full complement of BCTCES capabilities.

**Battle Command Training Center**—Facilities provide the capability to conduct digital battle staff training for both Active and Reserve Components. BCTCs directly support execution of day-to-day operations and exercise support for all leader and battle staff training required by Army Training System, ARFORGEN, HQDA, and Army Command training directives. BCTC-F modernizes current battle simulations centers to increase training capabilities on C2 Systems, maintain digital battlestaff proficiency, and provide Live-Virtual-Constructive—Integrated Architecture connectivity. Most Army BCTCs are assigned training roles as "Hub" or "Spoke" within ATS. These roles are defined by each BCTC's training support relationships and responsibilities for Joint Land Component Constructive Training Capability and other LVC training and are described in the JLCCTC Distribution Plan. Improved training will come as new MCA facilities that began construction in fiscal year 2007 are completed.

**Virtual Simulation Training** is a part of Battle Command Training Support Programme that ensures a realistic, immersive training environment involving real people operating simulated systems using Man in-the-Loop simulations or Embedded Training capabilities. In the virtual environment, simulators and simulations operating on virtual geospecific or non-geospecific terrain replace real systems and can be linked with components of LVC-IA to provide a training environment that replicates the real thing. Virtual Simulation Training provides commanders with "walk" level training, sustainment training, gated training events, Leader Development, and mission-rehearsal capabilities. Virtual training also allows Soldiers to perform tasks too dangerous for live environments, such as calling for artillery fires on or near an occupied friendly position. It also facilitates retraining specific tasks until training objectives are met.

**Close Combat Tactical Trainer** is the ground Manoevre component of the Combined Arms Tactical Trainer family of simulators, and is a system of computerdriven combat simulators that provide a realistic virtual environment in which units train on and successfully accomplish their collective missions. Units Manoevre in high-fidelity manned modules replicating actual combat and support vehicles. These simulators are connected by a local area network and have the capability to be networked with multiple simulation facilities. Manned modules in CCTT replicate the vehicles and weapon systems of combined arms battalions, armored reconnaissance battalions, and armored cavalry squadrons. Since its fielding, requirements for training in CCTT have grown. New requirements include training in mounted Manoevre tasks in wheeled vehicles, dismounted Soldier tasks, and collective gunnery training. The CCTT Programme's Reconfigurable Vehicle Simulator, Reconfigurable Vehicle Tactical Trainer, and Dismounted Soldier manned modules replicate activities for combat, Combat Support, and Combat Service Support elements at team, squad- and platoon-level. They also provide the ability to train Brigade Combat Team reconnaissance, engineer and dismounted elements. Dismounted Soldier provides the capability to conduct dismounted Soldier operations (individual to company level) in the COE. Dismounted Soldier consists of nine Virtual Soldiers and up to 28 Virtual Soldier Multifunctional Workstations (VSMW). Virtual Soldier allows a Soldier to immerse himself into the virtual environment and train both cognitive and psycho motor tasks and skills. The VSMW enables Soldiers and leaders to expand the training audience to company level. Close Combat Tactical Trainer components provide commanders a highly tailorable, deployable, full dimension, collective combined arms virtual training and mission rehearsal system with a robust exercise development subsystem with AAR capability. CCTT is designed primarily for installation training facilities and supports virtual training requirements. It also meets the requirement for a home-station trainer as reflected in CATS and supports the Reset/Train-Ready- Available ARFORGEN process enabling BCT training readiness. The Close Combat Tactical Trainer TDR was rewritten as a Capabilities Production Document that includes reconfigurable wheeled vehicle simulators and dismounted Soldier trainer requirements in a single document. There are currently eight CCTT fixed sites at Active Component locations, seven fielded RVS suites or partial suites, 12 Modular-CCTT platoon sets in six states for Reserve Component use, and two M-CCTT platoon sets in Germany. A Reconfigurable Vehicle Simulator is composed of six manned modules housed in three trailers. Reconfigurable Vehicle Tactical Trailer fielding is scheduled to begin in fiscal year 2009, based on the FY08-13 POM. Fixed sites will be fielded with RVS, while RVTT will be fielded to locations without a CCTT fixed site. There are 27 RVTT suites required to support the Active and Reserve Component operational requirements.

**Aviation Combined Arms Tactical Trainer** is a mobile, transportable, multi-station simulation device that supports unit collective, combined arms training. AVCATT provides six cockpits configurable to any combination of AH-64A or D, OH-58D, UH-60A/L, and CH-47D. Exercise record/playback and simultaneous AAR capability ensures the capture of training lessons learned. AVCATT is Distributive Interactive Simulation compliant and compatible with other SE Core-enabled systems. Interactive exercises help commanders hone unit collective operations skills and rehearse wartime missions. Combat Aviation Brigades preparing for deployments to Iraq and Afghanistan have networked geographically separated AVCATT suites, allowing mission rehearsals with actual task organizations for deployment.

**Recent fielding changes by the Aviation**

Implementation Task Force ensures AVCATT is aligned with CAB location and task organization. AVCATT meets requirements for a home-station trainer and, when provided with a compatible local area terrain data base, has the potential to provide virtual capabilities for home station live fire gunnery training during advanced tables and combined arms live-fire exercises. Of 23 suites, 15 have been fielded to their planned locations, and five have been contracted for production and begin fielding this fiscal year. The remaining three will be contracted and fielded prior to the end of fiscal year 2009. A fourth system has been added to the overall requirement, and when funded will be delivered to Alaska.

**Non-rated Crew Member Manned Module** is a virtual training system that is reconfigurable (UH-60 and CH- 47), self-contained, transportable, and interoperable with AVCATT. It will provide training for helicopter door gunners and other non-rated crew members of cargo and utility helicopters in door gunnery, sling-load operations, crew coordination and actions on contact in a virtual environment. The prototype was delivered to Fort Campbell, Kentucky where it underwent testing in coordination with the U.S. Army Aviation Warfighting Center to determine if full rate production is warranted. The system is currently being used to support deployment raining for 101st Combat Aviation Brigade, then will support deployment training for 34th CAB, followed by159th CAB. Funding for the NCMT prototype was received through a Congressional add. USAAWC provided a positive training assessment for NCMT, and the AVCATT Capability Production Document in staffing at DA includes NCM3 as a requirement. Additional funding is being Programmemed in the 10-15 timeframe to produce 48 NCM3 modules (two modules per AVCATT).

**Engagement Skills Trainer 2000** uses computer generated imagery to train and sustain individual marksmanship, squad and team fire distribution and control, and judgmental use of force skills. EST is used at force-generating installations, operational unit home-stations, and at forward-deployed sites. Deploying units also use it to sustain small-unit critical collective skills proficiency when not able to conduct live-fire training. The Programme completed fielding of five new escalation of force/ graduated response scenarios in 2007.

**Synthetic Environment Core** is the Army's virtual component of LVC-TE, integrating common components of virtual simulations and linking the virtual environment to the LVC TE. Key to the Army's training transformation plan and a complementary training system for the FCS, SE Core will develop new software and integrate existing hardware and software products to create the Army's common virtual environment. This will be done by linking system and non-system virtual simulations into a fully integrated training virtual capability. SE Core requirements include virtual simulation architecture, One Semi-Automated Forces integration as the common SAF, master terrain database production facilities; and common virtual environment, which allows the Army to execute combined arms and Joint training and mission planning and rehearsals at homestation and at deployed locations.

**Call for Fire Trainer:** The Call For Fire Trainer is a lightweight, rapidly deployable, observed fire training system that provides simulated battlefield training for Fire Support Specialists, Joint Fires Observers, and Soldiers at the institutional and unit level. The system provides simulated battlefield training to Forward Observers in four configurations: 1:4, 1:12, 1:30, and the Joint Fires and Effects Trainer System. The JFETS at US Army Field Artillery School provides an immersive environment for Army and Joint observed fires training that accurately replicate the Contemporary Operating Environment. As of October 2007, 126 CFFTs have been fielded.

**Live, Virtual, Constructive Integrated Training Environment** is an effort to template a common LVC infrastructure at Ft. Bliss/ WSMR by fiscal year 2010 in support of developing the Army's LVC Integrated Training Environment. The Live, Virtual, Constructive Integrated Training Environment (LVC-ITE) is comprised of an installation's training and operational network infrastructure along with an integrating LVC architecture that allows Army units to seamlessly train across the Live, Virtual and Constructive training environments and populate their Battle Command systems for mission rehearsals and training. This foundational structure and framework governs the relationships, principles, guidelines, and standards for interoperability of LVC components and C2 systems.

**The LVC ITE** is comprised of LVC training support systems, ranges, facilities, personnel and equipment, and a management structure and organization along with communications networks, gateways, interfaces and translators that allow exchange of data across training environments. The LVC-ITE will also support interoperability of the training and testing communities as appropriate along with ties to Future Combat Systems requirements. Continuing LVC-ITE efforts are linked directly to the LVC-IA initiative which will be field to selected locations by fiscal year 2016.

## Soldier Training Support Programmes

**Soldier Training Support Programmes** provide enablers that facilitate CATS-prescribed execution of individual and collective training for units and by Programmes of Instruction at Army Schools. It synchronizes requirements and resources necessary for combat and material development of these training enablers. It also provides personnel, facilities, capabilities, and operational support for Soldier training, and identifies emerging requirements associated with modularity, transformation, and rebasing. The following are the major Programmes of Record.

**Medical Simulation Training Centers** enhances functional medical skills required to save lives during combat operations. MSTC is a centralized medical training facility located at high-density population installations that provide state-of-the-art LVC training on Combat Medical Advanced Skills Training for medical personnel and Combat Life Saver training for non-medical personnel. The MSTC is where lessons learned in Operations Iraqi Freedom and Enduring Freedom is taught through both didactic and hands-on tactical and technical medical training. These 18 sites, to include a deployable capability in Afghanistan, are completing fielding in fiscal year 2008, with technical refresh being Programme during the FY10-15 POM years.

**Basic Electronics Maintenance Trainer** is a standalone, non-system training device that supports critical electronics training for 45 Military Occupational Specialties in all aspects of basic electronics, including theory and hands-on application. BEMTS allows instructors to assign lessons to either a class or individual students and track their progress. The Programme is fully funded beginning fiscal year 2008, with fielding beginning with Fort Gordon, Georgia; and Fort Leonard Wood, Missouri, and finish with RC training sites. Funding in the FY 10-15 POM will be required to refresh the approximately 1,353 procured systems.

**Instrumentable Multiple Integrated Laser Engagement Systems** provides tactical engagement simulation for direct-fire, force-on-force training using eye-safe laser "bullets." I-MILES Programme is a modernization that provides a more adaptable and user-friendly capability. Enhancements include discrete player identification for all participants, enhanced audio-visual cueing effects, increased bore sight retention and accuracy, event recording and display, increased Programmeability of weapon characteristics, and an external data port to make it easier to connect and provide event data to live integrated systems. The I-MILES Programme consists of five component systems: Individual Weapons Systems; Independent Target System Wireless Independent Target System; Combat Vehicle Systems, Shoulder Launched Munitions and Controller Devices. The Army's MILES Minimum Essential Requirement is 329,442 devices. Total I-MILES requirement to replace MILES is 217,087 devices. The Programme is post-milestone C. Fiscal years 2008-13 funding levels require 39 years to complete MILES replacement.

Engagement Skills Trainer 2000 uses computer generated imagery to train and sustain individual marksmanship, squad and team fire distribution and control, and judgmental use of force skills. EST is used at force-generating installations, operational unit home-stations, and at forward-deployed sites. Deploying units also use it to sustain small-unit critical collective skills proficiency when not able to conduct live-fire training.

**Laser Marksmanship Training System** is an eye-safe, laser-based marksmanship skill proficiency trainer that supports direct-fire weapons from handguns through machine guns. Capabilities include training for basic rifle and pistol marksmanship; and machine-gun, counter-sniper, and tactical training; as well as nightfighting using NVS for all weapons, thermal sights and NBC operations. The system is inexpensive, portable, and configurable to conform to a variety of training requirements and space limitations. It provides an easily deployable marksmanship trainer which mitigates live-fire limitations and supplements EST 2000 capabilities in support of ARFORGEN and OIF/ OEF training requirements. The Programme is fielded 86 percent (286 of 333 systems) for the Active Army.

**Call for Fire Trainer** uses simulated military equipment to provide high-fidelity simulated battlefield scenarios for training observed fire tasks to Soldiers, regardless of MOS. CFFT trains

Soldiers to call for and adjust indirect fire, and trains forward observers (MOS 13F) on the 19 basic call-for-fire tasks. CFFT also supports Type II and III Close Air Support training. In stand-alone mode, CFFT is capable of training up to 30 students. CFFT will replace current GUARDFIST system. One Tactical Engagement Simulation System is a family of tactical engagement simulation systems that supports force-on-force and force-on-target training and operational test exercises at brigade and below, in all BOSs, at home station, MCTC, and deployed sites. OneTESS overcomes MILES limitations by supporting training of proper engagement procedures; simulating weapon systems accuracy and effects; and stimulating detectors, sensors, monitors and countermeasures. OneTESS will provide a common training and testing TES capability and will establish TES architecture and standards for live tactical engagement systems. It will be the tactical engagement component for the Family of Live Training Systems, and Common Training Instrumentation Architecture. FCS will incorporate the OneTESS capability. System demonstration and Limited User's Test are scheduled for fiscal years 2007 and 2008. Milestone C is scheduled for fiscal year 2009. The Programme is not currently funded for production during fiscal years 2008-13; production funding must be readdressed during the FY10-15 POM process with priority to field to the CTCs.

**Home Station Instrumentation Training System** is a part of the LT2-FTS that will provide a deployable instrumented company-level training capability at home station that can be expanded to support battalion training. It provides objective data collection of unit performance in force-on-force, force-on-target, and live-fire training so units can better support and assess brigade Reset and ready phase training as part of the ARFORGEN cycle. First fielding of Objective HITS is in fiscal year 2010.

**Joint Fires and Effects Trainer System** is an immersive trainer which integrates CFFT to place Forward Observers in a virtual setting that accurately replicates current battlefield COE. JFETS has evolved to a prototype trainer. More than 3,000 officers, NCOs, and Soldiers from the Field Artillery School, operational units, and coalition partners have employed JFETS. It emulates conditions not achievable in the current generation of simulators. The experience is active, as opposed to passive, and is capable of training the Joint fires observer, regardless of Service. The system manipulates visual and physical space to give the observer the experience of being in and surrounded by a specific environment. JFETS is composed of: the Urban Terrain Module, configured to be a room overlooking a Middle Eastern city; the Open Terrain Module, configured to represent open desert or other terrain as required; the Fires and Effects Command Module; Close Air Support Trainer consisting of a 300-degree visual perspective; and the AAR room. As common gunnery architecture and One SAF capabilities spiral, JFETS will be able to connect to training systems across the Services and allow virtual training, both individual and collective. JFETS is an institutional requirement from the Field Artillery School.

## Combat Training Centers Modernization Programme

The Combat Training Centers remain a cornerstone of Army training and readiness. The CTC Modernization Programme provides needed capabilities to meet evolving ARFORGEN training requirements, replaces obsolete systems, and standardizes CTC training support capabilities to provide full spectrum training. The CTC Programme continues to transform to meet the Modular Force training and Army Force Generation readiness requirements. The Army's transformation to modular units and application of the ARFORGEN force management process has affected the Combat Training Centers by changing the training audience's structure and organic capabilities, as well as increasing the demand for CTC training with more modular units and a more frequent CTC training strategy. The development of an Exportable Training Capability is required to meet the increased throughput requirements driven by the ARFORGEN process and takes the CTC experience to other venues.

The *Combat Training Center Master Plan* describes how it will transition to meet the requirements of the Modular Force and ARFORGEN and contains the details for the CTC Modernization

Programme. The CTC MP describes the CTC requirements by CTC Pillar for the POM to sustain and improve the CTC capability to replicate the ever-changing Contemporary Operating Environment while simultaneously integrating more Joint, interagency, intergovernmental and multinational training tasks. However, current funding in CTC modernization prevents the execution of the CTC Modernization Programme with many Programmes recently determined to be unexecutable. Funding reductions in previous POM cycles have undermined acquisition strategies and delayed fielding of new capabilities to support the current and Future Force requirements.

Combat Training Centers Modernization Programme consists of Opposing Forces vehicle Fleets (technicals, tracked, wheeled, aviation [UAV and rotary wing], etc.); Instrumentation, Training Aids, Devices, Simulators, and Simulations; Battle Command (C4ISR and Information Assurance [IA]) and training facilities (MOUT, TAF, land expansion, live fire expansion; etc.) supporting the three Manoevre CTCs; OC Aviation; and the Exportable Training Capabilities.

**Common Training Instrumentation Architecture** is a component-based architecture that sets common standards, interfaces and protocols within the family of Army Live training systems and with other Live, Virtual and Constructive training systems. CTIA is the foundation architecture for the Army's Live Training Transformation family of training systems product line for training instrumentation and tactical engagement simulation systems that support home station training, deployed and Manoevre CTC live-training requirements, and interoperability with other Joint training systems. CTIA's component-based, productline architecture supports a high-level of component reuse among live training systems, promotes cost effective modernization, stove-pipe systems and supports FutureForce training requirements. Common Training Instrumentation Architecture is a FCS complimentary system and supports the Army's Campaign Plan and DoD Training Transformation. It has completed the fifth year of development. Several Army live training systems (Digital Ranges, CTC OIS, and Home station Instrumented Training System) are being developed using CTIA. Version 1.5 of the architecture has embedded DoD's Test and Training Enabling Architecture software, allowing CTIA-based live training systems to be interoperable with other TENA-based Joint test and training systems.

**Combat Training Center Objective Instrumentation System** is a major component of the Live Training Transformation and is compliant with CTIA. The CTC OIS replaces the current instrumentation systems at NTC, JRTC and JMRC. It is an integrated system of computer software, hardware, workstations, databases, voice and video recording, production and presentation equipment, interface devices and communication systems. The system is configured to collect, report, store, manage, process and display event data for 2,000 instrumented players with capability to expand to 15,000 instrumented players/entities. Combat Training Center Objective Instrumentation System will accomplish the following functions: exercise planning; system preparation; exercise management; training performance feedback and system support. Without CTC OIS, Soldiers and units will not receive high-fidelity cause and effect analysis/After Action Reviews of training at the Manoevre Combat Training Centers. Current stovepipe instrumentation systems at the MCTCs are obsolete with numerous single points of failures. Moreover, they are not fully and seamlessly interoperable with Joint and Live-Virtual-Constructive training systems. The current strategy is to maintain the current instrumentation system through life cycle maintenance while continuing a Research, Development, Testing and Evaluation Programme to determine an objective solution.

**Combat Training Center Objective Instrumentation System Life Cycle Management** provides RDTE for Life Cycle Management of current instrumentation systems at NTC, JRTC and JMRC until OIS is fielded. The Programme ensures optimal performance and integrity of the CTC Instrumentation System through a planned Obsolescence Elimination and Technology Refresh Programme. Failure to fund jeopardizes operation of CTC Instrumentation Systems until CTC OIS can be fielded. Requirement will be resubmitted for the FY10- 15 POM.

**CTC Modernization OMA** provides funding to support life cycle management of existing Programme, not covered under the RDA funding. It also provides OMA funding for CTC Modernization Programme MCA Projects and Army Battle Command System Software Licensing. Lack of funding impacts the Programme's ability to provide flexibility in funding non-Worldwide Contractor Logistics Support, non-OPTEMPO OMA requirements plus flexibility to provide funding required for MCA projects at MCTCs. Requirement will be resubmitted for the FY10-15 POM.

**CTC Live Fire Modernization Programme** provides for development and acquisition of replacement targets, lifters, and audiovisual- cueing devices on MCTC live fire ranges. It transforms CTC Live operations to doctrinally correct non-linear and noncontiguous operations. Without this Programme, units will not be able to perform live fire operations at MCTCs that replicate the current operational environment. Requirement will be resubmitted for the FY10-15 POM.

**NTC Military Operations in Urban Terrain MCA and Instrumentation System** provides increased capability to conduct full spectrum operations/ training at the National Training Center. It allows force-on-force urban operations training. It provides facilities and instrumentation that provides automated data collection and feedback for AAR; C2 of the MOUT exercise; and gives Observer Controller/Trainers the ability to monitor the unit's approach and actions. Additional funding is required in fiscal years 2012-13 to complete the instrumentation effort. Instrumentation requirements will be resubmitted in FY10-15 POM.

**Exportable Training Capability Instrumentation System** provides a deployable instrumentation package to support the Exportable Training Capability concept. Instrumentation is employed by the ETC OPS GRP and can be used at a Power Projection Platform, Power Generation Platform, or other location as required. The system will support exercise control, data collection, analysis, and feedback in a LVC construct for up to a BCT. This Programme provides the ITADSS pillar of the Exportable Training Capability. If this capability is not available, units will not receive objective force on force training or feedback for AARs at an ETC event. This has direct impact to the CTC Programme being able to fully implement its requirements for the ARFORGEN training and readiness model. Requirement will be resubmitted in FY10-15 POM if funding is not provided before then.

**CTC Information Assurance** provides for upgrade, replacement, or acquisition of necessary physical and information assurance security measures to meet ongoing and changing requirements for securing the CTC HICON and instrumentation systems. Includes acquisition and upgrades for filters, firewalls, software patches and physical security measures to meet DoD and Army security requirements. It will assist in migration to the CTC OIS by mitigating legacy security vulnerabilities of current instrumentation systems at the Manoevre CTCs. If not funded, the Programme will not be able to provide hardware and software systems needed to comply with mandatory regulatory information assurance requirements. Requirement will be resubmitted for funding in FY10-15 POM.

**C4ISR** Acquisition/Integration provides upgrades and/or acquires C4ISR (Battle Command) systems and components as technology changes occur within existing C4ISR HICON systems and as new systems are fielded to units rotating through the CTCs. This Programme supports acquisition and integration of new systems into the CTC HICON and OIS capabilities to enable the CTCs to interface with rotational unit C4ISR systems. Without funding, the Programme will not be able to ensure CTC Battle Command capabilities are updated as Army and Joint Battle Command systems evolve. Requirement will be resubmitted for funding in FY10-15 POM.

**OPFOR/Contemporary Operational Environment Combat Wheeled Vehicle Programme** provides wheeled vehicles for Opposing Force and Civilians on the Battlefield at Manoevre CTCs to replicate Combat/CS/CSS and commercial vehicles encountered on modern battlefields. It uses a common M1113 HMMWV chassis or other commercial vehicles. These systems reflect changing real-world conditions and provide full spectrum capability to MCTC Opposing Forces. The current fleet of OPFOR/COE vehicles at the MCTCs is composed of Visually Modified HMMWVs and civilian vehicles procured from DRMO and various civilian sources that are not sustainable over the long term. An integrated Programme is required to address procurement and sustainment of these vehicles. The addition of these vehicles will better replicate current operational environments and give the MCTCs a representative OPFOR that can operate throughout the full spectrum of combat operations. Requirement will be resubmitted for funding in FY10-15 POM.

**JRTC MOUT MCA** and Instrumentation Systems upgrades allow JRTC MOUT to meet future world environment and instrumentation requirements. Improvements include instrumentation that provides more discreet and accurate information necessary in a MOUT environment. The JRTC MOUT site has been in place for 15+ years and requires refresh of equipment and technology to remain relevant in the changing COE. Without funding, units will not be able to train as they fight and will not receive accurate training feedback prior actual combat if not funded. Requirement will be resubmitted for funding in FY10-15 POM.

**OPFOR/COE Vehicle Systems Modernization** provides RDTE to develop and test future OPFOR systems required at CTCs. It also upgrades current OPFOR Surrogate Vehicles and other major weapons systems and platforms. This maintains currency and relevancy under the changing COE. If this Programme is not funded, units participating in MCTC rotations will not face a realistic OPFOR. Requirement will be resubmitted for funding in FY10-15 POM.

**CTC Tactical Engagement System Acquisition** fields One Tactical Engagement System to the CTCs replacing existing laser based Multiple Integrated Laser Engagement Systems. OneTESS provides the OC/T situational awareness on player location and engagement activity. This acquires the newest available TESS for the CTCs. For Soldiers to train as they fight at MCTCs, they must be equipped with engagement simulation equipment that mirrors operational capabilities as closely as possible. Requirement will be resubmitted for funding in FY10-15 POM.

**CTC Aviation** provides RDTE to integrate specific CTC aviation training requirements for the Light Utility Helicopter which will replace UH-1 and OH-58 at MCTCs. LUHs support both Observer Controller/ Trainer and Opposing Force aviation missions. Items include tactical secure FM radios, GPS, IR/IR search light, Night Vision Systems, secure OCCS radios, 360 degree FLIR, BFT, VOX, OPFOR recognition both Electronically and visually, etc. It also integrates TESS with OPFOR LUHs. OPFOR aviation provides OPFOR rotary-wing aviation that replicate emerging threats. OC/ T aviation provides the OC/Ts with capability to control the event/ exercise and provides an AAR for aviation assets at a Manoevre CTC rotation. Both OPFOR and OC/T aircraft will be fielded as part of the LUH plan which is scheduled to begin in fiscal year 2008 timeframe. Failure to fund this effort could delay replacement of an OC and OPFOR capable aircraft at CTCs. Programme Managers will continue to pursue funding in fiscal years 2008-13 to meet LUH fielding dates, and if unsuccessful, the requirement for funding will be resubmitted in fiscal years 2010-15.

**Watercraft Simulators:** The current strategy for training Army Mariners is built on an integrated approach that includes institutional and unit training, as well as continuing professional development and certifications IAW AR 56-9. Given the cost of vessel operations and the feasibility of real-world training at distant ports and operating sites, a key element of the Army Watercraft training strategy is now and will continue to be the extensive use of simulations and simulators. Currently, the Army operates two vessel simulation facilities—one on the East Coast at Fort Eustis, Virginia, and on the West Coast at Mare Island, California. These facilities provide a wide range of simulations, to include integrated bridge operation for all Army vessels, inclement weather and damage control operations, and the ability to simulate a number of ports around the world. The facility at Fort Eustis includes an engine room simulator that provides operations and trouble shooting training.

## Training Support for FCSProgramme

The FCS System-of-Systems must be capable of simultaneously supporting operations, mission rehearsals, and training of separate audiences. FCS provides opportunities to fundamentally change

Army training. The Army's goal—to train anywhere, anytime—is best achieved by providing Embedded Training (ET) capability in all FCS. To that end, ET is the primary option for FCS-equipped BCT training in all training domains—institutional, operational, and self-development, including Army CTCs and JNTC. ET is being developed as an integral part of the FCS manned platform and C4ISR architectures, not as a set of add-on boxes and Software applications. Embedded Live-Virtual-Constructive training is an increment 1 capability and a Key Performance Parameter. KPP #6 requires "...FCS FoS must have embedded individual and collective training capability that supports LVC training environments." ET will be designed in at Programme start to ensure it is developed in conjunction with other FCS components.

## Modeling and Simulation

Modeling and Simulation (M&S) is a vital enabler and contributor to the Army's capability to provide Relevant and Ready Landpower. Army M&S is a multidomain enabler of related, discontinuous activities that support the Army's Operating and Generating Forces both current and future. M&S supports the Warfighter through myriad processes and activities such as concept development, experimentation, development of material and non-material solutions (DOTMLPF), testing, training, operations and planning, and mission rehearsal. It is an integral support component to the Warfighter, in the current operational environment.

As the Army transforms itself in response to the changes taking place in the world-wide security environment investments in Army M&S, particularly model functionality, must keep pace with changes in the environment. Investments in our model capabilities will be strongly linked to gaps in the operational capabilities of Current and Future Forces to achieve the greatest possible return for our Army. Army and Joint overarching concepts will describe the strategic context that will inform current and future development of M&S capabilities, which in turn informs the development of Army Warfighting Capabilities.

The Army has invested significant funds on the development and employment of models and simulations. Today, those investments primarily focus on traditional warfare (i.e. force on force) activity and support the development of technology and systems. While these investments have resulted in cost avoidance for training, acquisition, testing and evaluation, and analysis Army's M&S is still lacking robust functionality in the cognitive or human aspects of conflict. As an example, the Army M&S capabilities are lacking in their representation of irregular warfare. The Army will focus intellectual capital and resources to evolve current M&S capabilities and develop new M&S capabilities so that capability developers and commanders in the field have a relevant useful core set of modeling and simulation (M&S) tools, data, and business processes. Army M&S must support and enable Army modernization and support the warfighter by facilitating:

- Early assessment of Current and Future Force capabilities across the full-spectrum of operations
- Analysis of warfighting requirements to address mature and emerging challenges
- Risk reduction throughout the acquisition processes
- Training support and embedded training capabilities that are integral to weapon system platforms and Battle Command
- Net-enabled Battle Command capabilities for the human and technical aspects
- Cost-effective experimentation and gaming to gain insights across human, organizational, and system capabilities
- Human, organizational, and systems test and evaluation.

In support of the current operational environment and transformation activities, the Headquarters Department of the Army will develop a comprehensive M&S Strategy, building upon existing plans, to ensure unity of effort and purpose in the development of Army M&S capabilities, across multiple M&S communities and leverage the linkages between M&S capabilities of our networks, platforms, and home-station training facilities. The Army must develop metrics to monitor M&S interoperability, affordability and cost effectiveness.

# Modernizing Material- What the Army is doing about the Future

## Responding to Current Force Capability Shortfalls

The Army has a number of processes that seek to identify and redress required capabilities over time. TRADOC Army Capabilities Integration Center (ARCIC) addresses Current Force capability shortfalls through two processes—the Current Force Capability Gap Analysis (CGA) and the Capabilities Development for Rapid Transition (CDRT).

## Current Force Capability Gap Analysis

The ARCIC, in coordination with TRADOC centers and schools and other proponents, conducts a semi annual Capabilities Gap Analysis. The CGA highlights capability shortcomings for senior leadership, provides input to supplemental funding decisions, and experimentation, influences industry research and development, identifies needs for science and technology research, and identifies potential spiral candidates from the science and technology base.

## CGA Procedure and Comment Process

The capabilities gap analysis is based on a macro level approach that identifies needed capabilities extracted from Joint and Army Lessons Learned, Army Operational Needs Statements, Request for Forces, Combatant Commander Integrated Priority List, and Joint Urgent Operational Needs Statements. Asymmetric Warfare Division (AWD) conducts research and prepares capability gap documents (via PowerPoint® charts), updating the previous version.

In coordination with TRADOC proponents, AWD attempts to identify and assess the DOTMLPF solutions that can collectively satisfy a required capability, and then identifies residual capability gaps for those required capabilities not completely met.

The ACD Director requests review and input/comments from deployed operational commanders. After the operational force quality assurance check is complete, the ACD Director requests review and comments from other ARCIC directorates, TRADOC proponents and other agencies as appropriate. The documents are posted on the Asymmetric Warfare Division, Army Knowledge Online website with instructions for downloading (each briefing contains hyperlinks to the multiple charts referenced in the briefing).

Stakeholders in Current Force CGA include: ASA (ALT), ARSTAF G-3/5/7 and G-8, TRADOC Centers and Schools, TRADOC Capability Managers and Programme Integration Offices, ARCIC, Army Test and Evaluation Center, Rapid Equipping Force, and the Research, Development and Engineering Command.

## Capabilities Development for Rapid Transition

The CDRT is a semi-annual, DA-level process intended to reduce the normal material development cycle by several years. HQDA G-3 co-sponsors the process whereby non-Programme of record acquisition Programme material systems currently in use in operational theaters are considered for possible accelerated material development and Joint Capability Integration Development System documentation to compete for POR funding in the POM. Those systems not recommended for POR funding are either identified as "niche systems" – those systems to be sustained in theater with supplemental funding – or "terminate" – systems for which HQDA will no longer sustain with funding, but which may be retained by the unit and sustained with unit funding. Operational units may also recommend changes to DOTMLPF, so the process addresses the entire spectrum of capabilities. Currently in its fifth iteration, CDRT thus far has used input from Operation Enduring Freedom and Operation Iraqi Freedom (OEF/OIF).

Material systems must meet specific criteria to be included in the CDRT process. Criteria requirements:

- In use in an operational theater
- Not an acquisition Programme
- Operational assessment completed

The CDRT process unfolds over a six month period. An initial candidate list is developed by TRADOC in conjunction with the

Army Asymmetric Warfare Office, the Rapid Equipping Force, HQDA G-2 and G- 3/5/7. This initial list is sent to the Operational Force for any additional inputs resulting in a final candidate list. The final list is then redistributed to the Operational Force to categorize as an acquistion Programme, niche or terminate candidate. After integration of input and initial analysis, the list becomes the recommended list, and is distributed to the CDRT community of interest for comment. The recommended list is briefed to a DA-level Council of Colonels (CoC) who make a recommendation that is briefed to senior TRADOC and Army leadership—e.g. TRADOC Quarterly Futures Review, the AR2B and/or the AROC. A decision briefing is presented to the Vice Chief of Staff, Army, who approves the systems to move through the JCIDS process in an accelerated manner. Capabilities other than material system—the DOTMLPF areas, follow the same approval path, however are implemented within their normal functional processes. For example, a recommended change in doctrine would be processed through the Combined Arms Center, TRADOC schools and centers, and ARCIC.

An example of a material system that worked through the CDRT process is the Armored Security Vehicle. Army units operating in OEF/OIF submitted Operational Needs Statements requesting a capability to enhance the survivability of convoy security forces, as the lead vehicles were the ones to incur the brunt of IEDs. The requirements were validated by HQDA G- 3/5/7, with equipment to remain in theater as Theater Provided Equipment. In November, 2004 the VCSA approved the ASV for rapid transition to an acquisition Programme. Today, it is a Programme. With hundreds of systems in use in theater. Other systems that started with ONS and are now Programmes include Raven (Small Unmanned Aircraft System) and the RG-31, Buffalo, and Husky IED Route Clearance Packages.

A number of organizations are involved in the CDRT process. They include:

- TRADOC, ARCIC, Asymmetric Warfare Division—coordinates CDRT as the TRADOC process lead, and co-chairs the CDRT Council of Colonels with Army Requirements Division (DAMO-CIC), HQDA G-37

- Army Requirements Division (DAMO-CIC), HQDA G-3/5/7—partner in process, assists in staffing the process across HQDA and the Army, assists in the development of the candidate list, co-chairs CoC, and assists in JCIDS development process
- ARCIC Directorates and Divisions—provide subject matter expert input to the process and assist in oversight management of JCIDS product development
- TRADOC G3/5/7—O6/GS15 representative on CoC and the SME for training capability issues
- TRADOC Proponents—provide subject matter expertise in the review of candidate final and recommended system and capabilities lists, brief systems/capabilities recommended for Programme of record to the CoC, conduct DOTMLPF assessment, and develop JCIDS documents for selected capabilities
- TRADOC Capability Managers—provide subject matter expert input to process ICW proponents and leads, assume responsibility for selected systems
- Center for Army Lessons Learned —provides Army lessons learned and initial impression reports
- Army Asymmetric Warfare Office and Rapid Equipping Force—partner in candidate list development, analysis of input, and member of CoC
- Research, Development and Engineering Command—assists in list development, and member of CoC
- Army Test and Evaluation Command —performs in theater assessments and member of CoC Assistant Secretary of the Army (Acquisition Logistics and Technology)—provides comments during staffing, member of CoC, assist via the PM/PEO community in system evaluations and in JCIDS development
- HQDA G8—provides input to analysis and preparation of system financial data, member of CoC
- TRADOC Chartered Integrated Capability Development Teams—assist in review of candidate system list, participate in CoC as required

## Identifying and Prioritizing Future Force Capability Shortfalls

The ARCIC, in concert with TRADOC HQ, Centers and Proponents, conducts an annual two-phased capabilities-based Future Force Capabilities Needs Analysis (CNA) coordinated with HQDA and Joint Staff. The CNA informs the Programme Objective Memorandum and the Army's capabilities development community.

During Phase I (Analysis Phase), TRADOC participants conduct a macro-level assessment of the Army's ability to achieve it's warfighting requirements, producing four products: 1) Prioritized List of Required Capabilities, 2) Prioritized List of Programmed DOTMLPF Solutions, 3) Prioritized List of Future Force Capability Gaps Across DOTMLPF, and 4) List of Developmental Priorities.

During Phase II (Product Use Phase) HQDA and TRADOC use these four products to inform capabilities developments and Programming processes, to include: POM (over all PEGs); Joint Capabilities Integration and Development System capabilities-based analyses; Joint Staff J-8 Capabilities Gap Analysis; Army Concept and Capability Developments Plan; Capabilities-Based Assessment processes (Functional Area Analysis, Functional Needs Analysis, and the Functional Solution Analysis); Total Army Analysis; *The Army Plan*; *Army Modernization Strategy*; *Science and Technology Strategy*; Concept, Scenario and Architecture development; Integrated Question List; Studies, Analysis, Modeling, Simulation and Experimentation plans; and related Current Force gap analysis.

An example of the impact of this process is the Sequoyah Foreign Language Translation System. Historically linguists have been unavailable in sufficient numbers to satisfy the language translation needs of the Joint force. This need was documented in the Operational Needs Statement process and subsequently associated with a gap derived from the Army concepts addressing increased situational awareness. Initiatives were evaluated to address the gap in the short-term, while a Programme of record was created to address the gap long-term. This Programme of record was assessed and supported in the CNA as a critical system to mitigate the risk to mission failure. The consequence of these efforts is that the Sequoyah is currently funded.

The collective results of these functional and organizational assessments conducted during the CNA articulate critical DOTMLPF capabilities and gaps that inform the Army's Future Force Modernization Strategy.

## Science and Technology

The Army's S&T investment strategy seeks to pursue technologies that will enable the Future Force while simultaneously seizing opportunities to enhance the Current Force. To achieve this strategy, we are developing technology through investments in the three components of S&T:

- For the far-term, conducting basic research to create new understanding for technologies that offer paradigm-shifting capabilities
- For the mid-term, translating applied research into militarily useful technology application
- In the near-term, demonstrating mature technology in relevant operational environments to speed technology transition into acquisition Programmes

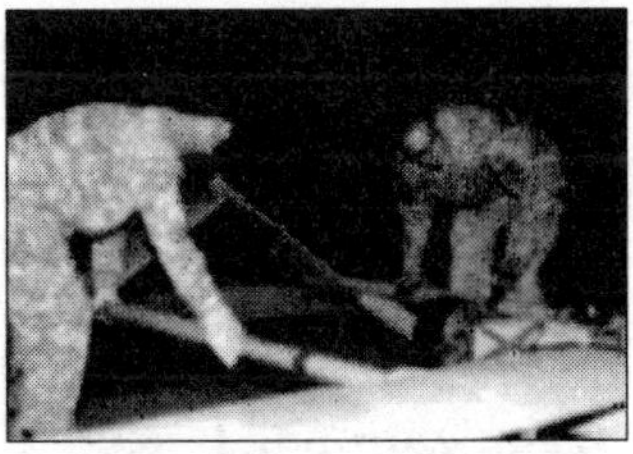

Our technology demonstrations prove concepts, inform the combat developments process, and provide the acquisition community with evidence of technology's readiness to satisfy system requirements. The entire Programme is adaptable and responsive to the needs of our Soldiers on today's battlefield and the lessons learned for future battlefields.

To enhance the Current Force, Army S&T is providing limited quantities of advanced technology prototypes to our Soldiers deployed in the fight. Operational security precludes the listing of specific S&T technology contributions to Global War on Terror (GWOT). These contributions have included force protection, command, control, communications, computers, and intelligence, surveillance and reconnaissance (C4ISR) and unmanned systems technologies among others. From a top level perspective the S&T community supports the GWOT in three ways. Soldiers benefit today from technologies that emerged from our past investments.

We exploit transition opportunities by accelerating mature technologies from on-going S&T efforts. We also leverage the expertise of our scientists and engineers to develop solutions to unforeseen problems encountered during current operations.

**Why is this important to the Army?**

Science and Technology serves two purposes in this developmental process. First, it provides a vision of the possible. This vision reflects what technology can bring to military operations derived from ideas, developed through concepts, to realized capabilities. Secondly, it develops the means necessary to implement these ideas, concepts, and capabilities. TRADOC is responsible for validating that the S&T Programmes are consistent with Army developmental efforts, both in content and priority from the perspective of Soldiers and leaders who employ warfighting capabilities. Additionally, TRADOC plays several roles in the process to ensure that promising capabilities from emerging technologies are transitioned to the Soldier, either through enabling concepts, Programmes of record or spiral insertion into the Current Force. They are listed below:

*a.* Staff Lead for Science and Technology. Within Headquarters TRADOC, the ARCIC's Accelerated and Capabilities Developments Directorate (ACDD) is responsible for TRADOC's involvement in the S&T process. The ACDD is also responsible for developing statements of Force Operating Capabilities (FOCs) derived from Joint and Army concepts and operational and organizational (O&O) plans. TRADOC ARCIC functional divisions, along with proponents and schools, participate in the S&T process by providing periodic reviews of new technology options for enhanced warfighting capabilities. Within ACDD, the, Science and Technology Division oversees the TRADOC S&T process and coordinates day-to-day S&T staff actions.

The current TRADOC Pamphlets (TP) 525-3- 0, The Army in Joint Operations, and the TP 525-66, Force Operating Capabilities (FOCs), provide focus to the *Army Science and Technology Master Plan* and warfighter experimentation. The ARCIC guidance document *Army Concept and Capability Developments Plan* provides a consolidated set of guidance for TRADOC Concept Development, Experimentation and Capability Development to establish the foundation for the future Modular Force. (http://www.tradoc.army.mil/tpubs/pamndx. htm)

TRADOC functional organizations, doctrine, training, and combat developers, as well as Army material developers, academia and industry use the FOCs as a reference to maintain responsiveness and viability in independent research and development. TRADOC FOCs are described later in this section.

*b.* Joint Capabilities Integration and Development System. Concepts are the foundation of the capabilities integration and development process. Concepts emanate from a vision of the future Modular Force and from the Chairman of the Joint Chiefs of Staff's Joint Operations Concepts that broadly describe the future Joint force 15 to 20 years from now and the related subordinate Joint concepts. The following concepts have direct linkage to National Military Strategy, National Security Strategy, Strategic Planning Guidance, and other national and DoD-level planning documents:

- Army concepts, described in TRADOC 525- series pamphlets, illustrate how the Future Force will operate and the capabilities that it will require to carry out full spectrum military operations against adversaries in the expected Joint Operational Environment
- Approved concepts serve as the foundation for architecture development and determination of (DOTMLPF) requirements through an evolutionary development process that produces needed capabilities

Army concepts describe future capabilities within a proposed structure of future military operations for a period of 5–15 years. These concepts are the basis for assessment that may include studies, experimentation, wargaming, analyses, testing and simulations leading to determination of DOTMLPF solution sets to gain the specific capabilities required in approved concepts. Approved TRADOC concepts, published as TRADOC pamphlets in the 525-series, guide the Capabilities Integration and Developments System requirements determination process for the Army by illustrating how Future Modular Forces will operate or be employed, their distinct attributes and design characteristics, and the capabilities that they must possess.

The JCIDS implements a capabilities-based approach that better leverages the expertise of all government agencies, industry and

academia to identify improvements to existing capabilities and to develop new warfighting capabilities when warranted. This approach requires a collaborative process that utilizes Joint concepts and integrated architectures to identify prioritized capability gaps and integrated (DOTMLPF) solutions (material and nonmaterial) to resolve those gaps. A description of JCIDS can be obtained at: https://acc.dau.mil/GetAttachment.aspx?id=42773&pname=file&aid=12042. The Army's CIDS process mirrors the Joint process and supports the Joint Requirements Oversight Council Programmatic processes for Joint experimentation and Joint resource change recommendations process contained in CJCSI 3180.01 found at: http://jitc.fhu.disa.mil/ jitc_dri/pdfs/3180_01.pdf. The Army's CIDS process depends on the concept development and experimentation process that translates strategic guidance and operational environments into warfighting concepts.

The purpose of CIDS analysis is to provide compelling evidence that allows Army leadership to make informed decisions. TRADOC conducts studies and analyses to assess concepts, determine required capabilities and capability gaps, and evaluate DOTMLPF initiatives to provide needed solutions. The DoD and Army vision of accelerated development, integration and fielding of DOTMLPF solutions requires significant investment of analytic resources to validate concepts and propose solutions. It is essential that those resources be applied wisely and efficiently.

The CIDS analysis process is composed of a structured, four-step methodology that identifies and defines tasks, capability gaps, capability needs and DOTMLPF approaches to providing those capabilities within a specified functional or operational area. Based on National Defence Policy and centered on a common Joint/Army warfighting construct, the analyses initiate the development of integrated capabilities from a common understanding of existing Joint force operations and of DOTMLPF capabilities and deficiencies.

*c*. The ARCIC ACDD supports the analyses to assess concepts, determine required capabilities and capability gaps and evaluate DOTMLPF initiatives to provide needed solutions. ARCIC conducts Gap Analysis, semi-annually, and the Capabilities Needs Analysis, annually, to identify the required capabilities for the Current and Future Force and then, through analysis of current capabilities versus desired capabilities, determines the capability gaps (Current Force challenges and future Modular Force needs). The capability gap analyses for Current and Future Modular Force and the derived Warfighter Outcome information is maintained in folders on the Science and Technology Enterprise Management (STEM) system. All Government users desiring a STEM account go to https://stem-collabsuite. altess.army.mil/

Existing technology (often mature prototypes or commercial off-the-shelf products) and non-technology solutions from DOTMLPF assessments can be used to address the gaps for the Current Force. The gap is narrowed for the Future Modular Force through a combination of existing technology and nontechnology solutions, with the ongoing S&T work represented in this master plan arrayed to address the residual future gaps.

The number of capabilities that the Army is required to have in the future is increasing given the broad nature of threats and the greater availability of technology to our adversaries. Many of the technologies and research the Army is pursuing are high-risk/highpayoff. This means that the private sector is not likely to sustain "risky" investments over the "long haul" to achieve desired technology breakthroughs for dramatic performance improvements and entirely new capabilities such as Excalibur precision munitions for artillery that nearly eliminates collateral damage to non-combatants. Today's Current Force has significant technology-enabled capability advantages as a result of the Army's past investments in S&T. Examples include the development of technologies for night vision, precision munitions, and individual Soldier protection. Scientists and engineers are expanding the limits of our understanding to provide our Soldiers, as well as our Joint and coalition partners, with technologies that enable transformational capabilities in the ongoing war on terror to ensure that the U.S. Army remains a victorious, relevant and ready land component of the Joint force.

## Force Operating Capabilities

Force Operating Capabilities articulate the capabilities the Army requires to execute Joint and Army concepts. They apply to both the current and the future Army, conducting full-spectrum operations on the information age battlefield and beyond. FOCs describe force-level capabilities that form the basis for future Modular Force warfighting requirements in DOTMLPF domains. FOCs provide the basis for analysis to define and refine requirements across the full spectrum of operations.

FOCs establish needs for the Army S&T community and are employed by TRADOC leadership in the conduct of S&T reviews of ATO candidates, including Special Access Programmes, as part of the Army Science and Technology Working Group and the Army Science and Technology Advisory Group forums. FOCs assist in focusing the Army's S&T investment priorities to support Future Force overall development and transformation. The FOCs are:

- Battle Command
- Battlespace Awareness
- Mounted/Dismounted Manoevre
- Air Manoevre
- LOS/BLOS/NLOS Lethality for Mounted/ Dismounted Operations
- Manoevre Support
- Protection
- Strategic Responsibility and Responsiveness
- Manoevre Sustainment
- Training, Leader Development, and Leader Education
- Human Dimension

The FOCs are fully described in TRADOC Pamphlet 525-66 (http://www.TRADOC.army.mil/tpubs/pams/ p525-66.pdf).

Army Organizations responsible for concept development and experimentation will take all necessary actions to allow full participation by the United Kingdom, Australia and Canada in experiments. These actions are necessary to support national and DOD policies toward these key allies, as well as the Army objective of enhancing U.S. and partner interoperability. The Army will use the solutions devised for the three allies as a starting point for achieving appropriate expanded access for other core partnerships.

## Relationship between Army Force Operating Capabilities and Joint Functional Concepts

The following paragraphs show the relationships between the Army FOCs and the Joint Functional Concepts, given the FOCs nested within the Joint Functional Concepts. These descriptions are the structured statements of operational capabilities that, when achieved in aggregate, fulfill the vision articulated in the Future Force Concepts and fulfill the Army contribution to the Joint Functional and Integrating Concepts. Although not a one-to-one alignment, the FOCs are associated with Joint Functional Concepts to facilitate transition of S&T enablers into functional capabilities through the Joint Functional Control Board process.

In addition, required capabilities for each FOC area can be linked back to tasks of Universal Joint Task List (UJTL) and Army Universal Task List (AUTL). These lists are available at: http://www.dtic.mil/doctrine/jel/cjcsd/cjcsm/m350004.pdf for UJTLs and http://www.army.mil/usapa/doctrine/Active_FM.html for AUTLs (FM- 7-15).

*a. Joint Functional Concepts: Command and Control, and Net-Centric Environment*

**BATTLE COMMAND** is the art and science of visualizing, describing, directing and leading forces in operations against a hostile, thinking and adaptive enemy. Future Battle Command will enable other advances in the future Modular Force, such as improvements in responsiveness, lethality, survivability, and mobility, to achieve a new way of operating, based on knowledge superior to that of our adversaries.

*b. Joint Functional Concept: Battlespace Awareness*

**BATTLESPACE AWARENESS** focuses on the ability of Joint force commanders and all force elements to understand the environment in which they operate and the adversaries they face. In the future, efforts to create superior battlespace awareness will involve a constellation of highly responsive sensors providing persistent coverage of adversary targets. A producer interactive network, continuously synchronized with operations, will enable users to subscribe to both realtime and archived fused data.

*c. Joint Functional Concept: Force Application*

**MOUNTED/DISMOUNTEDMANOEVRE** contributes to strategic, operational and tactical Manoevre—the defining capability of the Future Force. Capabilities are required for precise, decisive Manoevre, horizontal and vertical, day and night, in all terrain and weather conditions, synchronized with Army and Joint fires, and Reconnaissance, Surveillance and Target Acquisition. In future operations, decisive Manoevre will be central to entering the fight on our terms, seizing and retaining the initiative and finishing rapidly.

**AIR MANOEVRE** is critical to Joint operations. Army Aviation and Joint tactical air support must be closely integrated into ground Manoevre operations. Army Aviation plays a major role in the future Modular Force operations. Traditional aviation roles of attack, reconnaissance, and lift and cargo transport continue to be vital in the Future Modular Force. Key air Manoevre missions envisioned for future Modular Force are: Close Combat Attack, Interdiction Attack, Reconnaissance, Security, Vertical Manoevre and Air Movement.

**LINE-OF-SIGHT/BEYOND-LINE OF- SIGHT (LOS/BLOS) AND NONLINE OF SIGHT (NLOS) LETHALITY FOR MOUNTED/DISMOUNTED OPERATIONS.** Fires are categorized as LOS, BLOS, or NLOS. Engagement range is not directly tied to the definitions of LOS, BLOS, and NLOS fires. The method used determines the type of engagement. Future Force fire control and distribution requires networked responsive fires on-demand, engaging complex and simultaneous target sets, executed as preplanned or opportunity engagements.

*d. Joint Functional Concept Protection*

Protection is a process, a set of activities and capabilities by which the Future Modular Force protects personnel (combatant/ noncombatant), information, and physical assets against the full spectrum of threats. The Future Force will achieve this through the scaled and tailored selection and application of multi-layered, active and passive, lethal and non-lethal measures, across the spectrum of conflict, based on assessment of an acceptable level of risk. The Joint force must protect itself starting at point-of-origin, continuing through transit, employment, sustainment and redeployment. Force health protection is a mission capability element. The goal is to prevent adversaries from employing capabilities that would restrict or prevent the Future Modular Force from conducting decisive actions at a time and place of our choosing. Key protection activities are: detect, assess, warn, defend and recover.

Manoevre Support forces focus on ensuring future Modular Force freedom of Manoevre and protection throughout the theater of operation. Manoevre support capabilities are applied within operating areas, fully integrated within combined arms teams, to ensure continued friendly freedom of action and denial of enemy freedom of action. On a noncontiguous, three-dimensional battlefield, the idea of "Manoevreing" fires, sensor networks, distribution based sustainment and communications networks broadens the applications of Manoevre support capabilities. Manoevre support provides a wide range of integrated actions, both proactive and defensive, that support uninterrupted momentum, allow Manoevre forces to preserve combat power so that it may be best applied at decisive points and times, and foster rapid transitions in operations.

*e. Joint Functional Concept: Focused Logistics*

**STRATEGIC RESPONSIVENESS AND DEPLOYABILITY.** The Future Modular Force must, within a Joint context, be capable of rapidly deploying worldwide and arrive ready to fight or conduct other full spectrum operations immediately upon arrival. Current strategic deployment guidelines are to be capable of deploying to a distant theater to seize the initiative within 10 days, defeat the enemy within 30 days, and be prepared for deployment to another conflict elsewhere in the world 30 days later. In order to meet the strategic responsiveness and deployability capability, the Army, enabled by Army Power Projection Programme (AP3) initiatives, must be able to deploy and employ a Brigade Combat Team capability in 10 days, a nine BCT (Multi-Division) capability in 20 days, and a 15 BCT (Multi-Division) capability in 30 days.

**MANOEVRE SUSTAINMENT.** Army Concepts characterize Manoevre sustainment as a full spectrum capability that is strategically responsive, deployable, agile, versatile, and survivable throughout fullspectrum conflict. Manoevre sustainment units will conduct operational Manoevre from strategic distances, deploy through multiple austere points of entry, and rapidly establish Manoevre sustainment operations. They will arrive in the theater of operations immediately capable of supporting simultaneous, distributed and continuous Joint operations throughout the battlespace, day and night, in any terrain, protected from health threats. Future Force Manoevre sustainment operations are characterized by simultaneous operations distributed across the battlespace in accordance with the Manoevre commander's intent and operations plan. Superior situational understanding, based on advanced C4ISR capabilities and visibility of the distribution network, enables Manoevre sustainment organizations to operate within the battle rhythm of Manoevre commanders.

*f. Joint Functional Concepts: Joint Training Functional Concept*

**HUMAN DIMENSION (TRAINING, LEADER DEVELOPMENT AND EDUCATION).** The Soldier is the single most important aspect of the combat power of the Future Modular Force. The Future Modular Force Soldier is a combat Soldier first and foremost. Despite the expected proliferation of unmanned systems, Soldiers will remain the cornerstone for force design and employment. Soldiers, not equipment, accomplish missions and win wars. In order to achieve revolutionary effectiveness across the full spectrum of conflict, human engineering capabilities will enable the Future Modular Force to: decrease task complexity and execution times to improve performance while minimizing sensory, cognitive, and physical demands on the Soldier; and systems that have been human engineered to improve trainability.

Future Modular Force Soldiers and leaders must be multifunctional, and capable of fighting and winning decisively, as part of a Joint Force, on the full spectrum battlefields of the future. The demands of future conflict will continue to place great responsibility on future Army leaders at all levels, requiring mature judgment even while they are still gaining experience. Future battle will also require leaders who can operate with mission command in an environment of rapidly changing operational conditions, confronting a wide variety of threats. Future leaders must possess a Joint and expeditionary mindset, accepting change as a routine condition, and acquire proficiency in the use of a wide range of new technologies, particularly within the information arena. Army leaders will also need JIIM education and experience earlier in their careers than has been the norm in the past. Training capabilities will enable operators, maintainers, unit leaders, and staff planners to be trained in SOS functions, by leveraging networked, embedded, virtual, constructive, and live training modes anywhere, anytime. Training leader development and education regimens will develop thinking, confident, versatile, adaptive, and seasoned leaders. The FOCs identified for training, in order to fulfill the vision articulated in Joint and Army concepts fall into the following areas: leadership training and education; accessible training; realistic training; responsive training development and delivery; training for JIIM operations; managing unit performance; and providing universal training support.

TRADOC represents the warfighter in the S&T process. TRADOC validates that the S&T Programmes are consistent with the capabilities needed in the Current Force and the Future Modular Force. TRADOC plays a major role throughout the S&T development process.

## Leader Development: Preparing Agile and Adaptive Leaders

Leader development is the deliberate, continuous, sequential and progressive process, grounded on Army Values, which grows Soldiers and civilians into competent and confident leaders capable of decisive action. Leader development is accomplished through a lifelong learning process that takes place through operational experience in units, recurring experiences in the institutional Army (schools and training centers), and self-development. The focus of leader development is the future – the preparation of Soldiers and civilians for successive levels of leadership responsibility. Leader development is the mechanism by which the Army grows leaders who are adaptive and agile while providing purpose, direction and motivation to the force and all its components.

We will continuously assess and adjust the balance of leader competencies developed across the three training and leader development domains – operational, institutional and self-development. At present, the operational domain is developing leaders with significant capabilities to conduct counterinsurgency operations – the other domains must adjust to ensure our leaders build and sustain competency for major combat operations and limited intervention operations to support building the Army's strategic depth. Adaptation must occur through training in units, the Institutional Army, professional education, operational assignments and experiences, and self development. The Army will produce a steady flow of adaptive and competent, multi-skilled leaders who can lead the execution of full-spectrum operations, adapting their core skills for directed missions across the operational themes. We must identify the required functional competencies for full spectrum operations, and then provide the capability to develop them through our leader development Programme. Each of the three domains reinforces the others to produce leaders who are prepared to meet the challenges of the current and projected operating environments.

The initial focus for leader development is built on a base of junior leader competencies for their core functional skills. As leaders progress, focused developmental assignments, education, experiences, training and self-development broaden their skill sets and produce a "bench" of capable senior leaders. The Soldier will be—and has always been—the centerpiece of Army capabilities. Nothing is more important than our investment in training Soldiers and development of the leaders they will follow.

We are strong believers in life-long learning. We are using information technology to enhance Soldier and leader education in a time of war. Soldiers participate in more than 1,500 online courses to improve job proficiency and to work toward civilian degrees. Our Army Knowledge Online websites average more than one million visits per day, allowing Soldiers and leaders to collaborate and to share information regarding the lessons learned from combat and from training.

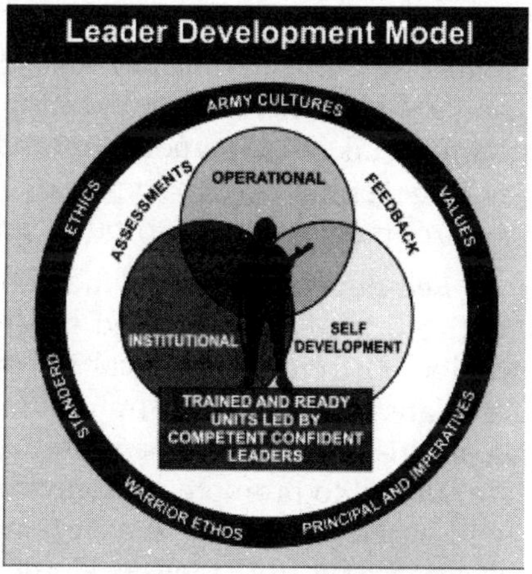


While new technology and the operational environment will be dynamic, the Army retains its doctrinal bedrock principles and imperatives: develop Warrior Ethos, train to standard, command responsibility for training, empower subordinates, put our best and brightest leaders in positions to develop emerging leaders, and commitment to expert assessment and feedback to ensure relevance and improvement. Warrior Ethos, grounded in the refusal to accept failure, is developed and sustained through discipline, commitment to Army values and ethics, and pride in the Army's heritage. We are, and will remain, a values-based institution. Our core values, integral to all training and leader development efforts, will not change. Significantly, the Army's values also directly support the Joint Service values articulated in *Joint Pub 1*: integrity, competence, physical courage, moral courage and teamwork.

Across the force, enhanced linguistic skills and increased understanding of other cultures will provide us a clear operational advantage. Our leaders will be equally adept at the employment of lethal and nonlethal approaches to accomplish the mission. Our training will challenge leaders with multiple scenarios designed to present fleeting opportunities, where dilemmas and uncertainty prevail. The focus of this training will enhance their ability to think and adapt their skills to the conditions they face. This capability requires creation of robust channels for collaboration between the Operational Force and the Generating Force. The key is to integrate our observations, insights and lessons learned into our three training and leader development domains.

Rigour will be maintained during initial entry training, providing the Operating Force with Soldiers and leaders ready to participate in collective training immediately upon arrival in units. In support of this collective training effort, the Army will sustain and improve the Combat Training Center capability to realistically portray the ever-changing operational environment, while simultaneously integrating unified action partners into training. Likewise, home station and deployed training capabilities will be enhanced to replicate a more robust operational environment in order to build and sustain critical skills.

Self-development activities, both command directed and self-initiated, will be supported by an integrated network that can deliver current and critical information and enables Soldiers, civilians and leaders to "train as we fight" anytime and anyplace. A multi-source assessment and feedback Programme has been developed to promote an Army culture for lifelong learning that will accelerate leader development through composite leader assessments and feedback, increasing awareness of Army expectations and reinforcing Army values and leader competencies. It will be a web-based 360 assessment and feedback tool that is integrated into the Warrior Knowledge Network and accessible to all Army leaders around the world, RC included.

An enabler available to support Army training is the Training Transformation (T2) effort, co-sponsored with OSD and the Joint Staff. Enhancing Army training with Joint National Training Capability and Joint Knowledge Development and Distribution Capability initiatives offers opportunities to include some Joint training requirements inherent within the concept of Joint interdependence. Joint interdependence is a key component of DoD's force design and sizing construct and comprehensive Joint training across all domains is required to achieve competence and confidence within the Joint interdependence construct. Significantly, T2 and the Defence Inter-agency Training Coordination Working Group under the Joint Staff J7 also provide some support to fully integrating Inter-Agency participation in our training in all domains, particularly in collective training at our CTCs.

Leaders will be able to dominate the Informational Environment by recognizing opportunities to exploit and attack adversaries' abilities to use information, and by defending friendly decision-making. They will be able to harness the capabilities of Information Operations in a coordinated and synergistic way in order to attain the critical enabler of Information Superiority. Army leaders will be trained to generate informational effects to shape the environment in support of a wide variety of options in support of mission accomplishment.

Our Battle Command systems and platforms will be interoperable and linked to the live, virtual and constructive (LVC) training network to support seamless transition from institutional and home station training through mission rehearsal to mission execution with minimal reconfiguration. This robust network will enable rapid preparation and employment of our forces, provide a Common Operational Picture and situational awareness to promote adaptation, and facilitate our ability to defeat our enemies innovatively and decisively. A key enabler is a cross-domain training network that leverages LandWarNet to create a realistic, adaptive, and collaborative training and mission rehearsal environment, accessible to both the operational and institutional Army.

## Combat Training Centers

The CTC Programme includes the Battle Command Training Programme (BCTP), Joint Multinational Readiness Center (JMRC), Joint Readiness Training Center (JRTC) and National Training Center (NTC), and integrates training with the Joint National Training Capability (JNTC).

Beginning this year, the CTC Programme will develop a CONUS Exportable Training Capability (ETC) that will support the Army Forces Generation process. Expanding the reach of the CTCs through an ETC is required to support the increased number of modular brigades (AC/USAR/NG) preparing to deploy, which also includes the multi—functional support brigades.

The ETC will not achieve operational capability until fiscal year 2010. The ETC will be manned with analysts and an OPFOR cadre and equipped with an instrumentation and after action review (AAR) capability that can be used either at home station (Power Projection Platform) for active units or an ARNG training area (Power Generation Platform) for the ARNG units. This ETC will deliver a training experience that is more rigorous and included improved feedback over the training normally provided at home station or ARNG training area.

CTC training rotations remain the Army's capstone training events for battalions, BCTs, divisions, corps and echelons above corps. Their focus remains unit readiness and leader development. The primary purpose of CTCs is to develop ready units and selfaware, adaptive leaders. CTCs accomplish this by integrating the contemporary operational environment and Joint, Inter-agency, Intergovernmental, and Multinational (JIIM) context into all training. This environment can include simultaneous, non-contiguous and continuous operations in a distributed, global, LVC training capability within a JIIM context. Army units experience a rigorous fight in offensive, defensive and stability operations against a freethinking and adaptable opposing force. The training scenario and events are arrayed to support specific training objectives and to stress the unit's Battle Command system.

Modernization efforts also include civilians on the battlefield as role players to replicate the human dimension of the COE, and building urban areas that reflect the environment our Soldiers will encounter. Instrumented feedback for both formal and informal after action reviews will enhance the quality of training and facilitate sharing of lessons learned to unit leaders, home station and deployed units, and our training centers and schools.

## Institutional Training

Army centers and schools are synchronizing capabilities to meet requirements as defined by the ARFORGEN process. Units require access to an array of institutionally developed training and education resources to enable full spectrum training across individual, staff, leader and collective training. The institutional army is working to lighten the commander's load and improve Army flexibility by creating, maintaining and storing learning resources to simultaneously support individual and collective training strategies for full spectrum operations. By providing products through both push packages and development of a learning repository system, Army knowledge centers support institutional training and operational training, with mobile training teams, individual and collective training support packages, lessons learned, exportable training and distributed learning capabilities. Warrior tasks, language proficiency, and cultural awareness and understanding are now key parts of both individual and unit training.

During initial military training, centers and schools will continue to train new recruits and officers, with emphasis on instilling Army Values, the Warrior Ethos and Soldier's Creed, and preparing them for their assignments. Civilian training has accelerated to develop an adaptive, competent Civilian Corps prepared to meet the future strategic environment and future leadership positions. Centers and schools will continue to anticipate and responsibly adapt training and leader development as the operational environment changes. The institutional army will constantly assess the dynamic and volatile COE and provide evolutionary, and where required, transformational modifications to our training Programmes and support systems to develop leaders through NCO, officer and civilian education Programmes.

**Initial Entry Training Re-design.** This initiative involves a comprehensive look at creating efficiencies in the training base to produce additional manpower by redesigning the conduct of initial entry training. These initiatives will produce trained and ready Soldiers at the right place, and the right time to effectively integrate with their first unit of assignment. To achieve this more dynamic throughput, the initial entry training community is testing several initiatives to determine feasibility. The end state for this redesign is that Soldiers spend less time in initial entry training and arrive at operational units sooner, without degradation of the critical skills required. A Center of Excellence has been proposed at Fort Jackson, South Carolina, in order to create a portal for information and improved operational synergy for all Army Training Centers ensuring a well established community of practice with assigned responsibility for all aspects of basic combat training. Command and control, standardization of instruction and quality assurance will improve as consolidation occurs over the next few years.

Work to improve Basic Combat Training will continue throughout the decade. Warrior Tasks and Battle Drills will be refined as the operational environment changes. Resource investment in this training will gradually increase to add to today's task-based training a series of structured vignettes designed to train the cognitive skills necessary to react to uncertainty with adaptability and flexibility. New methods to identify lessons learned, develop and approve new doctrine and Tactics, Techniques and Procedures, and rapidly integrate those lessons learned into Programmes of Instruction will be employed. Advanced training management technology will be used to track progress through basic training and provide a start point for the sustainment training required in Advanced Individual Training (AIT). This technology will track progress through AIT and be accessible by training managers at the Soldier's first unit of assignment.

**The Army School System** plays an important role in meeting the Army's expanded training mission. TASS is responsible for the vast majority of institutional training within the Army, and provides training to Soldiers in both the Active Component and the Reserve Component. Army Training System Courseware (TATS-C) is an on-going initiative to satisfy the need for expanding training technologies. All RC courses are converting to TATS-C to ensure critical tasks were taught to the same

standard regardless of the school. The system courseware includes MOS qualification, Army Leadership, functional, professional development, and civilian courses. The course's structure (phases, modules, tracks, lessons, tests) and media ensure standardization by training all Soldiers (regardless of component) on course critical tasks to task performance standard. A major outcome of this conversion will allow an active duty Soldier to take Army courses at a local armory if it is not available at his home station.

**Professional Military Education** is a progressive education system that prepares leaders for increased responsibilities and successful performance at the next higher level by developing the key knowledge, skills and attributes they require to operate successfully at that level in any environment. PME addresses educational requirements established by three key areas: The National Defence Strategy's four security challenges (irregular, traditional, catastrophic and disruptive), establishment of stability operations as a core Army mission with priority comparable to combat operations, and lessons learned from the Contemporary Operating Environment. The Army will continue to require Soldiers and leaders who are knowledgeable and experienced, to analyze their unit's ability to fight and sustain themselves, and are capable of adaptive thinking and decision-making in ambiguous environments. Modules on warfighting and irregular warfare will educate leaders on doctrine, tactics, techniques and procedures for decision making, and the employment of military units in combined arms operations in all emerging security challenges. These modules will be tactically focused, hands-on and execution-oriented, and culminating with an exercise that stresses and develops the leaders' ability to rapidly make decisions and to apply the elements of combat power throughout the full spectrum operations.

**Officer Education System.** OES is a sequence of PME for professionals in subjects that enhance knowledge of the science and art of war. The Army operates its officer PME system primarily to develop officers with expertise and knowledge appropriate to their grade, branch and occupational specialty. Embedded within the PME system, however, is a Programme of Joint Professional Military Education overseen by the Joint Staff and designed to fulfill the educational requirements for Joint officer management as mandated by the Goldwater-Nichols Act of 1986. Army OES is in compliance with the Officer Professional Military Education Policy, to ensure that OES graduates meet the requirements for Joint Professional Military Education.

Dramatic changes have been implemented across OES to meet the needs of a transforming Army and the realities of the Contemporary Operating Environment. All Programmes of instruction are structured to ensure that officer education continues to be current and relevant to the needs of the Army. The Army is developing a framework necessary to implement a world-class education system with distinct components for warrant officers, company and field grade commissioned officers in both the Active and Reserve Components. The Army will ultimately combine warrant officer training into common officer training as appropriate, whenever common officer skills are taught. Current OES modernization efforts are focused on increasing culture awareness and language training, and blending resident PME with distributed learning modules to shorten courses and give officers some flexibility with their assignments. An initiative being developed this year will increase JIIM opportunities for select officers. The Army is also working with the Joint staff to implement the National Security Professional Development Programme.

**THE NONCOMMISSIONED OFFICER.** The Army is developing broad skilled NCOs to support our Army today and into the future. Our goal is an innovative, competent professional enlisted leader grounded in Army values; who embodies the Warrior Ethos; champions continuous learning; and is capable of leading, training and motivating Soldiers. An NCO is an adaptive leader who is proficient in Joint and combined expeditionary warfare, full spectrum operations, and resilient to uncertain and ambiguous environments.

NCOs will continue to be the masters of leader tasks for their respective levels of responsibility and of individual and small unit training, and they will continue to be the recognized experts in field craft, basic marksmanship, Soldier care, and technical skills. Our educational system will train the right tasks at the right levels and will prepare the NCOs to operate in both the analog and digital environments. In addition to adapting NCO professional military education, the Army is developing a number of major initiatives, some of which are discussed below.

**Virtual Warrior University.** We are creating a Virtual Warrior University to integrate all training and education resources into one interface. Focused on the learner, the Warrior University will redefine learning as a dynamic construct that incorporates both training and education, simplified, streamlined and managed through a central, seamless integrated system for universal access.

**Career NCO Degrees Programme.** The CNCODP expands existing Civilian higher education degree choices to provide Career NCOs with a broad preparation degree option not tied to enrollment in a military occupation specialty degree. It will recognize college credit for military training and education, will maximize the transfer of credits between colleges, and be accredited.

**Army Career Tracker** is a new career management tool that will present a holistic view of a Soldier's training and assignment history and formal/informal education paths. This provides the Soldier the capability to see, understand and use information about their occupational specialty to make decisions about training, education, and assignment opportunities. The ACT will enable Soldiers to manage their career, supervisors to provide effective mentoring and counseling, and commanders and their staff to plan for their Soldiers' development.

**NCO Education System.** The NCOES has undergone a radical transformation to better meet the needs of an Army at war and to develop NCOs. It has changed significantly in the recent past and will continue to transform to better develop leaders for current and future requirements of the Army. The Army is developing a Life-Long Learning Strategy for both Active Component and Reserve Component NCOs. This strategy consists of a Life Long Learning Model that educates leaders to conduct full spectrum operations, serve in a wide range of assignments at above grade positions (Train Ahead) and develops NCOs into broad skilled leaders. All of these steps are being taken to support the needs of operational units during the Reset phase of ARFORGEN.

**Warrior Leader Course.** Our next evolution for the WLC is to adapt content to include materials for success at both the team and squad levels. This version will incorporate relevant parts of the current BNCOC. The scope of tasks/competencies addressed in WLC will provide both the team and squad level perspective where appropriate.

**Basic NCO Course.** We will change BNCOC to an Advanced Leaders Course. Content for the ALC will include materials for success at both the squad and platoon level and should include relevant parts of the current ANCOC. The scope of tasks/competencies addressed in ALC will provide both the squad and platoon level perspective where appropriate. Tasks that focus primarily on the squad level will be evaluated for migration downward to the WLC.

**Advanced NCO Course.** We will also change ANCOC to a Senior Leaders Course. Content for the Senior Leaders Course will include materials required for success at both the platoon and company level. Relevant parts of the current First Sergeants Course should be migrated into the SLC. The scope of tasks/competencies addressed in SLC will provide both the platoon and company level perspective where appropriate. Tasks that are focused primarily at the platoon level will be evaluated for migration downward to the ALC.

**Senior Staff NCO Course.** This new course will provide staff skills for assignments above the brigade combat team level. Potential target audience would be SFC - SGM being assigned to staff assignments on Army and potentially Joint staff level. Manning and resourcing of the SSNCOC would be achieved by leveraging resources now associated with the First Sergeants Course.

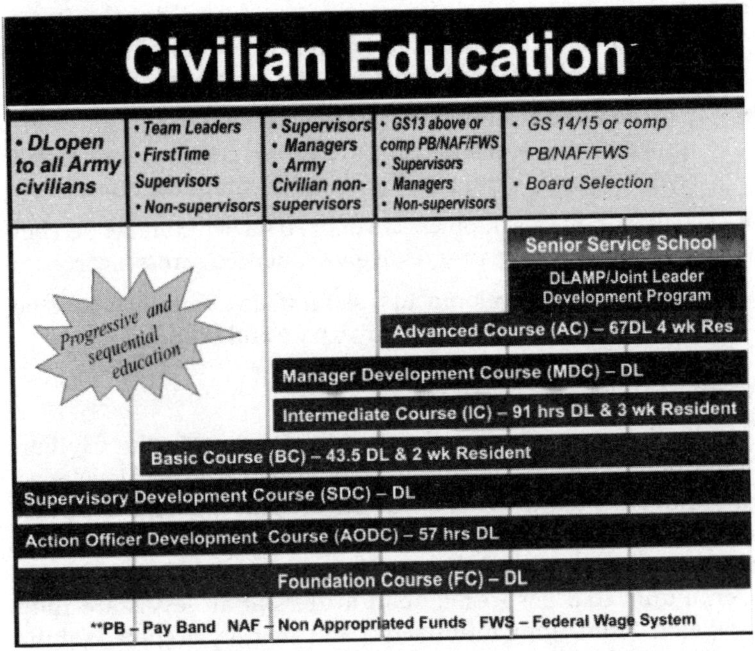


Figure B-5: Illustrated of the cources currently available in the CES

**Sergeants Major Course – Educating the MSG/SGM/ CSM.** The capstone of NCOES continues to be the Sergeants Major Course. The SMC will transform to meet the senior NCO professional development requirements of the Modular Force. It will foster the leadership skills to develop adaptive leaders within assigned organizations, and provide mastery of training management and conceptual learning skills.

**NCO Self-Development.** Army leaders have a responsibility as a part of the profession of arms to prepare themselves to serve the Nation to the best of their abilities. While Army leader education and training Programmes provide a foundation for competence, all leaders are responsible to extend their capabilities by applying the fundamental knowledge and skills through practice and reflection during exercises, operational experiences and performance of routine duties. Learning activities and self awareness beyond the school-house and training site are instrumental to enhance knowledge and skill performance for current and future leadership responsibilities.

- We are redefining self development and developing a structured and guided component. We are defining this new approach to self development as a three part Programme
- Structured Self Development is a defined set of required learning progressively sequenced across a career, closely linked to and synchronized with operational and institutional domains
- Guided Self Development is a defined set of recommended but optional learning, progressively sequenced across a career.
- Personal Self Development is self-initiated learning where the individual defines the objective, pace and process.

## Civilian Education System

Significant transformation has taken place in the Civilian Education System. A civilian education system has been developed and implemented to ensure that the civilian cohort is educated on skills needed to be effective members of the total Army. The CES is congruent with the DoD Joint Leader Development Continuum that ensures civilian leaders at all levels are fully prepared, "think Joint intuitively", and are fully prepared for the challenges of the future. The system provides a robust Programme of instruction to prepare civilians to assume more responsibility and a greater leadership role in the transformed Army as military positions are civilianized. The resident courses are augmented with distributed Learning (dL) to create blended course delivery. Civilians may complete any CES dL courseware as self development only. TRADOC is piloting a sustainment training for senior level civilians to bridge an identified gap in education and training between the Advanced Course and Senior Service College. Upon completion of the pilot and approval by the TRADOC Commander, the training will be integrated into the suite of CES courses.

## The Army's Distributed Learning Programme

Distributed Learning (dL) is the delivery of standardized individual, collective, and self-development training to Soldiers and units at the right place and right time, using multiple means and technologies, with synchronous and asynchronous student-instructor interaction. dL provides students, leaders and units with access to essential information and training anytime and anywhere.

The Army Distributed Learning Programme is a Department of the Army Programme that was approved for implementation in 1996. TADLP is funded to field and sustain digital training facilities, Army National Guard distributed learning class rooms, courseware redesign, Army Classroom XXI training modernization, Basic Combat Training/One Station Unit Training complex, deployed digital training campuses, the Army Learning Management System, and Information Technology Training (e-Learning). The mission of TADLP is to improve training, enhance force readiness and support Army transformation by exploiting current and emerging technologies to aid the development of self-aware and adaptive leaders through lifelong learning, and the delivery of training and education to Soldiers and leaders at anytime and any place.

Distributed Learning supports the training and education goals and objectives of major Army Programmes. It is an integral component of the three domains (operational, institutional and self-development) of the Army training system, and complies with the guidance and priorities provided in *The Army Plan*.

Distributed learning methods include, but are not limited to, implementing training by: simulators; simulations; correspondence courses; audio conferencing; video Tele-training (VTT), and interactive multimedia instruction (IMI) completed at home, in a DL facility at an installation, or in a unit deployed at an operational site. TADLP DTFs and ARNG DLCs have been fielded throughout CONUS and OCONUS to provide access to training to both the AC and RC.

**Infrastructure.** DTFs provide Soldiers with an onbase location to access web-based, job related and professional courses away from the workplace and distractions of home. DTFs include networked computers that support CD-ROM based training, Video Tele-training equipment to support room based courseware transmission from remote sites, computer servers to support the network and provide a highspeed gateway from the classroom to Army intranets and the internet. Functional capabilities include a student learning space consisting of electronic messaging and DTF scheduling and collaboration tools.

DLCs are a state-of-the-art communications and learning-delivery system designed to support the National Guard's traditional and expanding missions at home and abroad. Using DLC resources, Soldiers can study foreign languages and improve skills in reading, writing, critical thinking and information technology. There are more than 300 specially designed multimedia classrooms throughout the country, linked by a terrestrial network and emerging satellite technologies.

**Courseware.** TADLP includes DA military and Civilian training and education: military occupational specialty courses; additional skill identifier, skill qualification identifier, and language identifier code courses; reclassification courses; officer functional area and branch qualification courses; warrant officer technical certification; PME courses for OES, WOES, and NCOES; the Army civilian training, education, and development system; and functional training, task based training, self-development and education courses that can be delivered by dL.

**The Classroom XXI Programme (CRXXI):** CRXXI provides the capability to uplink digital training from the schoolhouse to Reserve Component Soldiers, forward deployed campuses, other TRADOC schoolhouses, and digital training facilities. CRXXI technology provides Solders with 24/7 reach back capability for training access anytime/anywhere.

**BCT/OSUT Starship Complex:** BCT/OSUT offers Soldiers a place to live and train while providing instructors with a digital training presentation platform that provides access to digitally formatted training materials to optimize training.

**Army Learning Management System:** Army personnel can access training from anywhere they have access to a computer and the Internet with the development of the new Army LMS, which is currently being fielded at TRADOC installations world-wide. From the office, home or DTF, Soldier's will be able to meet their distributed learning needs 24/7 and have access to: content, course catalogs and schedules, collaborative resources and training history. The LMS provides Army leadership at senior and unit levels, training officers and NCOs with the ability to manage their Soldier's careers from one location, saving time and money, and providing them with a powerful tool to manage their Soldiers' training more efficiently. Soldiers will also have the ability to track their own training history. The combined capabilities of DLS and the Army LMS will make training more efficient, delivery more flexible, and provide Soldiers the ability to track their own training history. The Army LMS is designed to touch every Soldier and civilian in the US Army, and will be the single source for Soldiers and their leaders to see training deficiencies, and to be able to address and direct their Soldiers to take the training they need to correct those deficiencies.

**Information Technology Training (e-Learning):** The Army e-Learning Programme provides free training for every Active Army, National Guard, Reservist, ROTC Cadet and Department of the Army Civilian with access to over 1,500 web-based information technology, business, leadership, and personal development courses. These courses are accessible 24/7 from anywhere using an internet connection. Army e-Learning benefits include: opportunities for enlisted personnel promotion points, over 40 certification Programmes such as MCSE, A+, CISSP, Cisco, Oracle and more with personal mentoring, continuous learning points for civilian acquisition workforce, and some college course accreditation.

# Personnel Services and Management Modernization—An Evolving All-Volunteer Force

In concert with restoring enduring balance and modernizing the force, we continue to sustain and transform the Army Human Resource Enterprise, field the Army Modular Force and grow the All-Volunteer Force. Ensuring the right quality and quantity of personnel—whether Soldier, Army Civilian Corps employee or contractor—is at the right place and right time is testing our future personnel system. Transforming the Human Resource Enterprise changes the way the Army manages and services its manpower (forces and structure). This includes AC and RC and their Families, Army Civilian Corps employees, veterans, retirees and contractors. It includes the transformation of personnel and HR organizations, manpower and personnel Programmes, policies, processes and systems, to ensure Joint readiness and interoperability, while continuing to meet the service-specific requirements of our All-Volunteer Force.

### Human Resource Enterprise Transformation

The streamlining of battlespace personnel/unit footprint improves the speed and quality of HR support to Soldiers on the battlefield. The Defence Integrated Military Human Resources System and other integrated HR systems will serve as the information technology platforms through which we will accomplish many of these support functions. The Army currently relies on five major databases and over one hundred different applications, subsystems, reports and queries to manage manpower and personnel services. Many of these databases and subsystems use different data standards and protocols, making modernization and integration complex and expensive.

A single, integrated military personnel and pay management system is critical because it will allow better tracking of Soldiers from home station through mobilization to the battlefield and back; it will enable us to manage and safeguard sensitive personal identity and friendly force information in a media-rich environment; and it will enable us to better monitor and manage the Operational Tempo of individual Soldiers.

The Army personnel community continues to improve data quality, reduce redundant manual input of common data elements and eliminate manpower intensive analysis of raw information. These improvements—complemented with efficiencies realized from the enterprise approach to Army HR systems, business process reengineering, leveraged web technology, data cleansing and preparing for a multi-component DoD pay and personnel system—will improve strategic responsiveness, enable Army transformation, enhance personnel services and provide reach capability, thus enabling reductions in redundant layers of personnel staff on the battlefield.

Additionally, the Army is restructuring through Base Realignment and Closure (BRAC), which will divest the Army of unnecessary installation infrastructure and will use the resultant savings to improve the fighting capabilities and quality of life for military forces. As a result of BRAC, Army Human Resources Command will relocate and consolidate all functions at Fort Knox, Kentucky, where it will co-locate with U.S. Army Recruiting Command and U.S. Army Accessions Command to form the Army HR Center of Excellence. GDPR will restation about 70,000 Soldiers from bases in Europe and Korea back to CONUS.

## The Enterprise Approach

The Human Capital Management (HCM) Domain continues to strengthen M&RA/G1 governance and portfolio management policies to enable focused, capabilities-based information technology investment decisions for the enterprise. Complementing the HCM Domain's investment decision making processes is an enterprise architecture that defines the operations, systems and technical views for the Army's human resources enterprise. The enterprise architecture is focused on the future state of the enterprise and establishes a baseline for the Domain's enterprise transition plan. The architecture includes the first working instantiation of the Army's Service Oriented Architecture with the Human Resource Command's cutting edge implementation of an Enterprise Service Bus. The enterprise's SOA architecture will provide greater flexibility for the integration of persistent systems with DIMHRS during its debut in October 2008 and will significantly reduce risk. Even with successful DIMHRS implementation, the requirement for a number of persistent systems to support manpower, training, casualty management and initial entry requirements remain.

HR Enterprise Transformation employs the Lean Six Sigma (L6S) methodology for improving the process flow of how we acquire, distribute, develop, deploy, compensate, sustain and structure all categories of personnel in all components. It enables us to optimize how we organize, equip, train and employ our personnel, units/agencies and systems on both the battlefield and in garrison.

### Personnel Services Delivery Redesign

As the Army's HR response to transformation, PSDR leverages web-based systems, connectivity and bandwidth to support our expeditionary Army. This redesign eliminates support layers and minimizes support unit footprints in the battle space. PSDR embeds critical personnel functions in the S-1 section, enabling the brigade to bridge directly to CONUS-based HR professionals to accomplish personnel services tasks such as creating modular, scalable and flexible new theater-level Adjutant General units to support casualty, postal, reception, replacement, return to duty, R&R and redeployment (R5). PSDR eliminates the need to unplug personnel services capabilities from a garrison structure to support wartime deployments, empowering commanders to provide HR services directly to their Soldiers. The Army is employing a four-phase PSDR implementation plan with the completion of redesign for all components by fiscal year 2009. Implementation is synchronized with the AMF Plan, operational deployments, *Army Campaign Plan*, Global Defence Posture Review, Installation Management Command (IMCOM) and Force Stabilization.

## Manning the Force

The Army continues to address the necessary refinements concerning the proper mix of manpower among the military, Civilian Corps and contract support requirements. This ongoing refinement process ensures that Army clearly delineates core and non-core functions in the effort to outsource or privatize noncore functions.

Unit Focused Stability sets the condition for the Army to build more deployable combat units. The Army will continue to be manned to achieve and maintain readiness, combat effectiveness, deployability and stability in support of Army priorities. However, the primary focus for all personnel resources is manning transition teams, deployed and deploying forces.

The Army will establish policies for the length, frequency of tours and number of deployments for the AC/RC. This will lead to a thorough force structure analysis that will result in recommended force structure adjustments, including the identified required adjustments to the AC/RC force mix. The metric for success for all actions will be the decrease of turmoil on units, Soldiers and Families, resulting in increased combat readiness throughout the Army.

## Force Stabilization

The driving concept behind Force Stabilization is to produce highly cohesive combat teams capable of increased operational effectiveness while decreasing turbulence and increasing predictability and stability for Soldiers and their Families. To achieve unit cohesion and higher operational capability in our combat units, the Army must:

- Synchronize assignments of large numbers of Soldiers with training and employment of units
- Manage personnel gains and losses to reduce daily personnel turnover stemming from the individual replacement system
- Manage force modernization and force structure changes within the Force Stabilization concept

Force Stabilization is supported by two manning strategies: Stabilization and Unit Focused Stability. With Stabilization, all

Soldiers CONUS-based are eligible to be stabilized at their current assigned post for longer periods and will be moved by HRC, based on needs of the Army, leader development, and individual preference. Although Soldiers in higherdensity military occupational specialties and at larger installations are likely to be stabilized longer than those in lower-density MOSs or at smaller installations, all Soldiers can expect to be assigned to their posts for greater periods of time than previously. Stabilization meets the Chief of Staff Army's (CSA) intent to stabilize Soldiers for longer periods and reduce permanent changes of station, while offering Soldiers and Families in CONUS predictability and stability in the unit and community.

Unit Focused Stability serves as a key personnel enabler for supporting the Army Force Generation readiness methodology. Unit Focused Stability is supported by two manning methods, cyclic and lifecycle manning, which are applied based on unit mission, operational requirements and the overall situation. The CSA has approved cyclic manning as a method but not yet for implementation. Lifecycle manning has been approved by the CSA and will affect all Manoevre BCTs. In coordination with G-3, Army G-1 has established the lifecycle implementation schedule, based on current and future operational deployment and redeployment time lines, as well as the current modular transformation schedule.

Currently, 19 BCTs underwent lifecycle management, with the goal of executing LM for all BCTs (except those in Korea and Germany) by fiscal year 2011. Under the LM model, Soldier assignments to that unit are synchronized to its established 36-month lifecycle. Soldiers arrive, train and deploy together during the unit lifecycle, providing commanders and Soldiers with a predictable environment where they will be able to build, train and sustain high-performing, cohesive teams. Because each Soldier's timeline will be synchronized with the unit's lifecycle, issues of nondeployability will be reduced, as should turbulence caused by PCS/Expiration Term of Service until the end of the unit life-cycle. Also, RC Soldiers who are not affiliated with a unit (IRR and IWP) will be screened, supported, developed and trained in accordance with the Deployment Cycle Support Process. Together, these strategies support Force Stabilization and provide the Combatant Commander with more deployable, combat-ready forces while also benefiting the Soldier and his family at home.

## Fully implement the Army Force Generation (ARFORGEN) Process

The Army is committed to fully manning, equipping and training the force to 100% of the Nation's requirements. In an environment of constrained resources, the Army prioritizes distribution of resources to units preparing to deploy and for critical domestic mission requirements. The Army uses the Army Force Generation model to project changes in priorities as units move through a structured progression of increased unit readiness over time. This structured model results in recurring periods of availability of trained, ready and cohesive units prepared for operational deployment in support of Combatant Commander's requirements. Operational requirements drive training and readiness objectives and priorities that support synchronization of institutional functions to man, organize, equip, train, sustain, source, mobilize and deploy cohesive, well led, well equipped and well trained units.

The *Army Campaign Plan* uses ARFORGEN as the process to provide Combatant Commanders and Civil Authorities with trained and ready Modular Expeditionary Forces, tailored to Joint mission requirements, and capable of conducting full spectrum land operations in persistent conflict. ARFORGEN's central focus is on management of forces for employment and next-to-deploy units.

Following the ARFORGEN cycle will greatly contribute to predictability for Soldiers and Families. Units rotate through three ARFORGEN force pools identified as Reset/Train, Ready and Available to meet operational requirements. The Reset/Train phase allows Soldiers to Reset with Families, go to professional development schools, and transfer to new units. During this phase units also receive personnel replacements and conduct individual and small unit training.

Units in the Ready Force pool continue mission-specific collective training and are eligible if necessary to meet Joint requirements. Units in the Available force pool are in their planned deployment windows and are fully trained, equipped and resourced to meet operational requirements.

Units are task organized in modular expeditionary design or force packages tailored to specific mission requirements. Due to current unit equipping shortages, the Army equips units from a combination of sources, including the unit's on hand equipment, new production, depot production and cross-leveling. When a unit enters the ARFORGEN pool they turn over much of their equipment for repair and they transfer some equipment to units that are significantly closer to their next deployment date. Also, because of Armywide equipment shortages, some equipment is not available to units until after they arrive in theater and receive equipment from Theater Provided Equipment.

ARFORGEN is designed to be a three-year cycle for the AC and a five-year cycle for the RC. The rate of deployment for AC units currently a two-year cycle with BCTs averaging one year at home in a combined Reset/Train and Ready pool before they enter the Available pool and deploy for up to 15 months. To support the GWOT, we must have legal processes that allow for routine periods of employment and potential contingency operations as part of the ARFORGEN cycle—a structured progression of increased unit readiness over time.

### Active Army Strength Forecaster

A2SF is a suite of newly redesigned suite of models employing the latest algorithms and IT to provide state-of-the-art strength management and forecasting for the active Army. A2SF increases flexibility in modeling manpower policies and Programmes; provides greater accessibility through web-based technology; improves projection accuracy; and reduces operation and maintenance costs. Continuing system maintenance, enhancements, and adjustments ensure the system remains current and responsive to Army forecasting requirements as the future evolves. A2SF capabilities include:

- Provide monthly historical tracking, required strength reporting and accounting as required by Congress, Title 10 and OSD
- Provide continuously reformulated forecasts for monthly projections of losses (by type), accessions, reenlistments, strengths by identity (Officer/Enlisted/USMA Cadets), strengths by grade, gender, skill, Operating Strength, "TTHS" strength and Operating Strength Deviation

- Incorporate policies and Programmes enunciated by DMPM and changes in the Force Structure into Strength forecasts
- Provide base strength for distribution planning by HRC, development of USAREC accession missions, DMPM reenlistment goals, formulation of the President's Budget, guidance regarding force maintenance and balance by skill (including application of enlistment/re-enlistment bonus funding) and promotion selection objective recommendations
- Produce the Active Army Military Manpower Programme, which portrays the future evolution of the Active force through the POM years

A2SF forecasts support the Army's accession, retention, reclassification and training mission, as well as provide data in support of the Army's resource allocation models, the training models and the enlisted distribution models. Reports from these models provide data for use by the Army Budget Office in development of the Military Personnel, Army appropriation requirements, Human Resource Senior leader decisions and policies, congressional inquiries and every aspect of personnel management.

## Recruiting

The Army can grow only if it can recruit. Significant initiatives to modernize the supporting information systems for this critical mission are ongoing. Army recruiters must be able to show detailed information on the full range of job opportunities, duty locations, training availability and incentives to perspective recruits. It is understood that the Total Army Force includes Active, Reserve and National Guard, as well as Army retirees recalled to active service. Each of these components has distinctive needs which must be considered in balancing the Programme for the Total Force.

To set conditions for sustained success in achieving annual recruiting missions, US Army Accessions Command must:

- Recruit and train for today's Army, with a view towards preparing for tomorrow's challenges
- Instill discipline, Army Values and Warrior Ethos
- Incorporate enduring lessons learned from a combat-seasoned force, sustain a comprehensive research agenda, innovate and

adapt to leverage advancing technology and the human potential of our volunteers

- Seek out, share, and embrace best practices, and constantly seek to establish more effective relationships with our Soldiers, our leaders, our Army and the American People we serve.

Furthermore, our approach must appeal to recruits, influencers, Civilian personnel, Soldiers and leaders alike, uphold the Army values, and foster attitudes that are motivated by a desire to serve our country, committed to the challenging work we do and adaptable to the changing dynamics of our mission.

Spurred by the developments of the Accessions Summit held October 2007, USAAC has begun down the path to fundamentally change the accessions process by addressing the cultural and organizational framework. Partnering with the entire accessions community of interest, the command will focus on the following areas to "Grow the Army" and sustain the All-Volunteer Force:

- Change the Army marketing and advertising approach
- Explore opportunities that expand the current market to include high quality legal immigrants
- Increase component recruiting integration
- Invest in education and health Programmes
- Review officer accessions and support transition to officer command structure
- Resource the Generating Force to better support Army accessions requirements
- Increase AMEDD (Health Services Professionals) recruiting.

The Army is expanding the capability to provide this individualized counseling beyond the Military Entrance Processing Station and directly to 18,000 AC, ARNG, and USAR recruiters and staff members by web-enabling the recruiting systems. Additional web-enabling initiatives are underway to allow interested civilians to query Army job opportunities without the immediate or direct assistance of an Army recruiter.

Concurrently, the technical infrastructure must be upgraded to meet the user response requirements and to maintain compatibility with modern operating systems and security requirements. By fully utilizing crosscommand assets and modern computing technologies, the recruiting systems will have continuity of operations from separate Midwest and East Coast facilities. The Army will continue to improve the accession process as technology changes.

Recruiting Objectives for 2008 and beyond: The Army is testing a flexible values-based incentive called the Army Advantage Fund to gain a competitive advantage for attracting eligible individuals who would have otherwise not considered the Army as a career choice.

The AAF incentive offers qualified individuals a lump sum utilized as equity towards home or business ownership for a specified term of service.

## Retention

For units, retention continues to be the unit commander's Programme for maintaining unit readiness and stability. It is mission critical to provide worldwide access to deployed and CONUS units to match the needs and desires of individual Soldiers. Army unit strength and Soldier retention policies and incentives are constantly being updated. Updates such as stoploss, reenlistment incentive criteria, changes to MOS, training availability and RC unit vacancies must accurately replicate throughout the Army systems, and be available immediately to unit commanders and Soldiers within the re-enlistment eligibility window. It is an imperative that the Army maintains critical 'technical' skills. This extends beyond the traditional medical and legal communities. Special compensation is also the most logical way to retain personnel with engineering, technology and communications skills.

The Army recognizes that restoring balance is all about people: Soldiers, their Families and the civilian workforce. Our Soldiers and their Families depend on the Army for care, support and services equal to the sacrifices they make, in this era of persistent conflict. Our Nation depends on the best quality Soldiers and Families defending freedom. Addressing the needs of Soldiers and their Families is essential to recruiting, training, and retaining a force with the capacity and depth to meet current demands.

Army Civilian Corps Planned modernization enhancements to personnel Programmes and systems affecting the Civilian workforce are captured in four primary strategic objectives:

Development of diverse, world-class enterprise leaders who effectively manage and lead people in a Joint environment

Sustainment of a diverse and agile Civilian Corps capable of seamless integration into the Total Force

Development of a mission-focused, results-oriented workforce that is strategically aligned and customer focused, providing measurable, leading edge results

These enhancements will be accomplished through the deployment of the National Security Personnel System, Army Leaders for the 21st Century, New Army Civilian Human Resource Environment and through business transformation using L6S.

## National Security Personnel System

NSPS represents a landmark transformation of civilian personnel management by changing the way the Army attracts, retains, rewards, and develops its civilian employees. This is a system that will give us improved opportunities to accomplish the challenges we face now and in the future by:

- National Security Personnel SystemHolding supervisors and employees accountable for results tied to mission requirements
- Providing broad pay bands to allow employees to be easily transferred to other work assignments and opportunities
- Motivating employees by rewarding them for performance and contributions
- Simplifying and streamlining recruitment and internal hiring and staffing processes
- Promoting skill development and advancement opportunities, while maintaining employee rights and legal entitlements.

NSPS is a phased process. Each phase is known as a Spiral, and each Spiral may have multiple increments. On 30 April 2006, DoD converted approximately 11,000 non-bargaining unit employees. The Army has now successfully transitioned over 68,000 nonbargaining unit employees to NSPS and another 700

are scheduled to be included by April 2008. Robust NSPS training efforts will continue worldwide in fiscal year 2008 to train many thousands of converted Civilian Corps employees. Military leaders and supervising civilians must also be trained in order to appraise the performance of civilian employees.

**Revitalize Soldiers and Families**

Attending to the needs of our Soldiers and their Families is critical to an expeditionary Army at war. The Army is launching a comprehensive package of Soldier and Family initiatives that will enhance the strength and resiliency of Soldiers and their Families. The Army is also continuing its efforts toward revitalizing our Soldiers and Families through full resourcing and implementation of the Army Medical Action Plan and the Soldier Family Action Plan. Additionally, the Army is aggressively reviewing and modifying policies and procedures in concert with pursuing legislative proposals seeking amendments and new authorities to more effectively meet the needs of the All-Volunteer Force. These enduring efforts will ensure that the needs of our Soldiers, civilians, Families and survivors are balanced against the needs of an Army at war.

**The Army Covenant: Enhancing the Resiliency and Well-Being of our Soldiers, Civilians and their Families**

Providing for the well-being of the Army Family is a fundamental leadership obligation. The well-being of our Soldiers, civilians and their Families is based on major life domains such as their standard of living, health, career, community life, and personal and family life. A sense of well-being in these major life domains enables Soldiers to focus on and perform the Army's mission, establishes a quality work-life balance and enhances their commitment to serve in the All-Volunteer Force. The Army must continue to assess and improve Programmes and services that provide for the needs of its Soldiers and their Families.

Providing support for the wellbeing of our people strengthens the Army's ability to compete for human capital while also affecting organizational outcomes such as recruiting, retention, readiness and morale.

The Army Family Covenant represents a $1.4 billion commitment to improve the quality of life for Army Families. It formally recognizes the sacrifices made on the home front while the Army is at war and pledges to standardize funding for existing Family Programmes and services. The covenant also seeks to increase the accessibility and quality of health care, improve Soldier and Family housing, ensure excellence in schools, youth services and child care and expand education and employment opportunities for Family members.

In the last two to three years, the Army has privatized and improved almost 80,000 homes on 36 installations and opened 40 new childcare centers, with another 22 on the way. The Army also recently spent $50 million to hire new healthcare providers for Soldiers and their Families, and is working with lawmakers to help Army spouses gain priority for civil service jobs. There are also family readiness support assistants at the battalion level.

## Soldier Benefit System Website

The SBS website (http://myarmybenefits.us.army. mil) is the Army's official one-stop resource for all benefits information in two distinct areas. Built on an expandable platform, the SBS website contains general benefits information that is easy to use, current and accessible to the general public, Soldiers, Family members and retirees. When accessed via the Army Knowledge Online (AKO) site SBS provides a password protected environment for all active duty Soldiers, linked to current DEERS data. This feature provides personalized survivor, disability, and retirement benefits reports. Additional website features include customized fact sheets of essential benefits information, in both English and Spanish, on over 100 topics; local benefit resources at all major Army installations worldwide; survivor planning with personalize reports that projects the lifetime stream for the Family's benefits that would be provided to beneficiaries upon the death of a Soldier on active duty; personalized retirement and survivor planning with features that allow Soldiers to perform "what if" drills.

The most recent expanded capabilities include a clear, accurate, integrated benefits report for Casualty Assistance Officers to provide surviving Family members and an interactive tool for Army Wounded Warriors to calculate his/her estimated disability rating and disability retirement income based on the combat and combat-related injuries listed. An additional module under development provides an Army Wounded Warrior sustaining income feature which provides income estimates while Soldiers are hospitalized and a disability calculator enhancements feature that expands the current seven combat/combatrelated categories targeting those with injuries less than 30% disability rating.

## Soldier and Family Assistance Centers

Soldier and Family Assistance Centers (SFACs) are user-friendly centers offering critical support services to Warriors in Transition (WTs), following injuries or combat wounds, while defending our Nation. This holistic approach to attending to the needs of WTs and their Families brings their most frequently needed services, to one location, near their medical treatment facility. Advantages provided by SFACs include:

- Cut time to services, giving Soldiers quicker access to help
- One-Stop Shops for: employment assistance, social services, legal assistance, military personnel, finance and education services
- More Than One-Stop—the SFAC also gives WTs and Family members access to travel claims processing, Department of Veterans Affairs, Army Wounded Warrior resources and a friendly helping hand
- Nurturing, morale-building, and convenient place to help WTs heal challenges
- Instill discipline, Army Values and Warrior Ethos.

Army Leadership mandated improvement in services for WTs and Families; SFACs are one of many essential responses to that mandate. Many facilities have been set up and new directors have been assigned, throughout the United States and in Eurόpe. Those directors and their Army Community Services Directors meet early in December to map their plans for the future.

Installations are currently building or renovating structures that will become the SFAC hubs, and most report being ready to operate fully by the end of January 2008. Extensive training for all SFAC staff on care, support, and services is on-going. Europe will also serve a widely-dispersed population of Warriors in transition through garrison assets.

This Programme helps the Army by taking care of Soldiers and Families, as well as by showing the Army's commitment to those whose sacrifices make the Army strong. SFAC facilities, often referred to as campuses, are a user-friendly environment where WTs and their Families can devote all their energies to the mission of healing and transitioning—either back to their units or to new lives as productive citizens. Additional services are being planned as the SFAC mission grows to meet greater demand. For more information: http://www.imcom.army. mil/site/command/armyfamily.asp

## Family Readiness Groups and Special Initiative

Family Readiness Groups (FRG) function as a communications mechanism, bringing facts to the families from command, and serving as an informal chain of concern to bring issues back up to command. They are integral to the morale and support of Soldiers and Families before, during and after deployments. It is structured based on the needs of the unit; some FRGs are large, very active and all encompassing to include parents, friends and significant others in their information chain while others are small and tailored only to the immediate requirements of a non-deployed unit.

A new system, the Virtual Family Readiness Group (vFRG) web system, provides all of the functionality of a traditional FRG in an ad-hoc and on-line setting to meet the needs of geographically dispersed units and Families. Unlike FRGs that are immediately located with the unit, the vFRG links the deployed Soldier, their Family, the FRG leader, the unit commander, the rear detachment and other family readiness personnel on their own controlled access web portal to facilitate the exchange of information and provide a sense of community, using technology to automate manual processes and provide enhanced services and communications.

Over 1,100 vFRGs are established linking Families on the home front to those forward deployed. The Army has limited development of vFRG sites to units at the battalion-level and higher in an effort to serve the most Soldiers and Families across the Active, Guard and Reserve. Waivers are available for separate companies and other non-battalion units with special needs. The vFRG is being redesigned to address feedback from users and administrators and improve end user experience. Marketing of these resources to commanders and Families is an integral part of the way ahead.

Family Readiness Groups are critical to maintaining the strength, morale and information chain for Soldiers, Families and commands. Elements such as the vFRG Programme have proven to be overwhelming successes as additional information sources directed to Family members of Soldiers within the command. FRGs leverage command and Families; vFRG leverages technology for providing up-to-date information and connecting Families and commands. For more information: http://www.armyfrg.org

## Improved Care for Warriors in Transition

### *US Army Wounded Warrior Programme* (AW2)

The focus of the AW2 Programme is on the most severely wounded, injured and ill population throughout the Wounded Warrior Lifecycle, from evacuation through the transition back to the force or to Veteran status, indefinitely. The Army recognized that those Soldiers suffering from illness or injuries incurred after 10 September 2001 in support of the Global War on Terrorism that need it most will be supported with the assistance, advocacy, and support they need when and where they need it. AW2

Soldiers are those who have received, or are expected to receive a 30% PEB finding for at least one Special Category/ Enabling Care condition in categories such as: Amputation; Blindness/ Vision Loss; Spinal Cord Injury/ Paralysis; Post Traumatic Stress Disorder (PTSD); Permanent Disfigurement; Severe Burns; Traumatic Brain Injury (TBI). These categories fall within the "Special Category (SPECAT) patients" defined in AR 40-400 "Patient Administration."

The Soldier Family Management Specialist (SFMS) is the "boots on the ground" AW2 Agent to assist, support and advise Soldiers and their Families during medical treatment, in navigating federal, state and private benefit systems; and link them with selected financial, educational, employment, legal and medical resources. Since the WTU Triad is the primary support entity for the SFMS it is fully supported by AW2 Staff Specialists who are Subject Matter Experts in critical area as such as Medical, Military Human Resources, Finance, Employment and Strategic Communications.

For AW2 Soldiers the TRIAD support system includes the AW2 SFMS. The TRIAD and SFAC personnel must understand the capabilities the AW2 Programme provides for the most seriously wounded, injured, ill Soldiers and their Families. The TRIAD will refer Soldiers they believe to be AW2 injury eligible to the AW2 SFMS and incorporate the SFMS into the TRIAD support system. For Soldiers that are already identified as AW2, the AW2 SFMS and the TRIAD will perform a case review. The TRIAD (especially the NCM) and AW2 SFMS will communicate issues, concerns and Soldier status. The AW2 Programme is also a resource for the TRIAD to leverage additional assistance for regulatory and policy roadblocks they may encounter. The AW2 SFMS is the single point of contact for referring AW2 Soldiers to and interaction with the Federal Recovery Coordinator. AW2 serves as an advocate and change agent to implement lessons learned to adjust policy and increase the responsiveness and effectiveness of our medical and benefit systems. These services to Soldiers are not limited by geography or physical locations or constrained by recovery or rehabilitation timelines – AW2 provides counseling and assistance throughout the lifetime of the Soldier.

AW2 works with Soldiers in coordination with Army Career and Alumni Programme on career plans and employment opportunities beyond their Army careers. It helps keep Soldiers in the Army by educating and facilitating COAD/COAR application efforts. AW2 has well established partnerships with veteran service organizations, non-profits and other individual and corporate partners for the individual benefit of Soldiers and Families.

Soldiers are tracked and managed utilizing an application within the Wounded Warrior Accountability System (WWAS) that operates on real-time, authoritative data directly from the source to empower AW2 with the total Soldier situation.

## Wounded Warrior Accountability System

As a result of the February 2005 U.S. General Accounting Office Report, the Wounded Warrior Accountability System was created to track and account for our severely wounded, injured and ill Soldiers. This integrated data architecture has been designed to provide accurate and timely data from authoritative sources and to track Soldiers through the Wounded Warrior Lifecycle, which begins at point of injury, through medical treatment and rehabilitation, to the Medical Evaluation Board and Physical Evaluation Board processes, through return-to-duty or transition to civilian life. The system is a single source for tracking, managing, and reporting while eliminating or reducing data inconsistencies and redundancies and increasing data accuracy. In the end, it improves support of the Wounded Warrior and their Family. WWAS currently supports operations for the AW2 Programme as well as the Wounded Soldier and Family Hotline. Changes are being implemented to provide Warrior Transition Unit leadership and case managers with access to WWAS data and application capabilities— further integrating support mechanisms for our Wounded Warriors. WWAS is also working to integrate data with the Department of Veterans Affairs, Social Security Administration, Department of Labor, Defence Eligibility Enrollment System and Defence Integrated Military Human Resources System.

## Warrior in Transition

A Warrior in Transition (WT) is a Medical Holdover, Active Duty Medical Extension, Medical Hold, and any other active-duty Soldier who requires a Medical Evaluation Board, or has complex medical needs requiring six months, or more, of treatment or rehabilitation.

Initial Entry Training (IET) Soldiers are eligible only if they require a Medical Evaluation Board or when deemed appropriate, by the local MEDCOM commander and the IET Soldier's commander. A Soldier's mission, while assigned to a Warrior Transition Unit (WTU), is to heal. Soldiers assigned to a WTU may have work assignments in the unit; such work may not take precedent over the Soldier's therapy and treatment. Unit commanders must clear UCMJ actions, other legal actions, investigations, property/hand receipt issues and Line of Duty determinations, prior to the transfer to the WTUs. (FRAGO 1 Annexure S to EXORD 118-07).

**Warriors in Transition duties:**

- Work as hard to heal as they work on defending freedom
- Follow instructions of their "Triad of Care:" physician, nurse case manager and squad leader of the WTU.

The Army continues to open assistance centers to centralize services. We continue to work with the Department of Veterans Affairs to streamline procedures, eliminate duplication, and provide maximum benefits allowed to WTs.

- WTs get priority at installations
- WTs top lists for quarters, to ensure they get high-quality housing, close to services they need, with minimal delay
- WTUs provide centralized support and rehabilitation; Soldier and Family
- Assistance Centers (SFACs) perform most other services to meet WTs' and their Families' needs
- Finance and other issues get resolved without delay; WTs or their advocates need only ask.

Changes in the Army's health care delivery system have become visible, even to the untrained eye. What's more, the Warriors in Transition and Families under the care of that system have begun to feel the results of those changes.

- Warriors in Transition and their Families focus on Healing
- WTs get individualized treatment from the Triad of Care
- A physician, nurse case manager, and military squad leader participate actively in the Soldier's and Family's healing process

- The WT responds better because of the attention the Triad pays to details
- Morale increases as success occurs more quickly
- The Army has adopted many procedures from private sector health care and from lessons learned in military treatment facilities, to open communication channels between WTs and medical decision-makers:
- Encourage WTs and Families to express exactly what their needs are
- Treat each person according to those individual needs
- Ensure Triad members communicate with one another on the treatment
- Ombudsman listen to WTs, Families, and the Triad, when things don't work the way they should, then recommend improvements in the process.

## More changes

Continuing to listen will refine the processes now in place which work so well. The Army will add specialized caregivers as they become available in the system and will continue to add services as resources permit. This will give WTs greater access, within the WTU, to more services and give Family members more opportunities to get involved directly in the healing process.

A Soldier's morale is one of the most powerful motivating factors in the arsenal. Any setback, no matter how slight, often can get in the way of the Soldier's performance, no matter what the duty. When the Army shows its investment in Warriors in Transition, they invest more in their own recovery and they achieve success more quickly, more completely, and more permanently.

For more information: http://www.armymedicine. army.mil/amap/amap.html

## Warrior Transition Unit Cadre

The Warrior Transition Unit (WTU) cadre makes sure Warriors in Transition are well cared for and receive the medical treatment, services, and support needed during recovery. The Army's Warrior Ethos describes it best: "Never Leave a Fallen Comrade." Here's how:

- Encourage WTs to focus on healing
- Get Soldiers to medical appointments, therapy sessions and on track with treatment plans
- Lead WTs through the full spectrum of administrative and Family support services, like pay, housing, benefits, transportation, vocational training and life skills coaching
- Provide meaningful duties for WTs able to participate
- The Army has assigned top-notch staff and cadre to manage the 35 activated WTUs and nine Community Based Health Organizations. These specially designed activities provide holistic care to wounded, ill, and injured Soldiers and their Families better than ever:
- Approved special duty pay for Squad Leaders and Platoon Sergeants
- Trained cadre in specialty skills for serving their fellow Soldiers in need
- Increased promotion opportunities for cadre members serving in WTUs
- Stabilized cadre tour assignments to ensure continuity for WTs

Plans call for cadre training improvements. With that, WTs and cadre will be able to provide feedback to the Army, as a way to help develop better care and treatment delivery for future WTs. Topping the list are increased professional development and training opportunities for cadre members.

Soldiers are the best advocates for their Soldiers. They can help guide Warriors and Families, in need of healing, through the benefits and services process. Since more than 70 percent of Soldiers who are wounded, ill, and injured have the potential to return to military duty, the Army needs the WTU cadre to help maintain the military environment while providing compassionate service to their fellow Soldier. The Army has made a commitment to serve each of these Soldiers and their Families for life, and vows never to violate the Warrior Ethos: "Never Leave a Fallen Comrade."

Warrior Transition Unit Cadre information: http://www.armymedicine.army.mil/amap/amap.html

## Community Based Health Care Organization Programme (COHCO)

The Army has a new Programme called The Community Based Health Care Organization. This Programme allows a recuperating Reserve Component Soldier to obtain services from medical facilities near home, while remaining on active duty. CBHCOs provide Reserve Component Warriors in Transition high-quality health care and administrative processing through nine CBHCO units, managing more than 1,300 Soldiers, who live in all parts of the country.

Mobilized Army National Guard (ARNG) and Reserve Soldiers work within CBHCOs, exercising command and control and clinical oversight, for their component's WTs undergoing medical treatment, through Military or TRICARE network providers in their local area. Army Medical Command's four Regional Medical Commands manage the CBHCO Programme and the care WTs receive.

Experienced nurse case managers coordinate healthcare appointments, track WT's progress, and ensure care meets Army, and TRICARE, standards. More than 350 ARNG, and many AR Soldiers, are assigned as cadre in support of CBHCOs, alongside their fellow RC health care professionals.

The Army Reserve and ARNG continue to support the CBHCO mission by mobilizing both C2 and Army Medical Department personnel, from a number of states, to work with the CBHCO WTs. This support brings Reserve Component expertise to health care, and to the individual requirements faced by these WTs. The Army Reserve and the ARNG remain committed to supporting the medical needs of their Warriors in Transition and Families. The RC also will continue to extend services to deployed Soldiers' Families throughout the mobilization cycle. For more information: http://www.armymedicine.army.mil/tools/links.html

## Improved Support For Families Of Fallen Soldiers

### *Army Long Term Family Case Management*

Families of deceased active-duty Soldiers can receive an extended level of support from a long-term care Programme the

Army launched 18 months ago. The Army Long Term Family Case Management Programme provides long-term support to Families of fallen Soldiers by helping them through the often painful and sometimes arduous steps toward receiving benefits and various other types of support. In the past, casualty assistance officers generally made themselves available to Families at the early stages of the mourning process, at least through a fallen Soldier's interment. But in the months and years following the loss of a loved one, unresolved issues and questions often surface regarding benefits and support services. Now support coordinators with Army Long Term Family Case Management contact the Family about six months following the loss of a loved one. The coordinator maintains an "open dialogue" with Family members for as long as they find it helpful. As part of ongoing efforts to better assist Families of fallen Soldiers, Army Long Term Family Case Management added 11 new categories to the Support Programme section on its Web site. Each category contains brief summaries and contact information for both National and local Programmes related to careers, children and youth, counseling, finances, emotional support, education, healthcare, legal assistance, military and government, peer support, religion and substance abuse.

Army Long Term Family Case Management's support coordinators personally provide ongoing support to Families of fallen Soldiers the months and years following their loss. ALTFCM is a service provided by the Army's Casualty and Mortuary Affairs Operation Center. To date, ALTFCM has served over 5,000 Family members and distributed more than 600 million dollars in retroactive benefits.

The Programme also follows Congressional legislation that pertains to benefits Programmes offered to Families of deceased Soldiers. The information can be found in the Support Programmes section of www.ALTFCM.army.mil. Families of fallen Soldiers are encouraged to contact ALTFCM for personal assistance, or benefit concerns, by calling toll-free 1-866-272-5841; visiting the Web site, or by e-mail to http://www.ALTFCM.army.mil

# Facilities Modernization—Posturing Installations to Balance Warfighter Readiness and Quality of Life

The Office of the Assistant Chief of Staff for Installation Management (OACSIM) is committed to ensuring that Soldiers and units are provided with the facilities and infrastructure necessary to support a 21st Century Army. OACSIM must balance meeting construction demands while maintaining or enhancing services to Soldiers and their Families.

## Installation Modernization Strategy

The combined affects of fielding the Modular Force, Base Realignment and Closure (BRAC), Global Defence Posture Realignment and Grow the Army has resulted in the largest construction Programme since World War II. The Army cannot afford delays in delivering facilities that support the arrival of modernized equipment before they are ready to be housed, maintained, trained or sustained. OACSIM and its executing agents, the Installation Management Command (IMCOM) and the US Army Corps of Engineers (USACE), continue to seek innovative solutions to ensure installation infrastructure and facility requirements are properly identified and validated. Achieving a high degree of synchronization between these three agencies in order to provide functionally and operationally relevant facilities is the key. Facilities now set the conditions for sustaining, training, maintaining, deploying and recovering units and are enabled to adapt to insertion of Future Force technologies as they are ready to be adopted.

Our installations must support a mix of Current and Future Forces. Modernized facilities are using a new generation of adaptive, multi-purpose standard designs. As such, new generation facility standards and criteria are based on validated facility requirements identified for the 2015-2020 Army in coordination with the Army Staff proponent for the facility type. Inherent with this approach is the goal to reduce repetitive construction through flexible and reconfigurable facility designs. These "flexible" designs maximize space utilization as more than one function or task is performed in the same space with little to no modification.

Many of these facilities are also incorporating a high degree of digital data and communications connectivity enabling units with unprecedented situational awareness. Digitally enabled facilities support reach operations and reduce the deployed force footprint. They also provide a resource multiplier by the using the same digital capabilities to conduct mission planning and rehearsal, and embedded or distributed training. OACSIM and USACE are developing new facility standard designs that are mission focused, digitally enabled, reducing the time to prepare, deploy and Reset.

In order to speed up the delivery of facilities, USACE developed the Military Construction Transformation process (MILCON Transformation or MT). This MILCON delivery strategy is targeted towards capturing industry methods and practices to deliver facilities faster, safer, greener and more economically. As USACE moves through the third transition year in 2008, the MT process continues to be refined as observations and lessons learned are incorporated into the next project to be executed. MT has also offered an opportunity to strike a balance and achieve a more equitable distribution of Army MILCON resources to meet fielding and stationing timelines as well as the flexibility to adapt to change.

IMCOM is also assisting USACE with implementing the MT process by maximizing the opportunity to improve the "look and feel" of installations. The construction demand facing the Army provides a one-time opportunity to achieve a common within the "look and feel" of our installations. As whole sections of installations are developed, IMCOM will improve the appearance of installations that fosters an identity for Soldiers and their Families to relate to, and a community for which they can be proud.

IMCOM continues to harness the "individuality" or diversity of each installation as it aggressively implements facility modernization. Not all installations are suited to meet a broad range of capabilities, characteristics or capacities on a single installation, nor should they. This is especially true given the magnitude from the combined affects of Modular Force fielding, restationing our forward deployed forces, or implementation of Base Realignment and Closure (BRAC). IMCOM continues to maximize the unique strengths, capabilities and capacities of individual installations to meet an operational or mission function while using the advantages of others within a geographic region that are better suited to fill gaps and shortfalls in capability or capacity.

## Modernization of Living and Working Environments

At the same time the Army executes its huge construction Programme, the increasing operational tempo of the Army in its war on terrorism increases the need for expanded Family support Programmes and services. Our Soldiers are deploying to an unprecedented amount of locations performing missions that can reach 12-15 month durations. This places a significant level of stress on service member Families. Living and working environments must be modernized to facilitate productivity and high morale while minimizing frustration and stress induced by sub standard living and working conditions.

Restationing Soldiers from all over the world has increased emphasis placed on Soldier barracks capacity and many installations. The latest barracks standard provides greater space and privacy along with telephone and cable-ready receptacles. The connectivity provided offers Soldiers an opportunity to continue their skills training or education at their own pace and intensity. New or renovated barracks also contain higher quality furniture, more washing machines and clothes dryers and increased parking along with greater open space and outdoor recreational facilities.

Barracks are not the only installation area undergoing major change. The Army has embarked on a concerted effort to improve facilities dedicated to preparing our wounded Soldiers to return to active service or transition to civilian life. These facilities are being developed in a "campus" architecture placing quarters, services and case management in a consolidated location whenever possible. The Army's objective is for these facilities to be within walking distance to each other and with consideration for Family participation and support as Soldiers and their Families prepare to move forward in their lives.

Family housing areas are also undergoing extraordinary improvements. The Residential Communities Initiative (RCI) is probably the most visible change on our installations. The RCI plan includes 45 installations (grouped into 35 projects)— more than 98 percent of the Army's current CONUSbased Family housing inventory, with an end state of 90,200 homes. Thirty-three installations—more than 71,500 end state homes —made the transition to privatized operations; and projects for three more installations totaling approximately 5,000 homes were transferred to the private sector in fiscal year 2007. The Army will use $955 million of appropriations and obtain $9.4 billion of private capital to construct/renovate housing for these 36 installations. An additional nine installations involving close to 13,800 end state homes are either in solicitation or under development.

OACSIM has increased its delivery of services and Family Programmes to meet the needs of the Army's current OPTEMPO. Installations are providing improved community and Family services to ensure the well-being of Soldiers and their Families. Providing these services to both our active and reserve Families alike extends beyond traditional installation boundaries or fences.

The restationing of over a third of the Army has created new requirements for childcare, youth activities, and physical fitness facilities. New facilities standards and standard designs are nearing completion for these facility types to incorporate the latest technologies and techniques to improve overall services to the Army community. IMCOM is working closely with the surrounding communities through integration of services and support wherever it makes sense. This strategy offers the opportunity to move resources and apply them to other shortfall areas in a comprehensive, integrated capital investment plan. At the same time, Soldiers and their Families enjoy the synergistic benefit resulting from the improved or strengthened civil-military community environment.

## Modernized Installation Management

OACSIM's objective remains the development and transformation to a system of installation capabilities and resources to support a CONUS-based projection of forces. Installations and communities will become increasingly integrated and mutually supportive. Regional, city and installation master planners will work together to leverage common infrastructure and services to create mutual benefits and decrease operating costs. Surrounding communities may provide medical, dependent education, recreational or emergency services to mitigate lack of on-post capabilities. Civilian and military communities may augment each other in mutual support agreements, thereby maximizing resource investments within a community or region.

Environmental strategies, land use and stewardship continue to be more fully integrated into mainstream installation management practices, business processes and base support services both on post and in coordination with state and local governments. Common and mutually supportive goals in land use and environmental considerations become less divisive as perspectives and appreciation for the benefits of close community ties outweigh the occasional disadvantages of close proximity to military installations.

Protecting our Soldiers, their Families, and our civilian workforce is a critical dimension of balancing the demands of a transforming Army at war. Access control points for all installations continue to be modernized to aggressively meet the realities of today's anti-terrorism and force protection needs. The Technology Standards Group of OACSIM is exploring beneficial methods, concepts and opportunities of incorporating advanced technologies such as biometrics; smart cards; entity tracking;

networked sensors; chemical, biological, radiological, nuclear and high yield explosives; and weapons or munitions detection capabilities. By linking local, state and federal law enforcement activities, security capabilities are enhanced as well as our installation force protection posture. As installation services (e.g., fire, education, etc) become integrated with the surrounding community, we must examine security considerations that extend beyond the installation boundary.

At the heart of balancing all of these installation demands and implementing these installation strategies is the need to improve, and in some cases, develop new business processes and practices. Installation infrastructure and facilities implications must be considered if the Army is going to synchronize decisions and implementation milestones. OACSIM, in coordination with ARSTAF proponents across all DOTMLPF domains, continues to refine the process by which facility requirements are validated and implemented. This unified ARSTAF effort is imperative to ensuring that we have the right installation infrastructure and facility mix at the right place and time is vital to continued Army readiness and modernization.

OACSIM has identified business processes that adapt to changing priorities. OACSIM and IMCOM are developing or improving policies and Programmatic strategies that support validation and verification of facility and infrastructure requirements. Synchronizing the myriad stationing and fielding timelines across all DOTMLPF domains is essential to minimizing distractions on Soldiers, disruptions to Families, and implementing an orderly transition to relevant facilities and installation infrastructure.

Some consolidation of activities at the regional level has been implemented and other concepts and initiatives continue to be refined. IMCOM is committed to providing Programmes that sustain quality installations, Family support, and assure the well-being of the entire Army Family. Soldiers enjoy the "peace of mind" that their Families are secure and cared for when they are deployed as each installation transitions to the new garrison model for common levels of support. IMCOM continues to seek opportunities for relieving operational commanders from the time—consuming tasks of running a "city" and managing the delicate balance of operational resources and training with infrastructure and facilities sustainment.

Senior Army leaders remain committed to improving resourcing gaps in base operations, sustainment, restoration and modernization. Consolidation of installation management under a central organization has contributed significantly to better understanding and Defence of these resources. As Army modernization evolves and technology is placed into the hands of Soldiers, so will installations evolve. The installation management and facilities engineering communities are committed to providing robust, mission relevant facilities that meet training, mobilizing and deploying the force, sustaining and reconstituting the force and caring for our total Army Family. The role of Army installations in sustaining a premier, expeditionary Army remains a fundamental imperative for Army Transformation and the war on terrorism.

## Commitment to Excellence

We will meet the criticality of need and execute construction through MT – quicker, sustainable, greener and at reduced overall delivery cost using life-cycle management and investment methods. We will maintain the duration of support necessary to ensure deployed forces are fully supported across the entire Army mission spectrum. Using multipurpose, adaptive facility standards with appropriate levels of connectivity and flexibility to accommodate transformation to the 21st Century Army with the robust platforms needed to meet global commitments.

Installations exist to support warfighters and their Families well-being. The installation management community remains dedicated to meeting the challenge of providing quality, mission-ready installations.

# Index